The Stars in Your Family

ALSO AVAILABLE
FROM THE ASTRO ROOM DIVISION
OF HAY HOUSE

ASTROLOGY REALLY WORKS! — by The Magi Society

You might wish to cut out or copy the
handy astrological guide below and
keep it with you for easy reference.

♈	**Aries:**	March 21–April 19
♉	**Taurus:**	April 20–May 20
♊	**Gemini:**	May 21–June 20
♋	**Cancer:**	June 21–July 22
♌	**Leo:**	July 23–August 22
♍	**Virgo:**	August 23–September 22
♎	**Libra:**	September 23–October 22
♏	**Scorpio:**	October 23–November 21
♐	**Sagittarius:**	November 22–December 21
♑	**Capricorn:**	December 22–January 19
♒	**Aquarius:**	January 20–February 18
♓	**Pisces:**	February 19–March 20

Fire signs:	Aries, Leo, Sagittarius
Earth signs:	Taurus, Virgo, Capricorn
Air signs:	Gemini, Libra, Aquarius
Water signs:	Cancer, Scorpio, Pisces

The Stars in Your Family

HOW ASTROLOGY AFFECTS RELATIONSHIPS BETWEEN PARENTS AND CHILDREN

Sylvia Friedman

A division of
Hay House, Inc.
Carlsbad, CA

Published and distributed in the United States by:

Hay House, Inc., P.O. Box 5100, Carlsbad, CA 92018-5100
(800) 654-5126

Edited by: Jill Kramer
Designed by: Highpoint, Claremont, CA

Library of Congress Cataloging-in-Publication Data

Friedman, Sylvia.
    The stars in your family : how astrology affects relationships
between parents and children / Sylvia Friedman.
        p.   cm.
    ISBN 1-56170-139-4 (trade paper)
      1. Astrology and psychology.   2. Typology (Psychology)--Miscellanea.
3. Parent and child--Miscellanea. 4. Parenting--Miscellanea.   I. Title.
BF1729.P8F75   1995
133.5'8155924--dc20   95-14485
                                                    CIP

ISBN 1-56170-139-4

99 98 97 96 95   6 5 4 3 2
First Printing, September 1995
Second Printing, December, 1995

Contents

Preface i
Acknowledgments iii
Introduction vii

How to Use This Book xvii

Chapter One
ARIES THE RAM
(March 21–April 19)
THE ARIES PERSONALITY 1
PARENT AND CHILD:
    Aries Parent/Aries Child 5
    Taurus Parent/Aries Child 7
    Gemini Parent/Aries Child 9
    Cancer Parent/Aries Child 10
    Leo Parent/Aries Child 12
    Virgo Parent/Aries Child 14
    Libra Parent/Aries Child 15
    Scorpio Parent/Aries Child 17
    Sagittarius Parent/Aries Child 19
    Capricorn Parent/Aries Child 20
    Aquarius Parent/Aries Child 22
    Pisces Parent/Aries Child 23
    SUMMARY 25

Chapter Two
TAURUS THE BULL
(April 20–May 20)
THE TAURUS PERSONALITY 27
PARENT AND CHILD:
    Aries Parent/Taurus Child 35
    Taurus Parent/Taurus Child 37
    Gemini Parent/Taurus Child 38
    Cancer Parent/Taurus Child 40
    Leo Parent/Taurus Child 42
    Virgo Parent/Taurus Child 45
    Libra Parent/Taurus Child 47
    Scorpio Parent/Taurus Child 48
    Sagittarius Parent/Taurus Child 50
    Capricorn Parent/Taurus Child 52
    Aquarius Parent/Taurus Child 54
    Pisces Parent/Taurus Child 55
    SUMMARY 57

Chapter Three
GEMINI THE TWINS
(May 21–June 20)
THE GEMINI PERSONALITY 61
PARENT AND CHILD:
    Aries Parent/Gemini Child 67
    Taurus Parent/Gemini Child 69
    Gemini Parent/Gemini Child 72
    Cancer Parent/Gemini Child 74
    Leo Parent/Gemini Child 76
    Virgo Parent/Gemini Child 78
    Libra Parent/Gemini Child 80
    Scorpio Parent/Gemini Child 81
    Sagittarius Parent/Gemini Child . . . 84
    Capricorn Parent/Gemini Child 85
    Aquarius Parent/Gemini Child 87
    Pisces Parent/Gemini Child 89
    SUMMARY 91

Chapter Four
CANCER THE CRAB
(June 21–July 22)
THE CANCER PERSONALITY 93
PARENT AND CHILD:
    Aries Parent/Cancer Child 99
    Taurus Parent/Cancer Child 101
    Gemini Parent/Cancer Child 103
    Cancer Parent/Cancer Child 105
    Leo Parent/Cancer Child 109
    Virgo Parent/Cancer Child 111
    Libra Parent/Cancer Child 113
    Scorpio Parent/Cancer Child 115
    Sagittarius Parent/Cancer Child 116
    Capricorn Parent/Cancer Child 118
    Aquarius Parent/Cancer Child 120
    Pisces Parent/Cancer Child 121
    SUMMARY 123

Chapter Five
LEO THE LION
(July 23–August 22)
THE LEO PERSONALITY 125
PARENT AND CHILD:
    Aries Parent/Leo Child 128
    Taurus Parent/Leo Child 131
    Gemini Parent/Leo Child 133

Cancer Parent/Leo Child. 134
Leo Parent/Leo Child 136
Virgo Parent/Leo Child 138
Libra Parent/Leo Child 140
Scorpio Parent/Leo Child 142
Sagittarius Parent/Leo Child 143
Capricorn Parent/Leo Child 145
Aquarius Parent/Leo Child. 147
Pisces Parent/Leo Child 149
SUMMARY 151

Chapter Six
VIRGO THE VIRGIN
(August 23–September 22)

THE VIRGO PERSONALITY 153
PARENT AND CHILD:
Aries Parent/Virgo Child 158
Taurus Parent/Virgo Child 159
Gemini Parent/Virgo Child. 161
Cancer Parent/Virgo Child 163
Leo Parent/Virgo Child 164
Virgo Parent/Virgo Child 166
Libra Parent/Virgo Child. 167
Scorpio Parent/Virgo Child 169
Sagittarius Parent/Virgo Child 170
Capricorn Parent/Virgo Child. 172
Aquarius Parent/Virgo Child 173
Pisces Parent/Virgo Child. 175
SUMMARY 177

Chapter Seven
LIBRA THE SCALES
(September 23–October 22)

THE LIBRA PERSONALITY. 179
PARENT AND CHILD:
Aries Parent/Libra Child. 184
Taurus Parent/Libra Child 186
Gemini Parent/Libra Child 188
Cancer Parent/Libra Child 191
Leo Parent/Libra Child 193
Virgo Parent/Libra Child. 195
Libra Parent/Libra Child. 197
Scorpio Parent/Libra Child. 198
Sagittarius Parent/Libra Child 200
Capricorn Parent/Libra Child. 202
Aquarius Parent/Libra Child 203
Pisces Parent/Libra Child. 205
SUMMARY 207

Chapter Eight
SCORPIO THE SCORPION
(October 23–November 21)

THE SCORPIO PERSONALITY 209
PARENT AND CHILD:
Aries Parent/Scorpio Child 214
Taurus Parent/Scorpio Child 215
Gemini Parent/Scorpio Child. 217
Cancer Parent/Scorpio Child 220
Leo Parent/Scorpio Child 222
Virgo Parent/Scorpio Child 224
Libra Parent/Scorpio Child. 226
Scorpio Parent/Scorpio Child 228
Sagittarius Parent/Scorpio Child . . . 230
Capricorn Parent/Scorpio Child. . . . 232
Aquarius Parent/Scorpio Child 234
Pisces Parent/Scorpio Child. 236
SUMMARY 239

Chapter Nine
SAGITTARIUS THE ARCHER
(November 22–December 21)

THE SAGITTARIUS PERSONALITY 241
PARENT AND CHILD:
Aries Parent/Sagittarius Child 246
Taurus Parent/Sagittarius Child. . . . 248
Gemini Parent/Sagittarius Child . . . 249
Cancer Parent/Sagittarius Child. . . . 251
Leo Parent/Sagittarius Child 254
Virgo Parent/Sagittarius Child 256
Libra Parent/Sagittarius Child 258
Scorpio Parent/Sagittarius Child . . . 260
Sagittarius Parent/Sagittarius Child . 263
Capricorn Parent/Sagittarius Child . 265
Aquarius Parent/Sagittarius Child . . 267
Pisces Parent/Sagittarius Child 269
SUMMARY 271

Chapter Ten
CAPRICORN THE GOAT
(December 22–January 19)

THE CAPRICORN PERSONALITY. 273
PARENT AND CHILD:
Aries Parent/Capricorn Child. 276
Taurus Parent/Capricorn Child 279
Gemini Parent/Capricorn Child 281
Cancer Parent/Capricorn Child 283
Leo Parent/Capricorn Child 286

Virgo Parent/Capricorn Child...... 288
Libra Parent/Capricorn Child...... 289
Scorpio Parent/Capricorn Child.... 292
Sagittarius Parent/Capricorn Child . 294
Capricorn Parent/Capricorn Child.. 296
Aquarius Parent/Capricorn Child .. 298
Pisces Parent/Capricorn Child..... 300
SUMMARY 302

Chapter Eleven
AQUARIUS THE WATER BEARER
(January 20–February 18)
THE AQUARIUS PERSONALITY 303
PARENT AND CHILD:
Aries Parent/Aquarius Child 308
Taurus Parent/Aquarius Child 310
Gemini Parent/Aquarius Child..... 312
Cancer Parent/Aquarius Child 314
Leo Parent/Aquarius Child........ 316
Virgo Parent/Aquarius Child 318
Libra Parent/Aquarius Child 320
Scorpio Parent/Aquarius Child 322
Sagittarius Parent/Aquarius Child.. 324
Capricorn Parent/Aquarius Child .. 326
Aquarius Parent/Aquarius Child ... 327
Pisces Parent/Aquarius Child...... 329
SUMMARY 331

Chapter Twelve
PISCES THE FISH
(February 19–March 20)
THE PISCES PERSONALITY 333
PARENT AND CHILD:
Aries Parent/Pisces Child......... 338
Taurus Parent/Pisces Child........ 340
Gemini Parent/Pisces Child 342
Cancer Parent/Pisces Child 345
Leo Parent/Pisces Child 347
Virgo Parent/Pisces Child......... 349
Libra Parent/Pisces Child......... 351
Scorpio Parent/Pisces Child....... 353
Sagittarius Parent/Pisces Child 355
Capricorn Parent/Pisces Child..... 358
Aquarius Parent/Pisces Child...... 359
Pisces Parent/Pisces Child 361
SUMMARY 363

APPENDIX 365

Afterword 367
About the Author 369

Preface

*"What lies behind us
and what lies before us
are tiny matters compared
to what lies within us."*

— THOREAU

This book is not going to comprise an intricate explanation of astrology. It does not explain the complex mathematical relationships between the Sun, Moon, and the Ascendents, or detail information about the planets. Instead, my goal is to structure knowledge for the novice or layperson, focusing on the benefit of the powerful Sun Sign (the all-encompassing self). I want to help parents learn to recognize and deal with the special set of traits and characteristics that are within their child or children, each being born under a specific sun sign precisely positioned in the heavens, on the date of his or her birth.

Each of our children is gifted with certain natural abilities, and these gifts must not be suppressed. If they are, this situation can lead to feelings of personal repression that will invariably hurt our children for the rest of their lives. Parents first need to understand how their own self-repression has affected their quality of life. They must not allow their own past experiences (which include their respective backgrounds and environmental influences) to stifle their children. They must come to terms with the past in order to live with the future. *Acceptance* is a huge word in our society; but *self-acceptance* is the only way for parents to guide their children toward facing a healthy future.

Most people who know very little or nothing at all about the study of astrology still find it both fascinating and scary. My experiences, whether they entail enjoying food at a good restaurant, sharing conversation at a cocktail party, or having fun at a picnic, are forever enlightening and humorous. It begins when someone is told that I am an astrologer. The first challenging question posed to me is: "Tell me about myself!" It's so interesting to watch the expressions on these people's faces as I begin to explain their personality, through their sun sign. The familiar begins to ring a surprising bell, which soon produces their second statement: "Please be kind!"

I laugh, and usually ask, "What's so scary about wanting to understand your personality and behavior?"

Most answer, "Nothing—but sometimes it's better not to know!" I tell them that it isn't astrology that's scary, it's self-awareness that is! Self-awareness can instigate personal risk-taking and change. That's definitely intimidating!

I want to clarify that I am not here to judge individual personalities; my purpose is to explain them. My years of experience as a practicing astrologer, with a natural ability to intuitively interpret my clients' astrological charts, have led me to become a Counselor in Human Behavior. I counsel individuals, couples (both single and married), as well as parents, whom I work with on opening up areas of communication, especially with their children. My particular concentration has been on repression in personal communication and the fear of confrontation.

Children must be the priority of the future! It is essential that all parents understand how their own background of family repression can be a negative force when raising a child. Poor communication will ultimately impede a child's personal freedom and self-confidence.

My experience as a counselor has shown me that 90 percent of my clients, who are now parents, or who will become parents, are *victims* of their parents! The unhealthy lessons that they have learned throughout their childhood can personally and functionally repress the children whom they are trying to raise. Mom and Dad must not parent through their own egos and through self-control. Children are born innocent and respond as though they were watered-down clay, formed or shaped in the hands of their parents. Excessive control mechanisms exhibited by Mom and Dad are simply the result of their own personal insecurity.

Of course, most parents do not intentionally victimize their children, as they are not consciously in touch with their own control techniques. What parents must realize is that by transferring their unresolved problems to their children, they are not giving credence to their individuality. Parents must work very hard to open their minds and look inside, always searching to seek an understanding of their own personality and behavior patterns. Making this effort will not only develop their children's potential, but secure their own mental health as well. I believe so completely in the validity of astrology with respect to personality, individuality, and behavior, that I need to educate, inspire, and motivate...which explains my rationale for the writing of this book.

I hope it brings you all the answers you're looking for!

Sylvia Friedman
Chicago, Illinois
1995

Acknowledgments

To my son Layne for his unconditional love, and the innumerable days and nights he spent in the preparation of this book!

To my loving daughter Alissa, who is always there to share my feelings, and for the myriad days and nights she typed corrections!

To Michael Moss: I could not have written this book without you!

To Cynthia Reynolds: Your special friendship, motivating force, and belief in me kept me going!

To Vicki and Michael Karagianis: Your home was always open to me. Your devotion and loyalty will never be forgotten!

To Kathleen Kelly: Your deep understanding of my needs, and your total trust in my ability to help people, has been an inspiration.

To Hope Daniels: Your friendship, generosity, and guidance got me through some very difficult times.

To Margie Tinerella: The spirituality, understanding, and mental affinity that we shared throughout this time has given me great comfort!

To Carol Gies: For the very special friendship that continues to grow, and an idea a minute!

To Marilyn Benson: For the love and generosity that never stops.

To my extended family: Lenore, Marci, Ken, Danny, and Joey, for the comfort of knowing that you are always there!

To Sue Chernoff, who has never let me down!

To Louise Hay, for her support and sincere acceptance of my work!

To Reid Tracy: It's wonderful to have a practical, stable, and wise man in my corner.

To Jill Kramer, whose many talents have made my life as an author very easy!

To Jeannie Liberati: It's such a comfort to know that you are out there selling my book!

To Kristina Queen, for your excitement and dedication to the promotion of this book.

To Polly Tracy, for her belief in the value of my book!

And to all the other special people at Hay House who supported this effort!

Thank you!

DEDICATED TO MY PARENTS AND CHILDREN

Introduction

Parent/child relationships have always been, and always will continue to be, difficult. I must admit that through all of the years I've worked with people, I'm still astounded by the lack of knowledge, compromise, and understanding that exists and which contributes to the ongoing dilemma within families. Astrology has been a valuable and practical psychological tool, which has given me an uncanny and welcome understanding of human beings. My experiences have led me to believe that I can illuminate, and be of help to, parents who are raising their children from birth to infinity.

As a divorced mother raising my children, I innately placed my emphasis on love and caring, but it was not enough. I had to find that extra dimension—an insightful support system! As I began to study and intuitively perceive the value of the astrological personality, I knew that I had found what I needed and did not have— a nurturing, knowledgeable "fairy godmother."

Through personal experience and continued study of my Aquarian son (key phrase: "I know," and God forbid I told him he didn't), and my Taurus daughter (key phrases: "I have" and "I want more"), I learned that having what I call "Astrological Advance Notice" of my two children's personalities gave me a true picture or, better said, a deeper insight into their traits, characteristics, and behavior. This special understanding taught me how to compromise and how not to parent my children through ego and control. This philosophy has been the key to our success as a family comprised of a single parent and two children.

Once you read this book, it is my hope that you will use it over and over again as a reference guide when you have a question about your child's personality and behavior. The contents will provide a wealth of information about your child or children and yourself, and show you how to build compatibility through understanding. My children are my greatest accomplishment, and I am still there for them every step of the way (even when they may not want me to be).

To all parents and children alike: My hope is that this book will provide you with the kind of information that can help inspire much-needed communication between parents and children, so that none of you will ever have to say: "I wish someone had told me this long ago!"

My Beginnings

Now, I'd like to tell you about a little girl named Sylvia, who has since grown into the author of this book. The following story is true. Little Sylvia's courage, need for communication, and her striving for happiness and love, remain with her. They most assuredly have been the motivating factors in her life, although life itself has been excellent therapy.

☆   ☆   ☆

I believe from the moment I was born, although I can't attest to it, my dream was to be a star—not an astrological star, but a star whose glow would light up a stage or screen. My mother's constant complaint was that my drama could keep her busy an entire day! Speaking of drama, I'd like to share a moment in time that has saved me from negative thoughts or deep depression when life's paths were not perfectly drawn. The flashback of this story always makes me smile, especially when I reach frightening detours and curves in the road.

When I was five years old, my parents took me to a huge banquet. It was a dinner dance at the end of the season at my father's lodge, where he was the president. It was a very important function, since he was also the chairman of the event. I remember that I was all dressed up in a beautiful black velvet dress with a white lace collar. Since we were quite poor, my mother had to save a lot of her money to buy me that dress. Undoubtedly, nobody else brought their children, especially a five year old, but my father believed that for every special moment he had, his pride and joy had to be present. I really loved him for that!

Well, I was walking around having a wonderful time talking to people who looked like they were wondering what a five-year-old kid was doing there, when I started to feel bored. I walked over to my father's table and began to tug at his jacket and said, "Daddy, I want to sing!" I had been fascinated by the large orchestra on the stage for quite some time before I approached my father. I thought to myself, Wouldn't it be fun to sing in front of all of my father's friends?

"So," my father asked, "you want to sing?"

"Yes, Daddy," I said. "I want to sing on the stage!"

"What are you talking about?" my mother demanded. "You can't go up on that stage and sing!"

"If she wants to go and sing on that stage," my father replied, "then let her go!"

I walked directly up to the stage and began to look up at the orchestra leader. I kept staring up at him and said, "I want to sing!" I don't believe he heard me the first few times, but I kept repeating: "Sir, I want to sing!"

He looked around and said, "That's nice, little girl." But I wasn't going to take no for an answer. I was determined to sing in front of all of those people. I heard him grunt, and then he grudgingly asked, "You really want to sing?"

I said, "Yes! And I want to make everyone happy!" He half-smiled and lifted me up onto the stage. It was a large banquet hall, and I remember thinking that it was so much fun being lifted up that high.

"What do you want to sing, and what's your name?" the orchestra leader asked.

I replied, "God Bless America, and my name is Sylvia." My father taught me that song. He was so proud to come to America from Poland and genuinely loved living in this wonderful country. The leader asked, "God Bless America?" and again I answered "Yes!" He took what I believe was a microphone and placed it in front of me and lifted me up onto a chair. I don't remember being very excited, just nervous.

Then his voice came over the microphone: "Ladies and gentlemen, may I have your attention?" Finally, after saying "ladies and gentlemen" several times, everyone finally stopped talking. The orchestra leader continued: "Ladies and gentlemen, I have a little girl right here on the stage who wants to sing for you." After a moment, I saw faces turn toward me, and a murmur built up in the room.

I shall never forget that orchestra leader—he became so determined to let me sing, he would not stop talking. "Ladies and gentlemen, I have a lovely girl on this stage who wants to sing for you. Her name is Sylvia, and she wants to sing 'God Bless America.'" All of a sudden, there was silence and applause. They were applauding before I sang. I thought to myself, Wow, isn't it wonderful to get all this attention! The orchestra leader looked over at me and said, "All right, Sylvia, sing!"

I was standing on that chair, shaking inside, but never once did I reveal my trepidation to the audience. I began to sing, and the orchestra followed. When I finished that song, a tremendous burst of applause permeated the room, and I thought to myself, Look how happy all of those people are!

I wanted to share this story with you, as it was a turning point in my life. At five years old, daring life, I took a risk and had to accept the results of exposing myself to the outside world. Most of us can recollect a moment in time when we felt a recognition of self, and hopefully your parents were there to appreciate that feeling!

My Parents, Sophie and Hyman Chess

My Virgo father was foreign born, with powerful instincts. He was a man before his time, not particularly educated, but his feelings about people were that they should be free to be who they are, and who they were born to be. He naturally understood my need to be independent and gave me permission to think for myself.

I was born an Aries, April 17th, sign of the Ram, a free spirit who needs personal attention and stability in the home. My father's belief in me was the string that held on to the balloon. I could not fly away without him. His spirit continued to be the celebration of my self-confidence. My Capricorn mother, on the other hand, was very concerned with her image; how she was perceived in life was everything to her. She loved me, but could not compromise her need for approval. Everything had to be perfect and under her control. Therefore, she could not understand my need for individuality and freedom. There were many special moments in our lives, but life with her *could* have been better.

Cohesive family spirit and understanding is where it all begins! This story and my belief in family is another reason for my writing this book. If my mother were alive today and could read this book, perhaps our life together could have grown through willful compromise. In the case of my father, perhaps he could have gone far beyond his instinctive ability. My free spirit lives, and my father is responsible. My mother gave me all that she could, except that she never really understood me. This book is dedicated to my parents, and to all parents who wish to make the effort and go the distance with their children.

A Need for Approval

Most of the clients who have come to see me seem to have the same problem that springs to the surface: the compulsive need for the approval of the world around them. This is a painful issue that takes time to be resolved. Surprisingly, most people begin to deal with this problem after they've reached their forties. They turn to therapy when a need to take charge of their own lives becomes apparent.

After listening to my clients, I have found that most of them were victimized by the egotism of a parent, or possibly both parents. Parents raise children with their own selves in mind, rather than trying to understand that every child is unique and needs to function through his or her own personality, traits, and behavior.

Parents must not view their children as a way to achieve their own lost dreams. Children can lose their special individuality (when parents try to take control of their lives) by issuing "great expectations." If parental egotism prevails, children will continually live with an inner question: "Do my parents really love ME?" Children who feel that they can never meet their parents' expectations can easily develop into "pleasers"—people who need to be loved by everyone. These children never feel as if anything they do is good enough, and they grow up with inner rebellion and resentment. Always trying to obtain their parents' love, they often say yes to their mother's and father's dreams, when what they want to say is no! As the years pass, these children can develop a deep problem with the decision-making process. They may take forever to make an important decision, and opportunities can be lost. Fear and self-doubt can win out if children are not allowed to express their own individuality.

Parents must respect and recognize their children's innate traits, talents, and abilities. It is their responsibility to have the consideration and courage to let go of their own egos. They must support and validate their children, as validation nurtures self-approval, and self-approval tempers the need to be all things to all people. When children are allowed to make their own decisions under the guidance of parents who recognize the importance of their kids' *own* dreams, blame and resentment will be replaced by love and respect.

☆   ☆   ☆

An Introduction to Decans

Before we embark on the study of each individual child's sun sign, I think it's important to tell you about something in astrology called the *decan* (pronounced *dek'-on*). The decan is a span of time that divides each sign into three 10-day sections. For example, in the sign of Aries, the first decan is from March 21st to the 30th; the second decan is from March 31st to April 9th; and the third is from April 10th to the 20th. I know I must sound like a broken record as I continue to repeat that *individuality* is the "lead performer" in the play named astrology—but each decan within every sun sign does reveal and represent significant differences in the impression of that sign's personality!

As I complete a study of each client's astrological chart, I find that no matter what their birth sign is, I must consider the decan category in my psychological overview. For example:

- *The first decan* is the most understated, inwardly intense, rigid, and ambitious in the sun sign category;

- *The second decan* is the easiest to handle, somewhat passive and lethargic, and not as assertive as its two companion decans; and

- *The third decan* is more creative and daring than the first two—a bit on the wild side—and seemingly fascinated with the dark aspects of life.

All of the other traits, characteristics, and behaviors associated with the person's sign will prevail, but I could not omit this special information, as it is another delineator included in the individuality premise associated with astrology.

Male Versus Female Behavior

Most of my clients ask me this question at the very first reading they receive: "Why does the male behavior of a sun sign appear to be so different from the female?" My answer is that astrology does not discriminate with respect to gender— that is, it is not like apples and bananas, with the man being tough and the woman soft and mushy. A boy or girl is not born tough or soft, and I am not referring to physiology or genetics. Within the same sun sign, he or she is individually born with the same traits, characteristics, inherent talents, and behavior. I believe children's interactions with people, and experiences in the outside world during the growing process have a great deal to do with their parents' visions or expectations. Boys are not born "blue," and girls are not born "pink." I should point out that I'm talking about environment, not heredity.

For example, a man can come from a very intense and emotional ethnic background, but will be conditioned to personally repress or deny his emotions. It's not fair, is it? If a boy is born with an emotional inclination, why should he be forced to go against the grain of his normal instincts? The philosophy that "He's a man" has nothing to do with emotion and feeling! It's like he's using biofeedback, trying to control his own body with the aid of brain waves, stemming from fear and a desire for personal control. The consistent practice of personal communication and confrontation within a family is the real solution for all concerned—whether the individuals concerned are male or female!

Will I Get Along With My Baby?

I am always prepared for my clients' never-ending questions about their relationships with their children: "Will I get along with my baby?" or "Why does Kathy respond to my personality better than Timmy does?" Parents cannot pre-evaluate how their ideas, feelings, or behavior will connect with their children before they are born, although I do recommend (if at all possible) astrologically planning the birth of your children. Compatibility can be achieved so much easier when parents can see that their teachings and guidance spark an immediate "I get it" signal from their children.

One cannot plan the positions of the ascendent or planets during a child's birth, as no one can predict the actual time. However, we can plan to bear children in the right month and decan that relates to a particular sign. This subject reminds me of a phone call I received recently.

I picked up the ringing phone to hear the voice of Ellen, a very emotional (and pregnant) fire sign client. Ellen is a Sagittarius, so her hysteria was minor in comparison to her fire partners, Aries and Leo. She said, "I'm getting to the end of Libra! What if I have a Scorpio baby? My God, water and fire, what will I do? Our wavelengths and personalities will be totally different! You know I have very little patience."

"Ellen," I told her calmly, "you will just have to handle the situation and learn to compromise. Remember, you, as the parent, will have the power of astrological wisdom and understanding!"

There was a pause, and then she laughed. "Am I being silly?"

I replied, "No, you may just have to work harder." We engaged in a little more discussion and then said goodbye.

Several days later, I heard a happy voice on the telephone exclaiming, "Sylvia, I made it! I have a Libra baby! What a relief."

"You would have managed either way, " I assured her. And I meant it.

Foundations of Personality

An astrological wavelength is primarily associated with the "element" describing the sun sign. The element is the substance, foundation, or groundwork of an individual's personality. It is the rising curtain, the beginning, the essence, of a child's response to life. The element is pivotal and is fundamental to family compatibility.

If your element is the same or complementary to that of your child, you have already won a major battle, as you are naturally bonded mentally and emotionally.

The "fire" element is represented by Aries, Leo, and Sagittarius. I refer to these signs as "the emotionals" because their first response is feeling (the heart first). Their key phrases, in order, are: "I am," "I will," and "I see." Here are some of the words that describe "fire": *bright, energetic, intense, warm* (in color), *passionate, directional, climbing upward* (with vigor and enthusiasm), *exciting, defiant, confident, daring, confrontational, self-reliant,* and *determined.*

The "earth" element is represented by Taurus, Capricorn, and Virgo. I refer to them as "the utilitarians" because their first response is practical (they practice first). Their key phrases, in order, are: "I possess," "I use," and "I analyze." Some of the words that describe "earth" are: *grounded foundation, material, stable, solid roots, dark* and *rich, narcissistic, analytical, exploratory.*

The "air" element consists of Aquarius, Libra, and Gemini. I refer to them as the "thinkers or "logicals" because their first response relates to the thought process ("give me the facts and nothing but the facts; what is the bottom line?") Their key phrases, in order, are: "I know," "I balance," and "I think." The words that describe "air" are: *original, free, abstract, independent, visionary, hollow, distant* (as if living in their own world), *weightless, ethereal,* and *passive*—one who paddles in his or her own canoe.

The "water" elements are born under Cancer, Pisces, and Scorpio. I refer to them as translucent, or "the moodies" because their first reaction is anxiety and worry (they are also emotional and sensitive, but they fear revealing this part of their personality). Their key phrases, in order, are: "I feel," "I believe," and "I desire." Words that describe water include: *transparent, gentle, calm, tranquil, troubled, temperate, serviceable, vulnerable, splashy, cool,* and *sympathetic.*

Compatibility-wise, be prepared for water to exasperate fire, as water will stifle fire's spirit by subconsciously trying to put it out—that is, there is too much manipulation there! You can combine air with fire, as air will operate as a fan propelling the fire, blowing it higher and brighter. True compatibility is fire with fire, air with air, earth with earth, and water with water. Now, remember that I said that the element represents the *beginning,* and *similar elements* will nourish compatibility. This innate similarity will be a bonding spirit, which can be the focus of healthy relationships. All of the other blendings will take a degree of work and compromise.

Parents who are on the same wavelength as their children will have fewer problems and an intrinsic understanding. The principal goal of a family should be directed toward personal compatibility. Therefore, it's important to know which sun signs are naturally compatible and which are not. In the psychology of astrology, one's beliefs, opinions, and emotional condition stem from an initial reaction—the element describing the sun sign. The remainder of one's personality, whether it has to do with one's stability, harmony, equilibrium, assertiveness, intensity, or dominance (and all other traits to be considered) is strongly influenced by the sun sign, environment, and life experience.

The emotionals *feel* first, the logicals *think* first, the utilitarians *practice* first, and the moodies tend to be *negative* first. Parents cannot always plan the birth of their children and most do not, so it is essential to understand what your child's wavelength might be, particularly if it is not in conjunction with yours. Possessing this information is definitely one of the keys to understanding a child.

What Am I Going to Do?!

I'd like to relate a story about four friends of mine (Marci, Ken, Danny, and Joey) that illustrates how important being on the same wavelength is.

Marci is a wonderful Gemini mother who adores her children; and Ken is a sensitive and caring Aquarian who gives a special meaning to the word *Daddy,* through his soft and loving expression. Danny was their first born; unplanned both biologically and astrologically, he came into the world a Gemini.

Together, they were a family of logical thinkers, because all of them had "a given compatibility," and Danny just fit right in! One day Danny wanted to start playing a game when it was time to go to bed, and he understood that his mother's words were clear, direct, and reasonable when she said, "No, Danny!" He just looked at her, winced, and stopped dead in his tracks. He wasn't frightened—her comment just seemed right to him!

Danny, Marci, and Ken did very well together, since all of them were on the same wavelength. Two years passed quickly, and Marci and Ken decided to have another baby. He was Joey, an unplanned Sagittarius (by *unplanned,* I mean that his parents did not try to conceive him at a certain time so that he would end up being a specific sign). Oh my, an emotional fire sign in a house of logic and thinking! What was this child to do—or better yet, what were Ken and Marci to do? Of course, as little Joey began to grow, this free-spirited, self-willed little person did not listen to the word *no* because to him this restriction did not seem reasonable. He needed to dare and explore and would not react well to sensible discipline. In fact, he would do just the opposite of Marci's reprimand. She would say no and he would continue on as though he had not heard a thing!

Marci groaned as she said to me, "What am I going to do? Danny is so good. He just listens. I can explain things to him, and he just seems to naturally agree with me. Joey *doesn't* listen; he just whines and cries to try and get his way."

I told her, "Marci, Joey is emotional. Simple no's won't work with him. He needs your attention, whether it be negative or positive. He probably will respond much better if you change the inflection of your voice. Just change your tone and pitch when you discipline him. He will respond! Whatever you do or say, do not constantly call him a bad boy, or he will set out to prove you right."

Marci is now consistently working to understand Joey and his emotions. Her logic still gets confused and annoyed by Joey's whining and crying, though. Logical people can have trouble relating to emotion. Marci's first reaction in dealing with Joey is to think to herself, Don't whine, Joey, just give me the facts, and I'll resolve the problem. After all, the same thought process worked with Danny. That's because Danny is a thinker. It makes it so easy—a piece of cake. Now Marci understands that her first reaction will not always be similar to Joey's, and she has to develop different tactics to deal with his emotional nature. It may never provide her with the security she feels with Danny's behavior, but as a mom, Marci will gladly compromise some of her logic to nurture Joey's emotional behavior, in order to build a healthy relationship. After all, air does fan the fire!

How to Use This Book

Each of the 12 chapters in *The Stars in Your Family* will focus on the personality of the astrological sign that the sun was in at the time of each individual's birth. It begins with the fiery, independent Aries, and ends with the sensitive, idealistic Pisces. The descriptive subheads depict the traits, characteristics, and behavioral patterns of each child, parent, grandmother and grandfather—you can use this book to find out about *any* parent/child relationship, no matter what age the person is. (So, when I use the words *child* or *children,* know that I *could* conceivably be referring to 60-year-old children!)

For example, under Aries, you will read the subhead "Motivators of the Zodiac," and this description will tell you that an Aries, who needs to lead, and appears first in the zodiac, will not enjoy secondary positions. You might wish to first glance at the subheads throughout the book before reading the entire text to get an idea of the main characteristics common to each individual.

As you continue reading each chapter, you will find a section called "Parent and Child," which will feature 12 sets of parents, who are, or may be, raising the child featured in the chapter—for example: The Sagittarius Parent/The Virgo Child, or The Aries Parent/The Pisces Child. The information will include parent/child compatibility, the foundation of the child's personality, and can help parents to recognize the inherent insecurity within each child. Once parents begin to understand what's behind a child's particular lack of assurance, subject to his or her own fear or self-doubt, they can learn to avoid problems that may occur without having this kind of advance notice!

The categories listed within the parent/child section apply to both the female and male parent—for example: The Aries Mom/The Virgo Child, or The Capricorn Dad/The Aquarius Child. Both parents need to understand how to treat their children in order to build healthy and fulfilling relationships.

This book offers you a special opportunity to understand how to raise children with respect to who they are, rather than based on unrealistic expectations of what you expect them to be. In addition, parents will begin to recognize themselves, and how they may have been treated by their parents; and grandparents will receive information that can help them learn how to communicate with their grandchildren, as well.

The Stars in Your Family deals with the traits, characteristics, insecurities, and behavioral patterns that relate to four kinds of personalities: fire, earth, air, and water. Even though each person is placed in an individual category, each one is different, and tends to stand in his or her own light. The book is about families: moms, dads, children, grandparents, aunts, uncles, cousins, and friends—virtually anyone whom you would like to better understand!

(**An editorial note:** I have used the plural "children" and "Mom and Dad/parents" for the most part throughout this book for ease of usage and to avoid awkward "he or she" references. However, this book, of course, applies to single-parent families, and those with one or more children.)

*"If I knew that tomorrow the world
would go to pieces, I would
still plant an apple tree."*
— MARTIN LUTHER

Chapter One

....

♈ ARIES THE RAM

MARCH 21–APRIL 19   **ELEMENT:** Fire   **KEY PHRASE:** "I am"

....

THE ARIES PERSONALITY

Some years ago, my friend Sandy and I were sitting in the park, as we did most afternoons when our children were small. On this particular day, Sandy began to talk about her three-year-old son Alan's character flaws.

Sandy asked, "Why does Alan need to take the lead with all of his friends? When he plays in the sandbox, I hear him shouting orders and giving instructions on how to build sturdy mountains and deep holes. Every time I try to help him with his puzzles, he seems impatient and bored. And he appears to have a problem finishing what he starts. I don't know why I worry so much, but there is a lot to think about when you raise a child!"

Sandy and I had a lengthy discussion regarding the psychological meaning behind her son's behavior. Yet, if I were to talk to her about it today (22 years later with an extensive knowledge of astrology), I would have told her, "Sandy, I would like you to understand that Alan was born an Aries, the first sun sign in the zodiac, and he will never enjoy secondary positions. He has a gift for leadership, and it would not be wise to stifle that ability.

"If he gets a little bossy in the sandbox, that's when your part begins. Tell him he must be patient and tolerant of other people's feelings, even when they may not work as fast as he would like them to. Nipping his critical nature in the bud will hopefully prevent him from hurting others without realizing it. And about those puzzles—again, patience is not one of his virtues.

"If his interest is not piqued quickly, he will get bored and want to go on to other projects. Encourage him to finish what he starts. You must start to influence him early on. Go over each step of a project or game, and show him how he can personally achieve his goal. When he reaches the last step, he will be very proud of his accomplishment."

Finally, I would have told her to always stress a positive attitude with her Aries son, in addition to nurturing his independence, initiative, and originality—although he must be taught how to temper these special qualities with patience, acceptance, and tact.

When Mom feels that first kick or nudge in her stomach, that natural movement will be a silent signal to warn her that when her Aries baby comes into the world, he or she, more than any other child, will be on a continual quest for love and attention. Cold and silent treatment is a no-no! This behavior will threaten this child's idealistic and naive desire to trust. Without trust, Mr. or Ms. Aries will inwardly retreat, and begin to fear verbalizing his or her personal feelings.

Young Aries children are very emotional and sensitive and will immediately respond to a lack of warmth on the part of Mom and Dad; cold behavior connotes personal criticism. The lucky parents of these children (who were born strong and eternally optimistic) would be wise to follow their lead. By supporting their powerful desire and ability to go forward, parents can ensure their children's success and potential. Their boundless energy will inspire them to be involved with ten things at one time, and they'll love every minute of life's uphill roller coaster. Aries children have an unrestrained zest for life, but they can be late bloomers when it comes to emotional maturity. Always remember that they crave an unusual amount of loving attention, personal validation, and stability in the home (even though these freedom-seeking children may leave their parents at an early age).

The Motivators of the Zodiac

Aries individuals, more than any other sun sign, need to be first. They are, after all, the first sign in the zodiac! They do not enjoy secondary positions, and consider themselves to be the leaders of the pack. They will finish eating first, stand first in line to play a game, and try to sit in the first row—first before all others, with respect to time, order, rank, and importance.

Because being first is their primary intention, young Aries children should be structured toward a career that is based on accomplishment, whether it be creative or professional. They must be encouraged to build, as tearing down is not their forte. Their excitement is in the thrill of pioneering—to lead the way, to be first or earliest in any field of inquiry or enterprise. Their greatest pleasure will be to initiate, or guide, those who may be frightened or hesitant. This is their particular style and talent. Parents cannot make the mistake of thinking that an Aries will be happy following another's lead, or in being told what to do. Although teamwork is their dream, and while "working together" to achieve a desired goal is always preferable, they always tend to remind you who's in charge. Mom and Dad will have to show young Aries children that they cannot force others to do their bidding. Years of study have proven that Aries children are the motivators of the zodiac, but these kids must be taught to logically understand opposition and obstacles.

Happily Argumentative

The Aries child has extraordinary will power and can be brutally honest. Being ruled by Mars—which is the planet of action—these children are born fighters. Like the butting ram that symbolizes Aries, they enjoy the thrill of daily combat, and go out of their way to instigate an argument (many times they'll do it simply to get attention). This action is a form of control, and young Aries must be taught that he or she cannot control the responses of other people. Mom and Dad will begin to observe these fighting instincts from the very second their daring little mischief maker begins to speak.

Since parents of this argumentative personality will have to deal with an Aries child's inner need "for combat," I will offer some advice on how to intelligently handle this frustrating dilemma. First of all, Aries children really do not mean to offend. An Aries perceives most circumstances to be "right or wrong." Therefore, it is important to give them honest answers when they are in an offensive, challenging mode. They love to win, but they will respect and recognize the truth of any statement. Parents must not try to cover up or rationalize anything they do, as an Aries child will not fare well with rationalization. Young Aries will comply with truth and honesty. This is the only way to compete on their battleground! Once young Aries children feel that there is honesty and consistency in their household, they will respond to their parents' wishes, requirements, and rules.

A hint to parents who raise this fiery little personality: activity and combat are the plugs that spark their electricity. Please be careful not to suppress their effervescent spirits, as their motivation might suffer as a result. Parents must be sure to utilize their combative nature and pioneering instinct by fostering their desire to complete important tasks, as Aries children have little patience and tend to lose interest quickly.

Young Aries daredevils will begin to take risks very early in their lives, and it is imperative to respect and admire their courageous attitudes. When they do decide to try something new and difficult, they need their parents' support. They will love and appreciate the faith that is placed on their need for independence, and their ability to make the impossible work. If Mom and Dad have a personal fear of risk, they'll have to avoid transferring that fear into the minds of these action kids, or they'll miss out on the pleasure of watching their potential and productivity grow. Parents: help your Aries children use their warrior quality as an aid in achieving their goals, and always stress their need for (heaven forbid) patience and tact!

It's Black or White—There's No In-Between

Aries children (along with their compatible fire signs, Leo and Sagittarius) have difficulty understanding gray areas, and this is something that has to be developed. Aries tend to see the world in bold, black-and-white strokes; they either go in one strong direction or the other. The middle ground does not hold much weight as far as these little fireballs are concerned. Remember that these children are decisively directional and must have their questions answered. To put off Aries children is tantamount to turning your back on them. You may think that this is an extreme statement, but trust me, it isn't! Aries individuals need to resolve their problems and move on. Indecision exasperates them. If Mom and Dad do not make decisions quickly, Aries children will wonder what their parents' problem is. It's best to explain to an Aries child that Mom and Dad will need some time to be certain that they are making the right decision.

Communication is the way to make Aries children understand gray areas. Parents: reveal your wisdom—ask them what they think (they love trying to tell you what to do). Respect is very important to Aries children, and to consider their opinion is the perfect way to communicate with them. Listen to their ideas, but try to help them understand that they cannot control every situation. This is their major lesson. Parents must begin to temper their black-and-white tendencies early, as Aries children believe that their sense of right and wrong is part of their birthright. Working with the team of Aries and compromise can be a major challenge. It's vital to be consistent and patient when teaching life's gray areas to Aries children, as they do rebel when anyone tries to make them go against what they know is right (even when they aren't). "I'm wrong" is just not in their vocabulary, and they believe that the word *no* should definitely have the power to put someone in their proper place. However, as parents continue to both communicate and encourage, they will find that Aries children's attitudes will improve as they grow up (although their idealism and naivete can keep them emotional babies for a long time)!

Watch Out for Their Short Fuses!

Aries children are born impatient, and this impatience is usually the cause of their anger. If they see other children who will not learn from their mistakes, they instantly decide to themselves: "That's dumb!" In fact, they will appear to have tunnel vision. If this happens, watch out for their short fuses, followed by tantrums. If someone does not do something exactly as they wish and loses their trust, be prepared! Aries children can lose their tempers quickly, although they can be so charming that you can expect the people that they hurt to immediately forgive them. Mom and Dad must take their Aries children aside and explain to them that this kind of behavior will frighten the other children. Young Aries needs to be shown that their direct and sometimes abrasive quality can easily hurt the feelings of the other children. If someone sparks their compassionate nature, however, they will feel very sorry about their inappropriate behavior. A calm, stable parent is the answer for this little ball of energy. It's important for parents to let their Aries children know what type of behavior is inappropriate or inconsiderate. Mom and Dad must help them understand that they cannot get angry or lose control when someone does not react in a way that they believe is right, or does not follow their instructions to the letter when they give a command.

Aries children can have trouble recognizing peace of mind, as they feel things, and move here and there, in a flash. They must be told that there are times when they must WAIT. They need to acknowledge that some people can learn from their mistakes by working in their own time and at their own pace. Young Aries kids need to be encouraged to help and lead their friends. What is amazing and totally surprising is that it takes just one moment for the Aries child's impatience to get out of control, and in another moment it's possible to witness an instant miracle—Aries is the only sign in the zodiac that does not hold a grudge. Aries children tend to think to themselves: It's over! Let's go on to something else!

☆   ☆   ☆

PARENT AND CHILD

The Aries Parent/The Aries Child

Two Aries in one household, whether it be Mom or Dad, are a handful for the rest of the family. I have been telling you about this fiery child, and now we have a fiery parent, or perhaps two fiery parents. All will lead, none will follow! And if there should be a Pisces mom or dad in this group, heed my warning: he or she will need to pack up and run off to Alaska—neither one will be able to get a word in edgewise!

The primary lesson to learn in reading about Aries is that they will always present themselves as independent individualists. Remember that their key phrase is "I am," and as they grow, they will tell those around them "who they are" on a daily basis. The Aries parent has already gone through the slow process of partially growing up, but their inner child is indefinitely present. They are late bloomers in a world of reality. However, Aries are strong, loving parents, blessed with a good deal of wisdom when it comes to raising their children.

Because Aries parents will clearly see themselves in their Aries children, this similarity naturally gives them a special affinity. Their wavelength is solid, and

Mom and Dad will easily comprehend the traits and behavior of their Aries children. Why not? They are like peas in a pod. These speed-and-action people make life happen! A word of caution to the Aries parent: I'd like you to pull back and look at the one trait that you might like to change in your life in regards to raising your children. Experience has taught you that patience is not one of your virtues, and this anxiety may have hurt some of your relationships. The one special favor that you can do for your Aries children is to help them benefit from your past experience. Please...teach them patience! The Aries "Ram Theory" is to push firmly through life; therefore, envision parent and child acting together as a team for the common cause of developing patience. This task will provide a daily reminder that will finally put an end to the mutual lack of this trait.

The need for space and freedom will never be a problem in a family of Aries. I can just hear Mom and Dad saying to their Aries child: "Thank you for making your own decisions. I welcome your independence, but if you should need help, I'm right here!" Aries parents must appreciate the strong advantage they have with their Aries child. They have the ability to nurture and teach this "fire baby," while utilizing the lessons they have already learned. Together, they can synchronize their power.

One last bit of advice for parents: when you witness your young, fiery Aries children beginning to solve the problems of their small world, quietly step in and help them understand the frailty of others. Teach them that trying to help people change their thinking will open them up for disappointment. As an Aries, you have learned, through your own pain, that your tendency to play "Joan of Arc" did not change the personality or beliefs of any individual who wasn't open to change in the first place! Do you remember how frustrated you felt when faced with this dilemma? Aries parents must teach their children that *acceptance* is a word that Webster has not deleted from the dictionary!

The Aries Mom/The Aries Child

Mom will be happy to know that she has given birth to a child who shares many of her traits. Aries children will be quite comfortable being raised by this mother, as their ideas and thoughts are similar to hers. An Aries mom prefers her children to mature early and to reveal an independent nature. Well, her wish will become a reality as she raises her Aries children!

Mom doesn't baby her children; she usually treats them like young adults. Even though she is very protective and wants to shield her children from harm, she is inwardly relieved to find that they have the ability to take care of themselves. Both parent and child are direct and spontaneous. Therefore, young Aries will never object to Mom's action-oriented personality. Aries are late bloomers, and they never really want to grow up. This desire can cause them to be naive and unstable at times. It's up to Mom to try and set some rules and limits when she raises her Aries children. These fire kids need to develop self-discipline, as they have a tendency to scatter their energy. I know that Mom understands what I mean, as she has probably had this problem herself!

Mom and her child are both assertive and have minds of their own. Therefore, Mom needs to understand that she cannot dominate this child, as she knows that Aries kids will always fight for their own individuality. Both Mom and her Aries children will enjoy exploring life, and their interests will be similar. Their egos are strong, and, as I have often said, patience is not one of their virtues. Aries are leaders, and when two or more leaders live together, compromise is essential. Once Mom and her Aries children understand how easy it is for them to get along, they will build a solid relationship that will last for the rest of their lives!

The Aries Dad/The Aries Child

An Aries dad is usually someone to look up to. He is efficient, straightforward, and honest—he tells it like it is! An Aries child will believe in the truth and will need to do things right; therefore, Dad can be the perfect role model. An Aries father is emotional, but he may not always reveal his sensitivity. He believes that if you are a strong and independent person, you should not burden people with your problems. Many of my Aries male clients have had a lot of difficulty with relationships because they cannot talk about their feelings. Their family seems to misunderstand their good intentions since they appear to be cold and distant.

Dad needs to learn that it's important to reveal his very human side to his Aries children, as they need to experience his sensitive and compassionate nature. Aries children, just like Dad, can grow up believing that they can handle everything. These children need to learn that it's okay to ask for help, and that receiving is not a weakness. Everyone deserves to receive!

The Taurus Parent/The Aries Child

Taurus parents will represent foundation, roots, and stability for the "I never look before I leap" Aries child, so Mom and Dad will need to create a comfortable and peaceful home environment. But beware when fire children come to live in the home of a Taurus parent—their constant energy may be disruptive and chaotic! The Aries children's illuminating aura will bring an electrifying pizazz to the environment, as they really want to savor all of life. As a result, Taurus parents may try to impose their own need for safety upon this innate risk-taker. A Taurus parent can unobtrusively temper their Aries child's spontaneity by practically pointing out the dangers that lie ahead, when a decision is based only upon sheer emotion. The Taurus parent's stability will be effective and calming for these fire children, particularly in the formative years, when most of their actions or reactions will be based upon sudden impulse.

The Taurus parent's values include honesty, integrity, and tradition, and these qualities will be right in sync with an Aries child. Remember, a lot of the rules may be broken when an Aries begins to explore the world. Underneath it all, a Taurus mom or dad will truly respect and admire this adventurous quality, but their own fears and protective nature will provoke them to try and confine or thwart this daring behavior. Parents must understand, though, that confinement will hinder, rather than enhance, this relationship. My study of Taurus personalities has revealed that they have a protective nature that can be extreme, particularly with respect to their Aries children. It would be best for them to develop flexibility. You ask why? Because it's a lot better than becoming a nervous wreck!

The Taurus Mom/The Aries Child

A Taurus mom is friendly and charming. Her understanding nature is appreciated by her family and friends, as she will always try to listen to their problems. Mom is basically kind and compassionate, and her need to help is sincere and honest. Taurus women are very sensitive and easily hurt, even if they present themselves as cool, calm, and collected. They have a difficult time expressing their own personal needs, and this tendency can often build to an internal anger that stays with them for years and years. Aries children, conversely, are born fighters and risk-takers. They tend to leap before they look. A Taurus mom fears confrontation, and she's not comfortable with change on any level. After she develops her lifestyle, she likes to maintain the status quo.

Mom needs to understand that her young Aries will always gravitate toward change and adventure. Feeling safe and secure may be okay for Mom, but an Aries requires mental stimulation and excitement. Aries children do need a safe and secure environment to grow up in, as it offers the kind of stability that is so important for these childlike warriors. Mom needs to understand that she and her Aries children are different in their approach to life. Mom does not relish taking risks, and her pace can be slow next to her quick-thinking, energetic kids. If she can learn to enjoy her free-spirited, dramatic children, rather than trying to stifle their spontaneity, young Aries will be very grateful to have a mother who is so down to earth!

The Taurus Dad/The Aries Child

Dad is methodical and slow-moving, while his Aries children are impulsive and tend to run with the speed of lightning. On the one hand, Dad will be fascinated by his kids' spirit and fortitude; and on the other, these children can exhaust him.

Dad is, for the most part, a practical man whose behavior is usually consistent and strategic. He can also be an idealist who wants to follow his dreams; but a need for safety and security may get in his way. Taurus fathers are usually patient men who are determined to finish what they start, while their Aries children's lack of patience drives them to leap before they look.

It would be a miracle to see Aries children work slowly and carefully, but Dad is the man who can help them see the light in this regard. He can guide his young Aries kids toward a life based on commitment and self-discipline, and he can teach these children how to stay with a project until they have seen it through to the end.

Aries tend to get bored quickly, and they are not usually patient people. A Taurus dad is usually a stable man, and his ability to work with details is a real attribute when it comes to raising these kids.

Dad is realistic and tends to hold on to the material world, while his Aries kids want to believe that there is a rainbow around every corner. Dad needs to be careful not to stifle his children's feisty spirit because that special fire is the key to their leadership qualities. Dan can help these naive little fireballs understand that they will be wasting valuable energy by spending their time with people who are unworthy of their trust.

Dad needs peace and harmony in his life. Therefore, he will take the middle of the road to avoid personal confrontation. Aries children do not understand the gray areas of life, as they see things in black or white. Dad is a go-getter, and when he makes up his mind, his determination is limitless. He can help his kids work on self-discipline and commitment.

Dad will admire his Aries children's ability to act upon what they say without hesitation. He is an insightful man, and he would be wise to compliment and appreciate his Aries children's efforts without placing too much restraint on their zest for life.

The Gemini Parent/The Aries Child

The initial insight I have to give you about Gemini parents is that they are always logical and somewhat detached. This tendency will definitely exasperate Aries children, as they are basically emotional and attached. So how can children who need to share feelings reach a parent who needs to be logical? Since logic is the basis of the Gemini personality, emotions may confuse or scare them. If one gives Geminis the facts and asks for the bottom line, they are perfectly happy to resolve the problem. Aries children can deal with the bottom line, but instead of dealing with facts, their bottom line has to do with emotions. They want to express ideas and understand how they themselves and others feel.

The traits that the Gemini parent will share with these children are desires for knowledge, freedom, and space. The positive aspect in this parent/child relationship is that Aries children are not as demanding as some of the other sun-sign children. The negative aspect will be a lack of attention. If Aries children feel that they're not getting enough of it from their parents, they can begin to resent the inability of the Gemini parent to fulfill their emotional needs. They may view this characteristic as a lack of approval or love, and their self-image and personal security can suffer.

The Gemini Mom/The Aries Child

Mom may not be a natural housewife. She can feel quite strained when she has children, and will impose severe pressure upon herself to be perfect in every way. She will fight her own need for freedom and space on a daily basis, while imprinting her control and dominance onto her children. Aries children are usually very strong-minded, and they are not easily controlled or dominated. They need the opportunity to make their own choices and decisions.

Since Mom is very bright, she will recognize the fact that her fiery children are quite intelligent and that their energy is a match for hers. Mom needs to motivate these fire kids, instead of simply ordering them about.

Overall, it is the courageous nature of Aries children that fascinates Gemini Mom so much. She welcomes an action-oriented child who tends to take risks in life. Both she and her Aries kids will develop a mutually satisfying relationship due to this type of mental affinity. The one concern I have when an air parent raises a fire child, though, is that Mom is basically logical, while her kids are emotionally based. So, Mom needs to make every effort to cater to their need for attention and affection, particularly in times of confusion and crisis.

The Gemini Dad/The Aries Child

Dad and his Aries children can be great friends, as they share a powerful desire to learn. An Aries child can be a willing student, and a Gemini dad will enjoy the responsibility of teaching this bright child the importance of developing the mind. Dad can be a bit inconsistent in his behavior, as he does not like anyone to pin him down. He is a free spirit who gets very involved in pursuing his own interests, often without considering the fact that his children really need him. Dad would be wise to understand that Aries children need a lot of attention and that they are very sensitive. Even though young Aries children are very independent and don't enjoy possessive parents, they still want to share their feelings and ideas with a parent who can help to validate decisions and nurture their self-confidence.

Gemini fathers are usually cheerful and optimistic. They have a powerful zest for life, and they have the ability to fit in anywhere. Parent and child are both fast talkers, but Aries children tend to be more honest about their convictions. When Dad makes a promise, he must keep it, and when he offers his opinions, he needs to be firm. This is the best way to garner his kids' respect.

Dad is a very intelligent man whose logical mind can help his little fireballs be more objective and reasonable. Aries children tend to make decisions quickly before they look at the entire picture, and this impulsive quality can lead to ill-advised moves on their part. Dad can do a lot to prevent such occurrences from happening in the first place!

The Cancer Parent/The Aries Child

If I referred to Cancer the Crab, and Aries the Ram, would you think that they were compatible? Hardly! For example, the Cancer mother is an emotional lady whose life usually revolves around the home. If her home is not in order, *she* is not in order! When it comes to her children, she loves them so much that it hurts—especially when it comes to an Aries child. However, an Aries child wants comfortable love, not dominant love.

Aries children are energetic. In fact, their energy is a vital component of their mental "survival kits." Even when these fire children are in a state of collapse, they will still keep going. Who else can do ten things at a time and still look for more interests to keep them busy? These children need to lead, and their spirit cannot be stifled. That's why it's important for water parents to understand that they cannot possess these fire children. If Aries do not receive validation of their spirit, they will rebel.

Family is everything to Cancer parents. Their own lives will be put on hold if their children need them. They tend to overwhelm themselves with worry, and this behavior can be the cause of their negativity. Cancer parents need to be positive with their fire children, because their zest for life is uncontrollable.

Cancers tend to be fearful of the outside world, and that is why their home is their sanctuary. Aries children are courageous and tend to naively search for new horizons. They do not like being shackled to anyone or anything. Aries children need a lot of love and attention and will appreciate living in a comfortable home where they can find safety and security, but a home will never take the place of outside interests. It's important for Cancer parents to understand that their fire kids will always be looking for excitement and adventure.

Aries children need guidance when it comes to making impulsive decisions. They need to be taught to look at all the facts before jumping into the pond. Both Cancers and Aries are emotional, but the parents do not like surprises, whereas the children love the spontaneity of life. Cancer parents can be quite helpful when it comes to teaching their fire kids that it's important to finish what they start. An Aries personality denotes the promoter, who needs to conquer the big project and leave the details to someone else. This doesn't mean that they are not perfectionists, because they *do* want everything to be right. But Aries children need their Cancer parents' guidance when it comes to developing tolerance and patience, as they can be headstrong and stubborn once they make up their minds. The best way for Cancer parents to reach their Aries children is to give them the freedom to explore and to learn about life without restricting their ability to enthusiastically motivate those around them.

The Cancer Mom/The Aries Child

The Cancer mom can devour and absorb her children if she is not careful. She is sensitive and emotional and can endure great suffering on behalf of any belief, principle, or cause. She is an excessive giver, and will get angry when she feels that she is not receiving the attention that she thinks she deserves. This is primarily *her* need, and not that of her children. One might think that since Aries children are emotional and enjoy a lot of attention, parent and child would be a team. Not necessarily so! When Aries are little tots, they will not be in touch with this possessive quality in Mom, and will probably feel very secure in the home environment. But, as Aries children grow, personal conflict can occur. The inner strength and self-confidence of Aries children may scare this mother, and this insecurity will come out through manipulation and guilt. Cancer is a water sign, and as I have mentioned before, what does water do to fire? You're right—it puts it out!

If a Cancer mom gives birth to an Aries, she must realize that no one can possess this child. Aries children love emotional security, but if Mom's personal security is dependent on these kids, she will undoubtedly experience rejection.

The Cancer Dad/The Aries Child

The Cancer dad is a loving father, as long as he can have things his own way. Cancer dads can be strongly opinionated and judgmental. They do feel deeply, but they may have a fear of personal expression. In order to mask his sensitivity, the Cancer father may use what I call the "total control" method. He will show those kids whose house they live in! What happens to Aries children when this situation occurs? They will buck! What happens to the Cancer father when this situation occurs? Well, he turns into the baby in the family. Emotional immaturity isn't reserved just for children.

A Cancer dad will have to work harder when raising his Aries child. He needs to understand that there are two bosses in the household—one is the parent, and the other is the child. Since Aries children need freedom, Dad needs to loosen his reins a bit in order to achieve a compromise with these fire kids. The result will be a personally fulfilling relationship, as both parent and child can learn a great deal from each other.

My last bit of advice: if Dad does not learn to express his feelings, his children may never be sure of his love. As I have previously mentioned, Aries children must always be validated by their parents. The Cancer dad can base his family relationships on receiving the respect of his children. If he tries to subdue his need to dominate his environment, and will accept open communication with his offspring, he can get the recognition he needs.

The Leo Parent/The Aries Child

A Leo parent and an Aries child will definitely be in fire-sign heaven! Mom or Dad will be a buddy, a pal, a hang-out person—a true romantic figure. This Leo lion/lioness is on the same wavelength as their Aries child—what a great beginning! Both must watch their egos, and if they do so, life will be beautiful. A Leo parent can be a perfect role model for these kids, as Mom or Dad is self-sufficient, independent, energetic, and a love bunny. These parents will be so proud of their Aries children that these spirited kids will feel genuine support and caring. What Leo parents naturally give to their Aries children is validation.

Of course, both of these signs are emotional, so life will never be dull. This will be a house of action. For some of the other sun signs, it may not be easy to grow up in this home, but young Aries will think it's a dream come true. The Aries child and the Leo parent feel mutually dependent. Leo parents love to hear that young

Aries is a "chip off the old block." Statements such as: "She looks like you," "His voice is like yours," or "He's as bossy as you are," will keep Leo parents proud and happy. With an Aries child, Leo parents will have to be cautious about exercising their control, while assuming the responsibility as the king or queen.

If Mom and Dad always remember that they will always be special to little Aries, there should be no need to rule this domain with control. Aries kids will never have a problem expressing their individuality, and Leo parents will appreciate this spirit. Mom and Dad will always feel the need to rule, but will have to understand that *ruling* will eventually have to become *sharing* when it comes to living with an Aries.

The Leo Mom/The Aries Child

Young Aries kids will be the apple of Mom's eye. She will be very proud of her fire children because they will always be able to keep up with her. Both parent and child are quick thinkers who will usually agree on most issues. They don't waste time waiting for the right answer. Young Aries children will certainly give Mom a run for her money, as they definitely have their own opinions on things. They tend to depend on a Leo mother because she gets things done quickly. They will trust Mom to follow through on her promises, and parent and child will no doubt build an honest relationship.

Mom can be a risk-taker, but once she settles in, she doesn't like to change her lifestyle. Young Aries children, however, are always looking for change, and their courageous natures will constantly search for new adventures. On the one hand, Mom will admire these feisty little fire kids, and on the other, she may fear for their lives. Mom doesn't have to worry because young Aries will come to her to help with decisions, as long as she's fair. If she can honor and support her Aries children's talents and abilities, she will have the kind of relationship that she hoped for when she became a mother!

The Leo Dad/The Aries Child

It is known that fire signs need to lead, and they do not enjoy secondary positions. Leo Dad is a leader who tends to protect his children and wants to provide them with the best life possible. He has high expectations and standards for himself, which tend to be passed on to these children. Aries children will never mind a Leo father's ability to motivate them, but they will be dissatisfied if he tries to make all of their decisions. Dad needs to know that when he raises these strong children, it would be best to discuss the decisions that involve them and allow them to offer their opinions on these matters.

All fire signs have a lot of energy, and they tend to carry a youthful glow as long as they possibly can. My research has proven that Leos usually look 10 years younger than they are. Therefore, Dad will always be able to match young Aries' zest for life, and he will also have the ability to make things happen. Aries children will usually feel that their father is strong and powerful, and they tend to look up to Dad.

His need for domination may have to be tempered when he raises the Aries child, however, as a person under this sign can never be controlled.

The Virgo Parent/The Aries Child

Demand, demand, demand—Virgo parents simply do not have control over their need to give orders. Virgo parents claim that the reason for their inability to let go of anything is because all things within their surrounding environment, whether it be home or career, must be perfect. We all know that nothing or no one is perfect, but try to explain this statement to a Virgo. If Mom and Dad would understand that their own need for control and perfection must be tinged with understanding and support of their children's individual personalities, then their kids would not have to suffer. No human being can obey *every* instruction.

Children of Virgo parents, especially Aries children, will vehemently dislike the word *obey.* When a conservative Virgo parent tries to impose his or her will upon an Aries child, watch the fireworks, or should I say *arguments.* A Virgo is a disciplinarian, and an Aries is a free spirit. The Virgo parent's responsibility will be to develop a strategic plan of love in order to gain the confidence of this little person. Well, let me help you: Virgo's world is neat and tidy, efficient and organized, full of regular patterns and rigidity, and while this can be fine for a Capricorn child, these traits can be quite detrimental to an *Aries* child's zest for life.

Aries children will want to partake in all of life's experiences with a sense of freedom. If a Virgo parent squelches Aries' expansive vision, he or she will crush this kid's creativity. Virgo parents are devoted and untiring in taking care of their children. They want to raise them to be socially acceptable human beings. Virgos are practical and have a difficult time understanding the emotions or sensitivity of an Aries child. After all, what does emotion have to do with keeping the bathroom clean?

Aries children are born with their own clear ideas of right and wrong, and they can be perfectionists in their own right. It is not the "tidy tasks" that upset them; it is the stern orders they will receive from their Virgo mom or dad. A Virgo parent will learn that tact and kindness will go a long way with their Aries children!

The Virgo Mom/The Aries Child

A Virgo mom is analytical and intuitive. She can pick out the best dress when shopping or the freshest flowers for a dinner party, but most of all, she can recognize a person who is talented and bright. Mom will grow to respect her Aries children for their intelligence and agile minds. Parent and child can learn from each other as long as Mom tries to give young Aries the space to explore life, without watching every detail. Aries children look at the big picture, and they can quickly detect what's wrong with it. An Aries will be more interested in the message than all of the intricate details. A Virgo mother is also able to see what's wrong with the picture, but she is not as concerned with the message as she is with every minute detail. This is one of the biggest differences between mother and child: an Aries child is emotional and sensitive, where a Virgo mother is practical and critical.

Aries children are usually leaders who have pretty large egos. They try very hard to do everything right, but their need for freedom and a lack of patience can prevent them from concentrating on every detail. Young Aries kids can benefit from Mom's practical expertise and self-discipline, but they will not appreciate being told to live up to unreasonable expectations and standards. If Mom can try not to stifle her Aries kids' spirit and spontaneity, she can reach her fiery children by helping them understand the importance of discipline and patience.

The Virgo Dad/The Aries Child

A Virgo father has many positive qualities, but he has a terrible time letting go of anything. Dad believes that he can persuade anyone to change their mind through his never-ending determination to pursue his own course. It's important for Dad to understand that he cannot force Aries children into anything. Once Aries children make up their minds, they can be as stubborn as Dad. Dad would be wise to give his Aries kids a series of options to choose from when an important decision is necessary. Parent and child are both strong and opinionated. The Aries opinions usually filter through their emotions, while the Virgo's opinions come through practical theorizing.

Dad also needs to be careful about being too critical and judgmental, as Aries kids take everything personally. If Dad is honest and constructive with his assessments, his children will listen. On the other hand, if these kids feel like they're being attacked in some way, Dad's words will fall on deaf ears.

Overall, if Dad can help his Aries child understand the practicalities of life, instead of always reaching for the stars, a happy balance can definitely be reached between parent and child.

The Libra Parent/The Aries Child

Logical, fair, free-spirited, artistic, administrative, and harmonious—that is the Libra parent. Wait a minute…this statement is not entirely true—these parents *can* have problems releasing their anger. One of the reasons for this reluctance is that Libras often have a hard time saying what they feel at the time they feel it. Arguments can intimidate and frighten them; their sense of balance is shaken. When someone hurts them, they can begin to harbor resentments toward that person until they reach a boiling point. This inner cauldron will trigger their anger at an inappropriate time, and of course, they will be totally misunderstood.

Libra parents must endeavor to get to the root cause of, and therefore eliminate, their anger when raising Aries children. In my research, I've found that about one percent of Libras have dealt with the frustration that they have built up through childhood. People often have a hard time believing that this is the case with these sweet and caring individuals. When ire arises, their personalities can turn sour and abusive. Libra parents can do themselves a favor by working on expressing their hurt at the time they feel it, instead of building their resentment to a crescendo. This hidden volcano gradually increases in force, volume, or loudness, and suddenly it erupts with gusto. However, this does not have to be the case if these parents begin to take baby steps in order to confront what they feel. Personal confrontation will help to alleviate their anger and build their self-esteem.

Libra parents are helpful and servicing personalities who truly love their children. Libras are somewhat detached on an emotional level, and there is something of a "space cadet" hidden under all of that logic. These parents will admire and "fan the fire" of young Aries, but at times the direct and truthful demeanor of the Aries will embarrass them, upsetting their sense of balance. When this situation occurs, Libras begin to stifle Aries' assertive natures. If this happens, the Aries fire will turn into steam, so be careful Mom or Dad—this child's steam can scald you!

Libras, let me explain how to understand your Aries children when they appear to be ultra-aggressive. You, as parents, need to remember that the key phrase of an Aries child is "I am," which means "I am born with self-confidence." Self-confidence is a blessing that most people would like to share with the Aries personality. Since you Libra parents can be emotionally reserved, you need to learn to view your Aries children's combustion in a positive light. They are so much fun, after all!

Wise Libra parents can try to calmly temper their know-it-all attitudes if they should become overbearing. The temperance should never be severe, though, for it can stifle the spirit of leadership and self-confidence that is within an Aries child.

The Libra Mom/The Aries Child

Libra mothers are peaceloving, while their Aries children were born to make war! These fire children want to love everyone, but they tend to be argumentative. Mom is a natural mediator, and she can help encourage peace and harmony in the household. She may not always succeed, but these fire children will admire her efforts to soothe them.

Aries feel, while Mom thinks! These kids are spontaneous leaders, while Mom tends to be a diplomat. She is usually a liberal and good-natured woman who does not want to stifle her fire children's freedom. She just needs to be careful about being too critical or narrowminded when her Aries kids make impulsive choices. Libra mothers are usually intuitive, and they will understand their fire children's assertive personalities. Therefore, they would be wise to encourage their children's ability to act upon what they feel. However, she needs to explain to them that it's better to objectively think about all the aspects of a situation before being forced to deal with a mistake that can't be undone.

Mom may not choose to develop her artistic ability, but she will always encourage her children's creative side. Both Libra and Aries love beauty, and they are stimulated by different cultures. Aries children can be greatly motivated by Mom's natural aura of tranquility. They will admire Mom's ability to mediate and find the best in people. Aries children were not born to accept peace as a comfortable part of living. They are pioneers who move forward wanting to build or, if need be, rebuild the walls that may crumble around them. At times, Aries' powerful energy can tire Mom out, but she will continue to fan their fire. Libras are peacemakers, while Aries are fighters, and both need to learn from each other.

The Libra Dad/The Aries Child

Dad could be on the side of the law, or he could be frustrated with the legal system, depending on what his issue is on any particular day. Libra men believe in justice and will defend anyone that has been treated unfairly. It's wonderful that Dad will go out of his way to help someone else, but it bothers me that he has so much trouble fighting for himself. One problem that can occur when it comes to a Libra's need for peace is his fear of personal confrontation. One wonders how someone could believe in peace, yet build up so much internal anger. I think the answer is that Libra's sense of fairness is not always satisfied by reasonable solutions.

Aries children are not as inwardly angry as their Libra dads because they will confront their beliefs and talk about them. Once the anger has subsided, it's really gone, as an Aries does not harbor resentment. Dad can teach his Aries children how to balance their assertive behavior, while learning how to be objective. And, this Libra father's Aries children can inspire *him* with their positive self-image.

Dad is usually accurate and precise, and he attends to the most insignificant details, a task that comes naturally to him, as he's a very patient person. Aries children, on the other hand, are usually impatient and will happily leave minute details to someone else. Make no mistake—Aries can be perfectionists, but they are easily bored. Dad has the ability to teach his kids to finish what they start, and his kids can teach him how to lighten up a little!

The Scorpio Parent/The Aries Child

Scorpio parents must learn to curb their need to control everything when raising Aries children. I know that they cannot help giving orders (perhaps I should call it protection), but Aries kids will respond poorly to orders and to being overwhelmed by someone. The Scorpio parent must represent stability, not dictatorship. Now, Scorpio parents, don't be angry—I understand that your home is well organized, and you like to take care of your environment. But remember that although Aries children can also be domestic, their greatest interest is in the outside world.

No one can ever deny that most Scorpios love and desire children. Mom and Dad will be dedicated to raising their kids and teaching them the best manners in order to inspire appropriate public behavior. Aries children will appear to be wise and mature very early in life, but a Scorpio parent must be careful of the idealistic baby that lurks inside. Scorpios deal with reality, not fantasy, when it comes to parenting. Therefore, they view their Aries children as dreamers who need a great deal of discipline. However, some aspects of a Scorpio parent's discipline will appear negative to the Aries Ram. At those times, their horns will stand erect, and the fight will commence. The Aries spontaneity may be viewed as impulsive by the Scorpio parent. Scorpios will have to understand and appreciate that their Aries children will always be "free spirits" who are assertive and self-assured.

In fact, there may be a subconscious bit of envy on the part of these parents. If this envy does not turn into jealousy or create a sense of challenge in Scorpio parents (forcing the Aries to abide by their rules), a deep, mutually satisfying friendship will form the basis of this parent/child relationship!

The Scorpio Mom/The Aries Child

Mom takes care of her home and her children, both of which are her biggest priorities. Scorpio mothers have natural expertise when it comes to understanding household affairs. Aries children can suffer in the hands of a Scorpio mom if she refuses to believe that they do not enjoy living in a regimented environment. Mom needs to learn that her Aries children want the freedom to grow up in a home that is not filled with extreme rules and regulations. Aries children can benefit from Mom's efficiency and sense of organization, but they will not enjoy taking orders all of the time. A Scorpio mom wants to protect her children; therefore, she tends to watch over everything they do so they won't be hurt. She needs to realize that these kids do not thrive on this type of behavior. If Mom can share her expertise with her Aries children, while acknowledging that she is raising free spirits, parent and child can work together to accept one another's approach to life.

The Scorpio Dad/The Aries Child

Both Dad and his Aries children are emotional. In fact, Dad is even more intense when it comes to worrying and making mountains out of molehills. Aries children are not geared toward constant worry. They make a decision and don't take a long time to act upon that decision. This behavior begins at an early age. If Dad can learn to appreciate his intelligent and positive children, he can be very instrumental in guiding them in the right direction. If he chooses to try and control their thinking, however, he may end up in constant arguments with these fiery individuals. When a Scorpio dad raises Aries children, he would be wise to learn that these free spirits will not relate to being attacked or controlled.

Dad is a charming and intelligent man. He is also innovative and creative with his ideas. He and his Aries children can find a lot to talk about as they begin to grow. Dad definitely does admire kids who appear to be emotionally mature and self-sufficient. Yet, Scorpio Dad may tend to view his Aries children as immature because they are not always as serious about every detail of a situation as he is.

All in all, Dad will enjoy the Aries enthusiasm and positive approach to life; he just needs to be careful not to stifle his children's potential.

The Sagittarius Parent/The Aries Child

Free spirits walking hand in hand in the park—who are these charming, charismatic individuals? They are Mom and Dad Sagittarius, and their Aries children. This relationship can be beautiful if their competitive natures do not get in the way. The logical question might be: what kind of competition could exist between a Sagittarius parent and an Aries child? Answer: Battling egos.

Sagittarius and Aries do have an instant wavelength between them, and as you have previously read, this is always the beginning of a great relationship. Mom and Dad (particularly Dad) want to create an open home environment, where "doing your own thing" is allowed. An Aries can certainly live that lifestyle. A Sagittarius mom and her Aries children will enjoy intellectual and philosophical compatibility. They will learn from each other, but there will be times when Aries children can be a bit too intense and dramatic for their Sagittarius mother. However, the Sagittarius mother also has her own "on-stage," performing ability, and she too loves the limelight. Mother and children need to share their need for personal attention, as we definitely know that Aries kids will never accept secondary positions.

Sagittarius parents have a tendency to upstage their own children, trying to prove that they know all of the answers. Aries children will have a problem with this behavior. Mom and Dad need to understand that becoming parents of Aries children will give them the challenge of sharing their emotional intensity and inner strength. The key to compatibility in this family is "honest love and a sense of humor." This formula is certain to bring joy and laughter that will brighten each room of their home.

The Sagittarius Mom/The Aries Child

A fire parent and a fire child share a similar approach to life, which can be the beginning of a healthy relationship. Both Sagittarius Mom and her Aries children need to protect their freedom and individuality. Therefore, young Aries will be able to explore life without too much restriction. Mom can be very definite and exacting in reference to the way she runs her household, but she has a complete understanding of the need for humor and fun. Mom and her kids will be able to share their interests, both on an intellectual and creative level. Mom will always want to develop the young Aries mind, and these children will love to learn. Both Sagittarius Mom and her Aries kids need constant mental stimulation. They have a lot of energy and tend to get bored quickly. As a result, Mom will need to introduce her Aries kids to a variety of interesting subjects to stimulate their minds. If Mom can understand that she has to explain her decisions, and ask for young Aries' opinions on important issues, she will find that she has made friends for life!

The Sagittarius Dad/The Aries Child

Sagittarius Dad is a free spirit who could have been a pirate sailing the high seas. Aries kids, on the other hand, are also free spirits, but they would most likely remain on land in order to discover their adventurous natures. There is usually a powerful emotional bond between this parent and child. Dad is honest and protective, and young Aries will trust him to do the right thing.

Aries children need a lot of attention and stroking, even though they are independent and self-reliant. Dad is a very supportive man, but his own sense of self-control can temper his demonstrative nature to a great extent.

Sagittarius fathers and Aries children are usually very active and versatile. They both seek out the new and different on a regular basis. Even though this parent and child think alike, though, Aries are much more possessive of the people and things they care about. A Sagittarius father's freedom is extremely important to him, and he tends to distance himself from the people he loves, even though he is an emotional person on the whole. Dad would be wise to understand that he cannot distance himself from his Aries children. These fire kids want Dad to affirm their choices, nurture their self-confidence, and help them make sound decisions.

Parent and child tend to set their goals and then act upon them. They are both spontaneous, impulsive fireballs, leaders who do not like secondary positions. Dad and his Aries kids can build a healthy and loving relationship as long as Dad acknowledges that his heart belongs to his fiery children!

The Capricorn Parent/The Aries Child

Here they are—the serious Capricorn goats, who feel and act old before their time, ultimately stifling their bloom of youth. How will this parent reach the ever-young ram, looking for excitement and adventure? We have a bit of a problem with this pair. Home and domesticity—these are the Capricorn's comfort zones. These parents will soon find that trying to control their Aries children by making them feel guilty about even the smallest task will simply not work. A Capricorn parent must never try to guilt-trip these children, as this approach will backfire. Aries do not accept guilt—they ignore it. Frustration between parent and child will be a constant problem in the household if a Capricorn parent continues to climb the guilt-edged side of the mountain with respect to these fire kids. There will be chaos if the Aries self-esteem is thwarted by this parent.

The most special traits common to Aries individuals are their self-confidence and unconquered belief in what they say and do. If Aries children feel that judgment or unfair criticism is the basis of the parent/child relationship, they will fly the coop early in life, leaving the Capricorn parent grief-stricken in the process. These parents should know that, as a result of their fixed natures, they can appear blind to the needs of these spontaneous children, and they may create friction that will push these kids away.

Capricorn parents need to work on establishing direct, honest confrontation with their Aries children. Any manipulation for one's own purpose will cause resentment. Aries children will not respond to unfair punishment, and they will not express deep regret for wrongdoing unless given a valid reason. I will have to bank on the intelligence inherent in the Capricorn parent to recognize, respect, and accept these ever-searching children. All in all, Capricorn parents are stable and organized, and they need to concentrate on restoring their Aries children's equilibrium when emotional forces tend to displace it.

The Capricorn Mom/The Aries Child

Mom totally understands the value of practical thinking. She depends on it. Her Aries children may possess common sense, but their hearts lead the way. So what do we have? We may have a mother who can try to impose her will upon these children. Capricorn mothers are perfectionists who tend to be very hard on themselves. If Mom makes a mistake, she will ask herself over and over, "How could I have done that when I know better?"

My answer to her is, "You're only human." Aries individuals can also be perfectionists, and they do not have a lot of respect for anyone who makes too many mistakes. However, they will not obsess about their feelings. They will correct the problem and go on. In many ways, this parent and child may complement each other. Young Aries can teach Mom about letting go, and she can teach her child the value of self-discipline and patience. Capricorns will wait a long time to make the right choice, where an Aries will quickly take action. I know that there can be a middle ground for both parent and child. It's called *compromise!*

The Capricorn Dad/The Aries Child

A Capricorn man respects anyone who is optimistic, assertive, independent, and self-confident. Therefore, he will respect his Aries children. Dad is usually a very bright man who takes serious charge of his life. He is also very focused on building a safe and stable foundation for his family. Young Aries will feel comfortable having a father who is strong and protective, but these kids may have a problem with Dad's somewhat distant persona. Capricorn men have a difficult time showing their children how they feel, and they usually have a problem displaying affection. As such, they show their kids how much they love them by trying to provide the material things in life. Most Aries children do not feel that material things are as important as saying "I love you," though. They need that special attention, and if they do not get it, they can retreat into their own world.

Dad needs to try and communicate with his Aries children and be there to support their feelings and decisions without trying to impose too many practicalities. Doing so can stifle the Aries spirit and enthusiasm. It's important for Aries children to be offered practical guidance, but no one will ever teach them to give up doing their own thing. If Dad can try to temper his sometimes rigid nature when he raises these children, he can be a steady influence without making too many unreasonable demands.

The Aquarius Parent/The Aries Child

I think...you feel. I think...you feel. Logic and emotion—this is the battle between the Aquarius parent and an Aries child. What may salvage this relationship is their mutual desire to learn. Aquarius is an extremely bright sun sign, and the capacity for learning can be unsurmountable. If you remember, I've mentioned how detached and insular the Aquarius sun sign can be. Well, this is the main source of tension between an Aquarius parent and an Aries child.

An Aquarius may have a problem verbalizing emotions and may tend to shy away from intimacy. On the other hand, the Aries child welcomes intimacy and attention. The Aquarius individual will not immediately understand these needs. Fiery Aries children can often be too emotional for their Aquarius parents. Aries children just aren't logical. Their satisfaction in life lies in being involved with their own imagination. They will openly express the sentiment, "I appreciate you leaving me alone" to anyone who violates their space. Aries children will need an Aquarius parent's presence to help stabilize and calm their emotions. The Aquarius parent, on the other hand, ought to show concern for, and interest in, everything that their Aries children do.

Dad, most likely, will allow Mom to do most of the parenting, assuming that his children will eventually develop their own identities, as he was able to do. Mom will handle everything logically, be totally self-sacrificing, and will suppress her need to talk about how she feels. High intelligence is the key to personal compatibility for the Aquarius parent and an Aries child. They are both very different, but they are both very smart. The two minds will mix well, and life's lessons will be learned through the Aquarius parent's ability to stabilize their Aries children with wisdom, logic, and respect.

The Aquarius Mom/The Aries Child

Mom is usually a very honest woman whose independence is unsurpassed. In fact, she can almost be too independent, never asking for help from anyone. She has an easy, comfortable manner when she raises her children, and does not place any restriction on their individuality. This quality will please Aries children, who need the freedom to be their own people. Mom agrees with these fire kids' independent philosophy, and there will be no problems in this area.

Mom functions through her intellect, as emotion is not her base. Her Aries children's base *is* emotion, though, and they usually learn through their instincts. Young Aries is always willing to learn, but it's the heart before the head that counts. Many of my Aries female clients have told me that their Aquarius mothers were cold and distant and that there was a lack of interpersonal communication. I try to tell them that their mothers were not indifferent to their feelings, they just couldn't understand them. It's very important for an Aquarius mom to try and communicate with her Aries child in order to build a harmonious relationship. I know it's difficult, but I am confident that Mom's intelligence will guide her in the right direction.

Mom will always be there to support young Aries' education and encourage these children to explore. She's a visionary, and will enjoy watching her kids pursue their goals. Both parent and child have powerful egos and a need to control. Therefore, there can be some conflict if Mom doesn't learn to be flexible with her Aries children. Her suggestions and guidance will benefit them, as long as she understands that there will be times when their emotions may stand in the way. It's best for Mom and her children to compromise when important decisions come up in order to appreciate the mental affinity that will be shared between them.

The Aquarius Dad/The Aries Child

"I know," Dad said.

"I am," Aries replied.

When you put these key phrases together, what do you find? A logical know-it-all parent, and a self-confident know-it-all child. The truth is that they both really do know a lot, and it's up to both of them to share their blessings. The only difference is that Dad *thinks,* while his child *feels.* Once Dad can understand that emotion is a fact of life when raising his Aries children, he can be patient and considerate of their feelings.

Dad would be wise to explain that he cannot always relate to Aries' emotions, especially if there are any disagreements. Dad cannot begin to explain these feelings until little Aries begins to grow, however, so it's up to Dad to try not to distance himself. Dad and his Aries are both individualists who listen to their own drummer. The best way for these two to really find each other will be through Dad's ability to be a stable force in his Aries children's life. His calm, unassuming nature appeals to his Aries kids, and if Dad can try to nurture their emotions, this relationship can be a compatible one.

The Pisces Parent/The Aries Child

Pisces individuals are symbolized by two fish swimming in opposite directions, never making a decision. Can you blame anyone for referring to them as "wishy-washy"? I know that Pisces parents do not like to hear this sentiment expressed, but trust me, they understand their problem. Aries children born to a Pisces parent are a totally different breed—they will be quick as lightning, the ultimate decision makers. As these children begin to grow and learn, they will start to question everything a Pisces parent tells them to do, especially if the latter doesn't make up his or her mind quickly enough. Aries children are so directional in their thinking that they could never think of swimming in opposite directions.

Decision and respect are the two concepts that mark the real problem with this parent/child relationship. Mom and Dad Pisces, it's up to you to make your decisions and live by them. If you fear doing so, and continually delay or avoid taking charge, your Aries children will take over your home, and that's when the trouble starts. We have talked about water and fire throughout this chapter, and by now, you must realize that these elements can be troublesome when living together under the same roof. The wavelength does not remain stable. Emotion is what saves the Pisces parent, and Aries children will see that their parents have great big hearts, a quality which touches these fire kids.

As for Pisces parents, they admire the inner strength of their Aries children; however, they can often resent Aries' domineering personality. The compromise that the Pisces is forced to accept when competing with these kids can be exhausting. Imagine a three-year-old know-it-all running the show, while his or her Pisces parents cringe in despair.

Pisces parents need to put their respective feet down in order to gain the respect of these children. The Pisces honor is at stake. It will take a lot of work, as the opinions of these kids can rarely be swayed.

It's important to recognize that the Pisces personality is quite childlike and idealistic. Mix that with Aries children who believe that they are adults, even while living in a baby's body. Can a baby raise a baby? The answer is obvious—Mom and Dad need to grow up first. Don't worry, Pisces parents, your kindness and compassion will definitely spark the love of your Aries children, as long as they don't have to raise *you!*

The Pisces Mom/The Aries Child

Both Mom and her Aries child are emotional, and both can be dreamers. It's just that Aries children go after their dreams, while Pisces individuals usually keep them locked up in their hearts. There will be times when Mom's frustration with her assertive children can make her feel that she has no control. It's best for her to believe in her own strength, rather than trying to manipulate these fire kids. I have had many female Pisces clients who have come to me to help them control these dynamic children. I try to tell them that control is not the answer. If anything, it will cause their children to rebel against them. If a Pisces mother can show her Aries children that she is an extremely loving person who will support and encourage their decisions, these sensitive children will be happy to find a parent who cares so much.

Mom and her Aries children can be very creative, and they will enjoy music, art, and theater. Aries and Pisces both like to play, and there is the potential for so much fun between them. Mom needs to hold on to her sense of humor when young Aries exasperates her in order to raise these children with the kind of self-confident attitude that is crucial to her kids' personal growth.

The Pisces Dad/The Aries Child

Dad has strong emotions, but he tends to shy away from them. He often tries to impose a life of order and perfection upon himself as a substitute for his deep-seated feelings. This kind of perfectionistic attitude can turn into control, and I think that Dad takes unfair advantage of himself when he tries to avoid his emotions. It would be best for Dad to reveal his sensitivity and zest for life in order to openly communicate with his Aries children. Young Aries will respond to emotion, but will never respond to control.

Dad usually has a great sense of humor, so most people do not realize just how serious he really is. He hides behind a mask that few people are ever able to remove. Dad needs to build an honest and sincere relationship with his Aries children, as these kids really value the truth. If Dad can be there to resolve problems and support young Aries' important decisions, these kids will appreciate Dad's special concern.

SUMMARY

How can anyone attempt to sum up Aries children? If I were to use three words that best describe these fiery little persons, it would be *courage, enthusiasm,* and *truth.* Parents who raise Aries kids will quickly find that their personal independence and powerful will cannot be abused or shaken. Otherwise, the rebellion will be heard loud and clear.

One of the best ways for me to sum up the Aries personality in a nutshell is by relating a true story about my mother's friend Francis and her Aries daughter Shelly, who was a school friend of mine. This experience was so devastating for young Shelly that she repeated the explicit facts to me over and over for years afterward, thereby indelibly impressing the details of it in my mind.

When Shelly was a child, Francis was upset that her young daughter's hair was too straight and thick. Her long curls would fall apart very quickly, and she would constantly complain to my mother. So, one day my mother suggested, "Take Shelly to a beautician so she can give her a permanent."

Well, Francis thought this was a sound idea and decided to take Shelly to a local beauty shop, which happened to be in a dark and dingy basement apartment. In the middle of the living room was a tall free-standing machine that looked like a torture device. Fastened to this machine were long wires with curlers on either end.

The "victim" who was getting the permanent had to sit in a chair while the curlers were attached to her hair.

Shelly slowly climbed into the chair, and the beautician attached the curlers. After a short period of time, the beautician removed the curlers to unveil horribly short, frizzy, clumpy hair. As Shelly looked in the mirror at her new reflection, she began to cry hysterically. She screamed to her mother that she would never show her ugly hair to anyone. Shelly was eight years old, going on ninety. When she made up her mind, that was it. So, she decided that she should wear a hat on her head at school, at play, or wherever she was seen—she was determined that her hair would not be visible to the public. This vigil continued for one month until the frizzies seemed to calm down. You must know by now that Francis never gave her daughter another permanent. Shelly's wrath was too much to bear for this Libra mother. Since Libras do not enjoy fighting and intensely dislike loud voices, Shelly was allowed to wear the hat whenever and wherever she desired.

Suffering through that experience made Francis realize that her daughter had a definite mind of her own. How she missed this aspect of Shelly's personality from the beginning is still a mystery to me. Francis should have given Shelly a choice— did she or did she not want a permanent?

Moms will find that their Aries children have good taste and have very clear opinions about what they like. I remember asking Shelly how she explained to our friends at school (and everyone else) why she was wearing the hat. She said that she simply explained, "I don't really like to wear this hat, but I dislike wearing the frizzy hair underneath. The hat comes off when the hair grows out." That seemed sensible to her. Shelly's self-contained personality, already evident at age eight, gave her the impetus to follow through with her own convictions, even though she had to explain herself to everyone. Since the Aries key phrase is "I am," her thought was, "Here I am with this frizzy hair and that's not me."

Need I say more? Most moms would tell Francis that she was too easy on Shelly, but I believe that when she gave her daughter permission to wear the hat, she did the right thing. An Aries child is quite single-minded, and to stifle her spirit would be the same as releasing the gas from a balloon filled with helium!

Chapter Two

♉ TAURUS THE BULL

APRIL 20–MAY 20   **ELEMENT:** Earth   **KEY PHRASE:** "I have"

THE TAURUS PERSONALITY

"Love me, please don't leave me," is the motto of the Taurus child. To be forsaken or abandoned is the worst feeling in the world for *any* child, but for young Taureans, this emotion becomes forever etched in their minds. They tend to dramatize conditions that affect them by adding details, which can be fictional. A Taurean's emotional security is extremely fragile.

My Taurus daughter Alissa was delivered on April 23rd, via Caesarean section (C-section). In those days it was "once a C-Section, always a C-Section. (Her brother Layne came a few years earlier—I'll tell you about him later on.)

I remember shouting to my obstetrician as he delivered my baby, "I know that she has a lot of hair," and the nurse replied, with surprise in her voice, "That's right, a lot of brown hair. By the way, how do you know it's a girl?"

I answered, "I was expecting her."

That Little Girl Has Magic.

When I finally held Alissa in my arms and looked down at my Taurus baby's dovelike soft, sultry brown eyes, I thought that they appeared to be symbols of intensity, combined with innocence and gentility. A surge of emotion filtered through my body. I remember thinking, What a perfect baby.

Her radiant aura was accurately described by my cousin on her second birthday. He said, "That little girl has magic." Then he added, "She is so much more than a sweet, lovable child; she is magnetic. Her charm will attract many adoring subjects in years to come." His prophecy was absolutely accurate. I now call her a "male magnet."

It was always a pleasure raising Alissa until the moment came when she felt threatened by "emotional insecurity." Taurus children put parents to a daily test. It's called the "don't try to take away my security" test. When Mom and Dad say the word *no*, watch Taurus children's eyes begin to squint and narrow, slowly forming into slits. In a matter of seconds, watch these little darlings turn into furious, steaming bulls with ferocious tempers.

☆ ☆ ☆

One late evening, as I lay half asleep in my bed, I felt a tap on my shoulder. I looked up, with one eye open and saw Ms. Alissa, age four, standing next to my bed. She said, "I want to sleep with you and Daddy."

I said, "Lissy, you have a beautiful room with a comfortable bed. What's the matter?"

"There's ghosts on the wall," she replied.

I tried to comfort her. "Honey, there are no ghosts, they are just shadows."

Her eyes began to fold into her famous "squint and scrunch" look. "I'm not sleeping in that room, it's scary," she declared. I thought she was about to snort. (A note to all moms and dads of children of this sun sign—please be aware that the instant your Taurus children begin to verbalize, they will create mountains out of molehills!)

Finally, I said, "Lissa, that's silly, it's your imagination."

Glaring at me, with hands on her hips, she turned, and choosing to ignore my explanation, she climbed right onto the other side of the bed to sleep next to her father. He sleepily put his arms around her, and as she cuddled close to him, she forcefully poked me with her elbow. In that moment, I saw her magic turn into witchcraft. Taurus children, if their security is threatened, will insist on having their own way!

☆ ☆ ☆

Taurus—the Bull!

Why is this sun sign called Taurus the Bull? There are a multitude of reasons. You've heard the statements: "He's like a bull in a China Shop," "She's a bull at the gate," or "Take the bull by the horns." Well, each of these descriptions can apply to the Taurus personality. They are highly sensitive, complex, chaotic, turbulent, unchangeable, unyielding people, and if pushed to the wall, they will insist on having the last word. They have a tendency to dissect their personal decisions to death, and this habit can become an obsession.

"Can I do it?" "Will I be perfect?" Will I be good enough?" Parents must be aware of the probable Taurus answer: "No, I'm not good enough." They can really exhaust themselves.

Mom and Dad, listen carefully. It will be frustrating and demanding to persist in trying to convince your Taurus children that they are worthy. Telling them to have faith in their abilities actually presents a very difficult problem: they won't believe you. Lacking a belief in themselves can remain with them for a long time, even though they may appear very successful and self-assured on the surface.

Parents who raise Taurus children can help build their self-confidence by creating a stable home environment, which includes rules to live by and a sense of structure. Mom and Dad need to designate specific "pattern building" responsibilities at home such as hanging up clothes, cleaning bedrooms, and washing the dishes. And most of all, these kids should remain consistent in performing all their duties. This will start to prepare them for school. Structured responsibility will serve as a motivator, leading them in a stable direction in life.

Taurus children must also be challenged. They will discover that such projects are fun, and that household chores are definitely boring. Do not release them from their responsibilities, though! They must be made to feel that they are a part of the family team. Parents must teach a "home study" course called "Accountability 101," or their Taurus children may flounder for many years, trying to decide on a life path that will satisfy them. Since they find it difficult to believe in their natural talents and skills, this effort could be quite trying.

An Inflexible Nature

The inflexible nature of Taurus children is usually related to a fear of personal confrontation—they don't want anyone to tell them that they're wrong. If they *are* proven wrong, the hurt and embarrassed Taurus children will repress their feelings and then expect you to punish them. Parents need to understand that Taurus children can be rebellious. A Taurus will consistently resist verbal force and control. Honesty is the most important contributing factor in a relationship between parents and their Taurus children. The most important belief that Taurus kids hold is: Parents who speak the truth deserve respect.

Taurus children also have "stubborn fits." What do I consider a stubborn fit? That's when someone is unreasonably obstinate and very difficult to subdue.

Taureans fear the unknown as well, mostly on a personal level. I have a Ph.D. in life experience when it comes to the Taurus personality. When my daughter Alissa would have one of her fits, I would try to control my Aries impatience and ask, "Are you mad at me?" She usually didn't answer and would continue to pout. Of course, as a small child, she could never understand that her stubborn hysteria was indicative of the Taurus child's capacity for "instant anger."

Parents, believe it or not, at your most frustrating, exasperating moments, you must not lose your temper. Swallow hard and pull back. Remember: your Taurus children's anger is a call for your personal attention. The first thing you must do is try to divert their anger by using humor. Then, rehash the problem and clearly explain why you were upset in a reasonable, stable manner. Don't shout; however, be firm. Young Taureans will always need your approval, and if you tell them that you don't like something that they've done, that's the same thing as saying that you don't like *them*. Use the "calm and funny" approach—it works. A sense of humor will always distract their anger and mellow the Bull. Once you convince these stubborn kids that you sincerely want to guide and help them, you may receive another emotional test—but they will never again feign deafness when it comes to heeding your advice.

A special note: these Taurus Bulls can make you so angry that you may want to give them "time outs" during an argument. Don't bother—this strategy will just compound their stubbornness. It's more important to let them know that you are in their corner. A cold, calculating, insensitive posture will only enhance their anger and fear. Always remember that most Taureans do not understand the words *constructive criticism,* as any type of reproach seems to validate their greatest fear: "I am not capable." This is a major dilemma with Taurus children, so it's crucial that they are taught to believe in themselves!

A Desire for Independence

"Don't do it for me, or I will try to avoid my responsibilities." These words are hidden in the Taurus mind, but they project the plea of a Taurus child. One day, my Leo friend, Teri, referring to Margie, her Taurus daughter, looked at me with pain in her eyes and asked, "Do I have to watch every word I say to her?"

As a Leo, Teri is fiery, quick on the trigger, and very direct. She moves fast, talks fast, and is…just plain fast. Her patience for her teenage daughter had run out for the hundredth time, and she was venting her exasperation to me. "Margie is so slow!" she exclaimed. "She lives in her own world. I tell her, 'Margie, please clean up your room, it's a mess.' And she says to me, 'Okay, sure,' and two days later nothing's happened. Is she slow or just lazy?"

I replied, "A little of both."

Teri shook her head. "I know my impatient nature is going to force me to clean up after her. I don't want to, but I just can't stand that mess."

I countered, "No Teri, you will not clean up after her, or she will expect you to take care of her for the rest of her life. If you had set up household rules, established accountability, and given her responsibility when she was young, this situation might not have arisen. You cannot waver from your own values or expectations."

Her silence became disquieting, and finally she muttered, "Oh, that's great. What do I do now?"

I suggested, "You have to sit her down and explain the facts to her. "Say: 'Listen Margie, I know I have been too lenient with you, and it may be my fault, but it's never too late for me to change. When I ask you to please clean up your room, I mean it. From now on, I'm going to give you a time limit. And if that time constriction is not honored, I will think of a punishment to fit the crime. In this family, we help, not hurt each other.'"

If Teri had continued to clean that room for her daughter, she would have picked up on Teri's Achilles heel—her impatience. Unconsciously, Margie could manipulate Teri and have her do everything for her—and if Margie felt that she could get away with murder as a young girl, why wouldn't she feel that she could escape responsibility in the future?

When the parent takes over, this behavior can become a real danger for Taurus children. As these kids grow, they will not believe that they can handle responsibility, since they don't have the experience. Overly protective, solicitous parents will only minimize their self-esteem and increase their emotional insecurity.

Taurus children let their parents know that they will always want them to be there for them, so it's important for Mom and Dad to reassure them that this will always be the case. However, if parents encourage their dependency, these kids will resent Mom and Dad forever!

Smooth and Sensual

One of the definitions in the dictionary for *sensuality* is "the arousing or exciting of the senses." The word *smooth* has many definitions, but I would choose "having an even, uninterrupted movement or flow." A little Taurus girl can grow into a smooth and sensual woman—think about Cher and Michelle Pfeiffer. A little Taurus boy can grow into a believable, charismatic man—think about Henry Fonda, James Stewart, Al Pacino, Daniel Day-Lewis, or Jerry Seinfeld.

In the girl child, we see a "protect me" sign written all over her. In a boy child, we see "macho man, with sensitivity" written all over him. Those who perceive these qualities in Taurus children will be magically drawn to them.

Most people find Taureans attractive, complicated, and somewhat of a mystery. One cannot grasp what they are thinking because they are so analytical that they don't even know themselves! They constantly search for the illuminating answer to the question: "What do I do for the rest of my life?" Even though their smooth, sensual "star" qualities help attract many admirers, they constantly question whether or not they're good enough at what they do.

Talents and Skills

Parents of Taurus children must teach them to focus. A lack of discipline can work against them because they enjoy being lazy. These earth children, more than their Capricorn and Virgo counterparts, will need Mom and Dad's assistance in order to assess their goals and to find significant direction in their lives.

Taureans value inspirational guidance. More than individuals of any other sign, they need to develop their natural talents and skills through a diverse education. This type of intellectual stimulation serves to build their self-confidence and will lead the way toward setting future goals and actualizing dreams. Once on this road, Taurus children will want to try out a variety of endeavors; parents need to remember to encourage them to finish what they start. It may be a struggle—in fact, Mom or Dad will have to be exceptionally patient with their Taurus children, but their perseverance will be the key to helping these kids handle life's lessons. Parents' encouragement now will save a great deal of personal uncertainty in the future.

As Mom and Dad progress with respect to their parenting skills, it's important for them to acknowledge that creativity is the spark that ignites the Taurus spirit. It can be music, dance, theater, or any field that requires imagination. Once again, these areas can be developed through education, and Mom and Dad should nurture this child's talent. Think of Barbra Streisand, Audrey Hepburn, Zubin Mehta, and Shirley MacLaine—all Taureans. I'm not saying that these children should be movie stars or creative artists, what they actually do doesn't really matter. What is important is having the ability to help young Taureans recognize their abilities.

One note of advice to parents: don't ever force your Taurus child to become involved in activities that they don't have a predilection for just because *you* do, or you may hear "I don't like dance class—my legs hurt. I don't like the guitar—I get warts on my fingers. I don't like gymnastics—I'm not coordinated." What's behind all of these excuses is a simple lack of self-confidence—or simple lack of interest. These little worrywarts quickly decide that they won't be good enough and give up before they start—unless it's *their* decision to try something. Whatever their final choices, discipline is imperative, as young Taureans will only discover their talents through hard work.

Also, parents should never ask their little Taureans, in exasperation, "What's the matter with you?" They will recoil and take it personally. Believe me, I have lived through this saga, and it is an exasperating test for any parent. However, in the end, if parents will just sustain their support and encouragement, Taurus children will grow into confident adults.

The Taurus Temper

Taurus children have a built-in combustibility. Don't be fooled by the sweet demeanor of these loving children, as their angry feelings will rarely be overt. But, when the flames do ignite, through a build-up of internal tension and resentment—watch out! The moment that Taurus children unleash their frustrations, their parents might do well to head for the hills—or at least another room! As the years have passed, I now find it humorous to talk about the "indelible impressions" made by my Taurus daughter Alissa. A representative story follows.

On this particular day in December, any weatherman would say that Chicago was "snowed in." Alissa and I were having a powerful argument about her household responsibilities, specifically on the subject of washing dishes—that is who was supposed to do them. There we were in the heat of a very heated battle, when she finally reached her peak of rage. She turned and rushed out of the house, running down the stairs barefoot in her flannel pajamas—needing to escape my wrath. The best way she could do this was to seek refuge in her girlfriend Christy's house. Christy lived down the block, but you had to go through an alley to get there.

I fully understood how much attention and approval my daughter needed, since I had been rising this "stubborn sweetheart" for nearly 15 years. I knew what I had to do. I took great pride in being a "Star Psychologist" when it came to dealing with this child. So, I, too left the house, running after her, down the alley, barefoot, on stones and snow, in my nightgown. I still cannot fathom my Aries energy, but there I was at her girlfriend's house, minutes after she arrived. I began knocking on the door, shouting, "Alissa, come out here right now!"

Her girlfriend Christy, a young Leo, innocently said, "Alissa isn't here, Mrs. Friedman." Christy was determined to protect her friend.

I vehemently replied, "Christy, if Lissa does not come out here this moment, I will come in and get her." Now, Christy feared for her life. There were a few moments of silence, and finally, the door opened and a bedraggled child slowly came out, her head down. There was this "sorry look" on her face and she said, "Mommy, I knew you really loved me."

I shook my head in resignation. "Lissa, your tests will be the death of me." She smiled, and then put her arms around me. We walked back to our house, in the snow, through the alley, over the stones, arm in arm. I often wonder…how did we avoid being hospitalized for double pneumonia?

Parents may think I'm a bit crazy, but Alissa's faith in my love and my "blind perseverance," have definitely given me the title of her "confidante extraordinaire."

The only way to work with the hysterical side of these Taurus children is to keep them believing that your support will always be there. One would think this would be "a given" if you were a caring parent, but that's not necessarily true. Nothing is a given with the zodiac's most sensitive earth child.

And Possessive, Too!

Taurus children are quite possessive. They will declare ownership over all property. Little girls will save all of their stuffed animals, dolls, wrapping paper, and poems. Little boys will keep all of their sports memorabilia, favorite toys, and personal mementos. And they will keep these things forever. "I have" is the Taurus key phrase, and when they have something or someone as a possession, Taureans hold on to them for dear life; as they get older, this tendency seems to worsen.

We know that most people sentimentally keep their belongings for a period of time, finally leaving room only for the memories that are most important to them. Not with Taureans, however—memories remain in their conscious minds forever as a part of their nature. As young children, Taureans become attached to little things. As they mature, the "things" grow in size, whether they are connected to memorabilia or relationships.

Taurus children can obsessively dwell on their thoughts and feelings. Their hopes and dreams—whether expressed or unexpressed—are as clear in their minds as a painting or photograph. They must be encouraged to express their ideas, or their nervous systems will be affected. This situation can cause physical problems that usually manifest themselves in the digestive tract. Excessive negative thinking can also contribute to their already vulnerable and insecure natures. It is very important for Mom and Dad to give their Taurus children permission to speak about what they think and feel—even the stuff that may be negative.

Parents can also help their Taurus children by curtailing frequent criticism. Trust me, young Taurus will never forget the cruel things that are said to them and they will tend to embellish these statements in fantastic stories in the future. They won't intentionally try to color others' words; it's just the way that they remember the incident.

One of the most endearing qualities of Taureans is their unwavering sense of loyalty. If they make a solemn promise, pledge their love, or vow to keep a secret, they will most certainly follow through on it. But...if any individual to whom they have shown their loyalty later deserts or betrays them, the bond between the two can be destroyed. If someone deceives Taurus children, they will lose their trust in that person, but once loyalty is established, that person can do no wrong.

All in all, parents who have talented, unique Taurus children are definitely fortunate, and one of the best ways to help them build fulfilling lives is to help them *lessen their loads!*

☆ ☆ ☆

PARENT AND CHILD

The Aries Parent/The Taurus Child

To all Aries parents: you know from reading the stories that I've presented so far that I am the proud Aries mother of a Taurus daughter. My personal experience has shown me that it is both a challenge and a joy to raise this child. It's never easy raising any child, but with a Taurus, you can be sure that you'll never suffer from boredom. This sweet little troublemaker will give you a run for your money.

The one special gift that an Aries mother or father naturally has is the power to love deeply. Their protective nature is built-in. These traits and feelings may be the savior in the relationship. Dad needs to be careful, as his natural strength and cool personality may intimidate his Taurus child. Mom's personality may have a similar effect, but her honest and expressive quality will bind the relationship.

What happens when a strong, impatient, fast-thinking, fast-moving parent has a methodical, patient, stubborn slowpoke for a child? Nerves and exasperation abound. Aries parents must learn to allow their Taurus children to move within their own time and space. They need to accept the fact that they will never be able to change their rate of movement. When they are very young, until the time they enter school, these children are sweet, delightful, cuddly, and often shy. Kindergarten is usually a breeze, but then parents will really have to prepare their Taureans for first grade, a time when they will have to contend with discipline and order, which will be inflicted upon them by a stranger—the teacher.

What will the reaction of young Taureans be when they don't receive the sole, undivided attention of the authority figure, but instead, have to share him or her with other kids? Well, I'll tell you: they'll begin to create chaos, and it doesn't matter whether it's positive or negative, as long as they can raise their voices above the crowd. Taureans can become theatrical and funny... or, they can cause trouble. Once they start their antics, one teacher may find them whimsical, and another will think that they're ludicrous. If a teacher thinks a Taurus child's behavior is inappropriate, though, it's actually because he or she wants to control the behavior without examining the underlying cause of the problem. It is difficult to work with a child who has an insatiable need for attention, as there are so many children to consider. A wise teacher would understand that a little special attention will go a long way. Recognition and appreciation of the Taurus child's work can be the difference between frustration and satisfaction.

Aries parents love perfectly behaved children. And until now, their little darling has been perfect, but here comes another test. What can an Aries parent do when faced with the rebellious Taurus child? Just breathe deeply and hold back on criticism—that's what! Mom and Dad must understand that little Taurus needs to make a huge adjustment in order to deal with the pressures of attending school for the first time. If they automatically punish this rebellious behavior, their Taurus children's attitude will only get worse.

The Aries Mom/The Taurus Child

It's very easy for an impatient and action-oriented mother to get the job done when her sweet, slow-moving children's tendency is to take their time. Mom means well, but she needs to step back and wait for her young Taureans to do the chores she has asked them to do. Taurus children are not only slow and methodical in their approach to life, but they can be a bit lazy. It's best that parents not encourage this trait. Once young Taurus understands that Mom can do everything, this child is just as happy to let her take over.

A Taurus wears an invisible sign that says "protect me," so a responsible Aries mother follows through. It is very important for Mom to understand that young Taurus needs to learn how to be responsible at an early age. If everything is done for these children when they are very young, they begin to feel as though they are incompetent. Taurus children have a problem believing in themselves, and they need to learn that they are, in fact, very capable, in order to build their self-esteem. Mom is a wonderful leader, and she can be an excellent role model for her earth child...as long as she lets go!

The Aries Dad/The Taurus Child

Dad is an individualist—first, last, and always! He likes to do things his way, and he rarely asks for help. He is very decisive, and at times he can be impulsive and spontaneous. Dad is usually a strong man who wants to lead. His Taurus children dream of being individualists, but their need for apporval and pleasing everyone around them tends to get in their way. It's very important for Aries dads to help their Taurus children understand that it's all right to say no when they don't want to do something. Taurus children take a long time to make a decision because they are hard on themselves and want to be perfect. They are very sensitive and easily embarrassed if they make a mistake. When I work with Taurus clients, I ask them over and over again, "What would happen to you if you made a mistake?" A few of the answers I get are, "People may think that I'm not good enough, or not as smart as I should be." I then ask, "Who says you *should* be anything?"

Taureans have a problem "believing in themselves," and they need their parents to set a healthy example without intimidating them. Most Aries fathers are very giving, but they tend to be impatient, and when they raise a Taurus, they really need to develop a lot of patience. Taurus children do not move fast, while Aries fathers are quick—men of action. Dad needs to accept the fact that his earth children need to work in their own time and space. He cannot force these sensitive kids into anything. Aries fathers can be very instrumental in helping their children make their own decisions (even if they're small ones), and these dads can motivate their kids to act upon them. If these fathers handle everything, their Taurus children will become much too dependent on them. Dad tends to take over because he is self-confident and aggressive, but when he raises these kids, he needs to back off in order to help them develop self-confidence.

Dad will be very attracted to his Taurus kids, as they are usually personable and vulnerable. This father is a natural caretaker, but I suggest that he guide and motivate, rather than control. By doing so, his Taurus children will feel that any final decisions were made through teamwork and cooperation between parent and child.

The Taurus Parent/The Taurus Child

This parent and child represent the "Safety and Security Duo"—they are the touchy-feely comfort couple. They do think, feel, and behave in a similar fashion, the sensitive child reflecting the emotional parent. Taureans project all their emotional behavior through what they absorb in their home life. If Mom and Dad grew up in a home with warm, loving parents who tried to understand their behavior, then the Taurus child will value and impart the same warmth, love, and understanding. However, a different personality will be revealed if Mom and Dad were raised by cold, detached parents; in such a case, the Taurus child can become an exact replica of those qualities. And in life, their personalities will reflect the environment that they live in.

Parents, whatever "raising technique" may have been present in your own parents' home, your own technique when raising this child should be warm, nurturing, and comfortable. A cold and negative atmosphere will frighten and intimidate Taurus children. Their perception of fear and intimidation will always be out of proportion; it's important to them that their home is a loving and safe place.

Always try to touch, kiss, and hug your Taurus child on a regular basis. If your personality happens to be reserved or remote, really make an effort to work on your attitude, and always try to give your Taurus children positive feedback. If these kids are raised in a cold atmosphere, they will quickly decide that it is not personally safe to touch or feel. And once they make this determination, they might take on a cold demeanor themselves. So, Mom and Dad, please make an effort to show warmth and affection to your Taurus children. Give them the opportunity to have what your parents may not have been able to give you—that is, assurance and confidence!

The Taurus Mom/The Taurus Child

Mom wants to create a home environment that reflects her need for comfort and security. She is a practical woman, and once her lifestyle is intact, she doesn't want anything in it to change. In fact, she holds on to everything, even when she knows that it's time to let go. Well, she is raising a child who feels the same way that she does. Young Taureans will be very pleased to live in a comfortable home that is safe and secure. Mom will never have to force them into anything, as these kids will usually agree to disagree.

My research has proven that most Taureans question everything that they do. This is one of the reasons they tend to suffer on a personal level. Many successful Taureans thrive in the professional and creative world, as they have great ideas, but when it comes to their personal lives, they tend to say very little when they feel hurt. Therefore, their level of self-esteem can be low. If Mom has a similar problem, she will know that it's important for her to teach her children to stand up for what they believe when it comes to interpersonal relationships.

Taurus children need to feel that it's okay to defend themselves when they believe they are right. Since they need a lot of attention and have a difficult time asking for anything, they tend to punish the people who do not take care of their needs. Mom needs to tell her earth children that it's okay to talk about their hurt feelings, instead of building internal anger. If Mom can work on her children's hostile feelings at a young age, she will save these Taureans a lot of grief during the formative years.

The Taurus Dad/The Taurus Child

Dad is both practical and sensitive. He can appear to be laid-back and friendly, or he can come across as an outgoing salesman. It doesn't matter which type he is, though—either way he tends to be very hard on himself. Dad may have a great sense of humor, but he is deadly serious about how he runs his life.

He and his Taurus children have much in common because they tend to share the same values in life. If Dad believes in his talents and abilities, he can be very successful; but if he tends to doubt himself, he may always be looking for the right road.

Both Dad and his Taurus children will be stubborn, and their horns can lock. On the one hand, Taurus children are insecure, and on the other, they want to be the bosses in any situation. Dad needs to understand that his children need his attention and his guidance when it comes to their insecurity and bossiness. One can only hope that Dad's parents gave him the assurance that he himself needed in his youth. If Dad makes an effort to understand that his Taurus children's insecurity lies behind their stubborn nature, he will bend, giving his children the support needed to feel safe and secure.

The Gemini Parent/The Taurus Child

What does a Taurus child do with a parent who lives through logic? It is a fact that the Gemini key phrase is "I think." Their minds are always going. Half of the time, Geminis are full of life, and the rest of the time, they're extremely solemn. Geminis are not referred to as twin personalities for no reason. I call them the schizophrenics of the zodiac. They are serious and moody when overwhelmed, communicative and interested when they want to learn something, and they can appear cool where emotion is concerned. We must not judge them, as thinkers are not feelers. Too much emotion can confuse and scare them.

Their saving grace is that they are sentimental, with a desire to save old photographs, cards, and letters to bring back pleasant memories. They are very sympathetic to human frailty, and appear to have a longing for experiences, things, or friendships belonging to the past.

For the serious Gemini, a family is an investment. For the restless, searching Gemini, a family can become a burden. Whichever one applies to you, Gemini parent, please remember that while raising a Taurus child, you should unfold the responsible and protective side your nature. Taureans want you near them. You can't afford to tune out mentally. Geminis are exceptionally bright, and they love to have fun.

Mom and Dad will enjoy their precocious Taurus children, instantly recognizing their innate wisdom and early maturity. Taurus children are old souls in many ways, but don't let this early maturity fool you—they will take a long time to grow up. I call them the "late bloomers" of the zodiac. The Gemini parent and the Taurus child are a fun couple who have a lot in common—after all, two split personalities should have an easy time understanding each other. The main problems that can occur between this parent and a Taurus child are due to the fact that Gemini parents are primarily loners who will not always understand having to give undivided attention to their children. This behavior will cause insecurity within the sensitive Taurus. To prevent this problem, Mom and Dad need to work on making an effort to compliment, encourage, protect, and support their Taurus children.

Gemini parents cannot afford to detach themselves emotionally. For a Gemini, this task can be very difficult. Remember: Geminis want the facts and nothing but the facts. The best way for Gemini parents to communicate with their Taurus children is to take on the role of educator, inspiring them to learn.

The Gemini Mom/The Taurus Child

Mom is usually an independent realist who works hard and has fun at the same time. Taurus children are also realists and understand the practicalities of life, but they are very sensitive and serious about their lives. Mom can be a good role model for her Taurus kids because she tends to encourage self-discipline, perseverance, and ambition. Her logical mind may not always tune into her children's sensitivity; therefore, she will need to work on being considerate of their feelings. Mom's reasonable nature is very important to her Taurus children, as they can become unreasonable when they feel hurt. It's best for Mom to listen to her earth children's problems, rather than dismissing their need for attention. This could be quite a task for a logical mother!

Mom will feel protective when she is near her soft, vulnerable children, and these earth kids will respond to her sparkling personality. A Gemini mother comes off as cool, calm, and collected. If you look inside, you can see the deep intensity that lurks within. Unfortunately, Taurus children can mistake "cool" for "cold," and they may feel that Mom doesn't care. That is far from the truth, but Mom cannot passively respond to these kids, as they will mistake this behavior for a lack of love.

All in all, this pair will learn a lot from each other and benefit from their complementary qualities!

The Gemini Dad/The Taurus Child

A Gemini father often builds his self-esteem through his career. At times, this may be a bit self-indulgent because his family needs him. Dad, more than Mom, relies on his logic, objectivity, and reason. Give him the facts, and he will solve the problem. Dad will need to modify some of his habits when he raises these Taurus children, though, as they do not depend on facts. These kids tend to take forever to resolve problems and make decisions. They tend to dissect everything, and sometimes they miss out on opportunities because they're so afraid of making mistakes.

Dad can be very instrumental in helping his children get to the bottom line of situations. He is a sensible visionary who can see the big picture and make up his mind quickly. However, Dad needs to understand that his Taurus kids tend to put a lot of pressure on themselves. In fact, he has the same problem at times. So, he has the capacity to help ease his children's load, as well as his own.

Dad is a lot of fun, and he's also a great pal. He will need to control his tendency to be critical and make quick judgments, though, because Taurus children tend to take everything personally. These kids are easily intimidated, so Dad needs to be reasonable and gentle when he offers advice. Parent and child can develop a healthy and honest relationship as long as Dad recognizes his earth children's need for personal attention.

The Cancer Parent/The Taurus Child

A Cancer parent will be naturally loving and affectionate. Home and children are where it's at for this Mom and Dad. They will instinctively provide the background, culture, and home environment needed for their Taurus children to thrive, but there is one trait that Cancers have that can cause their kids to run in the other direction. A Taurus child needs to be loved, not smothered. Mom and Dad will not mean to overprotect these sensitive earth children, but Cancer parents have a tendency to do so. Cancer parents need to control their home environment, and they like to keep everything neatly in its place. I can just hear their words: "This is my house, so everything in it must reflect me; therefore, I assume that everything in my home becomes my personal possession." Mom and Dad, please note: you will not be able to control Taurus children as though they are possessions in your home!

If Cancer parents try to smother or manipulate their Taurus children, the relationship will suffer. Cancer parents regard the home as a shelter to protect them from the outside world. Please understand, parents: your Taurus children will often return to this shelter, but don't encourage them to use it as a refuge. It will stifle their personal growth.

In an attempt to keep everything under control, Cancer parents may appear to have suspicious natures. Suspicion will bring out the rebel that exists within their Taurus children, however. Cancers do not trust people easily; their own sensitivity is so great that it leaves them open to being deeply hurt by others. But young

Taureans will dislike feeling that they are not trustworthy, and then Cancer parents will have an open, armed resistance on their hands. Mom and Dad must set a pattern of family trust, and let go of their fear of interpersonal communication.

A final note: a Taurus is not a born domestic and may feel a certain resistance to cooking and cleaning; this characteristic should not be used as a basis for parental judgment. Taurus children can easily learn how to manage a home, but their parents' tone of voice must not imply force. Cancer parents need to reveal their tenderhearted, maternal or paternal natures so that their Taurus children's hearts will be won over.

The Cancer Mom/The Taurus Child

Mom's home and her children are the most important priorities in her life. She can build a successful career because she is very smart and efficient, but her personal security comes through her family and the close relationships formed therein. Mom will pay a lot of attention to her Taurus children, and they will benefit from the kind of nurturing she offers. Since safety and security are Taurus children's highest priorities, this Mom will never let them down.

The best advice I can offer Mom with respect to her Taurus children is: "Do not be overprotective." Mom does not mean to control her children, but since they are so important to her, she wants to be involved in everything they are doing. Young Taurus children will not mind Mom's protection, but they will require the freedom to "have their own space" and explore life. Mom would be happy if her Taurus children never left her because she is very attached to these earth kids, but if she is not careful, they will depend on her for everything, and that will damage their self-confidence. Mom has the ability to guide and support her young Taureans so that they set off in the right direction in life.

The Cancer Dad/The Taurus Child

Dad will be comfortable with his Taurus kids because they are so lovable and cuddly. A Cancer father is emotional, so he has the ability to give his Taurus children the attention they need. A home is very important to Dad; it is really the only place that he can relax. He is usually hard-working and perfectionistic, and his emotional nature tends to make him inwardly intense.

Dad needs to be careful that his high expectations and standards do not overwhelm his sensitive Taurus children as they grow. Taureans have a problem when anyone expects them to be perfect, or when they are forced to do anything. Taurus children can be quite stubborn and rebellious, but Dad can thwart this behavior by using an honest and gentle approach with respect to his kids' goals and achievements. Taurus youngsters tend to be insecure, and this insecurity can only be compounded by a parent who does not explain his reasons for making a decision that will involve these earth children. Taurus kids will always trust dads who are considerate of their feelings and support their decisions.

The Leo Parent/The Taurus Child

Leo the Lion and Taurus the Bull—what does this combination bring to mind? The battle for autonomy is one thing. Watch those wills lock. The key phrases of Leo ("I will") and Taurus ("I have") should tell this tale without having to say very much. The Leo parent's need for *control* versus the Taurus child's resentment when it comes to being obligated to do anything is a perplexing situation. Fire-sign parents, who include Aries, Leo, and Sagittarius, all have a need to control, and most of them never realize how overwhelming they can be with their children.

Both Leo Mom and Dad are definitely leaders. They are men and women who act upon what they say. These roaring pussycats can lose patience with their Taurus children if they do not always behave. I don't want Mom and Dad to misunderstand and think that I believe that either of them are ogres. I don't. I know that Leo parents are two of the most loving parents there are. Leos are known as the kings or queens of the zodiac, and they believe that their homes, children, and investments are all part of their kingdom. A Taurus child and a Leo parent run neck-and-neck when it comes to being stubborn. And who do you think needs to bend? I'm certain that you know the answer—it will have to be the king and queen. In my opinion, all parents have the responsibility to try to both understand and help their children with their problems as they're growing up. And when it comes to problems, the Leo mom or dad will always be there. A bit of advice, Leo parents: when you do take on a problem with your Taurus child, don't act too hardheaded—try a little tenderness. Your Taurus child is overly sensitive and will have a negative reaction toward a dictatorship. Mom and Dad's approach to running the household must be tempered by allowing these kids to have their own points of view.

Leo parents are very loving, and their children are everything to them. The most wonderful quality Leo parents have is the ability to motivate and teach. They have the resources to present a variety of challenges to their Taurus children, and these kids will definitely respond. These children will always want to win favor and attention, and the way in which Leo parents can enhance their self-confidence is to appreciate their efforts.

A Leo tends to be naturally confident and independent, two qualities that a Taurus child will benefit from. However, this does not mean that young Taureans will ever stop dissecting their own personal decisions. These kids will always have a problem understanding that they don't have to be perfect. A Leo mother and father can provide the motivation and leadership to help their Taurus children believe in themselves. And this is how to do so, Leo parents: Don't lose patience with your children, don't make all their decisions for them. By dominating your kingdom now, you'll make it more difficult for them to make decisions later in life. Give these children a chance to participate in all aspects of life.

The Leo Mom/The Taurus Child

Most fire signs are attracted to Taurus children because they are so sweet and vulnerable. Therefore, when Leo, Aries, or Sagittarius parents raise these earth kids, they tend to do too much. Taurus children can become dependent on strong parents because they can make life very comfortable for them. For example, Mom is a strong and loving woman who will always do a lot for her children. Many Taurus children lose their self-confidence when they have such a tough act to follow. The best thing that a Leo mom can do for her Taurus children is to teach them to believe in their talents and abilities. It's best for Mom to encourage her young Taureans to take steps on their own in order to build the kind of self-esteem they deserve.

Most Taurus children have little tolerance for things that are not beautiful. Therefore, they love to dress up and look pretty or handsome. Mom also loves aesthetically pleasing surroundings and likes to look good, but it's important for her to teach her earth children that's it's important to believe in who they are, rather than how they look. Taurus children can be very insecure when it comes to their decisions because they need to be perfect. Mom should let them know that they can make a mistake without being criticized. Earth children (Taureans, Capricorns, and Virgos) all tend to take things very personally.

Taurus children are blessed with charming, easygoing personalities. Most people love their kind and sincere natures. But they do possess two traits that can be exasperating: they are stubborn, and they get angry quickly with little provocation. So, it's important for Mom to encourage these kids to talk about their feelings as soon as they can. Otherwise, they will harbor their resentment, and their anger can get in the way of their productivity.

☆   ☆   ☆

I was having dinner with my Leo friend, Annette, and her Taurus daughter, Sue. We usually met at our favorite restaurant once a week. Annette was in rare form, and her 18-year-old daughter had to listen to her comments most of the evening. "Don't crumple your napkin!" her mother told her. "Be careful, Sue, you stained the tablecloth!" She continued, "Why did you wear that dress for dinner? It's much too slinky!"

Sue was starting to boil, but Annette didn't let up.

"What happened to your hair? Why is it so straggly?"

I thought Sue was going to hit her mother, but instead she asked her a sensible question. "Will I ever be the perfect daughter you want, Mother?"

My friend replied, "I can't believe you said that—I love you just the way you are!"

There I was sitting in the middle of this drama, and I felt that I had to say something. "Annette, do you realize how you sound when you criticize your daughter?"

She answered, *"I'm not criticizing her. I just want her to have good manners and wear something that complements her wonderful figure!"*

I asked Annette, "How did you feel when your own mother used to say those things to you?"

She stared at me and finally answered, "You know, I never thought I was much like my mother."

Sue broke into the conversation, "I'm 18 years old. Will I ever be good enough for you? Mom, if you can't control how I eat, what I wear, and how I think, you're just not happy!"

As usual, I was in the position of being the mediator and said, "Annette, you don't seem to understand that the more you tell Sue how to conduct herself, the worse she will become. You cannot control a person's life, or you can ruin it!" I thought to myself, Can you imagine waiting 18 years to openly discuss this problem!

All of a sudden Annette began to cry, and she looked at Sue and exclaimed, "I'm so sorry!"

"Annette," I told her, "it's never too late to stop this kind of criticism. I know that Sue loves you because you are very considerate and loving, but how can she possibly feel good about herself when you constantly tell her what to do? Let her grow up!"

There was a long silence, and finally Sue blurted out, "That was perfect!"

I looked at them and said, "Now let's all have a sensible discussion." We talked for a long time…and it was worth it! This honest and intimate conversation was a real breakthrough in their relationship.

The Leo Dad/The Taurus Child

It's not always easy to live up to Dad. After all, he *is* the king of the zodiac. Most rulers think they are doing the best for their people, but there are times when they are just too domineering. Dad needs to give his young Taureans love and attention without trying to control them. Dad does not always mean to control, but sometimes he just can't help it. Dad can develop a wonderfully sensitive relationship with his Taurus children if he tries to teach them to be independent and self-reliant. These Taureans will be eternally grateful for his guidance.

Dad can take some lessons from his Taurus children when it comes to tolerance. These earth kids work slowly and persistently, while Dad is quick, impatient, and needs immediate gratification. Dad will need to develop patience with his Taurus children, as they will do things in their own time. If he tries to force them into anything, they will rebel. Dad is dramatic and a man of extremes, whereas his earth children tend to avoid them, and rather, choose the safe and secure road. Dad would be wise to understand that his earth children's approach to life is different than his.

If he can support and motivate his young Taurean, he will have accomplished the impossible dream!

The Virgo Parent/The Taurus Child

Virgo parents are grounded in the real world, so when someone does not live up to their expectations of life, the disappointment can be shattering. These parents can be very demanding, particularly if their instructions are not followed to the letter. Have no fear, they will be as hard on themselves as they are on others, though. The true lesson for a Virgo parent is that all people do not function as they do. A Taurus child's dreams and fantasies are always a part of their parents' lives, but the clash between this parent and child can strike with a loud bang. This revolt will come when Mom and Dad try to impose their perfectionist ways on young Taurus.

Taurus children are just plain stubborn, and this trait is a part of their personality that will never be eliminated. Virgo parents will realize this fact very early on. Even though Virgo parents will always seek harmony in the relationship, they always seems to pick out their children's minutest mistakes. Virgo parents feel this way because they are always looking for ways to improve everything, a behavior pattern that is simply a part of their nature. However, this attitude just won't work with a Taurus child. Virgo parents must be careful not to impose their nervous intensity onto their Taurus children, as a young Taurus will sense it immediately. Virgos appear to be calm, cool, and collected, but this is not the true picture. They tend to be obsessive and are determined to achieve their goals. A Taurus child can become neurotic living with such a nervous wreck.

The best advantage Virgo parents have when dealing with Taurus children is their wonderful ability to provide comfort and luxury. Virgo parents can create the most beautiful surroundings for their children. There is a strong sense of compatibility when it comes to their mutual love of beauty on all levels. Luckily, the wavelength of these two personalities is similar, with both of them being practical. The real difference between the two signs is the conflict between Taurus sensitivity and Virgo reality. If a Virgo parent begins to make excessive demands on a Taurus child, that child will think, Go ahead, push me, I don't care...I will move when I want to. Give me orders, I don't care...I will rebel.

Virgos' key phrase ("I analyze") is a concise description of the way they tend to think, feel, and behave. Psychologically, the Virgo is a very curious person who wants to learn about the mind and how it works. Virgo parents must use their acute mental skills to help understand their Taurus children. Virgo parents will be bonded to these vulnerable earth children, as their sweet and lovable qualities are so appealing. Mom and Dad must remember, however, that their Taurus children will not stay sweet for long if they do not ease up on their demands. If criticism is replaced with sound, constructive ideas on how to correct life's problems, Taurus children will respond very well.

The Virgo Mom/The Taurus Child

Both Mom and her Taurus children are practical people who tend to share the same values. Mom will make sure that young Taurus is taken care of, and she can be a perfect mother. But that may be the problem. A Taurus child also has a need to be perfect. Both parent and child have a tendency to be much too hard on themselves. It's up to Mom to try and ease up on her demanding nature when she raises Taurus children. These kids are easily overwhelmed and can begin to retreat from too many demands. In addition, they do not respond well to criticism. I know that Mom cannot always control her critical nature, but it can often hurt her children's self-esteem. Mom would never intentionally hurt her children, as they mean everything to her, but it's time that she realized she can have more fun if she stops making herself crazy. Taurus children are not difficult to raise. If Mom gives them the feeling of safety and security that they need, she will be these earth kids' best friend.

The Virgo Dad/The Taurus Child

Dad is one of the most protective signs in the zodiac. He works to provide a very solid foundation for his family, and young Taurus will never fault him for that. Dad is responsible, but his sense of reason is based on fact, rather than emotion. He and his Taurus child are both earth signs and tend to be practical, but the main difference between a Virgo and a Taurus is the latter's deep sensitivity. As such, Dad needs to watch his tendency to criticize and demand, because young Taurus is easily intimidated. He needs to take a soft approach when it comes to discipline, as this earth child is prone to being hurt.

Most Taurus children dissect all of their own feelings and decisions, and they are afraid to move forward because they don't want to make mistakes. They tend to parent themselves because they want to be perfect. It's important for Dad to help his earth children believe in their own decisions in order to enhance their self-confidence. Dad needs to be honest and sensible before imposing his will on these sensitive children, as this behavior can be harmful to their personal security. Taureans are the most stubborn signs in the zodiac, so these kids may need to please Dad, but they will resent having to do anything that scares them.

Dad tends to express his love in a subtle way. He is not very demonstrative, but he will do anything he can for his children. Therefore, I suggest that he try to be very attentive and supportive when his earth children need him. Taurus kids often scatter their energies; they can procrastinate and will work on projects at the last possible minute. Dad is very efficient and can be a great help by teaching his earth children how to plan and organize their projects. Once Taurus children are shown that being haphazard can be harmful, these intuitive kids are wise enough to accept a parent who wants to help set them on an easier path!

The Libra Parent/The Taurus Child

Libra parents and Taurus children are an easygoing group. Both signs feel that rushing around is not their style. Taurus children will never hear "Let's go" from their Libra parents. They just enjoy hanging out. A lot of love and spirituality will bind this parent and child, as both of them will harmonically fill each other's needs. A Libra mom and dad will never mind giving their Taurus kids a lot of attention, as it will be a great way to share their mutual need for contentment.

Libras are experts at making people feel at ease. Mom, more than Dad, will be a social animal who will instinctively develop a comfort zone around her Taurus children. Dad is a very protective guy who will admire his charming little Taurus daughter, and his Taurus son will be pleased with their relationship since Dad will be totally in sync with the competitive nature of his little boy. The Libra parent and the Taurus child can be a very good team, as they share several innate similarities: 1) They have a strong need for approval, 2) Both need to have a lot of love in their lives, and 3) They can suppress the external signs of anger even when people mistreat them. Instead of dealing directly with difficult people, both of these signs tend to harbor resentment against them.

A Libra mom or dad who is fortunate enough to have a Taurus child should grant these little persons a great gift: teach them to work on healing internal strife. Also, these parents should guide these kids, always trying to communicate honest feelings. A Libra parent should not worry about being misunderstood, as their kids can be trusted with true emotions. Parent and child will find satisfaction in their shared sense of values, humor, and privacy. This healthy pairing will be based on mutual respect for the truth. A sense of justice and fair play will be the two most important features of this relationship.

The Libra Mom/The Taurus Child

Taurus children need to keep their feet on the ground, while a Libra mom tends to look for broader horizons. Mom's natural ability to be objective is her key to raising her Taurus children. These earth children need a lot of attention, and they can be very stubborn and somewhat temperamental. That is, they can create nonexistent dramas and tend to blow things way out of proportion. Mom is very diplomatic, and she tends to assuage her Taurus children's feelings by calmly responding to their theatrical antics.

Both parent and child love beauty and nature, and they are clever, inventive, and creative. Mom is very successful when she works with other people, and her Taurus children will follow in her footsteps. The reason I call Libras the "sensitive thinkers" is because they want to serve humanity, and their knack for diplomacy can positively influence those in their world. Taurus children also have service-oriented personalities, and most people are attracted to their amiable personalities.

Young Taurus can learn a lot from Mom, as she is interested in developing the mind. There is a little girl inside of Mom who always reminds her to play, and her Taurus kids will enjoy this part of her personality. If Mom can remember that Taurus children need a lot of affection and attention when they are hurt and confused, she can help to eliminate their irrational fears and soothe their emotional wounds!

The Libra Dad/The Taurus Child

Dad is comfortable with children, as he tends to understand how they think. After all, he is a little boy at heart! Dad is also a teacher, and he will gladly invest his time and energy into someone who wants to learn. Taurus children will appreciate a parent who has the patience to help with homework, with important decisions, and who will empathize with them during their insecure moments. Dad is a very protective man, and he can sense when his kids are upset. He will always find a way to be there when they are troubled, and these earth children will welcome his attention.

Dad serves as an objective mentor, rather than as an analyst. This characteristic can be beneficial to his Taurus children, who tend to dissect everything—they are very hard on themselves. They fear making decisions, because there is always the possibility that a mistake will be made. Dad naturally offers them safety and security, as that is a mediator's job—he can do it in his sleep!

There are times when Taurus children will obsess over their feelings, and this type of behavior can exasperate Dad, because being a logical man, he just wants to assess the situation and then come to a solution. Dad has a way of turning chaos into reason, and his complex Taurus children are certainly lucky to have him in their lives!

The Scorpio Parent/The Taurus Child

Scorpio parents become protective and overly emotional when they raise their children. They want to be the greatest parents ever, and they feel that if they watch their children so very, very closely, nothing will happen to them. As a result, they tend to run a tight ship. As the Scorpio parents' children grow up, they are expected to participate in household chores, develop peerless social skills, and work up to their greatest potential. Taurus personalities can benefit from the knowledge that they have to be responsible in the home, and they understand the importance of presenting themselves in the best light when they're out in public. However, they can be intimidated by anyone who is overly demanding with respect to their personal and professional accomplishments.

It's okay to make these earth kids accountable for their actions, but they will rebel if they are pushed too far. They need gentle prodding, but they relish the opportunity to offer their own opinions and make their own decisions. Taurus children become too dependent on parents who do everything for them. When they do succeed at something, though, Taureans need to be praised for their achievements!

Scorpio parents usually provide a safe and secure home for their children. These earth kids will definitely find comfort in growing up with parents who like to keep things running smoothly, with very little change in their lifestyles. The real problem Taurus children can have when being raised by Scorpio parents is living up to Mom and Dad's high expectations. Since Taureans tend to dissect everything they do, they can be their own worst enemies. Their obsessive thinking will take the form of: "Am I smart enough?" and "Did I do the right thing?" Scorpio (water) parents need to be cautious when criticizing their earth kids, as it takes very little to make them feel insecure, and their self-esteem is easily tarnished.

The Scorpio Mom/The Taurus Child

Scorpio mothers are "Moms" in every sense of the word. They love their maternal role. They have a natural instinct when it comes to caretaking, no matter what age their children are. Taurus children can be 50 years old, and a Scorpio mother will still be asking them to call her when they get home. Scorpio women are definitely the major caretakers of the zodiac. Taurus children will appreciate the way their Scorpio mother sets up specific rules and structure in the household. Taurus children will definitely not be allowed to get away with laziness. But be careful, Mom, or your Taurus children may try to manipulate you into taking care of all their needs, sensing that you are a sucker for all little kids.

The soft, sweet, vulnerable quality that a little Taurus exudes will entice the Scorpio mother; in fact, this mom can be overly attentive to all of her children. She just adores them. After all, if you were born to be a mother, your family would be of the utmost importance to you, too! The only problem that this mother can have in regards to raising a Taurus child is that she tends to have an overprotective nature. I can hear the Scorpio mother saying things such as: "Put your scarf on, or you'll catch cold," "Do you have your lunch and your milk money?," and "Now, remember, stand at the door facing the playground when I pick you up from school."

A Scorpio mom means well, and when it comes to young Taurus children, this quality will definitely make them feel nurtured. The only problem with giving the types of instructions mentioned above to Taurus kids is: 1) they will forget the scarf at school, 2) lose the milk money, or 3) stand at the door facing the street. This behavior will drive Mom crazy, as specific details are very important to her. The plight of the Scorpio mother is that she will have to work very hard to improve her Taurus children's memory, as these kids can happily exist in their own private world!

The Scorpio Dad/The Taurus Child

A Scorpio father has a different effect on the Taurus child than does a Scorpio mother. He is a very private and secretive man. Mom can also share this trait, but for Dad, it is more pronounced. He is not interested in giving orders in reference to milk money and such. He can control others through the mysterious aura that he exudes. Taurus children may never understand what Dad is thinking about and, as a result, these kids can become quite insecure in this relationship. If Dad does not express his feelings to his son or daughter, the love issue will come to the foreground. Dad really does love this child very much, but he has a real problem verbalizing his thoughts. He may appear cold and austere on the surface, but underneath he is very emotional and intense.

Dad is a strong person who will have no problem resolving a crisis in his family, and he will always be very interested in what his children are doing. He can be quite judgmental, however, and the one thing Taurus children do not appreciate is a parent sitting in judgment of what they do. Dad should try to be open in his conversations with his Taurus children, and flexible in his behavior. The one trait they both share is a great dry sense of humor; his Taurus children will always "get it."

The Sagittarius Parent/The Taurus Child

A Sagittarius parent can often be up in the clouds, while the earthy Taurus child needs to be "down to earth," so to speak. Mom and Dad need to come down to their children's level when they are raising them. Taurus children are usually realistic and practical and tend to reject unrealistic demands and impulsive actions. These earth kids need to feel that their parents are stable. Sagittarians love variety in life, while Taureans tend to resist change because they feel that their safety and security are easily threatened.

Sagittarians are usually kind, compassionate, and loving, but they can run short on patience. Sagitarrian moms and dads are decision makers who may feel frustrated by children who take a long time to make a decision. This is where Mom and Dad must step back and help their Taurus children believe that they have the ability to make sound decisions. It's important that they just gently guide their children, though, as young Taureans can become too dependent on assertive parents who try to take over their lives. Since Taurus children need a lot of attention, an impatient, quick-thinking parent may need to slow down for the sake of these children. It doesn't take much to make them feel insecure.

It's important for Sagittarius parents to work on doing one thing at a time when dealing with a Taurus child, rather than scattering their energy, or this kid's nerves may act up. Sagitarrian parents *are* very motivational, and young Taureans do need someone who can be enthusiastic and daring when it comes to prompting them to take action. So, Taurus children *will* respect a spirited parent. If Mom and Dad will meet these kids halfway, this parent/child relationship will blossom.

Sagittarius parents and Taurus children have great imaginations. They both have the power to create beautiful make-believe worlds in vivid detail. They really have fun together, as they are idealists who would love to live a fairy-tale existence. A Sagitarrian is also a very funny parent. Mom will have a marvelous sense of humor, and Dad may very well be the clown in the family. These traits will give these children a great deal of pleasure!

The Sagittarius Mom/The Taurus Child

If you asked a Sagittarian mother what she would like to accomplish when raising her children, she would probably shrug, and tell you, "It's just important that I be a role model." She is usually an excellent cook, with a clean house, although she tends to do far more chores than she'd prefer. She is a free spirit who can be quite self-sacrificing when it comes to the needs of those around her. Taking care of others makes her feel important, although she sometimes takes on this responsibility because she doesn't trust anybody to do the job as well as she can. Be careful, Sagittarius Mom: as the years go by, you may begin to resent this selfless role; try not to forget about *you*.

The Sagittarius mother has a natural ability when it comes to finding the right toy for a child to play with, the best day-care center for her child, or a top-notch school for her child to attend. Mom is a bright and curious woman who loves to have fun, and she is efficient and reliable. When it comes to her Taurus child, she can be a motivator who will instill her son or daughter with a feeling of competence, and this is the best lesson any mother can give to a child.

The Sagittarius mom and her Taurus child have a lot of fun together, but the one trait that can be a problem for a Sagittarius mother is her tendency to dramatize, complain, and worry. We don't want young Taureans to take on more negativity than they are already born with. First, Mom will complain…and then Taurus will complain…and ultimately, no one will be happy. It's up to Mom to maintain a positive attitude and a good sense of humor, and little Taurus will be glad to follow in her footsteps.

The Sagittarius Dad/The Taurus Child

Dad can become a romantic figure to his Taurus daughter, and a buddy to his Taurus son. The Sagittarius father is a natural rebel, so he tunes right in to any problem. He will assume responsibility for all intense dramas that occur in the family, but there definitely has to be a crisis before he gets involved. After handling whatever problem arises, he'll just go back to doing his own thing and leave the rest to Mom. Sagittarius fathers are emotional, sensitive, and caring, but they can have a problem expressing their feelings. This quality detracts from their relationship with their emotional Taurus children, however, making these kids wonder whether or not their father actually cares about them. Sagittarius fathers, you often have a great sense of humor, but just make sure you don't base your entire relationship on cracking jokes!

Also, Dad, you can be wonderful at bringing a lot of variety into your children's lives, and you have a knack for teaching them about the world around you. You can be a sports fanatic (who especially loves to sail), and you will find that your

Taurus child will enjoy the same interests. Because you do tend to go off on your own, though—that is, you have a need to distance yourself, your Taurus children might take this tendency the wrong way, thinking that the only way to deal with people is on a superficial level. Share all of the variety of life with your Taurus kids—you have the ability to realize your dreams *together!*

The Capricorn Parent/The Taurus Child

They climb every mountain, for at the top there lies a challenge that demands attention. Capricorns respond to trials and tests as babies respond to milk. The main problem suffered by a child who is born to Capricorn parents will be Mom and Dad's belief that they think they know everything. Here we have well-intentioned, but domineering, parents.

Capricorns and Taureans are born earthy and practical. Therefore, this parent and child begin their relationship with similar needs and values. Mom and Dad are self-reliant and determined. These parents make up their mind, and you can be sure that every project on the agenda will be completed. Capricorns cannot handle disappointment, so they need to work on tempering the high expectations that they place on their children. They are relentless in accomplishing all tasks, as anything less than perfection makes them nervous and unhappy.

Taurus children, on the other hand, have problems dealing with overly high expectations or too much pressure. They are *born* hard on themselves, and most of them tend to doubt their abilities. They worry about the need to be perfect, and they fear making mistakes. So, you can see that it's important for Capricorn parents to temper their critical, perfectionistic nature when raising these earth children. These parents need to learn how to respond adequately to their Taurus kids' need for attention and help them develop much-needed self-confidence.

As far as giving love is concerned, Capricorns usually display affection, but more so in material ways than in a demonstrative, physical manner. Taurus children, who are easily intimidated by parents who may appear cold and unfeeling, may take this behavior personally and conclude that they are not loved. So, Capricorn parents need to push past their hesitation to show affection and give their kids lots of hugs and kisses. It may not be easy at first, but the results will be well worth the effort.

Taurus children are truly fortunate to have Capricorn parents who can help them realize their goals. These kids have a tendency to be lazy, so with a Capricorn parent teaching them the value of personal responsibility, they will grow up to be valuable members of society!

The Capricorn Mom/The Taurus Child

A Taurus child does not enjoy being told *what* to do, *how* to do something, or to do something in a certain way. Capricorn mothers can have a tendency to boss around her little Taurus children, which can intimidate them and make them more nervous than they already are. Mom herself can also be a nervous personality, since she is a perfectionist. In this way, she be her own worst enemy, and she can eventually become a foe to her child, too. The Capricorn mother and her Taurus child have much in common, though—both are practical and naturally respect quality and excellence. Mom has impeccable taste, and she will impart this quality to her Taurus child, who instinctively loves beautiful things.

Capricorn mothers are the most determined women in the zodiac. Their strength of mind withstands all adversity. Taurus children are very comfortable living with this earth mother, as they enjoy the safe and secure life she provides. Mom can be quite outspoken and usually believes in her ability to know what's right. Therefore, she can give a lot of orders, and her expectations are very high. Capricorn mothers have a hard time backing off, and they may not always know when to stop pushing. Their own obsessive natures make them nervous. If Mom's behavior makes her anxious, you can just image what it can do to her sensitive child.

Mom's earth children will appreciate the fact that she is stable and consistent. They do not like things to change. Parent and child can have a special relationship if Mom is careful not to become too bossy and critical. Once a parent tries to control these earth children, they will stop talking about their real feelings.

A long time ago, a Taurus client told me, "I tell my Capricorn mother what she wants to hear, and keep the rest to myself!" Taurus children are practical, and their overall values are the same as Mom's. This is a healthy beginning, and they can be very compatible, but Mom's need to control everything can be a problem.

Taurus children need to set goals for themselves, and Mom can be an excellent role model in this regard, as she can help them be efficient and detail-oriented. Taurus children need to follow gentle rules, and they definitely need to assume responsibility. Mom can be the perfect lady to offer this challenge!

The Capricorn Dad/The Taurus Child

Dad is the provider, and he always seems to be working. To a Capricorn man, work can be the essence of his being. Don't get me wrong: Dad loves his family, and he desires a stable home life, but this stability (of the emotional sort) is most often provided by his wife. Dad tends to show love for his children by what he *does* for them; it seems to be easier than having to say "I love you." This part of the Capricorn personality can be very difficult for a Taurus child to bear. Taureans certainly do enjoy material things, but Dad needs to remember that with these kids, attention and affection must come first.

A Capricorn dad's ambition to succeed should not come before his children. I did a workshop recently, and one of the participants who happened to be a Taurus said, "My Capricorn father was always away from home—traveling or staying late at the office. I felt as though he had abandoned me!" A Capricorn father needs to provide financial security—both for himself and his family—but it's important for him to remember that he needs to balance his practical side by providing a tender, caring side that can help comfort his children.

The Aquarius Parent/The Taurus Child

"I'd rather do it myself" should be the motto of Aquarian parents, as this Mom or Dad can equate dependency with weakness. Aquarian parents' independence and self-sufficiency is very admirable, but they tend to go too far when it comes to their need to be alone. Aquarians are intelligent, and most of them are well aware of how hard they can be to reach. It's important for Mom and Dad to understand that Taurus children need a lot of attention; these kids will be uncomfortable having to deal with a quality that could make them feel unloved. I know how much Aquarians love their children, but my experience has been that their children view them as being cold. Aquarian parents need to work on that part of their personalities in order to build a healthy relationship with their Taurus sons and daughters.

Aquarians are usually liberal when they raise their children. They will not expect them to follow rigid rules, as they themselves like to be free. Parent and child can be quite compatible, since both are careful and move slowly. Both like to work at their own rate of speed. Taurus children are practical, while their Aquarius parents are logical. Mom and Dad tend to be reliable and dependable; two traits which will enhance young Taurus' personal security.

I have found that both Aquarian and Taurus individuals will do anything to maintain their peace of mind, and this can be a problem when they need to defend themselves. In addition, my experience has shown me that they are both pleasers who will say yes just to avoid an argument. It's strange to say that both Aquarians and Taurus have powerful egos when they won't fight for their personal needs, but they seem to believe that avoiding personal confrontation is better than making waves. This behavior tends to hurt their self-esteem, and many would rather stay stuck in a safety zone than take a risk. If Aquarian Mom and Dad have not learned to overcome this fear of confrontation, it's up to them to set an example for young Taurus. It's never too late! If these air parents can learn that it's okay to say no to those they love, and fight for themselves, they will not only enhance their real talents and abilities, they will be able to teach their earth children a powerful lesson!

The Aquarian Mom/The Taurus Child

Mom, as a homemaker, is so independent, so efficient, and so perfect: she cooks, she cleans, she bakes, and she carpools. Mom, in the professional world, is a creative manager, a salesperson, a traveler, and most likely, a computer genius. She has to be all things to all people. To her, harmony in the home is essential, and she often tunes out any outside conflicts or personal confrontation.

Taurus children who live in this house are fortunate because they will always be Mom's favorites. Do you want to know why? Because these kids, whether girls or boys, are so "protectable." Mom is a great caretaker, but she will renounce her need to care about everyone and everything else for the sake of these earth children. However, she mustn't do everything for her little Taureans, or they will unintentionally take advantage of her. Mom's natural instinct for providing comfort and pleasure for her children will be so great that young Taurus' sense of responsibility will go right out the window.

We know that Taureans are self-critical and can grow up to be extremely hard on themselves, but since Aquarian Mom tends to be logical and does not enjoy hysterics or self-inflicted drama, this part of her personality will be very helpful when raising these children. These kids will innately value Mom's attitude toward life, as she projects stability and dependability. Taurus children will also receive permission from Mom to pursue all avenues in life that lead to exploring their talents and abilities. One problem Taureans may encounter, though, is that Mom may have a problem forgiving and accepting mistakes, as she happens to be a perfectionist who has great expectations for her children.

The Aquarian mother who chooses to be a career woman is what I call the "problem one-percenter." She is usually a dominant woman who may head up her own business. This mother may underestimate the sensitivity of her Taurus child, so she would be wise to avoid being too critical or judgmental—this type of behavior can bring out the stubborn streak in a Taurus kid. Remember: this stubborn quality stems from insecurity. Aquarius Mom needs to be careful with her demands, or she and her Taurus child will argue throughout all their years together.

The Aquarius Dad/The Taurus Child

Dad is strong and generally lives in his own world. He becomes a friend to all of his children, but he tends to be a loner who enjoys "doing his own thing." This behavior may cause his young Taurus to feel neglected as a result of this lack of attention. A real plus in this relationship is Dad's ability to serve as a mentor and advisor, helping to intellectually solve all problems. He is usually bright and logical, but he may appear rather cool when it comes to emotion. He really can't help this behavior, but his Taurus child may wonder if he really cares. It may not always be easy for Dad to compliment his Taurus; therefore, he needs to learn to nurture his child's confidence by being there when needed.

Dad will try to attend all school events unless he is working, and since work is often a priority, he must really make a point of being attentive to his Taurus children. Dad may be partial to athletic pursuits, such as baseball, football or soccer, but he will also enjoy music, art, and dance recitals. When it comes to bringing up his child, the Aquarian dad will always want to do the right thing.

The Pisces Parent/The Taurus Child

There are several kinds of Pisces personalities; what type a person is depends on what decan he or she is born into. Those Pisces born in the first decan (February 19 to 29) tend to stringently adhere to detail and structure, planning out their lives thoroughly in order to protect themselves from making mistakes or having to deal with rejection. They can take on a cool and distant demeanor…but it's really a façade. This type of behavior is really not the best decision for someone who is born sensitive, creative, imaginative, and playful. These Pisces personalities must not be afraid of their feelings; as they represent one of the most spiritual signs of the zodiac. Pisces who are in the second and third decans (March 1 to 10, and March 11 to 20) tend to be more in touch with their creative talents, and these individuals are the ones who can be great parents for the Taurus child.

Most Pisces parents love comfort, kids, and beauty, and they usually have a special talent for music, art, and theater. Pisces and Taurus individuals are sensitive idealists who can be very compatible. These water parents are playful and want to please their children. Therefore, they usually give them a lot of attention. Taurus children thrive on Mom or Dad's philosophy of life, as it is very close to theirs. The main difficulty I have found with this parent and child is their tendency to worry that the worst will happen. They make mountains out of molehills, which can cause them to develop an overall negative attitude. Taurus children are very hard on themselves, and they do not need parents who will encourage their personal dramas. It's important for Mom or Dad to accentuate the positive in any situation in order to influence their earth children in the most productive way.

No one would ever doubt the loving nature of a Pisces parent, and Mom and Dad will want to be there for young Taurus, but they need to repress their secret sadness in order to preserve their inner strength. Taurus children can be dependent upon their parents to help them make decisions and motivate them to take chances. It's up to Pisces parents to understand that it's important to be decisive. They can easily encourage their children because they genuinely care about helping them develop their potential so that they can find the happiness they seek.

The Pisces Mom/The Taurus Child

A Pisces mom is caring and emotional. Most of these charming mermaids love children, although they may feel like frightened little girls when they take on the huge responsibility of giving birth to a baby. It's normal for most women to wonder if they will be good mothers, but with a Pisces mother—who needs to be a *perfect* parent—the entire process can be quite traumatic.

This playful mother and her Taurus baby will be instant friends. The gentle quality that this Mom will impart to her Taurus child is a joy to behold. A Taurus loves to be treated with compassion and gentility. A Pisces mom can project her spirituality and her artistic ability onto her Taurus children in order to help them develop the natural talents that reside within. This can be a beautiful relationship, built on creative bonding.

The detailed and structured Pisces personality is good at making decisions. As mentioned previously, a Taurus child needs to have a mom who can make sensible decisions, exercise discipline, and be a woman of action, or this earth kid will not give Mom the respect she requires to be a successful parent. The real problem for this mother and child may stem from the fact that they both lack self-confidence. Any Pisces mother who bears a Taurus child must first understand her own emotions, which may include negative characteristics, such as co-dependency, repression of her own ideas and feelings, secret sorrows, and a tendency toward being weak-willed. Young Taurus will sense this instability early in life.

Thank goodness a Pisces mom is usually very kind and will be happy to focus a lot of attention on her young Taurus. This attentiveness is a perfect starting point for a great relationship, but if Mom spends too much time questioning her own self-esteem, she won't be able to dissuade her Taurus children from overanalyzing all of their decisions. If parent and children spend their time dissecting their problems, they'll never get around to accomplishing anything!

The Pisces Dad/The Taurus Child

Dad usually comes across as easygoing—a most happy fella. This merman (a male mermaid) is good-natured and is very likely to try to help his fellow traveler on earth. When it comes to children outside of his family, he can be a pushover, but with his own Taurus kids, his behavior can lean toward being overly critical and judgmental, which will diminish these children's self-confidence. A Taurus needs approval, and this Pisces father doesn't easily approve of anything or anyone. Outwardly, his attitude may be saying "I'm Mister Nice Guy," but inwardly, he tends to be negative and self-critical, a sentiment that can be easily picked up by his sensitive Taurus kids. Dad needs to try to be more positive and less critical. A Pisces dad has the capacity to be playful and imaginative, so ideally, he and young Taurus can often share the same world—it's called Never-Neverland.

SUMMARY

Taurus children are born with a mixture of complex traits that demand a good deal of understanding. Once parents accept the fact that their kids are ultrasensitive and may have an unusual need for security and safety, they will be way ahead of the game when raising them.

As life goes on, Taurus children will love the comfort that their parents offer them, especially when life seems difficult. Comfort, on all levels, is their most important emotional need, as it provides relief from self-introspection and offers a form of relaxation that has a beneficial effect on the nervous system. Positive attention, in addition to a calm, stable home environment, will reinforce this comfort zone.

Parents need to recognize that nervous tendencies can be a problem early in life with their Taurus children, although they may not be evident right away. As these earth kids grow, they may appear to be unaffected by emotions, but this is just a sign of false bravado, as Taurus children tend to hide their real feelings. Taureans, more than most, are deeply affected by life's experiences and the mood of their home environment. (Audrey Hepburn, a Taurus, and one of the most beautiful actresses to appear on the silver screen, had a magic all her own. One can hardly believe that this lovely, gentle woman died of colon cancer. See—nerves *can* get out of hand with a Taurus.)

As parents develop more of an understanding of their Taurus children, they will notice a strong response to relaxation. When Taurus kids become idle or lazy, it is their way of releasing tension or anxiety. Laziness appears to be a protective quality that Taureans utilize to deal with life's challenges. Also, parents need to watch out for what I call the "morning experience." Most Taureans dislike the early part of the day and wake up crabby and nasty. It really doesn't pay to speak to them, as they won't hear a word you say until they get out of bed and splash some water on their faces. The "morning experience" will start as Taurus children enter kindergarten, as this is when the first sign of responsibility enters their minds. First their alarm clock will ring and ring, and then their parents will try to wake up sleepy Taurus. An inner signal is telling these children that they will have to be responsible, but they will pretend not to hear their parents' gentle requests to "Get up." Then, after a long moment, a sullen voice will respond, "Wake me in five minutes." As Taurus children get older, those five minutes will probably turn into twenty.

These lovable slowpokes can drive Mom and Dad crazy. The secret in getting young Taureans to move at a faster pace is in the art of approach. It's a waste of time and energy to lose patience or get angry with Taurus children, as they will just ignore their parents. The "morning experience" is just their way of trying to shirk personal responsibility. Mom and Dad may think that they have a few tricks up their sleeve, like strategically forgetting to wake them and then letting them deal with the consequences, but that really doesn't help. Taureans will wait until the last minute—whether it's getting to school on time or running up the school stairs to turn in a paper at three minutes to nine, when it's *due* at nine. So Taurus kids need to be encouraged not to procrastinate. Not every situation has to be a drama. When Mom and Dad can convince their young Taureans that they are bright enough to do whatever needs to be accomplished that day, the "morning experience" will cease to occur.

Taurus children can be quite adventurous, but when it comes to personal change, it's a different story. The road to success for parents is to understand that a Taurean's fear of change stems from their insecurity about their abilities. They tend to dwell on the same concerns again and again: "Will it work out?" "I don't know if I can do that." "Why can't I keep doing things the same way?"

Because of these children's need for acceptance, Mom and Dad need to learn to gently push without being intimidating. It would be wise to explain to these kids, using simple language, that change in life does not always have to be intimidating—it can be very positive and productive. If parents work on this "change strategy" when their Taurus children are young, it will help deter them from getting stuck in a "safe" syndrome. Since Taurus children can be tough, Mom and Dad must be prepared to present solid facts that substantiate any proposal for change. New ideas must be carefully presented to Taurus kids so that they will accept them without fear or rebellion, thereby opening themselves up to all the experiences that life has to offer!

"Science is organized knowledge.
Wisdom is organized life."
— IMMANUEL KANT

Chapter Three

....

♊ GEMINI THE TWINS

MAY 21–JUNE 20   **ELEMENT:** Air   **KEY PHRASE:** "I think"

....

THE GEMINI PERSONALITY

Geminis are named "the twins" because their personalities are twofold. What you see may not always be what you get. I'd like parents to understand that their own intelligence and mental agility will always be tested when raising these complex children. Gemini babies are "logical thinkers," and they will expect their parents to be excellent teachers who can provide them with fact-based, well thought-out answers.

If Geminis are not satisfied with their parents' answers to questions, their eyes may dance about for a moment, as they decide whether or not it's worth responding, which will depend on how interesting they judge the speaker to be. This is an excellent example of why Gemini children often retreat into their own world—they will quickly evaluate the mental competence of all individuals, dismissing those who do not live up to their expectations. So, it will be important for Mom and Dad to teach these children to accept people for who they are, and not for how smart they are perceived to be.

As Geminis grow, their parents should understand that they will be fascinated by learning, especially in such areas as writing, public speaking, and the sciences.

This quest for knowledge and their capacity to retain information, however, may cause Gemini children to subconsciously reject any assistance from Mom and Dad, unless they can live up to their high expectations. This trait can seem a bit arrogant, and is possibly the most unreasonable part of their nature.

Geminis are so bright that they often get restless; in fact, boredom sets in much more quickly in a Gemini than in any other sun sign. And since these children are born divided into two opposing parts, many parents may find it difficult to predict what they are thinking. One side of a Gemini child's personality will need a stable home life, complete with rules and responsibility, while the other will be battling to be out, about, and free.

Which one of these complex people will Mom or Dad raise? Is it the serious intellectual whose mind focuses on logical problem solving—that is, the corporate executive, the business entrepreneur, the attorney, or the politician? Or will it be the spontaneous, outgoing, creative communicator whose desire will be to excite an audience with his or her multifaceted talents? The communicator can sing, dance, act, compose music, and write lyrics, with the ability to move an audience to laughter or tears. Think of the diversity of John Kennedy, Sir Laurence Olivier, Judy Garland, Barry Manilow, and Henry Kissinger. What do these notable and talented Geminis have in common? They all share the *power of persuasion,* which radiates through an inherent charisma—a magical glow emanating from their words, style, and glamour.

Since the serious intellectual does not outwardly resemble the dynamic entertainer, each will receive a different kind of response from the outside world. But, do not be fooled—the intellectual's need for attention is just as great as the entertainer's. No matter which one of the Gemini twins is born to a particular set of parents, Mom and Dad must understand that each child will live in his or her own private world—always restless, reaching out to learn and explore.

An Alert and Serious Side

Gemini children are very aware of the world around them and quite serious about how they want to live their lives. Parents will begin to notice how they can mentally set themselves apart from the rest of the world at an early age. Even as small children, they've already convinced themselves that they're smarter than everyone else. Although they choose to "do their own thing," they will never ignore a provocative or exciting experience, no matter how insignificant it appears to be. After all, they're compelled by anything that will generate a reaction in themselves or others.

Since most of Geminis' experiences are filtered through their powerful need for mental stimulation, it would be wise for parents to concentrate on opening up as many vistas as possible in order to educate these curious children. However, because they learn and absorb information quickly, Geminis are inclined to want to move on to something new as soon as they feel the challenge is over. It's important to help

Gemini children understand that they can't master a subject overnight. These children must be encouraged to study, study, study!

Geminis live with a mental intensity that typically underlies a cool exterior. Therefore, parents must always encourage laughter in the home and try to find ways to do chores in an upbeat, playful, and humorous manner. Parents would be wise to teach these kids to cook, sing songs, and play silly games—any of these outlets can lighten the mental load of a Gemini.

Emotions Must Be Tempered

A parent who becomes too emotional will frighten Gemini children. Yelling, screaming, or displaying an overly possessive nature will inspire young Geminis to escape into their own logical world. The road to real communication will come when Mom and Dad can demonstrate that they can sensibly handle a problem. If parents want to win the trust of their Gemini children, they must apply logic, reason, and objectivity to their upbringing. However, if they wish to help their Gemini children understand that expressing emotion can be as important as pragmatism, it would be wise to emote warm and tender feelings in the home. From childhood on, an outpouring of love will help Gemini children appreciate the importance of human interaction.

So, parents, give your Geminis lots of hugs and kisses. They may seem annoyed by this behavior at first, but don't give up. It's not illogical to display affection. My research has proven that as Geminis grow into adults, they tend to keep themselves at an even greater emotional distance than when they were children—that is, they can appear cold. Therefore, as adults, they will have to work harder to develop intimacy in personal relationships. However, if parents make an effort to display affection in the home, and their Gemini children observe that this is just a normal part of life, they will learn how important it is to care about people.

Geminis do not set out to ignore the needs of others, it's just that they can be consumed by their own thoughts. Parents need to recognize that when these children seem to be living in their own little worlds, it's important to show interest in what they're thinking. Parents must be warned, however, that Gemini children may reject these advances. At this point, Mom and Dad must not try to force a response, but should simply try to keep the lines of communication open.

Parents need to understand that a Gemini child will naturally steer away from any situation that involves personal confrontation. If I had to predict the astrological sign of Mr. Spock (the Vulcan science officer from the original *Star Trek* series), I would have to say that he was a Gemini. After all, to him, emotion was illogical. It took Captain Kirk, the commander of the Enterprise (who I'm certain had to be an emotional Aries), a long time to understand Spock's behavior. Spock, always the logical Vulcan, would respond with confusion whenever Captain Kirk tried to resolve a situation through his feelings.

Parents may find it difficult to impose their own personal feelings or beliefs upon a young Gemini, as these children believe that they can resolve their own problems. Their independence is admirable, but if they're allowed to take this insular quality to an extreme, they may never be able to share their inner thoughts with anyone. Mom and Dad must try to help their young Geminis understand that it's okay to share their feelings with others, and hopefully, they will respond to the fact that sharing can be a learning experience.

Logic and objectivity are the keys to a Gemini's heart, while mental affinity and friendship form the basis for building solid relationships. Parents must let these children know that they understand how difficult it is for them to deal with their feelings. They can do this by encouraging them to talk and by being there when they are needed. Otherwise, these children may choose the path of least resistance—being alone.

A Restless Nature

Gemini children may find it difficult to relax. Since their minds are always going a mile a minute, parents of these kids will soon realize that they don't like keeping still. Once a goal is complete and the challenge is over, this child will move right on to the next project. Mom and Dad will also notice that they can spend just as much time and energy indulging in gloomy moods. The restless quality that is inherent in the Gemini personality is caused by boredom, which drives them to seek out multiple outlets for their creativity. In my experience, I have found that all Geminis are restless, without exception. Whether they are intellectuals or artists, there is an intense quality that is inherent in their personalities, even if they appear to be calm, cool, and collected.

Parents can earn the respect of these complex children by displaying their own self-confidence, courage, and reliability. At times, it will take both patience and acceptance to deal with the restless nature of these children and their ever-expanding need for versatility. It's a good idea for parents to get them out of the house, and offer them a variety of options so that they may explore life fully. They will thank their parents for all of the opportunities with which they've provided them and, as a result, they will adapt better to the outside world.

Listen to Me!

When Gemini children speak, they expect their parents to listen. When they are seeking approval, they want their parents to listen. When they are asking for friendship, they want them to listen. These needs can contrast greatly with their own behavior. Gemini children will spend a lot of time doing their own thing because being by themselves never bothers them—in fact, they seem to enjoy it. But parents, when they finally speak to you, they will want your complete attention. These children have opinions about everything, and they will gladly offer their advice on how they think a problem should be resolved. However, they can become easily insulted if they don't receive the positive response that they were looking for. They can pull away if one of their ideas is treated as though it were insignificant, or if their intelligence is not acknowledged. Do not dismiss Geminis before they finish expressing their opinions. By paying strict attention to what these children are expressing, you'll show that you both care for and respect them, even if it's necessary to point them in a wiser direction.

One might not guess that any personality that could stand so alone would need so much approval from others. Interest in what a Gemini child thinks can be crucial to the development of their self-esteem. However, this need can be unpredictable. For example, Allison, a young Gemini, was sitting all by herself in the kitchen playing, pleasantly alone in her own thoughts, when her mother suddenly heard, "I want company. I need some company." Why, after sitting alone for so long in the kitchen, did this little girl suddenly feel as though she were left all alone? As much as Allison enjoyed her own time, and needed to have her own personal space, eventually she realized that she was all alone; she needed to have some company with her in the room. So it's true—even complex Geminis can become lonely. Even though they can be happy in their solitary world, they can definitely become frightened if they spend too much time in that state.

☆ ☆ ☆

It was a warm and humid evening when my friend Maggie and I decided to walk along the beach, adjacent to the cottage that she owned in Michigan. "I'm such a patsy when I handle Jimmy." she wailed, complaining about her relationship with her 10-year-old son. "He knows he can get anything he wants from me."

I told her firmly, "Maggie, you're going to have to stop allowing your son to intimidate you." Maggie is a very emotional Pisces, and her son Jimmy is a brilliant Gemini with the ability to control his mother by being cold whenever she doesn't obey his commands.

She continued, "Whatever Jimmy wants, Jimmy gets. I am so angry that I let him do that to me."

I responded, "Maggie, your son is 10 years old. He is very aware that you're sensitive and he knows that you won't confront him. And, he can persuade you to get him whatever he wants because he knows that you don't want to argue with him. The little actor is so clever that he knows that every time he puts on his distant and cold routine, you'll fall for it."

Maggie nodded quietly, as I continued with my assessment. "His behavior appears to bring out your own insecurities, making you feel like you need his approval. The only way that you can end this game is to look him straight in the eyes and say, 'Jimmy, you don't need anything new right now, and I am not going to respond to this behavior anymore. It's over.'" I let Maggie absorb these words and then said, "Maggie, Jimmy will begin to respect you when you tell him that what he is doing to you is no longer acceptable."

Tears formed in her eyes as she asked hopefully "Do you really think so?"

I told her, "I know so."

Maggie and I went back to the cottage that night, and she thought about what I had said. It took about a week for her courage to build. The next time Jimmy played his game of intimidation, she gathered her strength and simply told him, "Jimmy, I am not going to respond when you're nasty. It's unacceptable, and it hurts my feelings. I deserve better treatment from you. Haven't I treated you well?" Jimmy remained silent. She continued, "From now on, unless I want to buy you a present, or you happen to need something that will help you in school, my answer when you ask me for something will be no."

This was the beginning of a better relationship between Maggie and her son Jimmy. She continued to discipline him, and he began to respect her opinions. She convinced him that she *did* have a mind of her own and that she had finally begun to recognize his game.

Gemini children can be easy to raise as long as both Mom and Dad understand that they are not compelled to do their kids' bidding. Children of this particular sun sign don't like to have to owe anyone anything. They believe that a debt is an obligation, and they don't like to be closely connected to anyone or anything that will stifle their independence and freedom. Now, do not get the impression that these special kids are never obliging. They will gladly do someone a favor as long as it is not bound by stifling conditions.

There is one major reason why Gemini children will distance themselves from their parents, and it comes down to one word: *no.* This word will make these kids feel that they are not worthy of being given an explanation, which serves to damage self-esteem. Mom and Dad need to explain to their young Geminis that there are good reasons behind the word *no.* The worst thing a parent can say to Gemini kids when they ask, "But why?" is…"BECAUSE I SAID SO!" Offering a valid reason is always the best way to counteract a child's feelings of unworthiness and insecurity.

PARENT AND CHILD

The Aries Parent/The Gemini Child

Aries parents can be strong mentors. They are born with two traits that are perfect prerequisites for developing a compatible relationship with their Gemini child: intelligence and leadership. Gemini children who are born to an Aries parent will soon realize that they have inherited a best friend!

Aries parents are emotional, and their Gemini children are logical; therefore, they may initially have a problem communicating. Although Geminis are attracted to emotional people, they are primarily thinkers who cannot display their feelings. As such, the emotional Aries parent needs to understand that getting these kids to listen to him or her will require sound, reasonable explanations and fairly meted-out discipline. Young Geminis may not overtly reveal their high-strung, nervous natures, though. Gemini children may appear passive, and then, all of a sudden, an explosive temper will flare up! This is usually how Geminis show their anger.

Both Aries and Geminis are independent, direct, and honest. Mom and Dad will not try to stifle this air kid's freedom. A Gemini responds well to parents who are straightforward and constructive when working out a problem. Gemini children respect their Aries parents because they are usually intelligent and strong. Aries individuals usually say what they mean, and once they make a decision, they stick to it. Gemini children really admire this kind of behavior.

Aries parents tend to have difficulty handling the Gemini's unpredictable nature. Aries are either black or white, right or wrong, They hate waiting for anything or anyone, and they need to share their thoughts openly. Geminis, on the other hand, have no real sense of time, they do their own thing, and they tend to be loners. Mom and Dad really need to take these characteristics to heart when raising their Geminis, to ensure a mutually satisfying relationship.

The Aries Mom/The Gemini Child

When raising a Gemini child, an Aries mother needs to work on her lack of patience. An Aries has many virtues, but patience isn't one of them. It's important for Aries parents to understand that their Gemini children are born to be logical thinkers and that they can spend a lot of time in their own world. When Mom observes this mode of behavior, which is a Gemini child's "detaching mechanism," she will have to adjust to the fact that this trait may persist for years. And, since an Aries mom is bound by close emotional ties, this thinker part of her Gemini's behavior will test her patience on a daily basis.

An Aries mother wants to know everything about her children, and Gemini children will resent any kind of interrogation. In fact, they will probably feel that Mom is intruding on their private space. Mom will have to work on tempering her insistence that her children answer every one of her questions completely, especially when her questions seem to overwhelm them. Geminis will feel quite comfortable providing their Aries mothers with information, as long as she is tactful in her approach. Her own need to be close to her children makes this mom a special person, but a controlling and emotional attitude will push these kids further into their own worlds. Therefore, Mom would be wise to understand that when her Gemini children want their own space, it's time to pull back. If Aries parents accept the fact that their Gemini children need private time, they will gain their confidence faster than most sun-sign parents.

Both mother and child can build an excellent relationship if Mom can learn to loosen the reins. She must learn to subdue her emotions and intelligently guide with restraint. An Aries mom's honesty and directness will help to lessen Gemini children's tendency to build walls around themselves. These kids will come to appreciate Mom's sound advice and self-confident attitude.

The Aries Dad/The Gemini Child

Here's a story that tells you something about the strong personality of an Aries dad.

Many years ago, my friend Mark was presented with the challenge of his life: he became a single parent left to raise Gemini twins.

Since each Gemini child is said to have a dual personality, this poor guy had to deal with four personalities. His daughter Ellen was the outgoing, personable entertainer, while his son Jason was the serious, studious intellectual. It might have been easier to have had two entertainers or two intellectuals. But given his situation, Mark revealed his unselfish and courageous nature.

Mark was a stable father with the ability to be a mentor, romantic figure, protector, and sportsman. Both he and the twins built up a special camaraderie that was carefully honed throughout the years. As a responsible father, Mark wanted to be there for his children so that they could feel his strength enveloping them.

Now a single parent with two little babies, he felt somewhat overwhelmed by the middle-of-the-night feedings and multiple diaper changings. Since he was an Aries with little patience, he became a nervous wreck. And in addition to all of this stress, he was building a business that was just in the preliminary stages. The business was very important to Mark, but it never took precedence over the twins.

While a nanny took care of the twins by day, Mark watched over them at night, and before long, he got these feeding times down and could change a diaper with his eyes closed. And, as the twins began to grow into little tots, Mark would try to get home at bedtime just to read them stories. He would then work in his home office till all hours of the night. But he never seemed to mind. There was no end to his energy. This man could do ten things at once and keep going.

The twins are now in their thirties, and Mark's behavior has earned their undying respect. Why not? He was always involved in their education, and he helped to guide them in the right direction without hovering too closely.

☆   ☆   ☆

Mark's personality was always marked by *reliability,* and this admirable trait was at the very top of the twins' list. They were secure in the feeling that their Dad would never desert them. His commitment was unbreakable. When a crisis arose, he handled it with conviction. The real difference between an Aries dad and an Aries mom is an ability to control his emotions. Dad can put his emotions on the back burner, allowing logic and common sense to take over.

The Taurus Parent/The Gemini Child

Taurus parents maintain a careful, steady approach to life. Once they create a lifestyle that's both safe and secure, they don't like changing it. But how will this affect a Gemini baby, who is born with a need to explore, and a restless temperament? It doesn't seem to be a match made in heaven, does it? In fact, a Gemini baby will be an eye-opening experience for this mom or dad. First of all, the pace of a Taurus household can be far too slow for Gemini children. Their energetic, action-oriented personalities will definitely want things to speed up.

At first, Taurus parents and their Gemini children seem as though they're not on the same wavelength. Taureans like their feet planted solidly on the ground, while Geminis have to keep moving. Gemini children will want to experience life to its fullest, while Taurus parents tend to be drawn to a more conventional and reliable lifestyle. Take heart, though. Even if Taurus parents and Gemini children are not naturally compatible, Mom and Dad's offer of support and stability will draw their kids towards them.

The special quality that Taurus parents have is evident in their ability to allow a child's own natural personality to unfold—and to nurture that personality into adulthood. Taureans have great patience, and to them, time is not of the essence—it simply goes by. This attitude may create a conflict when raising young Gemini, who may not agree with this theory. Gemini children never seem to have enough time for all of the things that they want to do. Therefore, Taurus parents should try to understand that these young balls of energy have mental time clocks that are different from theirs. They will admire the intelligence and spirit of their Geminis, but their ability to act too logically—that is, not allowing emotion to interfere with their thinking, may test a Taurus parent's never-ending patience.

Taurus parents are similar to Virgo parents when it comes to handling problems. Both tend to obsess and dissect their thoughts over and over. By overanalyzing everything, they can develop a self-deprecating nature, which can create a need for extreme attention and approval. When Taurus parents raise a Gemini child, they must work on being decisive and positive in their behavior. Gemini children need help with their decisions, and because they take life so seriously, they need to grow up in an optimistic, positive environment. Taurus parents believe life requires careful consideration; therefore, personal decisions aren't always easy. So, while a Taurus parent sees life as serious and *personal,* a Gemini child sees it as serious and *objective.* It's easier for a Gemini to go after a goal without getting personally involved. Taurus parents must combine their conventional natures with a dose of flexibility, in order to accept the free spirit within this child.

The most endearing part of Gemini children's personalities are their charm. This trait will always be compatible with a Taurus parent. The beauty of their respective personalities come together when they play with one another. Parent and child love to have fun, and their healthy laughter will ring with comfort and joy throughout the home.

Taureans are worrywarts who fret about everything and tend to build up nervous anxiety. Gemini children, on the other hand, are comfortable in a rational environment, and overwhelming anxiety will be difficult for them to handle.

Taurus parents must maintain their sense of humor when they raise this Gemini daredevil. A Taurus can have a quick temper, and humor can work as a tool to appropriately direct this anger. Taurus parents must understand that a sedentary life is not for Gemini children; in fact, at times, their lives can get out of control, as they enjoy a hectic schedule. Taurus parents can really help and guide their Gemini children in this regard, as Taureans have the practical sense to help stabilize Geminis' thinking. Once Geminis feel stable, they can make responsible decisions. Little Gemini children have to understand that if they always remain in their own world, they can hurt the people around them. They must be taught to consider the feelings of others, and Taurus parents can be helpful in showing the way. All in all, Taurus parents will be fascinated by the brilliance of these action-oriented little people.

The Taurus Mom/The Gemini Child

Mom, more than Dad, will sometimes find herself on the edge of her seat when raising the adventurous Gemini child. She will tend to oppose anything that involves risk because she always envisions the worst possible scenario. A story about my friend Sharon and her Gemini son Mack illustrates this point.

Sharon, a Taurus mother then in her late thirties, and I were sitting in her living room waiting to go out to dinner, when her 16-year-old son Mack queried, "Mom, can I take flying lessons from Bob's father?"

I will never forget the look on her face. She stared at him, open-mouthed, her eyes wide open, and exclaimed, "Not on your life!"

His response was rather laid back, as he logically concluded, "Mom, I know I can learn how to fly."

Sharon was staring at him in shock. "You're not flying with Bob's father. He's an eccentric."

Mack smiled, replying, "He may be eccentric, but he knows how to fly a plane. He's a great pilot." Sharon was adamant. "I won't allow you to fly—God knows what could happen to you." By this time, I began to notice a rebellious look on Mack's face. His irritation was obvious, and he wasn't happy with his mother's reaction. (In my opinion, given the Gemini personality, she was lucky he even asked for permission!)

I knew that I should have stayed out of this discussion, but I interjected, "Sharon, you know Mack is very bright. He always makes logical decisions, and his technical skills are exceptional. He definitely has the ability to understand the mechanical aspects of flying, and these lessons seem to be important to him. Not only that, but Bob's father has been a flying instructor for years. I think Mack will turn out to be an extremely competent pilot."

Sharon looked at me and quietly asked, "Sylvia, do you think that my reaction is unfair?"

I paused for a moment. "You never mean to be unfair," I answered, "but you do tend to worry too much. I think that Mack will be just fine."

George Bush was still President at the time, and knowing that Sharon didn't favor him, I said, "Sharon, President Bush flew jet bombers, and he was a Gemini."

She laughed out loud, and said, "Oh, that helps a lot." Finally, she concluded, "Maybe I am too much of a worrywart."

I had to stifle my laughter. "You know you are."

Sharon smiled, her expression now softening. "Okay, Mack, but you'd better be careful. I want you to have Bob's father call me with all of the details." Mack burst into a big grin and ran over to hug his mother. Then he ran over to hug me.

I warned, "You'd better not prove me wrong." Sharon wasn't aware of what I was thinking at the time, which was that Mack's need for this adventure would be a way for his mother to deal with her fear. I don't think that Mack could have resisted the temptation to go against his mother's wishes if she hadn't given in—his mind had been made up. I felt this would be the perfect opportunity for Sharon to understand that Mack was turning into a responsible young adult and was no longer a child whose every move had to be supervised. Most of all, I knew that Mack was technically brilliant and could be trusted to fly a plane.

☆ ☆ ☆

A Taurus mom must try to be fair when her first instinct towards her child's latest proposition for adventure is fear. She must accept the fact that her Gemini child will never stop looking for a new challenge. This acceptance will be difficult for her, to be sure, so she will have to work hard to overcome her worrywart tendencies. Only a Taurus mom can judge: is she just trying to be protective, or is she exercising too much control, trying to restrict her child's natural impulses? If she accepts the fact that freedom is the best gift she can give to her Gemini child, the adjustment won't be as difficult.

The Taurus Dad/The Gemini Child

Even if a Taurus dad appears to be quiet and reserved, he will always be fascinated by unusual and titillating experiences. Gemini children are very adventurous, and they are always in pursuit of challenge and excitement. I have mentioned before that there are two types of Taurus personalities and two types of Gemini personalities: the serious and intellectual type, and the creative actor type. If the intellectual Taurus dad should happen to raise theatrical Gemini children, Dad will need to learn how to be more open-minded with respect to their free-spirited nature. If the theatrical Taurus father should happen to raise intellectual Gemini children, Dad can help to develop their adventurous sides.

Taurus parents and Gemini children usually get along well together, but there are times when they exasperate each other because they can't figure each other out. So, it's crucial that they all learn to openly communicate with each other to get a handle on what's going on in each other's minds.

The Gemini Parent/The Gemini Child

Gemini parents should not have a problem raising Gemini children, since they all think logically and have a need for their own space. It is simply their way of life. Parents and child are governed more by mind than they are by emotions. Therefore, mental compatibility will be instantaneous. Mom and Dad will raise their Geminis with objectivity and reason, and these kids will joyfully respond.

I have mentioned previously that the Gemini personality can be upbeat and fun-loving or extremely serious and intellectual. If a Gemini parent is the extroverted, live-it-up type of personality, and he or she is raising a potentially serious intellectual, the extroverted Gemini can be particularly helpful in changing the attitude of this child. Lighthearted parents can inject a bit of fantasy and humor into their children's lives in order to dissuade them from always depending on logic. This approach can also help to ease the emotional intensity of this serious child.

Now, let's reverse the situation. If a Gemini parent is a serious intellectual who is raising a funloving, extroverted child, the rearing process should be reversed, stressing realistic, rather than idealistic, expectations. This parent can simply instill gentle rules, which balance the child's tendency to show off. Whatever the situation, be it funloving or serious, a Gemini child cannot lose with a Gemini parent.

One final issue that I would like to discuss with respect to Gemini parents is that of intimacy, which is crucial to the Gemini child's personal growth. Mom and Dad may not realize it, but open communication may be lacking in the relationship with their Gemini child. The funny thing is, the Gemini child may not even realize that this is a problem, as both parent and child are compatible (on the surface) without sharing a lot of emotion between them.

Gemini parents should try to work on the development of personal communication with their Gemini child. This effort could introduce the concept that feelings should not be discounted as the child grows into an adult. Now, this may be as difficult for the Gemini child as logic is comfortable for them. If a Gemini parent understands how important it is to work on communicating openly when raising this child, this little boy or girl will avoid being alone as much, a tendency that is a fundamental part of being a Gemini.

When Gemini children have the opportunity to interact with people on a daily basis, they will be able to improve all of the relationships in their lives and become more aware of the feelings of others. Gemini children will always search for a best friend, and a Gemini parent can easily fulfill that role.

The Gemini Mom/The Gemini Child

Both Mom and her Gemini children are logical and reasonable people. Education will be a priority in their lives, and Mom will naturally support her children's need to pursue a variety of interests. These air kids are quickly bored, and if the information they receive is not challenging, they move on to greener pastures. This can also happen with the relationships in their lives. Mom will fully understand her Gemini children's need to explore life, as she herself is continually searching for mental stimulation. Both Mom and her Gemini children have a lot of nervous energy and need to be out and about on a daily basis. Young Geminis need a mother who will challenge them. Therefore, Mom is the perfect parent, as she can ask the kinds of questions that make her child think.

Mom and her Gemini child are each represented by the Twins because they have two sides to their personality. They won't have a problem living together because they each take their dual personality for granted. I have called them the schizophrenics of the zodiac. One moment they are so reasonable and sensible, and the next they have lost their grip on reality and the ability to reason. When a parent raises Gemini children, their dual personalities can become apparent at an early age.

I know that Mom does not relate to emotion as well as she does to logic, but it's important for her to try and encourage her Gemini children to be attentive and considerate of people's feelings. Once Geminis accept the fact that emotion is not so scary, they may develop a less distant manner. Most of my Gemini clients tell me that feelings make them uncomfortable and tend to confuse them. It's important for Geminis to believe that it's okay to feel. This special understanding can help them build healthy relationships as they grow.

The Gemini Dad/The Gemini Child

Gemini men and women are usually very intelligent. They are air signs whose main pursuit is developing the intellect. A Gemini man can either pursue scientific endeavors, or he can be an expert when it comes to words. Many Gemini men are public speakers, writers, and lyricists. Dad can be an excellent role model for his Gemini child, as he is the perfect mentor and teacher. Parent and child will also develop a very close bond that will be very important to both of them. Dad can be a loner, and there will be times when he will enclose himself in his own private world. His Gemini child has the same tendency, and will probably never notice that Dad is doing his own thing. If Dad can make sure that he is always available to answer his Gemini children's questions and help them to make sensible decisions, Dad and young Gemini will forge a brilliant friendship.

The Cancer Parent/The Gemini Child

Cancer parents are emotional, loving, and supportive. They genuinely adore children, and their home is their sanctuary. When Cancer parents raise Gemini children, they are presented with a real challenge. They will have to learn when to step in, and when to back away. When counseling Cancer parents, I always admire their active interest in their families, but when it comes to raising Gemini children, they must learn to respect and value the independence that their kids need. This can be a crucial issue for a parent who can sometimes be a little too much of an authority figure.

Gemini children are not born on the same wavelength as their Cancer parents. The logical base of the Gemini is in conflict with the emotional base of the Cancer. Cancer parents often feel that they need to be a dominating influence on their children, and with this influence comes the tendency to always want to tell their kids what to do. This behavior will simply not work when raising Geminis.

Gemini children can counteract their Cancer parents' attitudes by finding ways to control their Mom and Dad. But how do they accomplish this feat? Simple—with logic and reason. The Geminis' practical minds will instinctively understand that they are dealing with Cancer softies. In fact, these logical Geminis are smart enough to sense that Mom and Dad have their own need to please. As parents, they want their children's love, and they can compromise themselves to get it. Here comes the trouble. Geminis want everything that life has to offer and more. Cancer parents can be pushovers, and these Gemini kids can push to the limit. Mom and Dad must understand that Geminis are thinkers who want things their own way and will not always recognize how a Cancer parent *feels*. These kids can easily control these "heart first" parents with logic and reason.

Gemini children need to grow up in a consistently run, stable environment where household rules are clearly established. Since these kids are creative, they'll want their Cancer parents to both listen to and support their many innovative ideas.

Cancer parents, I know that intimacy is important to you, but your Gemini children may not be as taken by this concept. In fact, they tend to be afraid of it. Therefore, parents may not always be able to get through to these logical little wheeler-dealers. So, they must use their intuition to determine the emotional needs of their Gemini children. As soon as little Geminis start to grow, they may recoil when confronted with temperament.

The Cancer Mom/The Gemini Child

A Cancer mom can be both emotional and temperamental. She may feel that her Gemini child's logical and cool behavior is difficult to handle. Mom wants to emotionally bond with her children, so she needs to learn that she can't take everything so personally when she raises them, as their impersonal nature is not directed at her. It's important for Mom to use a logical approach when she wants to get her Gemini children to listen. If practicality and objectivity are applied when raising these kids, they will value Mom's guidance and ask her to help with decisions. Mom needs to be aware that Geminis do not listen when they sense that they are being forced or manipulated into something. Mom will enjoy talking, and she has a lot to say. Gemini children tend to filter all the information that they hear, just absorbing the data that seems to reflect reason. The rest of what's said is quickly deleted, so it's best to get to the bottom line as quickly as possible.

A Cancer mom feels very safe in her home, and her Gemini children will need these supportive roots to come back to as they begin to spread their wings, but Mom needs to remember that even though Geminis love a place to hang their hats, nothing compares to their innate desire for freedom!

The Cancer Dad/The Gemini Child

The Cancer father is kind and considerate, and he needs to be the head of the family. He feels that he must protect his children and also try to control them. It's important for Dad to understand that he can never do this with his Gemini children, though. These children may listen when they are young, but that soon changes as they grow up.

Dad is also very emotional, but his feelings tend to frighten him. On the one side of the coin, his self-control will help him get along with his Gemini children, but if the coin flips over and Dad tries to restrict his Gemini children's freedom, they can retreat into their own world. And the more these kids back away, the more Dad's ego can get out of control. Dad will get angry if young Gemini ignores him, and he will try everything to thwart this tendency.

If Dad can learn to be a friend, as well as a father, to young Gemini, there will be fewer arguments. Geminis are very smart, and they are clear about their preferences at an early age. Dad can earn his Gemini children's respect by offering them a series of options when making a decision that involves their well-being. Dad needs to work on tempering his ego when he raises these kids, or conflicts will most certainly arise. Dad can truly reveal his inner strength by teaching his freedom-seeking air children the importance of self-discipline and setting limits in their lives. Once Dad learns that controlling a situation is not the way to raise his Gemini children, he can work on developing and maintaining a relationship that is built on loyalty and respect.

The Leo Parent/The Gemini Child

Leo parents can be described as hot potatoes. They can be easy to touch, or too hot to handle. At times, Mom and Dad can be a little too overheated for a Gemini child's cool composure. Even so, I still believe the team works well, as the Gemini child's breezy attitude fans the fervor of the Leo parent. This child just loves the energy displayed by Leo Mom or Dad. Leo parents exhibit a lot of vitality, and their ability to express themselves will mentally stimulate their young Gemini. *A meaningful speech* will always attract the Gemini personality.

A Leo is a passionate parent. This may not be as apparent with Leos who are in the first decan (July 23–August l), but still, this emotion is always present. When Gemini children live in a home reflecting the strong emotions generated by their Leo parents, they begin to understand the power of expressing their feelings. This experience will be a boon to these sensible thinkers, who base most of their decisions on logic. (Anyone should be able to see that logic and emotions mix like oil and water.) The thinking process is based on an orderly and established series of steps, which lead toward a desired goal. Too much thinking, however, can instill passivity, which can limit a Gemini's "peripheral vision"—that is, they will not pay enough attention to those around them. This can sorely affect all of their personal and professional relationships.

A Leo parent is purposeful, direct, and, just like his or her Gemini child, a quick thinker. Once Leo parents have determined the bottom line of any situation, their minds will be made up. To a Leo, it's black or white, right or wrong. The only time a Gemini child may be confused by this behavior is when a Leo parent becomes too emotional. You see, the real difference in the personalities of the Gemini-Leo parent/child duo is the idea that life is not always black or white—there *are* gray areas. And Geminis have a lot of gray. One gray area that can ring loud and clear is when young Geminis fall prey to their moods. And these children can sure be moody!

Since Leo parents are less likely to lapse into very distinct negative or manic moods, they may have a difficult time at first understanding little Gemini's personality. (It's heartening to know, though, that a Gemini becomes less outwardly moody as an adult.) Well, in the case of this child, Mom and Dad will definitely learn to adjust and will come to understand that it's only a temporary state of being. It's not much of a problem when young Geminis are in the process of learning something new, or when they are working on a project, as they are task-oriented people. The greater adjustment for the Leo parent can come when young Geminis have to get to an appointment on time, or whenever they have to plan ahead in their personal lives. Mom and Dad will need to encourage discipline in these areas.

Leo parents can handle themselves with great poise, and they can seem formal in appearance or manner. Whether it be Mom or Dad, both make powerful parents who will make deep investments in their children. Leo parents will have a lot to teach Gemini children, as long as they continue to recognize the difference in their children's approach to life. Leo parents will usually act upon what they say, while a Gemini child feels a great deal of trepidation when it comes to making a decision or a commitment.

Imagine sitting in an automobile when you shift it into neutral. The gears are now disengaged, and the engine has no idea where to go. "Neutral" places the vehicle in a position of not being able to go backward or forward. With Geminis, being in neutral can cause them a lot of problems when they're trying to make a decision. They have a habit of changing their minds because they fear having to commit. So, when raising their Gemini children, Leo parents should teach them how to deal with life in a very decisive manner. Advising them on the best way to make decisions will help them move forward in life.

The Leo Mom/The Gemini Child

There is passion within every Leo mother. Her powerful feelings may be hidden by her need for self-control, but they will always be there. Mom wants the best for her children, and with her energy, anything is possible.

Parent and child are different in their approach to life, overall. Mom believes in her feelings, and her Gemini child believes in things that are based on fact. Mom needs to learn that her Gemini kids will not readily respond to her feelings, as they do not trust emotion. Give Geminis the facts and just the facts, and their antennae begin to peak out.

Geminis feel that they can depend on Mom's inner strength and on her ability to provide a comfortable home. These kids won't think that Mom is asking them foolish questions, as they instinctively recognize that she is an intelligent woman. Young Geminis will admire her honest and direct manner. Mom needs to understand that she cannot become overly emotional with these kids, as they are frightened and confused by emotion. She would be wise to offer sensible explanations when she makes a decision, and she needs to give these children the opportunity to offer an opinion on all matters that concern them.

Mom needs to be aware of the fact that she is raising a child who needs time to make decisions. This part of her Gemini's personality may disturb her, as she likes to be close to her children. Mom needs to accept that emotional bonding is not easy when you raise a Gemini child, but Geminis tend to trust their Leo mothers, and their relationship is built on friendship that develops though honest communication.

The Leo Dad/The Gemini Child

Dad needs to be in control of his life; therefore, he can be a dominant figure in the household. When you believe you are born a king, this is natural behavior, right? Gemini children usually look up to a Leo father, as they admire his ability to lead. Dad is an emotional man with a lot of common sense. He can easily help his Gemini children make the right decisions, and he usually offers good advice. Dad needs to be careful about imposing his will onto these kids, though, as Geminis like to form their own opinions and can never be forced into anything. Dad's freedom is very important to him, so he can understand that his Gemini free-spirited children will always need to pursue their goals as they see fit. There are two important issues that will always come up with Gemini children: the need for individuality and the application of free will to their lives. Dad has the ability to guide his young Geminis in the right direction, and he can be of great assistance when it comes to these children's personal growth—just as long as he understands and respects the personality makeup of his daughter or son.

The Virgo Parent/The Gemini Child

The precocious, free-spirited Gemini now meets a very suitable parent. Opposites do attract, and this parent-and-child combination will be bonded by their differences. You may be asking yourself: how can two people be bonded by differences? Well, anyone who is familiar with Virgos knows how difficult it is for them to take anything lightly. They want to be extraordinary in everything they do, and their expectations of themselves are ridiculously high. I always begin my counseling with Virgo clients by making two statements: "Let go of the things you can't do anything about," and "Take a lot of vacations."

Gemini children want to live in a sensible and rational world—a world in which they can explore life, learn as much as they can, have complete freedom, and do their own thing without interference. Virgo parents enjoy living in a fairly traditional family environment, which would imply a certain sensibility; however, these earth parents are not always sensible. Virgos have a need to create their own inner dramas in order to get the job done. These dramas are based on excessive worry, unbelievable expectations with respect to themselves and others, and instant criticism of anything that's less than perfect. Now, is this a sensible and rational way to live? A Gemini child will never think so.

Virgo parents have a tendency to fear illness, and many can become hypochondriacs. Remember, if they get sick, that means they are no longer perfect. Showing worry over illness in front of Gemini children is an absolute no-no—these kids don't like getting emotional over being sick. Geminis are fitness conscious, and they will naturally want to stay in shape as they grow. Working out will be used as an outlet, or a need to release stress. But Gemini children will not appreciate their Virgo parents creating medical mountains out of molehills, as only a Virgo parent can do.

If a cold is treated like pneumonia, or if Mom and Dad act as if their child has a life-threatening fever when his or her temperature hits 99 degrees, a lot of strife will occur. However, when Gemini children do get sick, they will expect their parents to take care of them, and Virgo moms and dads are wonderful caregivers when they are able to calm their nerves.

The Virgo Mom/The Gemini Child

Gemini children may see Mom as being too fixed in her opinions, and this image can be quite intimidating for someone who finds change exciting. These kids may actively oppose any of Mom's demands that appear unreasonable. However, a Virgo mom can be a fine asset to her Gemini child if she can utilize her efficiency and strict attention to detail in order to help young Gemini accomplish tasks and reach goals. A Virgo mother enjoys her Gemini children's free-spirited nature, but she cannot resist trying to be in control of what happens in their lives. Mom needs to understand that this type of behavior would be a big mistake.

Gemini children can be quite attached to their mothers, which means that these Virgo moms can be quite influential in raising them. The best way for a Virgo mother to get along with these kids is by lessening her need for control and trying to explain her reasons for making a decision. Mom needs to understand that she can hurt her children by needing them to be as perfect as she is. If she can work on becoming less demanding, she can enjoy a very compatible relationship with her Gemini children. These kids will admire her ability to keep things in order, and they will appreciate her capacity to achieve important goals.

The Virgo Dad/The Gemini Child

Virgo fathers are usually practical, stable, solid, and dependable. They believe that they need to protect their children from all of the nuisances that are a part of daily life, but at times, they can go overboard. Children do not enjoy being *trained* to *perform properly*. A Virgo father has great intentions, but he can lose sight of his children's real needs. They want his guidance and his gentle wisdom, not an armed forces training manual. Since a Virgo father is an absolute perfectionist, he may sound like he's giving orders even if he doesn't mean to. He just expects things to be done right.

Virgo dads are loyal and dedicated, and I would describe their outlook on life as practical, rather than emotional. Therefore, they may not understand that a well-behaved, socially acceptable child does not need excessive training. There is not a child in the world, especially a Gemini, who will accept living by a set of rules without a good explanation.

Now, a Virgo dad has a lot of inner strength and can be very helpful to his children, but it is very important for him to realize that each child has his or her own individuality. When a Virgo dad has Gemini children, he will have to sit them down and try to explain his need for perfection, because a free-spirited Gemini cannot comfortably live with rules that have no exceptions. Dad will need to modify his personality when it comes to restricting this child's behavior, or face a lot of confrontation. Remember, Dad, your child can learn from your good manners, efficiency, determination, and morality. If you can allow your Gemini child to be spontaneous and free, your own life will become more of an adventure, as well.

The Libra Parent/The Gemini Child

A Libra will be a fine parent for a Gemini child. The Libra mother or father will have a great respect for freedom, and will never do anything to discourage Gemini's natural instinctive behavior. A Gemini will thrive on this approach. First of all, since Libras are always fighting for their own personal independence, they will dislike anyone or anything that tries to take that free will away from their child.

It is important for Libra parents to try to be forthright with co-workers or friends who have hurt them. If they hold things in for too long, a Libra is capable of becoming unreasonable and contradictory when dealing with their children at times when they will need their patience and understanding.

Geminis are quite definite in their opinions and can often give the impression of knowing it all. As they grow, young Geminis have a tendency to reveal a stubborn streak when things do not go their way. In fact, their annoyance and irritation is usually visible on their tight-lipped faces. When this situation occurs, a Libra parent should avoid appearing abrupt, angry, or sharp-tongued, without considering the consequences.

Libras are dreamers and may have a tendency to avoid responsibility. This mode of behavior can result from a lack of self-confidence with respect to the handling of their personal lives. Their need for balance in their lives—that is, the desire to have everyone and everything running on an even keel, makes them especially hard on themselves whenever they have to make a decision. I always tell my Libra clients that overanalyzing every detail of a situation before making a decision is a good way of never reaching one!

Libras are one of the most talented and creative signs in the zodiac, and I urge these individuals to recognize their natural ability to appreciate beauty, culture, nature, design, color, and so much more. There is very little a Libra cannot do on a creative level, especially Mom.

A Libra parent's need to balance personality and attitude will mesh with a Gemini's need for a rational home environment. Raising Gemini children will not be difficult for Libra parents as long as they can build their kids' confidence in them by being consistent in how they display their feelings. If they say what they mean at the time that they mean it, this kind of direct behavior will definitely win points with their Gemini children. A Gemini's mind is quick, and he or she can be on to the next subject and out the door before you've finished your thought.

The Libra Mom/The Gemini Child

Mom is artistic, and she can represent a romantic ideal to her Gemini son, serving as a role model for the type of woman he may seek in a relationship later in life. In addition, she has the ability to lead him in the right direction when he makes important decisions. She maintains the perspective that he tends to lose when his nerves take control. Mom's Gemini daughter will have a wonderful companion, and will never be lonely with this Libra mother by her side.

Mom has style and taste and will provide her Gemini children with an appreciation of beauty and culture. Since both mother and child need their own space, this allows for a special sense of freedom in the relationship. Mom has the ability to comfort and nurture her children, while they explore the world around them. Mom may need to work on her fear of making important decisions when her Gemini children come to her for help in resolving a problem. They will need her wisdom and guidance. A Libra mom has an uncanny instinct for the truth if she can just allow herself to act upon it. Once Mom understands that her ability to make decisions comes from self-confidence, she will learn how to feel good about herself and be an excellent mentor for her Gemini child.

The Libra Dad/The Gemini Child

Libra fathers are charming and playful. Their "little boy" quality is a distinguishing attribute. They adore their children, and their easygoing demeanor is very appealing. Gemini children will relate to their logical father, as both signs are characteristically reasonable and sensible. The one problem that can occur between parent and child is that Dad can fall prey to the clever maneuvers of his adventurous explorer. A Gemini moves fast, and Dad gravitates to this kind of energy. Libra dads can be a bit laid back, and there may be times when his little Gemini will need to push him along, trying to gently prod him into action. There is never a dull moment with this air kid. I better not call the children of Libras "little," though, as they like to treat all of their children as though they were adults.

Libra men are very likeable, but they can get moody when they have to make an important decision. At those times, they tend to pull back into their own world, without sharing their thoughts. A Libra dad needs to work on sharing his thoughts with his family in order to feel their support. If Dad can develop the ability to talk about his feelings, he can help his Gemini child, who will have a similar problem communicating. Gemini children will usually feel Dad's support and encouragement because their dreams tend to mesh with his.

The Scorpio Parent/The Gemini Child

"Help! Please let me say something." This may be the cry of Gemini children if their Scorpio parents do not allow them the opportunity to voice their own opinions. If we want to talk about a mother or father who wants to organize their children's lives, a Scorpio parent is the one.

Scorpio parents and their Gemini children share a mental affinity. They are both intelligent, cultured, curious, and love to travel, but in a parent/child relationship, they may run into a bit of trouble. The Scorpio parent is rules-oriented, and the Gemini child is a free spirit. Geminis want to do things right, but they will not respond to anyone who continually tells them what to do! After a while, Gemini children may pretend to be listening, but other thoughts will actually be floating through their minds.

Scorpio parents are loving and protective, but they tend to be possessive and controlling when raising their children. They will do anything they can for their kids, but they expect them to be very good little girls and boys who consistently do the right thing at the right time. Geminis are very high-strung and nervous, so too many orders tend to upset them. A Scorpio parent needs to understand that a Gemini child does not like to be forced into submission. Geminis are free spirits who move in their own time and space. This trait may exasperate Mom and Dad, but they need to understand that Geminis need to break the rules once in a while. Geminis need to be able to pursue their own interests, coming back to their parents for advice and encouragement, but not ever feeling stifled by an overbearing attitude.

Scorpios have a lot of patience, a characteristic that will certainly come in handy when raising their capricious air children. Scorpio parents should temper the discipline and set down reasonable, logical rules. If that is done, young Geminis will respect their ability to build a stable and well-run home and will work on creating a relationship based on mutual consideration.

The Scorpio Mom/The Gemini Child

Mom is the caretaker, and Dad is the boss. When it comes to making sure everything is organized, Mom is extremely competent. In fact, certain Scorpio mothers can get excited about the prospect of going to the cleaners or washing a load of towels. With a Gemini child, this Mom may have to pull back a bit on how strict her rules are. I understand that these moms are both resolute and determined, and if they make up their minds that they want their children to do something, they can be unbelievably focused. Fortunately, Gemini children will never mind someone taking excellent care of them, and they will easily welcome the feeling of stability. This Mom does everything so well, especially when anything domestic is concerned.

There are times, however, when Mom may drive her Gemini kids crazy with her orders and protestations: "Do this, and do that!" "Why didn't you put that away?" And the ever-popular: "I don't know what I am going to do with you!" Now, being asked to do something isn't what bothers young Gemini, as he or she can be very efficient; it's *how* Mom phrases her demand. Mom must be careful that there isn't a tone of chastisement in every word. Sensing that there is going to be a punishment involved in the completion of a chore that hasn't even been started can make a Gemini feel guilt-ridden. Once this happens, the child will begin to avoid helping Mom, tuning her off whenever she becomes too serious and restrictive.

Don't get me wrong: nobody has a bigger heart or has a desire to be more involved in an important cause than a Scorpio mother; she will help anyone who has a problem—adults, animals, children—you name it. She can give you her all, especially if she is allowed to take charge of the situation. A Gemini, however, will never respond well to anything that reeks of control. Therefore, Mom has to find a way to avoid butting heads with her Gemini child. This information is important for the Scorpio mom to know, because I believe she has the patience and intelligence to work with this child. I know that Mom wants the best for her children, but with her tremendous need for organization, she can make everyone in her environment feel responsible for following her orders.

My main concern when I talk about the Scorpio/Gemini duo is the fact that Gemini children are never actually children. As soon as the learning process begins, they quickly start to intellectually mature. They never appreciate being treated like babies. In most cases, Geminis rapidly rise to the top of their class because they have an advanced capacity for anything involving mental stimulation.

On the other hand, Scorpio mothers tend to believe that *all* of their children are babies until they have finally proven that they are grown up enough to make intelligent decisions. And in a Scorpio mother's estimation, that time may be *never*. In the case of a Gemini child, Mom will get very angry whenever she feels her "adult" child decides to avoid her instructions. She can lose her perspective. Now, I understand that this Mom can be very serious about her home. This is one of the ways that she likes to present her image to the outside world. While there is nothing wrong with her values, a Gemini may not be comfortable living in a controlled environment. With this bright kid, compromise is the key to compatibility.

A Scorpio mother is stable and protective, but the demands she places on herself are so heavy that this sensitive mother can wind up making herself too nervous. Most people won't be able to notice this reaction on the outside, as she always gets the job done, no matter what. To counteract being so hard on herself, Scorpio mothers should allow themselves to join with their Gemini children in their pursuit of the simple joys in life.

The Scorpio Dad/The Gemini Child

A Scorpio father is also a very effective parent in his own right. He exerts more control over himself than most other sun-sign dads because he is a very intense personality. When a man begins to control his feelings early in life, those repressed feelings can build up, creating an emotional cauldron. He believes he will become too vulnerable if he feels too much. These types of feelings make Scorpio Dad an extremely private person. A bit of advice to Dad: your emotions are profound and intense, and it would be wise not to stifle them, as one day this behavior may hurt you physically and emotionally.

Now, since a Gemini child tends to respond less to feelings then he or she does to logical thinking, Dad and child should get along very well. And like his or her

Scorpio father, a Gemini does not tend to intrude on anyone's privacy. This Gemini will also share Dad's deep inner intensity, but while a Scorpio is overwhelmed by emotion, a Gemini's profound emotional core stems from the strong desire to succeed at every endeavor.

A Scorpio father and child can get along beautifully if the former puts aside his need to dominate situations, and concentrates on developing a mental affinity with his child. He can teach his Gemini child all about life and the complex nature of the world, as he is a natural teacher who imparts his knowledge simply and gracefully—particularly when he has a good student. Sharing knowledge through their teacher/student roles will form the basis for an excellent Scorpio/Gemini relationship.

The Sagittarius Parent/The Gemini Child

"I want to see the world, as fast as I can." This could be the motto associated with Sagittarius parents. They are visionaries who will have lots of dreams and fantasies. This sure sounds good to Gemini children—they are also imaginative dreamers.

Sagittarius parents have an honest, direct way of communicating, and they will have a tendency to treat their children as friends, since that was the relationship they would have wanted with their *own* parents when they were growing up. Many Sagittarian children who had to live with controlling parents become adult "rebels" who relish their freedom.

A Sagittarian's energy is stimulated by exploration and learning. These parents need to move on in life to greener pastures from time to time, or they can become lethargic and unproductive. Anything dull or repetitious on a long-term basis can be quite destructive where Sagittarians are concerned.

Well, as you might have guessed, this parent\child duo has a lot in common. They are fast-thinking, quick-moving, and can comfortably sail on the same ship—two pirates seeking adventure on the high seas. Sagittarius parents will enthusiastically observe and cheer on the development of their Gemini children's hearts and minds, and this positive encouragement and reinforcement will help young Gemini move forward without any strings attached.

The Sagittarius Mom/The Gemini Child

Mom will invest a lot of time and energy into raising her children. Her Gemini children will have supreme confidence in her ability to help develop their minds. For example, Mom's a great help when it comes to finding out what libraries have the best materials and services. Education is very important to a Sagittarius mother, as her philosophy is "the more my kids learn, the better they will be." A Gemini child will definitely appreciate this kind of thinking. Mom is also a lot of fun; she comes up with innovative ways to find amusement in life, and she has a terrific sense of humor. At times, however, Mom may be less than diplomatic in her instructions, and she can appear to have a tough exterior. In reality, she's a softie, but she *is* used to doing things her way. Her Gemini children will not be intimidated by her actions, however, as their personalities relate very well to someone who is direct.

I must caution Mom to be careful about sacrificing her own personal feelings when she is raising her children. She loves attention, and she cannot dismiss this very special need. If Mom does not take care of herself and her own interests as her children grow, she may be sorry later on, when her children begin to build their own lives and she needs to define her own existence.

The Sagittarius Dad/The Gemini Child

Dad and his Gemini children will have brilliant discussions on idealism and philosophy. Dad is an emotional and sensitive man, while his Gemini child is logical and will concentrate on the facts. Both Dad and his Gemini child require mental stimulation and the opportunity to pursue challenging projects. Dad will always encourage young Gemini's desire to learn. Dad may go off into his own world from time to time, but he needs to be there to support his child's creative and diverse interests. Dad's energy and enthusiasm is right in line with the persona of this child, and young Gemini will enjoy sharing ideas and thoughts with him. In addition, Dad is a lot of fun; he is a joking, life-of-the-party type who is a welcome party guest, and this is a trait that the Gemini child admires quite a bit.

The Capricorn Parent/The Gemini Child

"Mom or Dad, please don't expect me to be exactly like you. Your way may not be my way!" It will be up to Capricorn parents to really appreciate and understand this sentiment when they live with a Gemini child. Capricorn parents enjoy creating a safe and comfortable environment for their children, and they will do everything possible to eliminate risk in their children's lives. Gemini children will be comforted by the stability inherent in this lifestyle, but they will not want to adhere to rigid conditions.

Capricorn parents can be strict in the demands that they place on both their children and themselves. They can't help it. Capricorns move hesitantly when it comes to personal change, and they like to live their lives at an even keel. When the boat rocks, they try to balance it. This is a perfectly happy lifestyle for Capricorns. In fact, they don't like surprises, even on their birthdays. (However, I think that Dad would enjoy *being* at the party, and Mom would prefer to run the whole show.) The fact is that there is no one better than a Capricorn when it comes to planning a party, because people of this sign truly understand how to utilize whatever (or whoever) is placed in front of them. Capricorn parents are both intelligent and intuitive, and they are able to quickly assess quality and substance.

Self-control can almost be a fetish with this practical personality. When I work with Capricorns, I keep repeating the same word: *flexibility...flexibility*. Parents, when it comes to raising energetic Gemini kids, you will have to work hard to understand that these kids are free spirits. Their need for variety may exasperate you, but it's only through healthy change that a Gemini child will feel creative and happy. These children do not enjoy playing with the same things over and over because their minds are always on the go. Parent and child can balance each other out by combining both stability and imagination.

Remember the key word: *flexibility*. Parents need to learn to bend when raising these children. Mom and Dad must be both pliable and adaptable to anything new that arises in their lives. By doing so, Capricorn parents will really enjoy the challenge of raising these brilliant Gemini children.

☆ ☆ ☆

My Capricorn friends, Hank and Lisa, were watching their Gemini daughter Cynthia perform in her junior high school play. They were both nervous because they wanted their daughter to be a star! As they watched the play, they began to shift nervously in their seats.

Lisa moved close to Hank, and said, "She's mixing up the lines! We worked with her for hours!"

Hank shook his head and asked incredulously, "How could she do that?"

Lisa shrugged. "It's out of our hands!" She said with disappointment, "A lot of hard work gone down the drain!" I was sitting next to Lisa, and I began to laugh.

Lisa turned toward me, and asked, "What's so funny?"

I answered, "You two! Your daughter is fine. So what if she's improvising her lines? She's only changing a few words!"

Lisa said, "But that's terrible. Isn't she being very inconsiderate of the people who are on stage with her?"

I told Lisa, "Cynthia is not being inconsiderate; she's just playing with the dialogue." I paused. "I know how hard and long you worked with her, but you can't get up there and recite her dialogue for her!"

Lisa reflected on this for a moment, and whispered, "Sylvia, if the lines are written, then they must be spoken as written."

"But Lisa," I explained, "your Gemini daughter has to do her own thing!" Both Lisa and Hank quieted down and didn't say a word the rest of the play.

When it was all over, Cynthia came out for a curtain call—and the applause was resounding. She stood up on that stage, bowing and smiling, and her parents were beaming from the audience.

"You're right, Sylvia," Lisa admitted, "she was just doing her own thing!

The Capricorn Mom/The Gemini Child

Mom is one of the most efficient women around, and she makes it her business to know something about everything. She usually develops a lifestyle that conforms to tradition and convention, and she definitely needs to be in control of her environment. She expects her family to adhere to her fixed ideas of how to run a home. Once a Capricorn mom makes up her mind, it takes a very persuasive person to alter her thinking. She's not in favor of change, as too many surprises scare her. I have often mentioned that Capricorns have difficulty understanding how to be flexible. A Capricorn mother who raises a Gemini child needs to be aware that maintaining flexibility is the only way to save herself from frustration. Gemini children will not mess up Mom's house, but their inconsistent ways of doing things can exasperate her.

Gemini children look toward the future; therefore, they do not feel that they need to make a commitment to living a conventional lifestyle. It's the "new" that fascinates them. They are very sentimental about the past, but the future is much more exciting. Mom will have to be willing to adapt when she raises Gemini children, as they won't have the desire to maintain the status quo in any aspect of their lives.

The Capricorn Dad/The Gemini Child

Dad has a great sense of humor, but he's extremely serious about how he deals with his life. He tends to be hard on himself; therefore, his expectations and standards are very high. Dad needs to realize that his Gemini children have different kinds of personalities. They do not function well with orders. Reasonable instruction will be just fine, thank you. Dad needs to bend a bit when he raises these kids. Fixed ideas.and opinions will not work with Geminis. They definitely have minds of their own.

Both parent and child have razor-sharp intellects, and they are both emotionally intense. Dad tends to obsess over his problems, while his Gemini never stops thinking. Geminis *do* know how to play, though, and that is their way of releasing tension. Dad's serious nature often prevents him from really letting go, so it's important for him to find ways to relax, as Gemini children will want someone to share their fun-loving ways.

It may be difficult for Dad to fully understand his Gemini's need for independence, as he tends to restrict his own freedom by placing too much pressure on himself. Dad can learn a lesson from his energetic, enthusiastic air child: how to balance his intensity by having more fun.

The Aquarius Parent/The Gemini Child

What a great team. "I give you permission to be as free as a bird." This is what an Aquarian parent will tell a Gemini child, because that's the kind of lifestyle an Aquarian enjoys. What more can a Gemini child ask for? However, I've found that there is one thing that seems to invade the Aquarian spirit, and that is a powerful need for approval. That desire has a way of overriding other concerns, because these water bearers will go to any length in order to defend themselves. This trait can be put to great benefit, however, as Aquarians often come to people's rescue. They have a strong sense of social responsibility and humanitarianism.

Aquarians are usually respectful of other people's ideas, but they will remain staunch in their thinking when they decide that they're right about something. They can become pinned down by their key phrase ("I know"), so another person has to gain both their trust and respect before they'll ever consider changing their minds.

Aquarian parents are cooperative and considerate, and these admirable qualities will serve as an example when dealing with the (possibly) self-involved Gemini child. When Geminis get immersed in their own thinking, they don't think about needing to cooperate with others, or having to be considerate of another person's feelings. During these moments, they just go about their own lives playing out whatever is in their heads. Aquarians can also act this way, but they tend to worry more about how the other person is feeling. This is especially true for an Aquarian mom.

Aquarians and Geminis have much in common. They both live within their own thoughts as a form of protection from the outside world. Both can easily be hurt by anything they view as negative, and since they strongly believe in what they think, they both take criticism very personally. Mom, however, does not display the insolence that Dad can sometimes project. While many Aquarian dads won't appear arrogant on the outside, they can still be quite adamant about their own beliefs when they're in an argument. They must be careful not to overcompensate, remembering that it's not important for them to get everyone's approval.

Gemini children can live up to their best potential in a free-spirited environment, but Aquarian parents will be sure to nurture the mind first. They strongly believe in the value of education, and like their Gemini children, they can be confused by the outpouring of too much emotion. Aquarius parents can be artistically eccentric, or they can be perfect peacocks, dressed in designer clothes. Either demeanor will be quite suitable to the Gemini child.

The Aquarius Mom/The Gemini Child

Mom is an idealist, but her logical mind helps her understand the realities of life. She is very bright and can easily adapt to taking care of her family. She does not raise her children with fixed ideas or extreme discipline. She is much more casual in her approach. Mom is a caretaker, and there are times when she can personally suffer because everyone depends on her so much. Asking for assistance is very important for this independent woman's well-being, but Mom has a hard time asking for anything because she is so independent and believes that she needs to help everyone else. She feels good when she can be of service, but eventually this attitude can frustrate her.

Gemini children will enjoy growing up with an Aquarian mom. She will never try to take away their freedom, and she will encourage their need for individuality.

Mom understands the importance of this concept because she believes in making her own decisions.

Even though Mom is the kind of mother who can do it all, she would be wise to assign special chores to her Gemini child, who will benefit from developing self-discipline. Young Gemini will not be offended by Mom's approach, though, as her rules will tend to be on the mild side, rather than of the rigid variety.

Mom is usually artistic and creative, even if she never chooses to use these talents. I am always frustrated by my Aquarius clients who do not choose to use their creative abilities. This creativity can be a wonderful asset for Mom as she raises her Geminis, since she can inspire these kids to use their innate artistic talents, as well.

The Aquarius Dad/The Gemini Child

Dad and his Gemini child will really understand each other. They both tend to protect their individuality and do not like anyone to rain on their parade. Parent and child are both keen thinkers, who will enjoy participating in the same kinds of activities. Young Gemini children will trust Dad to help with projects, as they will be quite comfortable with his methods of teaching. Parent and child are very compatible, as long as their egos remain intact. Both Geminis and Aquarians feel self-confident when it comes to their level of intelligence, and each can be defensive when criticized. It will be up to Dad to give young Gemini the option to come up with an answer before he does.

This dad and child tend to shy away from too much emotion, since their logic doesn't always mix well with strong feelings. However, Aquarius Dad and his Gemini child can both be very sentimental, holding on to the past, their family mementos, and their personal treasures. They also can feel nostalgic for past romances. In fact, the best way to reach this air sign duo is through their sentimentality.

The Pisces Parent/The Gemini Child

In my experience, I have found that there are two types of Pisces personalities. First, there are those who are assertive and outgoing and tend to hide their sensitivity by surrounding themselves with order and detail. They need to keep things under control. They set daily schedules and force themselves to be disciplined in order to make sure that everything is done right. They tend to be very hard on themselves whenever they make a mistake, even when these errors might not ever be noticed by anyone else. This trait can cause them continual frustration.

This type of Pisces is always busy, the kind of individual who has a problem saying no to anyone. Statements such as: "I've got to do this for John, and I've got to do that for Susan," and so on, consume a great deal of their time. A Gemini child is very clever and will try to control any situation where there are no limits placed on his or her needs. This smart kid can sense Mom and Dad's desire for love and approval, so a Gemini child may think, "Oh, boy, I can get Mom and Dad to do *anything* for me." Mom, more than Dad, will have to learn how to stand her ground.

She will be fine as long as she establishes honest, simple rules for young Gemini to follow.

The second type of Pisces is a sensitive dreamer. He or she can be an artist, writer, dancer, or actor. A creative Pisces is much more free-spirited than the type of Pisces who controls all of his or her feelings. Being negative is the one trait that both personalities have in common. All Pisces parents need to work on this behavior when raising children, particularly when bringing up a Gemini child. Pisces parents cannot allow their frustration to build up, as they can appear to be negative. They can also create problems for themselves by doing too much against their own will. Pisces parents have to learn when to back off and when to take their private time. Together with their children, they can share the joys of taking it easy.

While a Gemini tends to view the world logically, a Pisces view is based on both intuition and feeling. Pisces parents can be very loving, but at first, a Gemini may not respond to outward displays of affection. This child will have to get used to the idea, but eventually, he or she will understand that expressing affection is logical in its own unique way.

When Pisces parents raise their Gemini children, it will be important for them to value truth and honesty above all else, including their fear of interpersonal conflict. I've found that Pisces individuals may avoid the truth if they have to confront someone in order to express it. They need peace and harmony in their homes and may cover up difficult situations in order to keep everything running smoothly. (Remember, white lies have a way of turning into real lies, and pretty soon truth may be a thing of the past.) Shying away from the truth can diminish a Pisces' self-esteem and self-confidence. So, if Mom and Dad appear to waver in their decisions, young Gemini can become very uncomfortable and insecure. This child may come to doubt the value of the advice that's being offered. While dealing with confrontation within the family is difficult, and getting to the truth might make family members feel like they're zigzagging through an emotional maze, it ultimately leaves everyone feeling more at ease.

The Pisces Mom/The Gemini Child

Mom will always be there to support and encourage her children. She understands kids, because there is a part of her that remains the dreamy little girl who indulges in her fantasies.

Many Pisces mothers grow up to be perfectionists who are very hard on themselves. Perfection means that they must live up to their children's expectation of what a mother should be, but I don't think that little children really have any idea of what a mother *should* be. A Pisces is loving, kind, and compassionate, and these are very good prerequisites for being a mother. Many of my female Pisces clients fear that their children won't love them enough, so they do everything possible for them. Many Pisces mothers never learn how to say no, and they tend to suffer from deep inner frustration. Mom needs to work on standing up to her Gemini children, or they may take advantage of her. Geminis are strong personalities who can be self-indulgent if they know that they can have everything their way. Mom needs to be aware that she is raising a logical child, and emotional bonding may not be the answer in this relationship. If Mom can just be the charming, poised, creative lady she is, her Gemini child will adore her!

The Pisces Dad/The Gemini Child

Dad and his Gemini child are both charming and playful. I don't know which one is the better talker, since they both understand how to turn simple words into poetry. Parent and child are super salespeople who can speak to anybody. Both Dad and his Gemini children are both outgoing and personable, but *his* emotions tend to override his logic, while the Geminis' logic will always prevail. Dad and his Gemini child can be great friends, as they both love to have fun. There is one particularly important thing that Dad needs to do when he raises his Gemini child, though: he has to work on listening to every word his son or daughter says. A Pisces man tends to listen to what makes him feel comfortable, and then he can tune out the rest of the story. I know that this behavior is not intentional, but Gemini children are hurt when a parent does not listen to them. They will definitely ask a lot of questions, and they will expect to be given sensible responses.

An emotional parent and a logical child need to attempt to really understand each other, and it's usually up to the parent to build a healthy relationship. Both Dad and his Gemini children have difficulty talking about their feelings, and they can shy away from personal confrontation. Consequently, they need to learn how to approach life with honesty and sincerity, and they should always consider each other's feelings at every turn.

SUMMARY

Parents who search for clear-cut answers when trying to understand how to raise their Gemini children should realize that this quest can be exasperating. In the process of rearing these young thinkers, Mom and Dad will have to accept their kids' unpredictable behavior. I refer to the aspect of the Gemini personality that I call their "distancing mechanism." From time to time, this mechanism will click on—especially when Geminis want to be alone in their thinking. One doesn't always know when or why this is about to happen, and during these times, Geminis can appear detached or aloof when you speak to them. This behavior should never be taken personally, as they can pull away from anyone or anything that will interfere with their solitary thought processes.

When bringing up Gemini children, Mom and Dad should try to avoid posses-sive behavior—that is, they should never act like they own their kids. Geminis will always have a problem reacting to the demands of a controlling parent, particularly with parents who do not respect their individuality. The best way to secure a healthy parent/child relationship with these children is to present them with a se-ries of options when there is a problem to work out, and give them the power to choose. These children must be allowed their freedom. One of the primary concerns parents need to deal with when raising Gemini children is to help them understand that they don't always have to reach for the extremes in life. (They have a tendency to be attracted to situations that take them to great emotional highs and lows, since both seem to present a fascinating challenge for them.) It's a good idea to teach young Geminis that the moderate, middle ground in life can be achieved by com-municating their feelings openly and honestly, thus achieving a comfortable bal-ance in their lives.

*"Making a home is different
than doing housework."*
— ANONYMOUS

Chapter Four

....

♋ CANCER THE CRAB

JUNE 21–JULY 22   ELEMENT: Water   **KEY PHRASE:** "I feel"

....

THE CANCER PERSONALITY

Cancer children (who are often called Moon Children, because they are sensitive, reflective individuals who are ruled by the moon) are easy to raise as long as they grow up in a family environment that will not compound their own emotional fears. Parental validation is very important when rearing *any* child, but it is crucial for parents who bring up a Moon Child. Young Cancers will easily pick up and mimic the behavior of their parents, as they tend to be natural caretakers themselves. So how do you parent a parent? If you are a Mom or Dad wondering how to discipline this child, try not to be overly harsh and direct. Moon Children are extremely sensitive and can be excellent listeners, but they can become overwhelmed emotionally. Therefore, they can only respond to the use of logic when it comes to dealing with problems. Parents who are domineering will intimidate their Cancer children, who tend to take everything personally. If parents become too temperamental with these children, they will feel as if they're being punished even if that's not the intent, and this behavior will cause them to retreat into their own world.

Little Cancers can be too judgmental of other people's behavior, as they tend to base their own self-confidence on how well everyone else is doing rather than on how well they're doing themselves. That is why they always need their parents' approval. And, they may rebel if Mom and Dad do not pay enough attention to them. So, parents, please do not ignore your Cancer children, particularly if they're trying to explain something to you. They may take awhile before they get to the point, so you may need to maintain a patient demeanor. It's important to remember that Cancer children do not think in a linear fashion, so by allowing them to talk things out at their own pace, you'll give them the time to explain things to *themselves,* which will help them figure out their problems in their own way.

Parental encouragement has to be clear-cut and unambiguous when dealing with Cancer children. These kids must be taught to *ask* for what they need. They tend to give more than they receive, providing for everyone else's needs rather than looking after themselves. (Their thought pattern is that you don't have to worry about people saying no to you if you don't bother to ask for anything.) Cancer children can wind up being the "good guys," patiently waiting for others to come through for them—and they may find themselves waiting for a long time as a result. By teaching Cancer children to ask for what they need, they will not be so disappointed when their expectations aren't met.

I have said that Cancer children emulate and mimic their parents' behavior; therefore, Mom and Dad's ability to communicate the importance of truth within the family is necessary for these kids' personal growth. I believe that a parent's greatest accomplishment when raising these children is the development of family trust. These kids need to have gentle honesty applied to their lives. It would be wise to use a soft, kind approach when explaining that telling the truth will help and not hurt them, especially when it's related to family matters. These children will learn through the rules that are set down within the household.

Lessons of personal accountability are also necessary as these Cancer kids move toward adulthood. If taking responsibility for one's actions is an expected behavior, then Cancer children will always be truthful with their parents. Some children may fear confiding in their parents, and they may evade the truth because they think that being honest may get them into trouble. It's not that Cancer children would intentionally want to be deceitful, as they can feel quite guilty when they are dishonest, even if they just tell a white lie. It's just that the fear of getting punished is stronger than dealing with guilt.

When I work with the parents of Cancer children, I ask them to avoid using manipulative tactics when raising these kids. Trying to make them feel guilty will only backfire; however, by gently and directly asking them for the truth, parents can provide them with an avenue to give honest answers. Parents of young Cancers have difficulty believing that these nice kids can get into a lot of trouble as they reach their teenage years. (If they haven't been taught to express their feelings as children, keeping things inside may manifest later on in troublemaking activities.) Children who are encouraged to honestly express their thoughts tend to like themselves better. Moon Children will need constant assurance and reassurance that what they tell their parents will be treated with objectivity and care. I'd like Mom and Dad to know that personal accountability can be a difficult lesson for Cancer children, but once they are encouraged to honestly speak up whenever they've done something wrong, they will understand the value of personal responsibility.

Cancer children are very sweet and lovable when they are little tots, and as these kids grow, they often develop into kind, considerate, compassionate, efficient teens and young adults who often appear mature at an early age. Parents will never have to worry about them with respect to taking charge of any task or project—especially when it relates to the home or school. One of Mom and Dad's biggest concerns may be to help these kids recognize that everything in the world does not revolve around what they think. Other points of view have meaning, too. If they are taught to *share their thoughts* with other people, they can begin to understand the meaning of honest communication.

Cancers can be excellent managers, with fine administrative abilities. They usually interact well with others as long as they stick to their own gut instincts and don't worry whether or not others are judging them. My favorite line to my Cancer clients is: "You'll feel better about yourself if you can learn to let others know how you feel."

The Soul of a Comic

As Cancer children grow up, they tend to fall back on making jokes when they feel uncomfortable and sad. They really enjoy making people laugh, just like Cancer comics Bill Cosby and Robin Williams. How fast they keep the jokes flying will depend on the particular child's level of insecurity. A Cancer child can become overly insecure when he or she is born into a household that has a very bossy parent.

A Cancer's joking method is subconsciously used as a diversion. Male Cancers tend to hide from their feelings if they've been raised by a dominant mother figure. Mom's overwhelming expectations can inadvertently cause this youngster to feel inadequate. If parents can recognize when their Cancer child is joking around as a cover-up for feeling blue, they will begin to understand that the jokes have nothing to do with what this child really feels inside. The story below says a lot about the way Cancer sons often relate to their mothers.

☆　☆　☆

It was a Saturday evening, and I was performing at a dinner party for a group of newlyweds. We embarked on the subject of individual compatibility, and I began to evaluate each couple, talking with them about their relationship. I guess I surprised them with my accuracy, so they started calling out, "Tell us more!"

It was interesting that when I began to discuss the relationship between a young husband and wife named named Dale and Susan, I noticed that Dale (a Cancer) began to make a joke out of everything I said. One of his friends chastised him. "Come on, Dale, can't you be serious once in a while?"

So I replied, "He is very serious, but he's just having trouble with my analysis. It's too close for comfort." After that statement, Dale got very quiet.

His wife said, "Dale, listen to Sylvia, she knows you as well, or better, than I do." I didn't really feel comfortable with that statement, as I couldn't possibly have known him as well as his wife did.

Dale just looked at me questioningly, and asked, "How do you know these things about me?"

I replied, "I've been studying you for years."

He laughed and exclaimed, "I can't believe this!"

"Dale," I asked him, "do you think that what I have been saying about you is accurate?"

He nodded. "I think you're right on, especially about my mother. She is a domineering person."

I said, "Dale, if you begin giving yourself permission to get in touch with your real feelings, and make an effort to talk to your mother about them, your self-esteem will grow." His wife Susan nodded.

As I started to leave that night, Dale walked over to me and took my hand. "It would have been great to have you as a mother," he told me. "You say it like it is."

I smiled and thanked him. "Dale, if I have inspired you to think about yourself, then try to speak to your mother. Tell her how you'd like to be treated. It's never too late. Talk to your wife, and I am certain your compatibility will grow. If you can try to take some baby steps in this direction, then I have done my job."

A Good Reason to Be Called the Crab!

There really is a good reason for calling a Cancer "the Crab." These children can be moody, and they have a tendency to feel very sorry for themselves. If parents of Cancer children try to work on building healthy communication from the onset, they can be instrumental in helping these kids understand how they feel. It is so important for parents to encourage their Cancer children to talk about their problems so that they don't obsess over them. These sensitive kids will run a situation over and over again in their minds, and they really need their parents to listen to them. A Cancer who spends too much time alone tends to only see the negative side of an issue. Cancers like to keep their own counsel, and without support, they'll think that they've got the only opinion that's right.

Cancers will need both their parents to help them reach rational decisions if their emotions get out of control. These Moon Children can benefit from intelligent, interactive discussions, where everyone can agree to disagree. These talks will help a Cancer child formulate a much clearer perspective of any problem. As Cancers begin to define their own thinking, while comparing it with the energy and power of another's opinion, their outlook can be a lot more productive. Cancers who are taught to concentrate on positive thinking will not be as dominated by their moods and will work their way out of difficult situations in a much easier fashion.

Cancers Value Maturity

"I hope my parents will act like grown-ups." This will be little Cancer's wish as he or she enters the world. Cancer children want their parents to be self-confident, mature adults who can serve their needs in a responsible and consistent manner. Cancers wear their hearts on their sleeves, and they have a tendency to be suspicious of anyone who might hurt them. As a result, it takes them a long time to trust someone.

They really do not mean to sit in judgment of people, but they do. Their parents are not beyond suspicion, and Mom and Dad may have to present sufficient evidence and make rational explanations before their point is made. Cancer children can believe that they are grown-up at age four. These kids may give a lot of orders, and they expect their parents to obey. Parents of these children will need to be steadfast in their own beliefs and actions. They cannot fall prey to little Cancer's demands. If Mom and Dad start to become too indecisive, this child may take on the role of a parent.

A Cancer child will respond to parents who are sympathetic, compassionate, and emotionally strong; since they're so sensitive, they tend to turn away from parents who are too domineering. Remember, these kids need gentle honesty. Cancer children, more than any other sun sign, emulate their parents' behavior, and they can benefit or suffer as a result of their actions. Since much of a Cancer's personal identity is taken from his or her parents, it is very important for Mom and Dad to serve as healthy role models.

What kind of parent would serve this function for a Cancer child? Someone who is traditional, even a bit old-fashioned, and who is willing to give a lot of hugs and kisses. This behavior will provide a safe, comfortable atmosphere for Cancer children and help to give these youngsters the emotional support and affection that they need.

As I mentioned above, Cancer children enjoy being viewed as grown-ups, and they can be quite comfortable assuming the role of a parent. They will usually take on this role by giving their peers benefit of their sage advice. Parents will be proud of this grown-up attitude, as it will make their children appear very confident, efficient, and organized. However, Mom and Dad will have to intuitively understand that within this confident person still lurks a very sensitive child. At times, this trait can make a Cancer child seem like someone caught between two worlds—right between insightful parent and little kid. However, Cancers do tend to be more comfortable offering opinions about others because this behavior helps them avoid talking about their own feelings, thereby possibly opening themselves up to criticism. This is the time when parents can be there to help and guide their Cancer children. We all know that humans can be part parent and part child, and this is an accepted theory in standard psychology. In the case of Cancer kids, acceptance of their inner children would be healthy. A Cancer child will unintentionally lean toward becoming the parent and will quickly fear the need to reveal his or her own feelings. Young Cancers do want to talk about themselves; they just have to learn how to let their guard down and allow people in to help them.

☆　☆　☆

Theresa, a Cancer, was a very bright girl. She easily aced her school tests, and probably had the ability to do anything she wanted. A friend of mine in high school, both she and I shared the title of "Group Activity Leader" for the girl's chorus. Theresa had a great personality, and we would spend a lot of time talking to each other. She would always tell me her dreams of becoming a surgeon, as she liked the idea of saving people's lives. I remember telling her over and over again that I thought she was smart, kind, and compassionate and had just the right qualities for pursuing that career.

I know her parents loved her very much, but I don't believe they were able to understand her behavior. One moment she sounded like a grown-up person talking about her accomplishments, and in the next, she was crying and crying, wailing that she could never do anything right.

Now, her parents could not separate themselves from their own judgmental behavior. Her Mom was a very strong Aries who was very critical of Theresa whenever she did the slightest thing wrong. Picking the wrong color dress or arriving home five minutes late from school could all provoke her mother's wrath. Being a sensitive Cancer, Theresa became overly critical about herself, and when anything in her life went wrong, she began to imagine how everything in her life could unravel. The imagination is a wonderful thing, but if your internal dialogue is persistently negative, you need to change your thoughts—fast!

For Theresa, emotional escape seemed to be the only answer, and she began to take drugs and large quantities of alcohol as a remedy for her low self-esteem. This behavior eventually led to mental and sexual abuse. She hung around with the wrong people, and I think that she subconsciously knew that her unhealthy behavior was upsetting her mother. So while the rest of her friends went off to college, Theresa stayed home. She got a job, rented her own apartment, and seemed to continue on a vigil toward self-destruction.

I hadn't seen Theresa for about a year when I heard this story. It was a summer evening, and I guess she was out partying the night away. It was said that she got unbelievably drunk and wanted to drive home by herself. The people who were with Theresa told her that she couldn't drive home alone. She began to argue with them, and walked out. I don't know all of the specifics, but I do know that Theresa ended up driving in the wrong direction on Lake Shore Drive in Chicago. She skidded into an embankment, narrowly missing the oncoming cars.

The crash really shook up Theresa and her family; her mother slowly began to listen to her, and family counseling helped her learn to curb her instant anger and criticism. They came to understand that Theresa's profound sensitivity was uncontrollable, and that this lack of personal control scared her. They came to realize that she needed them to be sympathetic instead of critical. Whenever she was frightened, that's when she started acting immature, and that's when she needed her parents' support the most. It took a near tragedy, but everyone finally "got" it.

I was too young at that time to tell her parents what I could tell them now. I would have explained that Theresa's sensitivity is a gift, and this gift could one day help her achieve the personal and professional goals she wished for. After all, if she did become the doctor who saved people's lives, her sensitivity would have been a wonderful asset.

☆ ☆ ☆

PARENT AND CHILD

The Aries Parent/The Cancer Child

As you continue to read about Aries individuals, you will see that patience is not one of their virtues. An Aries parent is strong and courageous, a person who presents a solid and protective image to any child. Since most Aries parents tend to project an innate self-confidence, they want to believe that all of their children will naturally inherit this kind of personality. Therefore, they may have a problem accepting that their Cancer child may not be as outspoken as they are. Aries parents like to believe that love cures all, so there will be no doubt about how much effort they will put into loving their children. But their need to take control of any situation can sometimes be too much for the sensitive Cancer child.

Aries men are quick thinkers who enjoy adventure. They move forward with the speed of race car drivers. Aries women, too, enjoy doing many things at the same time, and almost everything they do is perfectly executed. Young Cancers can feel somewhat inadequate when confronted by Mom and Dad's need to take control of everything. This may become a battle of wills, as young Cancers, with their predilection for taking on parent roles at times, may also want to wield power. The only difference between an Aries and a Cancer is that Aries individuals will never stop until they get their point across; however, Cancers tend to retreat when their feelings have been hurt. Aries will think that they've won the argument until they realize that the Cancers have gone off and done whatever they wanted to do in the first place. Now, an Aries will not want to push away his or her Cancer child, so I suggest that Aries parents set limits when it comes to their aggressive natures; it's more important to understand a child than it is to always win the argument. (Even if you know you're right.)

Aries parents may have to compromise their own need for perfection in order to develop trust between themselves and their Cancer children. There are two special gifts that Aries parents have that they can give to their Cancer children: one is to try and nurture their self-confidence by not expecting them to be perfect, and the second is to make certain to compliment and reassure them when they're trying to accomplish a task or goal. Now, Mom will be wonderful with compliments and reassurance, but Dad may find it difficult to verbalize any expression of admiration or praise, because he tends to feel less comfortable expressing his feelings. I'd like to suggest that Dad try and make a few concessions when it comes to his stoic nature. He will feel great joy when his Cancer child looks up at him and smiles, as he offers that extra pat on the back.

On the other hand, if Aries parents become too tough or critical with their Cancer children, they may not want to confide in Mom and Dad. These children need to be told how good they are whenever they accomplish something; since an Aries is such a strong authority figure, they will often seek that approval. One thing an Aries parent can bring into a home is a sense of adventure. While a Cancer enjoys personal safety and a comfortable, secure home, an Aries can be the ultimate risk-taker, daring life on both a personal and professional level. I can just hear their advice: "Johnny, always be ready to take a risk as long as you set a definite goal for yourself." Giving Cancer children this special kind of permission to really live life may help them move out of their safety zones.

The Aries Mom/The Cancer Child

Mom is a strong woman, and she tends to dominate her environment. Her home is very important to her, but her outside interests place a close second. She sometimes forgets how special babies are because she wants her children to mature early so she can effectively communicate with them. A Cancer child may not be comfortable becoming independent at an early age, though. Water signs are very emotional, especially when they are young, and they need to be pampered. Mom does not always see life through the eyes of a child. This attitude is not intentional, as she can be quite affectionate and attentive. Cancer children need a lot of empathy, and there may be times when an Aries mom will lose patience with them. She needs to be aware that she is raising a very sensitive child who takes everything personally. She should try to be considerate of their early need for dependency, while helping them see that they do not have to make mountains out of molehills when a problem arises.

The Aries Dad/The Cancer Child

Cancer children are usually very intuitive, and they will quickly sense that Dad is a very protective and caring man. He isn't home all the time; therefore, he won't lose his patience at those times when he *is* home and they demand his attention. Dad is usually a dominant figure in the household, unless he's married to a fire sign such as Leo and Sagittarius. If two fire signs raise a Cancer child, they will have to work extra hard to develop patience. Dad is honest and direct, and he will not mince words. Cancer children are not as forthright in their approach to life, and they don't easily look at the bottom line of a situation. They can go on and on before they come to the point. Water children can exasperate fire parents because it takes them a while to make a decision, so it's up to Dad to help his Cancer children, pointing out that they don't have to obsess over everything again and again. Aries fathers are usually positive role models for their Cancer children. Since Cancers harbor a lot of fears, Dad can teach them to overcome them through the development of self-confidence and the nurturing of a courageous attitude.

The Taurus Parent/The Cancer Child

There is one word that is associated with a Taurus: *loyalty.* Taurus parents will be dedicated to providing a stable and comfortable home for their children, and they will always be there for them through both good times and bad. I can even hear the Cancer child exclaiming: "Wow, this is a pretty good parent I'm getting!" Taurus parents consistently provide a safe and stable environment for their Cancer child to come home to.

Taurus parents and Cancer children will have much in common, including their mutual need for roots, family, and a comfortable place to hang their hats. For all intents and purposes, a Taurus will be an ideal parent for a Cancer child, but there could be one significant problem: the parent may turn into the child, while the child may assume the role of the parent. Both Taurus and Cancer are born with the same inner frailty—they are extremely sensitive. In fact, both of these signs have a very thin skin when it comes to allowing their feelings to get hurt. So, it's vital that they let people know when they've hurt them, or they can start to build up resentments that increase over time. A Cancer can stay mad at you for a long time without you ever knowing it. Particularly when they grow into adulthood, Cancers need to realize that, in the long run, speaking up when they feel hurt or resentful is much more productive than being silent and seething within. They need to acknowledge and accept the fact that their feelings are as important as anyone else's. Cancers who keep their feelings to themselves wind up suffering from nervous tension and other physical and emotional ailments.

Taurus parents and Cancer children also share a fear of rejection, and since both parent and child are very sensitive, this is where the roles can reverse. Cancer children quickly sense any lack of self-confidence on the part of their parents, and their first instinct will be to try to take charge of the house. This behavior will make it difficult for the Taurus parent to exert discipline. While parents often need their children's approval as much as their children need theirs, it cannot be at the expense of the parents' own feelings. Taurus parents must let their Cancer children know when something is bothering them.

Taurus parents can be excellent confidantes, as they are very sincere and trustworthy. A Taurus mother is very intuitive, and she will be able to sense the vulnerability of her children. She can heal their wounds by being warm and comforting whenever these kids need her.

A Taurus dad will be a protector, making certain that every material need is met. He is sensitive, but he may have a problem revealing this part of his nature. Competition and challenge will energize him, although these traits won't necessarily be related to athletics. Sometimes he can derive the greatest excitement from acquiring knowledge and from pushing his abilities to the fullest.

Dad can also exhibit a lazy streak, and he may enjoy sleeping the day away. He may also have a tendency to be something of a "bad boy" who loves to play, leaving the household chores to Mom. At times like these, when he's off in his own world, his Cancer child may futilely seek his attention. I would like to suggest that Dad really make an effort to spend quality time with his Cancer kids, or they will simply spend most of their time with Mom. Dad's Cancer children will silently resent him if he ignores their needs, and they will disrespect his lethargy.

Taurus parents are basically devoted parents. They just need to examine their own needs carefully as well as those of their Cancer children to ensure that everyone is co-existing in a mutually satisfying fashion. The Cancer child should be allowed to *remain* a child and not take on the adult role, and the Taurus parents should be able to take on the parental responsibility with strength and decisiveness.

The Taurus Mom/The Cancer Child

Mom is an earthy woman who is both realistic and sensible. Home and family are very important to her because safety and security are her priorities in life. Cancer children need to live in a home that provides the personal security they need. Mom and her Cancer kids will get along well because her philosophy of life is similar to theirs. Taurus women are practical, but they are very intuitive. Mom will understand her Cancer children's profound sensitivity, even if they pretend that nothing is wrong. Cancer children can be demanding, and they need a lot of attention. Mom will not hesitate to take care of them, but there are times when these water children may go too far. They can be very bossy, and Mom needs to work on sifting out the important requests from the trivial ones. She also should teach these children that they cannot *demand* anything, but have to voice their needs in a calm and reasonable manner.

Also, Mom needs to acknowledge that Cancer children are just as hard on themselves as they are on others. This shouldn't be difficult for Mom, as she also tends to be self-critical. Mom can do her Cancer children a favor by releasing her problems when she cannot resolve them. She cannot worry about everything, as she needs to help her children understand that life does not always have to be a series of trials and tribulations. Cancers are so sensitive that their nervous systems can be adversely affected by their emotions, so it's up to Mom to provide a calming influence.

The Taurus Dad/The Cancer Child

Dad is usually a gentle guy who pretends that nothing ever bothers him. He wants to provide a fine life for his family, and his practical values are positive influences on his Cancer child. Dad and his Cancer child can both be stubborn when they make up their minds, but I believe that Dad will usually win the arguments. Dad is an especially honest man who believes in honor and integrity. He can be very instrumental in helping young Cancers learn the value of truth in their lives. Cancers are very sensitive, and they do not enjoy personal confrontation. There may be times that they will tell a white lie rather than tell the truth because they fear punishment so much. It's up to Dad to point out the importance of being truthful at all times and to be a shining example of this philosophy in his own home. Taurus Dad is, essentially, a born manager, so he can certainly steer his Cancer children in the right direction.

The Gemini Parent/The Cancer Child

What happens when you combine a Gemini parent and a Cancer child? This rational parent will have to teach his or her emotional child the value of logic. While this appears to be a challenge, reason and emotion can work together beautifully. Remember Gemini parents: Cancer children can become overwhelmed by their own emotions. Once you understand this dimension of your Cancer children's personalities, you'll know that your goal is not to make them feel less, but to use logic more. You can show them how they can progress through a problem by taking reasonable steps.

As they move into the toddler stage, a Cancer child can be quite demanding, which may interfere with this parent's need for quiet time. Geminis are restless, and they often enjoy spending their time alone, letting their minds wander. This can be a problem when raising Cancer children, as these kids will want their parents to pay attention to them whenever they need them. If these kids do not receive the response they want, they can become crabby, obstinate, and irritable. It will be natural for a Gemini parent to use gentle logic in order to control this behavior, though. And, young Cancers will learn that Mom and Dad mean business. They will quickly let this child know that whining or irritability is not acceptable. To a Gemini, you either take care of a problem or you don't. These parents can help their Cancer children understand that complaining about an issue or driving yourself crazy by running a situation over and over again in your head won't solve anything. When overwhelmed by emotion, Cancers must take positive action.

Geminis can often come across as serious, cool intellectuals, and they may seem somewhat passive. This kind of behavior will be difficult for a Cancer child to handle, as it can hinder their emotional development. Geminis and Cancers can both be moody, but there is one main difference between them: Geminis find it hard to explain why they feel the way they do; they just want to be left alone.

If you are a Gemini parent, it would be wise to try to let up on some of your own self-control as you raise your Cancer children. Remember: these kids are too young to understand the fact that you sometimes need time to be by yourself. You might wish to set aside specific time to spend with your children after your solitary stints so they won't feel neglected. If you do set aside this time, though, it's important that you stick to your promise, or your Cancer children will build up resentment toward you.

All in all, Gemini parents are basically outgoing and personable, and will not appear threatening at all, due to their upbeat and energetic natures. A Cancer child will be happy to have these parents around, because they are essentially charismatic "big kids" who are a lot of fun to be with. However, a Gemini parent can sometimes be moody, so Cancer children can easily become confused when they live with a parent who tells them "Let's play" one moment and "Go away" in the next. I know that Gemini parents would never intentionally hurt their children, but Cancer children do tend to take everything personally. Since consistency is very important to them, it would be wise for Gemini parents to work on developing this trait.

The Gemini Mom/The Cancer Child

Mom is usually a methodical homemaker who will create a beautiful environment for her family, but she will always search for stimulating outside activities that will have nothing to do with being domestic. It's important for her to be aware that her Cancer child's basic security comes through stability in the home and family and that these children feel most comfortable with a Mom who would naturally sacrifice her own needs in order to take care of them. At first, a Gemini mother may not believe in raising her children with this philosophy. She is very independent, and will always need to do her own thing. Her mind needs stimulation; and housework, obviously, is not the most exciting thing in the world.

Even though she has a need to pursue her own interests, Gemini Mom must also assure her Cancer children that their own needs are being adequately met. It may be confusing for a Gemini mother to realize that her Cancer children, while being so emotionally dependent on her, always seem to come up with all of the answers. Cancers are sensitive children who need a lot of attention, but they also have a tendency to judge Mom and Dad on every call they make. Whether they're playing the parent role or not, though, Cancer children will expect their Mom to be by their side, especially in their early years. They are the kind of children who want their mothers to be waiting for them with milk and cookies when they come home from school. If their mothers can't fulfill this role, many Cancer children can slowly and quietly start to become resentful. This type of dependent attitude may stifle a Gemini mother's free spirit.

I'd like to see Gemini Mom try and be objective when it comes to her Cancer child's need for attention. If she should return to work soon after her Cancer baby is born, she must choose a loving caretaker. Cancers fear strangers, and they would resent being taken care of by someone who is not an emotionally responsive person. Leaving a Cancer child in the hands of someone who is merely efficient, but not affectionate, will definitely cause problems within the household.

The Gemini Dad/The Cancer Child

A Gemini father may find it difficult to be physically demonstrative, as his logical mind does not always mesh with the idea of affection. Dad needs to try and communicate his love and caring to his Cancer child in any way he feels comfortable. One way in which he can show his affection is through his ability to protect his family.

Dad will always try to provide the best things in life for his children, who will join with him in his great quest for knowledge. He will be an excellent teacher, and as his Cancer children begin to grow and their minds become alert, Dad will be right there taking his little Cancers to museums, libraries, and bookstores. It would not be uncommon for them to all take a trek to Europe (with backpack, if necessary) just to enjoy the culture. Remember, Gemini Dad, your Cancer kids will definitely benefit from any educational experience you can offer them, but your hugs and kisses are very important, too!

The Cancer Parent/The Cancer Child

In this family, both the parents and children might be wearing rose-colored glasses. Cancers tend to see people as they want them to be, rather than as they really are. Their idealism can sometimes cloud their reason. A Cancer can tend to view the outside world in a predominantly negative fashion, yet they are idealists when it comes to their own personal lives. Since Cancer children are so sensitive, they can sometimes retreat into their own worlds when they get overwhelmed by emotion. Therefore, it's up to their Cancer parents to help these kids see the upside of life. This task may represent a Cancer parent's greatest challenge.

Those Cancers who do tend to view the world in an unrealistic manner may feel that people are not always living up to their strict standards, which can cause them to build up a lot of resentment. Cancers find it difficult to confront other people when they hurt them, and they wind up letting their feelings build up over time—at which point they may finally let out their frustration by yelling and screaming.

Cancers have to learn how to reveal their emotions to people at the time that they feel them, and not let too much time elapse. If they repress their anger for too long, their self-esteem will definitely suffer. (Cancers have a tendency to wait for people to wake up, recognize what they've done wrong, and apologize to them. Sometimes they have to wait a long time!) Therefore, it is important for Cancer parents to give their Cancer children the opportunity to express their honest emotions, without fear of criticism or judgment.

There is another reason why Cancers may find it difficult to confront their real feelings. They view themselves as caretakers, and they are comfortable taking responsibility for important matters that arise, whether these situations occur in the home or office, or elsewhere. If they are allowed to take over and do it all, they will not need to make other people accountable for not doing *their* part. My Cancer clients often complain about being disappointed or hurt by someone else's behavior. "How could John hurt me like that?," or "Why didn't Sherry tell me what she was going to do?"

I tell them, "Well, I think you knew what they were going to do before they did it. You just didn't listen to what your instincts were telling you."

Cancers have to learn how to confront what they may not want to hear. Otherwise, the price they pay for being passive is too high. It is as important for Cancer parents to work on trying to overcome their own fear of confrontation as it is to help their children with this problem. These parents can be of great service to their Cancer children, as they will be too young to be aware of this dimension of their personality.

Cancer parents' standards can be difficult to meet. Mom and Dad can be very hard on themselves, and this behavior can easily rub off on their sensitive Cancer children. They must be honest with themselves, and learn to accept situations and people as they really are, and then, as the loving, nurturing parents they can be, teach these lessons to their children.

The following story is a good example of the problem that Cancers have with confrontational issues:

I was having lunch at the Chicago Art Institute's crowded outdoor cafe when a nice young woman asked if I would mind sharing my table with her and her little girl. I said, "No, of course I wouldn't mind."

I guessed that the mother was in her late twenties, and her little girl was around three. They both had rich dark brown hair cut into short bobs, and huge dark brown eyes covered by long, thick lashes. They looked like two China dolls. Cancers are basically made up of two physical types: those with dark hair and dark, dramatic eyes; and those with light hair and clear green eyes that you can almost see through. These two definitely fit the former category.

I asked the little girl's mother, "Is your daughter a Cancer?"

She looked at me curiously and said, "A what?"

I explained, "I'm an astrologer, and your daughter looks like a Moon Child."

She replied, happily, "What a wonderful name—Moon Child." She introduced herself as Randi, and told me that her daughter's name was Trisha. Trisha's birthday was July 14th.

"Yes, she's a Moon Child." I grinned.

Randi asked, "How did you know that?"

I replied, "She looks like a Cancer."

Randi laughed and said, "I might also be one. My birthday is July 12th." I assured her that she was and told her that two beautiful dark-haired ladies born under the same sign will be great friends. "Oh, yes," she said, "our friendship has already begun."

As we were talking, the waitress came over to the table to take Randi and Trisha's order. Randi asked Trisha what she wanted to eat, but of course, Trisha was taking her time. The waitress began to tap her foot on the ground impatiently, and said in a rather sarcastic tone, "You better hurry up with your order. The cafe is closing."

Randi looked quickly over at Trisha, and then back to the waitress."Would you please give us a few minutes?" she asked her.

The waitress left and came back a few minutes later. "Does your little girl know what she wants? She doesn't have any more time," she said rudely.

Randi nervously spoke to her little girl. "Honey, what would you like to eat? The waitress is waiting for you." The little girl looked up at her and said, "I want a peanut butter and jelly sandwich."

The waitress looked up at her mother and said with irritation, "Do you mean it took her all of this time to choose a peanut butter and jelly sandwich?"

Randi just shrugged and said, "That's right. I'm sorry."

Well, even though Randi's behavior was none of my business, the astrologer in me had to help her. I asked Randi, "Didn't that attitude bother you?"

She nodded and said, "Of course it bothered me, but I didn't want to make a fuss."

I said, "Randi, don't you think the waitress should have been made accountable for her nasty behavior? She is here to serve you! She had no right to rush you like that."

Randi nodded. "I know you're right. I just got nervous and didn't want to start a fight."

"But wouldn't you have felt a lot better if you just said that you didn't appreciate being rushed, and that if she acts this nasty to everyone, her job might be in jeopardy?" I asked.

She replied, "I just can't confront those things!" Randi was a sweet person who was a prime example of the nonconfrontational Cancer.

She did add, "Sylvia, I want to thank you for bringing this to my attention. I may not have confronted the situation today, but perhaps after I think about my behavior, I won't back away the next time."

☆   ☆   ☆

The Cancer Mom/The Cancer Child

Cancer children really need to feel that Mom appreciates them. They are very sensitive and harbor many unrealistic fears, so Mom should understand that they will expect her attention. Cancer mothers and her Cancer children are similar in many ways, both being emotional, with a tendency to make mountains out of molehills. They worry a lot, which often results in problems with their digestive tract.

It's very important for Mom to be open and self-expressive with her Cancer children so that they will follow in her footsteps. Cancers can be timid when they are small children, so they need to feel safe and secure in the home that Mom has made for them. She usually provides a relaxed and beautiful environment for her children, one that they will return to with frequent visits even after they grow up.

Cancers do not enjoy change. Many of my Cancer clients have told me that they did not grow up in homes that provided a stable and secure feel. There were many disruptions in their lives, and these frequent adjustments made them somewhat distrustful and suspicious. As a result, their relationships have suffered.

So, you can see how important it is for a Cancer child to feel anchored in one place. A Cancer mother feels the same way, so she has the power to provide this safe haven for her child. This Cancer mother will most likely be a kind and compassionate woman who'll enjoy protecting her child. Young Cancer will feel goodness emanating from her and will welcome her affection and consideration.

Even though Cancers are gentle and sensitive, though, they can also be bossy. When they are small, they order their friends around, and when they grow into adulthood, they tend to control their relationships. It's vital for Mom to let her Cancer children know that they don't have to control everything. Cancer children have a tendency to do so because they get hurt easily and feel they need to dominate situations to avoid being rejected. Mom would be doing her Cancer children a huge favor by helping them understand that true happiness stems from giving and receiving!

The Cancer Dad/The Cancer Child

A Cancer dad's bark can often be bigger than his bite. He is usually very protective, and he can appear very masculine and strong. He will definitely try to defend his Cancer child, but he tends to hide his own emotions. Dad would rather have Mom deal with their children whenever they are troubled. Dad will have to do some real soul-searching in order to understand his own fear of dealing with his own feelings. Otherwise, he may develop a temper if he keeps repressing all of his emotions. I know that if he tries, he can fill the shoes of the strong, protective, and loving dad that his Cancer children need in their lives. By learning to work through and accept his feelings, he can start to appreciate his own sensitive nature. In fact, he has the capacity to become the most loving parent in the zodiac.

The Leo Parent/The Cancer Child

The Leo kings and queens of the zodiac may have to temper their royal demands when it comes to raising Cancer children. Since the Lion and Lioness operate with great energy and power, they may need to learn to be more diplomatic. No one would ever say that these parents are not loving, as they truly believe that love is the answer to healing all of their children's wounds. But while they feel this way about their children, some of them are hard-pressed to believe that they are truly loved *themselves*. This is one of the reasons that Leos tend to seek so much approval.

Now, you may be asking yourself the question: why would the king or queen need approval? I would have never believed that these personable cuddly cubs would ever doubt that anyone loved them. After all, a Leo can be all things to all people. Leos often believe that they are the only ones who can take care of everyone properly.

Leos are excellent caretakers because they are intelligent, strong, efficient, and organized. Most of them are outgoing, with magnetic, charismatic personalities. (There may be some exceptions in those born under the first decan, as they can be a bit reserved in their behavior.) Leos make very responsible parents, because they always want to do the right thing. The main contribution that they can give to their Cancer children is to recognize their accomplishments and appreciate who they are. This is very easy for Leos, actually, as they desire the same consideration from their own parents.

A Leo parent may have a tendency to lose patience with the more emotionally controlled Cancer child. Cancers can be overwhelmed by their own sensitivity, sometimes having trouble letting their parents know how they feel, and a Leo parent may have a problem understanding why this is the case. Leo parents believe that any child of theirs should grow up to be just like them—individuals who would naturally fight for what they believe in, act upon their ideas, and take control of their own destiny. Now, Cancers will fight for what they believe in when it comes to their own ideas, and they will act upon them, but they simply don't express themselves as dramatically as their Leo parents.

A Cancer child is soft and sensitive, so the Leo parent must be aware that this Moon Child does not respond well to harsh, direct confrontation. Leo parents are very direct and will not always realize that they can frighten their Cancer children with their sense of authority. A Leo does not think that using a direct approach is scary, but emotionally fragile children tend to respond better to diplomacy. If Cancer children feel that they are going to get a harsh lecture every time they get into a scrape, they may avoid telling their Leo parents the truth. This would be a mistake, though, as a Leo parent cannot tolerate being lied to. It will be up to the Leo parent to understand that a more gentle, direct posture will be necessary when teaching this child personal values.

The Leo Mom/The Cancer Child

A Cancer child is extremely sensitive and will need a lot of attention, and a Leo mom will definitely be there for private, quality time. She is very loving and always willing to help her children work up to their greatest potential. She will be an important factor in these kids' lives, as most Cancers tend to become very attached to their mothers. Cancer children are emotional and fearful, but many of their fears are unrealistic. It's important for Mom to pull back when her water children begin to make mountains out of molehills. She cannot cater to these fears, as these children will become too dependent upon her and never learn to work out their own problems. Mom needs to sit down and ask them why they are scared and then she needs to listen to their stories. Evern if they are reluctant to divulge their feelings, they need to be pressed until they open up. Once Mom gets in touch with her children's fears, she can help them understand the heart of the issue and perhaps gently inform them that the situation is not as dire as they have made it out to be.

Since most Leo mothers are strong women who can do many things at a time, Mom needs to restrain herself from always taking charge of every situation. If she does so, these young Cancers will begin to rely on her for *everything*, and then their self-esteem will suffer. Ultimately, Cancer children begin to resent strong mothers for making all of their decisions. When a fire sign and a water sign get together, there can be a lot of conflict. It's up to Mom to inspire her Cancer children to function in leadership roles in life and to encourage them to make their own decisions (with a little help from her, of course).

The Leo Dad/The Cancer Child

Dad is an emotional and loving man, and he is also strong and domineering at times. I know that Dad will never want to miss the special moments that he will have with this loving child, so he must temper his need to be controlling. Cancer children tend to be dependent on strong parents, and Dad may enjoy this intimacy when they are young, but when they grow up, they begin to rebel. Cancer children have no problem following Dad's rules as long as he doesn't intimidate them with his strength. Dad would be wise to offer his children the opportunity to choose from a series of options before he makes any decisions for them.

A Leo father is usually very intelligent and intuitive, and his knowledge can be a fabulous asset to his Cancer children. He can present a fine role model for them to follow—his daughters will view him as a romantic figure, and his sons will thrive when emulating his honest, direct, action-oriented personality. If Dad can help his

Cancer kids enhance their self-confidence, they will always be grateful to him. Cancers are hard on themselves, and they worry a lot. If they are not as productive as they would like to be, they fall into moods and retreat into their own shells. Dad needs to teach them to talk about their feelings before they become emotionally overwhelmed.

When a take-charge father is raising sensitive and emotionally dependent children, he needs to help them build their self-esteem so they can realize the personal, professional, and spiritual growth that is a part of their birthright!

The Virgo Parent/The Cancer Child

In this pair, we have soft, sensitive, emotional Cancer children paired with parents who will analyze their every move. Imagine a little Cancer girl sleeping in her crib. A Virgo father is standing over the crib, whispering to his wife, "She's not lying in the right position. Look, her hand is stuck under her tummy. I know she's not comfortable. Pull back the cover, and I'll straighten her up."

His wife then replies, "You don't need to straighten her up. Her hand isn't stuck. She's fine."

Virgo parents don't miss a trick when it comes to raising their children. The best part of a Virgo's personality is that he or she will notice the good in someone, along with the bad. These parents will instantly try to help come up with ways to correct any problem in order to get things right. They will quickly nurture the fine qualities inherent in their children. I'm sure you've noticed that I've often talked about the emotional sensitivity of a Cancer child. Therefore, Virgo parents' habit of analyzing someone's personality may cause their Cancer child to take Mom and Dad's intent the wrong way.

Virgo parents want to protect their children in order to keep them safe; therefore, they may overdo the dictates of good behavior, self-discipline, and order in the home. They believe that if their children behave well, they will be socially acceptable. My experience, when counseling the Virgo/Cancer duo, has taught me that a weak link can form in the relationship if Virgos fail to take a Cancer child's innate personality into consideration. Virgo parents need to understand that their children sometimes need empathy more than analysis. To Cancer children, feelings are what matter most. If Virgo parents are cognizant of this fact, they may ease up on their analysis of everything that concerns these kids' behavior. If children expect to receive criticism and judgment at every turn, they will cut off any communication from their parents and protect themselves by staying in a nonconfrontational world of their own.

Virgos depend on their practicality and insight, which is contradictory to the emotional nature of the Cancer child. Cancer children tend to question everything and rebel against strict rules of any kind. This rebellious part of their nature will not reveal itself when these kids are young; in fact, they will try to fit the mold of well-behaved kids. Cancer children do not want to make waves. They will be sweet and loving youngsters who usually obey the rules, but a long-term problem can result if they're not encouraged to express their emotions. I caution Virgo parents to be careful about ignoring the sensitivity of their Cancer children. Remember, Virgo Mom and Dad, you're very sensitive, too, but as adults, you deal with this emotion differently. Your Cancer children expect their emotional needs to be recognized, and if they're not, the parent/child relationship may be unfulfilling and distant. It's important to know that your children feel comfortable opening up to you!

The Virgo Mom/The Cancer Child

Cancer children are emotional and very sensitive. They begin to take on the woes of the world at an early age. Their Virgo mom is a practical woman whose clear thinking and scientific reasoning tend to make her the ultimate nurse. Both Cancers and Virgos tend to be caretakers, and family is usually the top priority in their lives. Therefore, this parent and child have the same basic philosophy—they concentrate on the people who are closest to them. Mom needs to understand that her Cancer children are gentle people who cannot modify their personal reactions. As these water children grow, they begin to hide from their real feelings because they are burdened with unrealistic fears.

Mom is realistic and reasonable, and if she tempers her outspoken nature, she can help her young Cancer look at the realities of life without trepidation. Cancer children can reap rewards when they are raised with a Virgo mom's standards of right and wrong. Since the home is so important to these kids, they will not feel uncomfortable performing household tasks. Mom can present guidelines with respect to efficiency and responsibility in order to help her children build a solid foundation for dealing with the outside world.

Mom believes in psychology. She analyzes everything, and the mind fascinates her. The best way a Virgo mom can build a healthy relationship with her Cancer children is to work on understanding how fragile they are. Too much control can stifle her water children, as these little crabs can crawl into their shells and be reluctant to come out. Therefore, Mom needs to tread lightly!

The Virgo Dad/The Cancer Child

Dad is a practical man who has an idea a minute. His curiosity helps him to constantly increase his wealth of knowledge, and education is very important to him. Since Dad is very bright, he can impart a good deal of information to his kids that will benefit them in all aspects of life.

Unfortunately, Dad has difficulty with personal communication, as practicality does not interact with emotion. It's very important for Dad to become a role model for his Cancer children, as they will have trouble expressing their feelings. Cancers are very emotional and fear rejection. Dad is not usually very demonstrative, but he needs to understand that a lack of attention can hurt young Cancer. I caution Dad to watch his exacting nature. Even though making demands on himself feels comfortable, he may fail to notice that his emotional children can begin to feel incompetent and insecure if they have to live up to Dad's high expectations. Remember, Dad, children tend to make mistakes because they have little experience in the outside world.

A Cancer child wants to be responsible, and will usually enjoy taking charge of any project. Dad can teach young Cancers the value of responsibility, but many Cancer children tend to want to be in control of things on their own terms. That can mean running the whole show themselves.

Dad can be an excellent example for his Cancer child when it comes to achieving goals in a rational and practical way, but he needs to ease up on his expectations of perfection. When Cancer children overburden themselves, their nervous systems react adversely, resulting in all types of emotional and physical health problems.

The Libra Parent/The Cancer Child

Libras fear isolation. They don't like being left by themselves, yet they can voluntarily set themselves apart from the world in order to privately resolve their problems. Libras need a great deal of support and approval, a characteristic they tend to regard as a weakness. Basically, they equate a need for approbation with a lack of personal strength. This belief can affect their ability to make personal decisions.

Libras are humanitarians who need to be needed; therefore, they can sacrifice their own desires for the sake of others. I believe this attitude is equally shared by both Libra men and women. Libras need appreciation and recognition, but they can have a difficult time accepting compliments. They do not feel comfortable with people who hover or make a fuss over them. It's best to gently enter their lives, as anyone who is too loud or abrasive can frighten or annoy them. Since they are so sensitive to criticism, they tend to take everything personally. If they came from a traditional home that provided comfort, beauty, and protection, they will try to provide a similar environment for their children. If they feel that they have come from a household where the parents lived in their own world and didn't pay enough attention to them, they may carry a feeling of resentment with them into adulthood, which certainly affects how they present themselves to the world. While they are often soft-spoken, buried feelings of resentment can result in a loud and obstreperous temperament. Libras have to learn how to release their feelings instead of letting them fester within them; they must realize that what they think and feel *does* matter!

In the Libra personality, I see two different types of people—those who have an artistic and spiritual nature (which helps them release their frustrations and express their need for approval), and those who are traditional, structured, and conservative (and who may have more trouble dealing with their feelings). The artistic Libra parent can bring beauty, fairness, and harmony into the life of their Cancer children. The conservative parent, on the other hand, may have a tendency to be too critical and controlling. A Cancer child may retreat from the conservative personality, but if these parents will make an effort to let go and be more free, they can easily move into the artistic and spiritual side of their nature.

Cancer children will probably feel at peace living with their artistic parent, while feeling somewhat restricted and dominated by the conservative one. Many Libras generally raise their children in an adult manner since they like them to be independent. Just remember, however, that little Cancer is not an adult yet, even though he or she might exhibit an early maturity, which I refer to as their "parental base." Even as kids, they have a tendency to act like parents, and Mom might observe that her Cancer children may try to reverse their roles. The artistic Mom may have to stress rules, limits, and boundaries in order to let these kids know who's really the boss. The conservative Mom has a built-in sense of order, and she will know how to dominate a situation. With Libra Mom around, little Cancers will really have to watch their *p*'s and *q*'s.

Libras are probably the most sensitive of all the air signs, but logic and reason are still at their base. They are thinkers who may be uncomfortable displaying affection. Therefore, it will be easier for them to raise their Cancer children as independent, self-sufficient, free spirits. However, a Cancer may misinterpret this attitude as being distant and inattentive. It will be important for Libra parents to work on building a close emotional relationship that nurtures their Cancer children in both cerebral and emotional ways.

The Libra Mom/The Cancer Child

Mom is a *thinker,* while her Cancer child *feels.* When a thinker raises a feeler who needs a lot of attention, the relationship will need some work. As always, I believe it's up to mothers to try and help build their children's self-confidence by giving them what they need. If the kids go too far, then it's up to Mom to nip them in the bud. A Cancer child needs a lot of affection.

Libra Mom will be attentive to her Cancer child, but it may be hard for her to be overly demonstrative. She is a strong humanitarian, and will do all she can for those who hurt, but her efforts with one-on-one intimacy may take some effort. Mom *does* want to help her children live up to their best potential, and she will be there to support their every effort. She is bright and creative, and she can help her Cancer children sensibly resolve their problems. Mom may have to stand up for herself at times when her little Cancer water sign becomes too demanding and bossy. Cancers need their parents to help them understand that they don't have to control everything and everyone in order to receive love.

The Libra Dad/The Cancer Child

Dad is usually a peaceful man who won't try to force his children into anything, although he may try to convince them to listen to his opinions, as he can be very persuasive. Libra men are usually fair and need to live in harmony with those in their world. Cancer children are very emotional and are easily hurt; therefore, there may be a conflict between these two. Cancer children need a lot of attention when they're young, and if they don't receive it, their emotions can get out of control. They may seem malleable or submissive when they are young, but they have excellent memories and tend to hold grudges for a long time if they look back and perceive that they were "done wrong" when they were young.

Libra Dad is a mediator who has the ability to calm anyone down. He can be inwardly nervous and intense himself, but his external charisma tends to hide his real feelings. Cancer children may not always think they want reasonable and sensible answers, but ultimately, they can benefit from a father who can objectively prove that hysteria doesn't make any sense.

The Scorpio Parent/The Cancer Child

Scorpio parents like to live their lives firmly in one position. They don't like to change if they can help it. "Let me control my life, and contentment will be mine" could be their motto. When Scorpio parents raise Cancer children, they would be wise to understand that this child's persona is very similar to theirs. Mom and Dad will have to be cognizant of the fact that Cancer children are often mature for their young age. Since Scorpio parents tend to scrutinize the actions of their children, they may forget to give their "wise beyond their years" child the benefit of the doubt when a problem arises. They don't always believe that their children are capable of doing something until they can *prove* they can do it. An ideal Scorpio parent will be one who believes in his or her children without requiring significant proof first.

Scorpios enjoy their children very much and are quite comfortable with the concept of family. They have a lot of love to give, and they profess everlasting devotion to their children. Cancer children are on the same wavelength as their Scorpio parents, but they may have a problem with Mom and Dad's strong-willed natures. Scorpio parents can be quite compatible with their Cancer children if their guidance does not manifest itself as a series of demands. Cancer children do not have many material needs, but they do need nurturing with respect to their emotional maturity. If Scorpio parents do not raise their children emphasizing freedom of choice, they can be viewed as being overly dominating and unrelenting. And, if a Scorpio parent becomes too dominant in the household, Cancer children can begin to feel insecure, and their self-esteem will suffer.

Scorpio parents really mean well when they exercise their protective nature over their children, but they may lose sight of what individuality really means to these kids. They would be wise to work on sharing their thoughts and ideas with their Cancer children, because even though Cancers are sensitive, they can also be assertive, and they definitely want the opportunity to succeed using their own initiative. Cancer children require rules and limits, but they fear punishment, which they view as a form of rejection. It's best for parents to provide their children with cogent explanations when they mete out discipline, without letting a trace of ridicule and humiliation seep into their voices. Cancer children are very proud and have a strong sense of dignity. Therefore, they need to feel that their parents will always love, respect, and forgive them.

The Scorpio Mom/The Cancer Child

A Scorpio mom's home is her castle, and she easily reigns over this domain. Domesticity is second nature to her, and she can provide the kind of safety and security that her Cancer children need. Parent and child are both sensitive, and even if they don't talk about their personal feelings, their reactions are easily stirred by emotion. Scorpio mothers are usually energetic and action-oriented. They are always busy, and when they're not, they look for something to do! My experience has taught me that Cancer children are attached to their mothers, and most of these moms have been dominating and strong. It's important for Mom to ask for her children's opinion with respect to decisions that concern them, as they are easily intimidated by strong parents. If Cancer children believe that their feelings count, their self-confidence can soar.

Cancer can be quiet and reserved when they're young, but as adults, they tend to take charge of their homes and professional lives. Mom is a private person, and so is her water child—neither parent nor child is comfortable talking about their feelings. Mom is a willing confidante who can provide her Cancer with excellent advice, but on a personal level, she listens better than she talks. It's very hard for Mom to communicate her personal feelings; therefore, she needs to work on giving herself permission to open up. If she does so, young Cancer will follow her lead. This kind of self-expression will be beneficial to both of them.

The Scorpio Dad/The Cancer Child

A Scorpio dad may have a hard time bending when he has already made up his mind. He can be quite rigid in his beliefs, because he assumes he already knows everything. It's very important for Dad to remember that he needs to give his Cancer children the option of making their own decisions. I am aware that Dad needs to be the master of his household, but if he becomes too dictatorial with his sensitive Cancers, their self-esteem will suffer.

Dad may be organized and efficient, but he will not adhere to anyone else's strict code of ethics. His own convictions are what count. He's a rebel who's out there fighting for his cause. Dad would be wise to help his Cancer children develop the kind of courage that he himself possesses when he believes in something. By developing this quality, Cancer children will feel more empowered in the world and also gain Dad's respect, which will make life easier for everyone in the home.

The Sagittarius Parent/The Cancer Child

"Keep it light, keep me on my toes, and keep me smiling." Sagittarius parents are bright, and they are always seeking new horizons to explore and conquer. They are individuals who love being mentally alert and physically active, and they love to laugh. (In fact, they often smile through their tears.) At times, they be a little sarcastic and can appear to be insensitive to the feelings of others, but underneath it all, they are not the cynics that they may seem to be. These fire signs are aware of everyone and everything.

Sagittarius parents will develop a positive relationship with their Cancer children if they can try to fine-tune their predilection for sarcasm. These parents tend to make a joke out of everything, especially in Dad's case. Sagittarius parents don't always realize that some of the things they say can be perceived as harsh by their sensitive Cancer children. They would be wise to remember that these kids take everything personally. When Cancer children feel that they are not being treated with kid gloves, they withdraw, only telling their parents what they think they want to hear. The best example a Sagittarius parent can set is to just tell it like it is—simply, kindly, and to the point.

The Sagittarius Mom/The Cancer Child

Mom believes in raising her children with a free hand. She may not care to be the president of a women's liberation group, but she is definitely her own person. She says it like it is, and her interest in continuing her education is great. Sagittarius moms are strong women who can be very direct when they ask their children to do something for them. They can also be opinionated and judgmental, but they try to be honest and forthright in their beliefs.

They can rule the roost when it comes to their households, but they work hard to provide an interesting lifestyle for their children. Mom finds pleasure in educating her children. She will teach them to respect academics, as she is always ready to further her own knowledge in any particular area.

Emotionally fragile Cancers can sometimes misinterpret Mom's behavior. Their feelings may get hurt when Mom becomes overly assertive. Even though they may be experiencing emotional pain, however, these children would rather silently rebel than say anything to Mom. This is one significant way in which parent and child are dissimilar in their behavior. Mom is a direct lady, and she doesn't like to create something out of nothing, while her Cancer child tends to make mountains out of molehills. Mom is a worrywart, but she is also a woman of action. As such, she tends to gets the job done. Mom is more patient than her fire counterparts, Aries and Leo, but her Cancer children may still frustrate her by not being honest about their feelings. I can hear her say, "Just tell me what you want!"

I would like to caution you fiery Sagittarius mothers that when you raise your "watery" Cancer children (who do not get to the point quickly), if you respond with impatience and disinterest, they will retreat into their own sensitive shells. They may not always understand your need to move on. As I've mentioned before, *water* and *fire* do not always have an easy time together, as water can extinguish the fiery spirit. However, Cancer children are very bright, so Sagittarius Mom will reap great rewards if she can exercise a little more patience.

The Sagittarius Dad/The Cancer Child

A Sagittarius dad functions as both protector and player. He expects Mom to do all the hard work, and then he tends to step in for the fun. A Cancer child will find his behavior less serious than Mom's; therefore, he will be less threatening. Cancers love to have fun as well, so they will enjoy the amusing times they share with their Sagittarius father. Dad can woo his Cancer daughter with his charm, humor, and protective nature—she will be Daddy's little girl. Dad can charm his son by trying to increase his self-confidence, and motivate him to succeed through his *own* efforts. Dad and his Cancer son will enjoy going to athletic events and collecting memorabilia. This can be a special pastime for both of them, as they both love sport and competition. A Sagittarius father will feel it's important for him to be there for his children, an essential part of successful parenting when raising a Cancer child. Cancer children will depend on Dad's strength and natural ability to handle any crisis that occurs in their lives. He won't disappoint them!

The Capricorn Parent/The Cancer Child

"I love you" are the three most important words a parent can express to any child, and it is probably those three words that Capricorn parents find the most difficult to express. They will write it on a birthday card or on an occasional note, but to verbally say "I love you" can be as difficult for them as climbing Mount Everest, and it will be even more difficult for Dad than it is for Mom.

Cancer children need love, attention, and affection, and their feelings take precedence over the mundane details of life. Young Cancer children fit right in with the traditional and practical lifestyle that their Capricorn parents provide, but they will quietly and secretly rebel against an excessive amount of "household control." They like to live in a home that is neat and clean, but they are not obsessed with perfection. Capricorn parents are very intelligent people, and I know that they will pass along positive habits to their Cancer children—without expecting them to be exactly like they are.

It doesn't take much to move a Cancer on an emotional level. I know that once Capricorn parents understand this fact, they will try not to tell these kids that they are too sensitive. A Capricorn can view their Cancer children's lack of emotional control as a weak point in their personality, since self-control and self-discipline are so important to the way Capricorns run their lives. To put down the fact that Cancer children are sensitive can be a huge mistake, leaving these kids with a terrible feeling of self-doubt.

Young Cancers have a need for spontaneity, and they are capable of great achievement, but Mom and Dad will have to use strategy in order to accelerate a Cancer's level of personal success. Cancers do very well when they receive practical guidance, although they do have to learn how to share the joy of their successes with others. These Moon Children can be proprietary or modest, depending on their level of personal security. Cancers and Capricorns share the same values when it comes to home, family, and possessions, and they both expect a degree of order and routine in their lives. The best lesson for Mom and Dad to learn when bringing up Cancer children is to be patient with them so as not to disrupt their ultrasensitive natures.

The Capricorn Mom/The Cancer Child

Mom's sincere dream is to be a wonderful mother. If she can, she will provide the best educational opportunities for her children in order to enhance their personal and professional growth. If her children are not ambitious, she will do everything she can to encourage them to focus on long-term goals. Capricorn Mom's children can benefit from her ability to organize and prioritize tasks. Mom's stable personality is ideal for securing her kids' desire to be raised in a comfortable and beautiful home. Mom will expect her Cancer children to grow up with proper social skills and etiquette so that they can fit into any situation in life with ease. Young Cancer won't have a problem living in the traditional, conventional environment that Mom has established, and as such, parent and child will co-exist amicably, assuming that Mom is careful not to be too demanding.

Cancer children will admire Mom's practical and efficient nature, and they will follow her lead as long as she gives them the opportunity to participate in the decisions that concern them. If Cancer children are not given the freedom to choose, they will begin to resent the person who is trying to seemingly control them. In addition, if their opinions are not given any weight, they will begin to doubt themselves and may develop an unhealthy dependency on the person "in charge." It's important for Mom to share her thoughts and ideas with her Cancer children in order build the kind of relationship that will be mutually satisfying for both.

The Capricorn Dad/The Cancer Child

Dad is very definite in his opinions. He is very interested in practical matters, and is hardworking, persevering, and industrious, so he needs a structured, organized lifestyle. He enjoys a comfortable home, and he's determined to maintain that level of ease. He has boundless determination, he will build a strong foundation for his family, and he is extremely protective of his children, who are of utmost importance to him. Capricorn fathers tend to spend a lot of their time away from home to build their careers, so it's vital when they raise their Cancer children to take some time off in order to give them the attention they need. If Capricorn dads let their professional lives take precedence over their personal lives, their relationships at home can suffer greatly. Cancer children need to have their father around them in order to share their ideas and interests.

Dad would never intentionally hurt his Cancer children, but his pragmatic nature stands in the way of his feelings. I would like Dad to recognize the sensitivity that is inherent in his kids' personalities, so that his gentler side can rule at the times when it's appropriate.

The Aquarius Parent/The Cancer Child

"It's heart to heart, not head to head." Aquarius parents enjoy mental stimulation, and they, along with the other air signs (Gemini and Libra) are thinkers. Cancer children are feelers, so they usually react first from the heart, as opposed to the head. Therefore, the Aquarian parent has some work to do.

It's important for Aquarian parents to understand that Cancer children need to feel heartfelt love in their relationship. Therefore, it's up to them to work on balancing their own need to communicate through the intellect, with their child's need for emotional response and empathy.

Aquarian parents are fair and liberal. They believe that life is based upon enhancing an individual's independence and freedom. "Don't rain on my parade, and I won't rain on yours," is their motto. Aquarians are self-imposed loners who will seek company when they decide it's appropriate and choose isolation when they feel a need for solitude. Cancer children should avoid taking this behavior personally, as it doesn't mean that they are being rejected in any way.

Cancer children will appreciate having objective and intelligent parents who believe in allowing them the freedom to be whom they want to be. They will also respect their parents' honest and ethical behavior. Aquarian moms and dads do, however, have a tendency to overthink their decisions, and do not always feel safe acting upon their gut reactions, as they have trouble believing that their feelings are totally reliable.

As far as the Aquarian/Cancer relationship is concerned, Aquarian parents will have to allow themselves to respond to their Cancer children's sensitivity. I am not asking Aquarian parents to first feel before they think because that type of behavior is not conducive to their personality, but they do need to be aware that their Cancer children *are* emotionally based individuals. When these parents raise Cancer children, they will observe how kind, helpful, and sympathetic these kids are, and Aquarian parents will appreciate and value these wonderful traits because they share these qualities, too. Aquarians may appear to be calm, cool, and collected on the outside, but on the inside, they are extremely intense, and very hard on themselves. This is because they are always trying to get to the truth at the heart of an issue.

The best part of the Aquarian/Cancer relationship is Mom and Dad's ability to provide these children with unconditional love. With an Aquarian, there are no strings attached. This will be the key to making their Cancer children feel secure. Aquarians can also instill a sense of peace and harmony into these sensitive kids. These parents will allow their Cancer children to talk about their feelings in an open atmosphere, where they will not have to fear angry outbursts or judgmental reactions.

Aquarian parents will teach their Cancer children not to harbor resentment. Aquarians abhor strife or violence of any kind, so they can be a positive influence as far as helping these kids sensibly discuss *why* they feel hurt or angry when these emotions crop up.

The Aquarius Mom/The Cancer Child

Mom usually takes care of everyone else in her home except herself. She is an excellent caretaker because she understands her family's basic wants and needs. In fact, their nurturing personas make Aquarians excellent nurses, and many do choose this profession as their life's work. Mom's Cancer children will appreciate her caring attitude and feel comforted by it as they progress in their lives.

Aquarian mothers can be very definite in their opinions. They are intelligent women who strongly believe in their own ideas and principles. It may take her a while to make up her mind, but once she does, it's very hard to get Aquarian Mom to change her mind. When Mom raises a Cancer child, it's important for her to understand that his or her opinions need to be taken seriously. When Mom does take the time to listen to what her little Cancers have to say, they will be assured that their opinions hold weight. As a result, their self-esteem and self-confidence will be enhanced, and a mutually satisfying relationship will be the result.

The Aquarius Dad/The Cancer Child

The Aquarian father can get involved with too many interests outside of the home, and he needs to be cautious about staying too far in the background when raising a Cancer child. All children need quality time, but Cancers, in particular, need a lot of individualized attention. I'm not asking Dad to give up all of his own interests, but it would be a good idea for him to achieve a balance between his family and his profession. I know that he has the wisdom to do so.

An Aquarian dad can sometimes lose sight of what's important in his personal life and become preoccupied with the world around him, always seeking out new and exciting adventures. He does not always know that his presence is needed at home, because he sees Mom seemingly taking care of everything. With his predilection for freedom and individuality, Dad has so much he can impart to his Cancer child. He just needs to take the time to do it!

The Pisces Parent/The Cancer Child

With Pisces and Cancer, we have an emotionally compatible match. Young Cancer is powerfully bonded to his or her Pisces parents. Pisces parents are idealistic and sensitive, and they intuitively sense their child's sensitivity. These water signs tend to base many of their decisions on intuition, and most of the time, they're right! (A Pisces can just look at someone and know how that person is feeling.)

One of the points I've mentioned about Cancer children is that it's important for them to have parents who are stable, solid, and conventional. Pisces parents are not born to convention—they are dreamers at heart! Some may introduce a lot of detail and order into their lives, but being practical isn't very important to them; they'd rather spend time in their beautiful fantasy worlds. This is when they need to remember that their Cancers need a lot of attention, and that these Moon Children will appreciate this water sign's creative nature. But when a situation becomes too emotional, Pisces parents may want to retreat into their own world; that's when they need to be patient and listen to their Cancer children when they need to talk about their feelings. Cancers are very earthbound, so Pisces parents can teach their children how to reach for the stars.

Pisces parents love children, and they enjoy raising a family. They also have a tendency to spoil their children by giving them everything they want, because they want to receive their everlasting love and approval. Since Pisces parents are great dreamers whose fantasies are usually creative and beautiful, they have a way of making life a delightful adventure for their children.

One interesting fact about Pisces is that they are very generous, and sometimes their Cancer children have a tendency to take them for granted. So, Mom and Dad will have to be on guard not to let their kids get the best of them, or resentments will start to form.

The Pisces Mom/The Cancer Child

A Pisces mother is a very giving person, and there is nothing that she wouldn't do for her children. Cancer children are very compatible with their Pisces mother, as her sensitivity will be right in line with theirs. However, Mom will have to work on her fear of confrontation, a trait that she shares with this child. Mom wants everything in life to be harmonious and peaceful, and she can often suffer by settling for "peace at any price."

Another thing that a Pisces mom has to learn is how to stand up for herself in order to enhance her self-esteem. If she does not learn how to defend herself, her Cancer children will pick up on this behavior and avoid releasing their feelings, as well. Cancer children will not benefit from this repression of emotions; however, they love their Pisces mother so much that they will follow her lead. I try to persuade my Pisces clients to really make an effort to speak their minds whenever they feel they are being treated unfairly. When Pisces are strong enough to let others know when they have been hurt, they will be making great strides in their life. Their Cancer children, who learn by example, will benefit, too!

The Pisces Dad/The Cancer Child

A Pisces dad and his Cancer children usually develop a warm and comfortable relationship. Dad is emotional, and he has a big heart. Most Pisces fathers are extremely generous, and they will be there to take care of their kids' needs. Even though young Cancers are sensitive and somewhat self-critical, they will find that the natural attraction between their Pisces father and themselves makes for a profound sense of security. These kids will trust Dad's ability to love them and be there for them when times are tough. Personal relationships are very important to water signs, so it's crucial for young Cancer to build a healthy relationship with their father at an early age in order to develop the trust that will no doubt endure well into adulthood. Cancers may tend to relate to their mothers a little more when it comes to receiving love and attention, but Dad will be a vital part of their lives, too (he is a great playmate, and Cancer kids will love this side of him!).

SUMMARY

When Cancer children are not given the opportunity to express their feelings as children, they may find it difficult to express honest emotions as they progress into adulthood. They worry that people might refute what they say or be offended. Presented with a difficult situation, they might tell a small white lie to spare someone's feelings, but that white lie can sometimes develop into a big one.

Now, no one can deny that Cancers have loving and affectionate natures, as they are the ultimate humanitarians. If it were up to them, they would do anything to eliminate all of the suffering in the world. They are considerate and responsible, but they sometimes tend to sacrifice their own needs for the sake of others. If they try to respect their own personal feelings, and their own need for attention, they can avoid turning into good-natured martyrs. This recognition of their need for self-expression can thwart a lot of frustration and happiness in the future. Cancer children will ultimately thank their parents—no matter what sun sign they are—for raising them to believe that their sensitivity is a treasured quality that should be appreciated and not derided.

Chapter Five

....

♌ LEO THE LION

JULY 23–AUGUST 22   **ELEMENT:** Fire   **KEY PHRASE:** "I will"

....

THE LEO PERSONALITY

"**I** WILL be the leader of the pack. Do you hear me, Mom and Dad?" Lions and Lionesses are the kings and queens of the zodiac, and *they will* be the rulers of their domain. When a Leo enters the universe—no matter whether it's a girl or boy—these children are destined to lead. Due to the power of their will, they are excellent at taking charge of any situation, and they know how to keep their ship under steady control.

As an Aries, I am definitely attracted to the Leo personality, and many of my best friends are those charismatic dynamos. When my Leo friends and I start talking, we seem to get lost in each other. We could walk together through the middle of traffic, with horns honking away and people screaming at us, and not even notice, because we are so totally immersed in conversation. Since we are both on the same wavelength, we laugh a lot and tend to boss each other around. Neither one of us likes to be placed in secondary positions.

There is a magnetic quality that surrounds a Leo; some describe it as a feeling of "drama"—the actor or actress looking to be center stage. They can be great romantic figures, the men dashing and heroic, the women brave and instinctive. These leaders present themselves as intellectual, funny, emotional, and intense, all at the same time. When you bring a Leo into the world, you'd better be ready for a bright flash of light. "Here I am, folks," the little Leo will exclaim, "ready to take the world by storm!"

A "Go Get 'Em" Attitude

Leo children are born independent, aggressive, determined, intelligent, and helpful. They want their parents to appreciate and nurture their "go get 'em" point of view. With this kind of support, these kids can become accomplished leaders who will make their mark in the world. If parents try to stifle their enthusiasm, these children can grow up with a great deal of insecurity. And once these children feel that it's difficult to receive the approval and support of their parents, they may never live up to their potential. This struggle can become a lifelong trial for them if these kids are not allowed the freedom to find their own way.

Leos are idealists who want to believe that the world is a wonderful place in which to live. If they are allowed to express their feelings and explore life with enthusiasm, they generally become quite self-contained, not terribly worried about the acceptance or rejection of other people. They are also quite simple in their desires. Just give them love, hugs and kisses, compliments, a comfortable home, room to achieve, and good friends, and that should do it. However, these kids can sometimes be so intense that others often mistakenly think that they are much more complicated than they really are.

Personal Needs

There is a very important aspect of a Leo's personality that needs to be recognized: self-worth. Leos have a habit of compromising their own personal needs, believing that taking care of others is more fulfilling than allowing someone to take care of them. Little Leos may crave the practical things in life—beautiful clothes, money to spend, and a good education, but they are often afraid to take care of their own emotional requirements. In fact, of the Leos I've counseled, many have chosen mates that are very dependent on their strength. I have often found that a Leo's need to have control over a situation or relationship seems to outweigh their need to receive love.

I have been told that Leos are self-involved; but that's far from the truth. I'm always amazed that individuals such as Leos, who need so much love and attention, don't concern themselves more with their own feelings. Leos don't always think that they deserve the things they dream about, so it's crucial that they develop this aspect of their personas—that is, the belief in themselves and their acknowledgment that they *do* matter as much as anyone else!

"I Want More!"

I was a guest in a group therapy session when I came across Ruthie, a Leo. She was a regular in this group, and her main dilemma was that nothing was ever enough for her. Each time we went around the room and talked about our problems, all Ruthie could do was laugh and say, "I want more." She thought that she was being funny, but I felt that this was her way of avoiding her real feelings.

Everyone in group was given permission to react to what they had heard, so I decided to ask Ruthie what "I want more" meant.

"I'm never satisfied," she explained, "because most of my relationships have been awful." The group shuffled a bit in their seats, as though they'd heard this before.

"Why?" I asked her.

"Because everyone is dependent on me!" she exclaimed.

"Do you like it that way?" I wondered.

She adamantly replied, "No! Let people take care of themselves!" Then she laughed again.

"Well, do you allow anyone to help or take care of you?" I asked.

Ruthie now became more serious. She said, "They feel like they don't have to, because they think I'm so strong."

"I don't believe that strength is your problem, " I told her. "I just don't think you let anyone in to help you." She slowly nodded her head. "Don't you feel that you deserve any help?" I asked.

Ruthie shrugged and said, "I guess I can't give up control."

I responded, "Perhaps if you learned not to keep all your feelings to yourself, you might let someone in, and that person might be very happy to take care of you."

She looked at me and jokingly said, "You mean that if I give someone permission to take care of me, I won't be able to tell the group that 'I want more?'"

I smiled and said, "You got it."

You see, it's very hard for Leos to give up their need for control. If they're always working to keep everything tightly managed, they won't have the time to think about their own feelings. Ruthie's story is about a grown woman who, at age 45, had only just learned the importance of appreciating her *self!*

The Caretaker Who Wants to Be Cared For

Leo children tend to be independent from the very beginning of their lives. They are born caretakers, always looking after everyone else, even if no one is looking after *them*. And they're always giving people the impression that they're feeling fine, even when they aren't. This is because they are very self-sufficient, but they can take this behavior to the extreme. As the kings and queens of the zodiac, they often believe that they must be all things to all people. Helping people *does* give them a lot of personal satisfaction; however, it's more important for them to allow people to share half of their load.

As children, Leos need a lot of affection and attention from their parents. Above all, these fire-sign kids need to be noticed. When they are well-behaved, they need to receive their parents' appreciation. This feedback helps them believe that they are special enough to receive love. Since Leos need to feel that they're worthy of love to such a great extent, their parents will have to avoid keeping them at an emotional distance. Affection is the key to opening their hearts, which will give them the confidence to ask for what they need in life. If Leos see that they can easily receive what they desire, they will believe that they are deserving of good.

"I Promise"

When a Leo says "I promise," those words can be etched in stone. And they don't like to promise anything unless they can deliver. After all, kings and queens are symbols of respect. They like to maintain their superior status, so they cannot risk going back on their word. If Leos promise you something, they will honor that promise, because to them, it's do or die.

Parents of Leo children should not risk making promises that they don't believe they can live up to. To a Leo—and this is the case from an early age—everything that's important and serious has to do with the words *I promise.* Little Leos will always remember what has been promised to them, so building trust with these kids will be based on whether or not someone has kept their word.

When parents are raising their Leo children, they may notice that these kids tend to avoid telling them whenever something has gone wrong, because they fear that their parents are going to rush to punish them. Leos don't believe in outright lying, so they just omit parts of the story. The best way for parents to handle this problem is by developing a bond of honesty that can grant freedom to both parent and child. If Leo children tell Mom and Dad a true story, they must believe that these parents will accept the situation and try to help them solve their problem. These kids will only lie if they expect their parents to be very critical and judgmental of them. Their rationale may be that telling the truth isn't worth it, because they think that their parents just won't understand.

PARENT AND CHILD

The Aries Parent/The Leo Child

These are the folks who can easily make a positive impact on the life of their Leo children. Aries/Leo is a match made in heaven, especially when it's a parent/child relationship. Aries parents have the capacity for love that Leos dream about. They can fulfill their emotional needs without much effort. *Giving and receiving happen naturally in a home where an Aries and a Leo co-exist.*

Aries parents will have the same amount of energy as their Leo children do. Aries are fast-moving early risers who start the day with an optimistic attitude. They feel that each day may add a new adventure to their lives. Their Leo child is definitely in tune with the attitude of this fiery parent. Both parent and child are leaders who have the ability to work as a team without feeling as though they have to outdo one another.

Leo children need strong role models, and the most impressive part of the Aries personality is that they maintain their convictions. Leos are courageous when it comes to adventure or their own ideas, but unlike their Aries parents, they shy from personal risk. However, their Aries parents will have the natural ability to motivate and nurture a Leo's self-confidence. This is one of the reasons why the Leo/Aries relationship is usually such a healthy one.

When Leo children lose their perspective and fail to see the importance of an issue, it doesn't take much more than a look from an Aries mother to set them straight. Both an Aries and Leo see the world in terms of black or white, and both share very strong notions about what's right and wrong. They don't usually see the gray area on issues; to a fire sign, this middle ground is too dull and nebulous. Aries parents do not have the patience to ponder a decision, and there is little hesitation when it comes to getting a job done. Their little Leo will think, What a relief. You understand me, without me having to tell you anything.

Aries parents will have a wonderful time raising their Leo children. A deep friendship will develop as the years go by. Leo kids will instinctively sense that they can speak openly to their parents without fearing an instant reprimand. Providing a set of options to their children is built into the Aries rearing technique, and little Leo will benefit from being allowed to provide input into decisions that are important to them. By providing this child with the freedom of choice, both parent and child can comfortably agree on a final outcome.

There is one trait that both a Leo and Aries have in common, and that is impatience. Neither parent nor child is born with this gift. They want everything yesterday, and they share the feeling that they have to painfully endure any problem that doesn't have an immediate solution. If something takes a long time, both a Leo and an Aries will suffer. Both of these signs are saying, "Come on, let's get the problem fixed and move on." So as long as they live together, these two won't have a problem.

Here's my advice to all Aries parents of Leo children: please do them a big favor and help them understand that everyone does not act as quickly as they do. Leo children must also be taught that they can learn from others. Like their parents, Leo children become exasperated with anyone who seems incompetent, slow moving, or who doesn't seem to accomplish things as perfectly as they do. As you can see, it's also important to teach these children not to be arrogant. Even though Leos often seem to be right, they must be shown the value of slowing down, stepping back, and listening to other people's ideas. Sometimes Leos rush ahead because they don't want to be challenged. What these children don't realize is that they might be hurting people's feelings. A Leo must understand that there is much to be learned by allowing others to share control of a situation.

The Aries Mom/The Leo Child

Mom and her Leo child are strongly bonded emotionally, and they tend to sense each other's feelings. Mom can be an excellent role model for young Leo, as she is intelligent, a natural leader, and a woman of action. Leo children tend to be very similar to their mothers, and it's easy for them to find comfort in this special relationship. Mom will be involved in many things, as her interests are varied, and young Leo will be happy to move along at her fast pace. A quick-thinking mom is perfect for this fiery child.

As young Leo begins to grow, there may be one difficulty between parent and child. That problem can revolve around their respective egos. Fire signs usually have large ones, and they all want to lead. Leo children will not mind following Mom's lead, but they will be annoyed if she makes all of the decisions. It's important for Mom to include her fiery children in the decision-making process when an issue involves them. In fact, it would be wise to let young Leos feel as though they were actually *making* the final decision.

Leo children are just as independent as their Aries mother, and they will begin to reveal this freedom of spirit at an early age. Mom will never be disturbed about her Leo's need for freedom, though. On the contrary, she will value it. As long as Mom is able to convince her kids that she appreciates their opinions, this relationship can be a blend of love and harmony.

The Aries Dad/The Leo Child

A Leo child will depend on Dad because he will act upon what he says. If Dad promises to do something for young Leo, he will do it. As you have read, Leos are very serious about what they promise, and they will value Dad's ability to conform to this way of thinking. Dad and his Leo child are both emotional, but Dad tends to hold back on his personal feelings, as communicating them makes him feel imperfect. It would be wise for Dad to try and share his feelings with this child, as young Leo will enjoy talking to Dad. Personal communication will enhance an already fine relationship. It is not wise for emotional people to repress their feelings, as one day they will feel that they have lost a lot on a personal level. Dad and his Leo child can be great friends, especially if they work on sharing their innermost thoughts with each other.

There are certain types of Aries parents (usually in the first and third decans— March 21–30; and April 10–20, respectively) who can appear to be a bit rigid and cool. Dad, more than Mom, has a need for structure and privacy, which can often be taken to an extreme. And Dad, please take my advice; you don't have to control your feelings with your Leo children. They would never deliberately take advantage of your good nature. Now, an Aries dad can appear stoic, and he can seem a little indifferent at times, but this is only what he shows the world. On the inside, he feels deeply. Since little Leos want to share everything with their father, these kids' feelings will be hurt if Dad keeps all of his emotions to himself.

Dad must allow himself to reveal the depth of his sensitivity, or a long-term emotional block can form between both him and his Leo child. If this Dad can understand that his Leo child is his true "partner in crime," he can open up his heart and give all of the love and affection that little Leo needs to receive.

The Taurus Parent/The Leo Child

Taurus parents like to take their time, and Leo children are ahead of their time. It's a combination between the slow- and the quick-moving. However, in spite of this dichotomy, these two do make a terrific team. As two creative beings, they both share a strong imagination and a wealth of great ideas. In fact, Taurus parents often forget how creative they are, as they tend to get immersed in the task of providing a comfortable and stable home for their children. They often focus specifically on what mundane goals need to be accomplished, while putting their artistic and musical abilities aside. While Leo children do need a comfortable, stable environment, they also benefit from parents who give themselves time to allow their own inventive imaginations to run free. Taureans have the ability to create whimsical adventures for their children, full of discovery and innovation.

As Taurus parents begin to raise their Leo children, they will have to deal with their own fear of change. Young Leo has an affinity for setting things in motion, and if Mom or Dad wants to slow little Leo down, the lion or lioness *will* roar. Taurean parents like to make changes very slowly and carefully, weighing all of the consequences of every decision. Taureans have to learn to trust themselves; they have excellent instincts, and need to give themselves a break. Instincts are everything to a Leo; this little caretaker is fast and decisive. While it is necessary to give weight to important decisions, a Taurus parent must be careful not to impose an overly obsessive attitude about them on these children, or else they may wind up stifling these kids' self-expression.

Taureans do move very quickly when they have finally pushed themselves to the limit, though, but this tendency to wait until the last minute may be a subconscious way of *forcing* themselves to make a decision. A Taurus can easily operate in this way, but a Leo would never feel comfortable completing an important task at the last minute. A Leo needs to create a plan, and like the captain of a ship, boldly undertake it. It is important for Taurus parents to understand that Leos have an exact sense of timing. As they begin to grow, they will want to wear a watch all of the time, in addition to the fact that they use their minds like a stopwatch. When it comes to completing a specific task or project, Leos become very aware of time, and it's important for them to always allocate enough time for themselves or else they'll start to become very nervous and intense when time starts to run out.

A Taurus mother needs to be flexible with her Leo child. She will enjoy this child's dutiful and dependable nature, but this son or daughter may be difficult for a Taurus mom to raise if she neglects to encourage and nurture the creative abilities of this little person. A Taurus dad, on the other hand, will have to temper his desire for young Leo to always behave in a calm, peaceful, easy fashion. A Leo child is adventurous, and he or she will probably need to try most things once. While it will be perfectly reasonable to attach sensible boundaries to this child's behavior, Mom and Dad just need to remember that Leo children will be a lot easier to raise if they allow their creative energy and imagination to flourish!

The Taurus Mom/The Leo Child

Mom's nature is far more peaceful than that of her fire child. She moves at a more methodical pace, and she will find that young Leo will begin to pass her by at an early age. Leo children can be demanding if their parents give in to their whims. At an early age, Mom needs to let her Leo children know that she will not be their slave. She is so good-natured that her somewhat bossy fire child can take advantage of her.

Mom will enjoy her Leo children because she will admire their leadership qualities, but she cannot let her fears stifle their spirit. Leo children need to be given the freedom to fully explore the world. A Taurus mom will encourage and support her kids, and these young Leos will appreciate the fact that she is a very caring woman.

There are times when these children may think that they are the parents in the family because Mom is a bit slow in making decisions. As such, it's best for Mom to temper her need to dissect everything, because she will find that her fire children have little patience. However, Mom will have a lot of fun with her Leo kids, because their optimism, energy, and enthusiasm will light up her life!

The Taurus Dad/The Leo Child

Dad is down to earth, and he would prefer living in the country as opposed to the city. He is more comfortable residing in a natural environment where tall shade trees and expansive backyards are standard equipment. A Leo child is more of a city person, however. He or she will appreciate the joys of country life, but would prefer visiting there just on the weekends. Both Dad and his Leo child love the simple pleasures, and they will concur when it comes to giving and receiving love, maintaining a comfortable home, enjoying good food, and sharing new and challenging experiences. The real difference between parent and child is the inner intensity that drives the fiery Leo child. Dad is a sensitive man who can be motivated by challenge and competition, but he is much more passive than a Leo. A Leo child may become impatient with Dad because he can take his time making decisions. Well, it's true that Dad certainly has a lot of patience, so he can help his Leo children by teaching them to be prudent before acting on impulse. Dad cannot expect his Leo children to totally change their thinking, but by applying practical lessons to their lives, he can help them look before they leap!

The Gemini Parent/The Leo Child

This air-sign parent will certainly enjoy fanning the enthusiasm and excitement of a fire-sign child. Little Leos are bundles of inner intensity, so Gemini parents can teach these children how to "take it easy" and not be so terribly hard on themselves.

Geminis are logical thinkers, and they need to be given the freedom to be by themselves and think things through. Leos, on the other hand, also require their own time and space, but they are always feeling responsible for the needs of others. These fireballs tend to take care of everyone but themselves. Therefore, they do not easily give themselves permission to be alone. A Gemini parent can teach his or her Leo children that it's all right to spend time alone, and that it's a very human way of dealing with one's personal problems. Making time for themselves is a very important lesson for Leo Lions and Lionesses to learn, as this practice can lessen their inner intensity.

There will be times when Gemini parents will have to depend on their intuition in order to assess whether or not their Leo children need attention. Since Geminis often operate within the confines of their own world, they will really have to make a point of doing so. If Leo children sense that their Gemini parents are distant, they may take this same approach when it comes to developing their own interpersonal relationships. Ultimately, a Gemini parent will be charmed by little Leo's charisma and enthusiasm.

The Gemini Mom/The Leo Child

When I speak of the Gemini/Leo relationship, I am talking about two independent, self-reliant people. A Gemini mother's main challenge will be dealing with her Leo children's emotional nature and tendency toward drama, since she may find these qualities somewhat annoying. She needs to be responsive to these kids when they act in this way, because if Leo children sense that their moms are distracted or are losing interest, they may, in the future, repress their emotions for fear of a negative response. Then, in turn, they will emulate Mom's distant behavior when dealing with other people.

A close relationship between Mom and child can start with interesting conversation, as a Gemini can often converse on many subjects intelligently. Both parent and child share a desire to learn all about the world and what it has to offer. Mom's logical mind can be very helpful when helping to define young Leo's choices. She can reasonably assess the value of any seemingly flighty decision this child wants to make. Remember, Leos tend to make their decisions instantly, but they do let their emotions take over, which can be a challenge for Gemini Mom. She tends to use logic when making her decisions, and she has the ability to rationally explain the pros and cons of any situation. Leo children are bright, intelligent thinkers who will understand her explanations and appreciate the fact that Mom is looking out for their best interests. But Mom is not just all business—she definitely enjoys spontaneous and free-spirited moments. She will often delight her Leo children by coming up with inventive and imaginative games for them to play.

The Gemini Dad/The Leo Child

A Gemini father can appear to be a serious fellow who has a tendency to intellectualize everything he does. This behavior can overwhelm his Leo child. They tend to both mentally and emotionally exhaust themselves as it is. However, Dad also possesses a brilliant, dry sense of humor, which often lightens things up. This theatrical side of Dad will be very compatible with his Leo children, as they both enjoy drama and intensity. A Leo daughter will want to be "Daddy's girl," and his son will have great admiration for his creative ability.

Dad is a thinker who has a logical approach to life. His fire children, though, tend to feel everything. Many Leos may tend to repress their emotions as they grow unless they are given permission to let these feelings out. Dad would be wise to acknowledge his Leo children's sensitivity, even if he has a difficult time acknowledging his own emotions.

The best way that Dad can help his Leo children come into their own power is to help them develop the creative sides of their personality by nurturing their interest in music, art, and theater. These pursuits will mesh well with the showmanlike quality in Dad's nature. Dad can also help his fire kids understand that it's not necessary to go to extremes every time they want to accomplish something. His own logical, reasonable demeanor can be an excellent example for his passionate and fiery children!

The Cancer Parent/The Leo Child

These parents will be loving, nurturing caretakers, and a Leo child will feel safe in their home. A Leo child needs to feel protected, and Cancer parents will be happy to provide any form of protection that can save their child from harm. They just have to be careful to not be too possessive. Mom, more than Dad, will need to discern what the fine line is between being protective and being possessive, though.

Leo children are independent and self-sufficient. Even before they learn to speak, they are physically acting out their need to be their own people. Once Leo children do learn how to speak, however, their parents will quickly notice how opinionated they can be. But remember, this part of their personality was decided upon as they entered the universe.

Now that we know that a Leo child is usually an assertive and forceful person, we know that it's important for parents to guide and teach, rather than manipulate them. It's best for Mom and Dad to offer honest and sensible explanations when trying to discipline this fire child. If a parent tries to force a Leo into submission, he or she will encounter rebellion. Leo children are usually magnetic, and they tend to energize those around them. They are leaders who like to win their battles. Both Cancers and Leos tend to control, and both can be bossy. There will be times when a parent's and child's will power is tested before an explosion occurs. It's best to approach a Leo child with honest and straightforward conversation. Cancer parents tend to see the gray areas, while Leos only see black or white!

The Cancer Mom/The Leo Child

A Cancer mother feels a need to exert control over her home environment, and since little Leo does live in her home, he or she will have to deal with Mom's tendency to dominate. However, essentially, Mom is a very good-hearted woman who can definitely spoil her children. In fact, if it were up to her, they would always stay in the house. Little Leo will love her attentive nature, but it will be necessary for her to use caution when it comes to nagging, or handing down too many orders. She may have a tendency to resort to manipulation if her children rebel, and Leo children will back off from anyone who tries to "trick them" into doing anything. An argument could very well be the result. If parents are just straightforward and direct when it comes to raising little Leos, they will reap the benefits, because Leo children really pay attention when they believe they're being dealt with honestly.

A Cancer mom needs to be constantly reassured that her son or daughter loves her, which is something that has confused me ever since I started to study astrology. Why would anyone who is so loving and affectionate have to wonder if her children loved her? However, as I learned more and more about Cancer women, I realized that motherhood and giving birth are the happiest moments in her life. It would be horrible for her to think that her children didn't love her as much as she loved them.

Mom has a tendency to wait on her children hand and foot. So, it is in this area where Mom will have to decide whether or not she is acting overly protective. At times, Mom must be careful not to put down young Leo's assertive and outgoing behavior; this would be a mistake. Trying to stifle Leos' personality can cause them to doubt themselves, as these little fireballs will really take Mom's criticism to heart. In general, Leos don't like being told what to do, since they feel this behavior is an insult to their intelligence. This is especially true in social situations, as Leos feel that they are instinctively charming, expressive, and friendly, and don't need much direction. However, Cancer moms can remind their little Leos that they should not be so stubborn that they refuse to accept the benefit of valuable lessons from others.

Cancer mothers may not be aware of the emotional insecurity inherent in their Leo children because they will try to hide these feelings. When moms first try to help them to learn something new and change their current ways of doing something, the first instinct of Leo children is to rebel, which can hurt their relationship.

Since all relationships are important to Cancer moms—particularly the ones with her children—she will need to acknowledge that Leos often have to learn lessons on their own, usually by trial and error. Subsequently, their sensible Cancer mom can then point them in the right direction.

Mom may be perceived as being cold at times, but if the truth be known, she is really very warm and giving, often to the extreme. It is this part of her personality that young Leo will find both endearing and lovable. Leos are not usually negative or moody people, but Cancers can have that tendency. Remember: Leo children need constant attention and won't understand when their Cancer moms are acting a little moody. This kind of behavior can upset their optimistic and positive Leo kids, as these little people will feel that their mother's behavior results from something they did. It would be wise for Cancer mothers to try and explain to their children why they are expressing the feelings that they are. If this is accomplished, these moms will have nothing to fear. Remember, Leo children will generally love and accept their parents for who they are.

The Cancer Dad/The Leo Child

Cancer fathers are both strongminded and loving. Most people like them because they are outgoing, friendly, and funny, but there is a dimension of their personality that will need some work when it comes to raising their Leo children. Cancers and Leos are both stubborn and have powerful egos. They both take all criticism personally, which can heighten their emotional insecurity. When a Cancer father's ego takes over in a parent-child relationship, he can become overly critical and bossy. A Leo child will not respond well to anyone who believes he has complete authority. After all, this little girl or boy that he is raising thinks he or she is royalty. This Dad may resent little Leo's strong and outspoken nature. Both parent and child appear to share the following philosophy: "It's my way or the highway." It will be up to a Cancer dad not to see his Leo child as the competition, and he will have to replace his ego with sensibility and reason. Many arguments can be avoided if Dad is wise enough to replace his need for control with honest conversation. His Leo daughter will receive a lot of attention because she is a strong personality, and Cancer men like to be around these types of women. If Dad is not careful, his little girl will wrap him around her finger.

Leos are smart, exciting, and feisty. At times, they can be too outspoken and think they know it all, but when Cancer parents explain things to them logically and let these kids know how they feel, they will have the keys to raising these fireballs.

The Leo Parent/The Leo Child

Imagine a beautifully structured home built with emotions, dreams, quick decisions, a good sense of right and wrong, impatience, drama, and flair. Wait a minute—now add a few rainbows and the sun. Perfect. This is the house where Leos live.

Leo children will be a reflection of their Leo parents, and this is exactly what Mom and Dad want. When a Leo raises a Leo, there is an instant camaraderie. They understand each other, as they are both emotional, intelligent, stubborn, direct, romantic, and dramatic. The spotlight will have to be large in order to fit these two Leos in it at the same time.

Leos need to have their own space so both parents and children will not feel uncomfortable taking their own private time. Their values are the same: love, hugs and kisses, intellectual affinity, hard work, financial security, fun, and individuality. One of the only problems that might arise with a Leo parent and child is a clash of wills. Both can be very stubborn when it comes to believing in their own opinions, and little Leos can start to boss their parents around. I never worry about Leo parents handling this situation, but I do worry about them spoiling their children and giving them too much. A Leo is usually overly generous and will always want to be supportive when it comes to raising a child.

Leo parents also need a lot of love, and they receive immense satisfaction when they see a smile on the faces of their little Leos. But once you give Leo children too much, they want more. Leo parents may need to learn that they will receive love just by being their strong, supportive selves. They don't have to keep buying things for this little fire sign. Leos ares kind, compassionate, and helpful, so if they are taught to spread their love around, they can act as motivating influences on those who don't have as much self-confidence.

The most important thing the parents can teach the children in this Leo/Leo duo is how to ask for what they want. My Leo clients who, by the way, are no longer children, are just now learning what it means to allow others to do things for them. I think that the most qualified person to teach Leo children that they should allow themselves to receive, as well as give, is a Leo parent. The Leo child will then trust the source of the information and get the most out of it. I understand how difficult it can be for Leo parents to teach their children about a subject that has probably been the hardest lesson of their lives. What's so interesting is that the experience of *give and take* can be terrific for both parent and child. Leo parents can give their Leo children the greatest lesson they will ever learn: how to carry this feeling of being supportive into the outside world.

The Leo Mom/The Leo Child

Mom is the enthusiastic confidante. She will be happy to share in all of her children's secrets. In fact, she's not happy if they're kept from her. She's not very good when it comes to talking about herself, as she is a very private person, but what works for her may not necessarily be what she wants for her children. Mom has a tendency to do too much for everyone; but with a Leo child, she will experience the joy of having a self-reliant, independent person living in her home. Mom and her Leo child can dream together, as they both enjoy playing in delightful fantasy worlds. The first decan (July 23–August 1) Leo mother will enjoy a clean house, as she likes to keep everything in its place. She is the one who will teach her Leo child the importance of order and efficiency. The most important ability that a Leo mother has is her capacity to visualize "a better place." She will work to improve the quality of life for both her children and her other family members, whether they be Leos or otherwise.

The Leo Dad/The Leo Child

At times, Dad can appear to be tough, but he will soften up for his Leo child. And little Leo will recognize this vulnerability, you can be sure! Dad has no problem revealing the "softie" part of his nature to his Leo child, because when it *does* come to making a decision, he can often be more stubborn than Mom. Once his mind is made up, that's it. Leo children will have the courage to stand up to Dad, although most of the time they will find themselves in agreement.

Leo dads who are born in the first and third decans (July 23–August 1; and August 12–22, respectively) usually tend to keep their feelings to themselves. They are inwardly intense and do not always display as much affection as they would like. It is important for a Leo dad to be attentive and affectionate to his Leo child, especially his daughter. His son will be his proud friend, and together, the two of them will believe that they can conquer the world!

The Virgo Parent/The Leo Child

Most people think that Leos are risk-takers, but anyone who really knows them will understand that their risks are usually calculated. Like the Cowardly Lion in *The Wizard of Oz*, Leos need to feel safe and secure at home, surrounded by their own family.

Virgo parents tend to be pragmatic people who like to stick to what works for them. They like to be at the helm when a decision is made in order to make sure that the ship is up to speed and maintaining a precise course. A Leo child also likes to be involved with things that work, but they tend to be more visionary than practical. Leos are spontaneous and enjoy the challenge of new adventures. Virgos, on the other hand, like to plan their adventures. They love to go on vacations, as time away relieves the pressure they put on themselves to be perfect. (My one goal in life is to see my overly meticulous dear Virgo friends throw away all of their Windex and paper towels!)

Leos and Virgos have much in common when it comes to keeping things structured. Therefore, little Leos won't mind that their parents like to live in a clean, orderly home. The main problem that can occur when Virgo parents raise their Leo children is when Virgos fail to provide their Leo kids with the freedom they need when it comes to making decisions. Leo children will be very frustrated if they have to do every chore, every game, and later in life, every career choice in the way their Virgo parents prefer.

No matter how practical they may become, Leos base everything on their emotions, while Virgos tend to base their decisions on practicality. This can be a problem. Even though it's important for Leo children to understand the practical side of any problem, they must not be made to feel embarrassed or afraid of making a decision based on what their emotions tell them. Virgo parents, please remember that your Leo kids will take your practical advice to heart, as long as you don't make them feel as if you're stifling their independence.

The Virgo Mom/The Leo Child

Leos will respect their Virgo mother for wanting to maintain a beautiful home, so they will have little problem adhering to her rules and regulations. The only time little Leos' temperature will rise is when Mom makes excessive demands upon them. If Leo kids are politely *asked* to do something, they won't mind doing it; but if they are *told,* they will stubbornly resist.

Virgo moms are hardworking and know how to get the job done fast. They play fairly, and they themselves will conform to rules that they have set for their children. Their home will provide the stable and safe environment that young Leo needs. My Virgo friends always tell me that they want to stop themselves from needing to keep everything perfect, but I never believe them because I know that keeping everything in its place gives them peace of mind. A Virgo mom is very hard on herself, as she has high expectations. These demands can sometimes be projected onto her children.

Leos need the freedom to think for themselves, as they have a tendency to make impulsive decisions. Unfortunately, *impulsive* is not a word that exists in a Virgo's vocabulary. And this is definitely where Mom comes in handy. She can be very helpful when it comes to reasonably explaining why impulsive acts can be impractical. She will also know how to present the facts so that the appropriate decision can be made. This mode of behavior works will while Leo children are young, but as they grow into adulthood, they will definitely want to make more decisions on their own.

Leo children see themselves as actors and actresses who will someday receive standing ovations from an adoring public. Since a Virgo mother tends to be logical and realistic, she doesn't always comprehend this need for drama and emotion. I'd like to suggest that Mom try to maintain an even keel when raising her Leo children. With her high standards, she is capable of teaching her Leo children the value of stability and order; but on the other hand, she needs to allow her little Leos the freedom to explore and search for their own place in the sun. And by utilizing Mom's practical "can do" approach to life, they will no doubt find it!

The Virgo Dad/The Leo Child

A Virgo dad can be an executive involved in the corporate world or a creative genius in the world of advertising and public relations, but no matter what his profession is, or how much time he invests in his career, he will always cherish and take care of his children. This earth sign is a true advocate of education. Dad will want his children to work toward receiving the highest academic achievement possible. In addition, he expects them to be kind to their fellow human beings and to behave admirably in public. Therefore, the rules of etiquette and decorum will be taught in the home.

Dad might have a tendency to be frugal, believing in the wise and prudent expenditure of money, but Leo kids won't have any problem with this attitude, as long as Dad will finance a good education for them and will allow them to choose the career that they are naturally guided to. Leos really do enjoy spending money, much to Dad's occasional frustration, but he has the ability to teach them the value of earning money by doing odd jobs. As they grow into adulthood, these children will appreciate Dad's shrewd financial acumen.

Leos need to be free to express themselves as they choose, and as they get older, Dad may have to accept that their ideas may not always be identical to his. Leos will work very hard to achieve, as they can also be perfectionists. Actually, most of Dad's values are compatible with the values of his Leo children, except for his need to be critical. Leos' feelings are easily hurt, and they don't respond well to criticism at all. We all know that Leos are emotional, so Virgo Dad will really have to try to work on understanding how his children feel, or he will come up against defensive children. Together, the respective practical and emotional sides of this duo will create a life that is full of great accomplishments.

The Libra Parent/The Leo Child

Libra parents admire and respect their Leo children's outgoing, decisive personalities, since their own predilection for examining every side of an issue when making a decision can create problems. Libras are also loving and considerate, but they have a tendency to push themselves too far. They can come up with dozens of chores to do for themselves, as well as undertaking everyone else's responsibilities, until they finally just collapse from exhaustion. Leos, on the other hand, are better at pacing themselves, but they never stop. Libra parents do not reveal their nervous tension on the surface; they just keep it nicely tucked inside themselves. They appear very calm and peaceful whenever they handle a situation, and they have the ability to create an aura of tranquility in the home. Since Leo children are also very intense and emotional, they will appreciate having parents who don't become anxious every time they are told about one of their Leo child's adventures. However, Libras do have to learn that it's all right to show people whom they care about that they are vulnerable, by letting them know how they feel.

The Libra Mom/The Leo Child

Libras can have trouble confronting people who've hurt their feelings. If they hold on to this anger too long, they wind up making themselves miserable in the long run. If they don't try to verbalize their feelings, they can become quite edgy and defensive, two qualities they wouldn't want to pass down to their intuitive and optimistic Leo children. Mom is a very important person in a Leo's life, as this child will adore this kind, compassionate air sign. Leos and Libras can be great friends, and Mom has the ability to nurture her Leo child. Fantasies and adventures together will create a life for this duo that can become a storybook of cherished dreams.

A Libra mom's need for balance and stability can be very instrumental in providing a beautiful and artistic environment for her Leo child. Her creative side will definitely harmonize with that of the theatrical and idealistic Leo.

The following story will reveal something about the innate creative nature of the Libra mom.

☆　☆　☆

I was speaking at a luncheon for the Lady Elks Club, and I like to incorporate questions from the audience in my speeches. A Libra lady named Emma stood up and asked me this question: "Why do people think I'm creative?"

I very simply answered, "Because you are."

She remarked, "I don't see myself that way. I wouldn't know how to sketch a tree."

Then I asked her, "Are you very dedicated to your home and to raising your children?"

She replied, "Of course I am."

"Do you do creative things for your family?"

She shrugged. "Like what?"

"Well," I asked her, "do you enjoy working with color and designing things?"

She responded, "Of course I do. I have always sewn my kids' costumes for school."

"So why don't you think you're creative?"

She answered, "Well, I never paint or sketch."

I suggested to her, "Emma, how about taking a ceramics class, where you could work with your hands molding and painting a bowl, or making a small statue?"

She admitted, "That does sounds fun."

I continued, "I always tell my Libra clients that they need to give themselves credit for the things they do. Emma, I look forward to admiring your work."

She thanked me, and a couple of months later, I received a beautiful ceramic bowl as a gift.

☆　☆　☆

The Libra Dad/The Leo Child

Libra dads usually have a pleasant, gentle manner. They appear to take life as it comes, but don't be fooled—on the inside, they can take life very seriously. A Libra father can be a workaholic, as he feels a strong responsibility to provide for his family. Dad needs to feel that his day's work has been completed, as he dislikes leaving a job undone. Young Leos will be unhappy, though, if Dad spends too much time away from home; they might start to think that he doesn't care. A Leo child needs Dad's attention and affection because he is such a calming influence. Even when he suffers from the Libra inner intensity and nerves, he will rarely display these feelings in front of his family.

Dad is a natural teacher, and he can be very instrumental in helping his Leo child appreciate the beauty in life. A Leo child is always in search of knowledge, and Dad will be a perfect catalyst for achieving this goal.

Dad has a logical base, so sometimes he can appear to be off in his own world, but the best way to really communicate with his Leo children and reassure them that he is there for them is to sit down and have heart-to-heart talks. His children will admire and respect his openness and be more likely to share their own feelings as a result!

The Scorpio Parent/The Leo Child

Scorpio parents are strong authority figures. Having children fits right in with their "take charge" personalities. There is no question that Scorpios love their children and that they can elevate the meaning of family to the highest level, but the first thing they need to understand when they raise Leo children is that these kids may not exactly be on the same wavelength. It basically goes back to the water and fire concept.

While it's true that there are many similarities in the Scorpio/Leo combination—they both enjoy a safe and secure home, cleanliness, organization, good food, and a passion for learning—the real conflict stems from the way in which these two signs choose to approach their lives. A Leo is an idealist who dares to dream, while a Scorpio is a realist, a water sign who is concerned with the truth and who views things as they really are. The only problem comes when reality has a tendency to diminish idealism.

The Scorpio Mom/The Leo Child

A Scorpio mom likes to do things for people, and her Leo children will be pleased that she knows how to take care of their basic needs. After all, a Scorpio mother is an excellent cook, and she knows how to maintain a beautiful home. King and queen Leo will adore anyone who enjoys taking care of them. However, a Scorpio mother *will* definitely expect them to uphold their end of the bargain, by keeping their rooms neat and putting away all their personal items.

From the start, young Leos will have minds of their own, so it's important for Mom to understand that she must give her Leo children the freedom to make their own decisions, as this type of interaction will contribute to a healthy relationship that will be characterized by a minimum of strife. The most significant word to describe how a Scorpio mother and Leo child can maintain peace and tranquility in the home is: *compromise!*

The Scorpio Dad/The Leo Child

A Scorpio father likes to control a situation, and so does his Leo child. Scorpio Dad has a lot of will power, and sure enough, his Leo child possesses this quality, too. And if you think that Dad can be domineering, he has a true partner in his Leo child. What can be done to balance out this potentially explosive situation?

Well, let me offer a few suggestions. When there are two strong personalities in a home, eventually one of them has to bend. The best way for a Scorpio dad to reach his Leo child is to avoid barking out orders and by loosening the reins. In this way, little Leos will learn how to make their own decisions. Scorpio dads are excellent problem solvers, and by listening to their Leo children, the two signs can work together to figure out any problem that arises. Leos need to be able to disagree with Dad, particularly as they enter adolescence. In fact, Dad will discover that his Leo children are gifted with intellectual maturity. Leo kids may not always reveal *emotional* maturity, but they do have an "old head" resting on their young shoulders.

If a Scorpio father can work on understanding how his Leo children feel about things, he will earn their respect and admiration. (The truth is that Dad is also quite emotional, even if he doesn't want anyone to know that secret.) Dad can be a strong influence in helping his young Leos accept the realities of life, as long as he does not push them into thinking exactly as he does. If he can try to emotionally tune into his Leo children's outlook on life, he will have a stronger connection to these little fireballs, and he will find it easier to get his own feelings and ideas across.

The Sagittarius Parent/The Leo Child

"I'm going to be raised by a free spirit." Imagine little Leo's excitement as he or she is brought home from the hospital. Like their little Leos, a Sagittarius parent is an adventurer with an independent attitude. Leos have no problem expressing themselves, and this parent will give them the freedom to say what they're thinking. Sagittarius parents dislike personal restrictions of any kind, and they will recognize the same desire in their Leo children.

Both Sagittarians and Leos tend to have rigid standards when it comes to their professional lives, and they work hard to get a job done. However, both dream of peacefully idling their days away on their own island. In fact, Sagittarius men love to sail, and if possible, they will try to own a boat of their own. To them, it's "Have boat, will travel."

Both Sagittarius parents and their Leo children are emotional, sensitive, fiery, and energetic. These sun-sign individuals share a natural bond, although the Sagittarian philosophy on life is not quite as intense as the Leo's. A Sagittarius is a loner who likes to live in his or her own world. Leos do need their space, but they like to spend more time with people. Both Sagittarius parents and Leo children are quite opinionated, and when they argue, both of them definitely think that they're the ones who are right. However, the nice part about most fire signs is that they fight clean. They have a strong sense of justice and fair play, and they will argue their case in a reasonable fashion. Sagittarians and Leos just have to avoid letting their egos get in the way of a beautiful relationship.

The Sagittarius Mom/The Leo Child

Sagittarians and Leos share many of the same values, and little Leos will appreciate the intelligence that they share with Sagittarius Mom. The home environment she provides will be largely free from tension and anxiety. Both Mom and child think in very definite terms (black or white, right or wrong) but a few shaded gray areas are present in Mom's personality. She has the ability to help her Leo child see both sides of any situation. Developing the mind, encouraging physical activities, and providing opportunities to learn form the basis for Mom's philosophy when raising her children.

Sagittarius Mom will have more patience than her Leo child, but sometimes she winds up tolerating too much from people. Instead of confronting those who have hurt her, she has a tendency to internalize her injured feelings. Now, Leo children are not thrilled about confronting people who have hurt them either, but since they don't seem to worry about things as much as Mom does, they simply find a way to resolve problems with a minimum of confrontation and anxiety. Since most fire signs want everything at the moment or yesterday, this parent and child can move quickly in order to get things done, ultimately learning to agree that they can disagree.

The Sagittarius Dad/The Leo Child

There are several roads that a Sagittarius dad may take in his professional life, and what he chooses usually seems to have a lot to do with how sensitive he is. When a Sagittarius man chooses to work in the corporate world, it's because he likes an environment where he can control the day-to-day events. In fact, he can appear to be a tough businessman on the outside, although that behavior does belie the sensitivity within.

Little Leos, however, may enjoy a more creative atmosphere, and Dad should not try to steer his children away from this side of their personalities. Very often, Leos excel in the world of art, advertising, theater, sales promotion, or photography. Leos who choose to work in the rigid corporate world can often wind up feeling stifled and unhappy.

Most of the time, a Sagittarius dad will leave the basic tasks of raising a child up to Mom. When he spends time with his Leo children, his responsibility is to try to be as openminded as possible, which will allow him to reveal both his sensitivity and his imagination. When Dad spends time inventing games with his children, encouraging his little Leos' own creative abilities and listening to these children when they have problems, he's going a long way toward enhancing an already compatible relationship!

The Capricorn Parent/The Leo Child

Capricorns are serious, steady, stable people. They have a brilliant talent for quickly recognizing quality in others. Many Capricorns are in upper management because they intuitively understand how to find the right person for the right job. Since they have excellent planning skills, they realize that this ability will make their lives a lot easier. Their Leo child, who is also a leader and very hard-working, will be right up there when it comes to understanding the need for quality and high standards in all areas. Capricorns tend to admire Leos, and they often end up married to them. They are attracted to the Lion's power and strength.

Both Capricorns and Leos have strong wills and unbelievable determination. Their egos loom large, and there are times when Capricorn the Goat, and Leo the Lion, clash. The main difference between them is that these earth parents have the ability to wait for what they want, while the fire children's impatience tends to force them to leap before they look. Leos always want to take center stage, even if they have a low-key approach to life. They can be stubborn, and they definitely do not like to take no for an answer! The usually believe that they have all the right answers at an early age.

Both Capricorns and Leos tend to be controlling because they both like to have things their own way. Capricorn parents can reach their Leo children by being straightforward and honest when they offer opinions and exercise discipline. They need to learn that being judgmental and manipulative will not change their Leos' behavior, but will just damage their self-confidence.

Leos are emotional and sensitive, and they need a lot of attention and affection. These Lions and Lionesses are kids at heart, and they happily respond to warmth and humor. They are easily hurt, and they take most things personally. Therefore, they need kind and approving parents to enhance their self-esteem. There are few people who recognize a Leo's profound sensitivity because they are so aggressive and independent, but beneath the surface, these children really want their parents to be there for them.

Capricorn parents really enjoy taking care of their children, but it's very important for them to understand that they cannot control a self-sufficient personality such as a Leo. Leos can be very demanding, but these little pussycats will purr when they are given the opportunity to lead and to make their own choices.

On the one hand, Leos are wise beyond their years; on the other hand, they are quite childish. If Capricorn parents can provide them with logical and sensible explanations for the decisions they make, these idealistic kids will truly benefit from their parents' guidance.

The Capricorn Mom/The Leo Child

A Capricorn mother's strongest desire is to make sure that her child is approved of by others, both personally and in the professional world. She believes that it's very important for a mother to sacrifice her own needs in order to assure the safety and security of her children. After all, marriage and family are the most important things in the world to her. Capricorns believe that they have the ability to convince anyone to change their mind about an issue, even after that person's mind is made up. It comes down to persistence and perseverance. (Capricorns have a lot of patience when it comes to explaining their side of the story.) Sometimes Capricorns need to give up the fight and learn to "agree to disagree," because ultimately they're the ones who can get hurt in the end. My strong suggestion to all of my Capricorn clients is that it's wise to simply let go of anything that looks as if it can't be resolved.

A Capricorn mother should remember that Leo children will never respond to anyone who tries to change their personality. These self-confident fireballs tend to be full of enthusiasm and spontaneity, and they don't appreciate anyone who tries to tone them down. Capricorns are realists, and they have the tendency to look at everything in practical terms. If the bills aren't paid right on time, if every errand isn't completed as scheduled by the end of the day, and if there isn't a definite plan in the works for any given situation, a Capricorn mother is thrown off track and can become very uneasy. Since Capricorns often need to keep everything organized, they tend to stifle the spirit of their little Leo dreamers by frequently pointing out what is not possible.

The most positive thing a Capricorn mother can do for her Leo children is to point them in the right direction, and then let her kids decide how they're going to get there. If Leo children sense that someone is trying to dampen their fiery spirits, they tend to hide their feelings from that person. (Capricorn mothers, if you want your little Leos to trust you, then you must allow them to express themselves without being overly critical or judgmental!)

It would be wise for Mom to recognize her Leo's need for affection. When it comes to running her household, her efficiency is admirable, but it will never make up for showing her child how she feels. Leos will love living in a comfortable home, but these kids need a personal connection. If they feel as if their feelings are being ignored or they're not getting enough attention, they will begin to "put up" with Mom, rather than appreciate all the work it takes to make their home comfortable.

A Leo child's frustration may very well result in insecurity and poor self-esteem. I need to repeat this statement over and over again: if Leo children do not have an opportunity to learn and live freely, they will retreat into themselves, keeping all of their feelings hidden under a protective shell.

It would be wise for Mom to understand that trust is sacred to Leo children, and they will turn away from anyone who does not allow them to be who they are. If Mom can use her powerful abilities to encourage her Leo child's intelligence, enthusiasm, free spirit, and courage, she can overcome one of the greatest challenges of her life.

The Capricorn Dad/The Leo Child

Dad will provide a fine life for his children, as he is a hard-working man who will toil as long as it takes to provide financial security for his family. Capricorn men usually have a difficult time expressing their feelings, so it isn't always easy for them to cater to their Leo children's personal needs. Capricorn dads may feel somewhat awkward displaying affection. It's much easier for them to buy their children toys or clothing than it is to allow themselves to kiss or hug them. What these dads need to realize is that they will experience great joy if they can just let themselves go in that area. It's important that Capricorns try to overcome their fears and force themselves to enter that unfamiliar area called *intimacy*. After a while, like anything else, the uncomfortable becomes comfortable, and displaying one's feelings openly in a physical manner can make life so much more gratifying in the long run.

Capricorns can also be both spiritual and powerfully articulate, and they can make excellent leaders. The late Dr. Martin Luther King, Jr. is a fine example of a Capricorn leader.

A Leo child can learn a lot from Dad, as this father is very realistic and is usually gifted with considerable business acumen. He is stable and solid, and ready to give advice on demand. He feels both great responsibility and duty towards his children. The Capricorn men who have chosen creative careers can utilize these talents to help themselves balance the more serious side of their natures. Once Dad can understand that his Leo children need his attention and crave interaction and free discussion, he will be able to be a vital part of a loving and openly communicative relationship.

The Aquarius Parent/The Leo Child

Aquarian parents are people who believe in the meaning of words. They are literate, straightforward, bottom-line people who seek absolute clarity in their lives. Their capacity for learning is limitless; they solve difficult problems with objectivity, as they have a powerful need to understand the truth. They are air signs who tend to place the people they care about on pedestals, but watch out, because, as we all know, people can fall off of ivory towers.

Little Leos will be in good hands, as their Aquarian parents are honest, direct, and very trustworthy. Unlike Capricorns and Virgos, Aquarians do not believe in a conventional approach when raising children. Convention interferes with their

individuality. Aquarians move to the beat of their own drummer, and they won't
allow anyone to stifle their spirit or ideas. They are similar to their counterparts,
Gemini and Libra, because they are also quick-thinking, idealistic dreamers. Aquarian parents will give their Leo children permission to be unique.

Leo children will soon recognize that these parents may be a little intimidated
by their enthusiasm and spontaneity. They may have to learn not to hold back the
spirit of their Leo children, and to give them the freedom to act upon their own
ideas. Too much of anything, especially emotion, can sometimes overwhelm Aquarians. They have to learn to just "jump in" and show these children how to accomplish their goals. Being both logical and scientific, Aquarians are excellent
teachers. Leos, however, can be stubborn when it comes to expressing their opinions, and an Aquarius parent, who tends to always seek peace and harmony at any
price, will have to ignore the tendency to simply give in. Once parents show these
children that they're not going to stifle them, they will gladly seek Mom and Dad's
advice because they genuinely want to know the best way to do things.

They are idealists, but Leos do not place their ideals before action. (Aquarian parents are idealistic, as well, although people will not readily perceive this from their
outward behavior.) They may live on their ideals, while idling their lives away. A
Leo's personality does not include procrastination. They are doers, and Mom and
Dad will have to try and give these children the freedom to act. The Aquarius personality reveals an inwardly shy and reserved nature. Therefore, these parents will
secretly admire the self-containment of the Leo personality; however, Aquarians are
cautious people who may fear that young Leo's ego will get out of hand. Leos do
stand up for what they believe, and they can become quite adamant in their opinions. Aquarians, on the other hand, may yield under pressure, because they do not
want to make waves—that is, they believe in peace and harmony at any price (mostly
theirs). Leos can be unyielding when they want to make a point. Therefore, parent
and child need to compromise, and of course Mom and Dad will serve as the teachers in the relationship. All in all, Aquarian parents have to temper their fear of action and emotion, while Leo children need to stabilize their often-impulsive natures.

The Aquarius Mom/The Leo Child

As with all air signs, Mom will believe that the mind is the first priority. An
Aquarian mother will enjoy continually learning all of her life, and she will impart this trait to her Leo child, who will respond beautifully. Intellectual accomplishment will not be difficult for this little fire child. However, Mom has to learn
not to intellectualize *everything* to the point where she doesn't pay attention to little Leo's emotional needs. A Leo child will always be emotionally intense, and there
is no mistaking this fact. I'd like to suggest that Aquarian moms allow their young
Leos to get their feelings out onto the table *first,* before trying to settle them down.
This will be a difficult task, as Mom's first instinct will be to back off. When parents and children begin life with a different emotional base, it will always be up

to the parents to make the effort to understand their child (only later will the grown-up child begin to understand his or her parents).

In the case of an Aquarius mom and her Leo child, I believe that she will do anything she can to develop a healthy relationship with her little fire-sign child, no matter how much work it takes!

The Aquarius Dad/The Leo Child

An Aquarian dad can be either easygoing or arrogant, depending on how insecure he is. When an Aquarian father overcompensates by trying to impose his opinions onto another person, he can be difficult to handle. Naturally, when Dad is relaxed, he will be much more compatible with his Leo child. After all, their can't be two know-it-alls in the same family.

Dad is very bright, and he can master almost anything he puts his mind to. Using his abilities for reasoning and objectivity, Dad can teach his Leo child how to think about any decision thoroughly before making it. Dad is a free spirit, but he may approach life in a more sedentary fashion than his Leo child. Leos in the second decan (August 2–11) may appear to be more mellow, but this Leo, too, is sure to be on the move.

Dad and Mom are both independent, but Dad can be more reclusive than his female counterpart. He likes his private time, a part of his personality that can frustrate his Leo children, particularly when they need Dad's attention. Leo children are quite independent, but they can start feeling insecure if they sense that someone is ignoring them. The best way for an Aquarian father and his Leo child to get along will be for Dad to compliment and encourage this little fireball. Young Leos thrive on praise, as they take great pride in their accomplishments. They will be pleased to have a father who listens to them and who won't insult their intelligence. If Dad can acknowledge that spending too much time by himself may harm his relationship with his Leo child, he will have won a major battle.

The Pisces Parent/The Leo Child

Look out, Mom and Dad. Your Leo children will give you a run for your money. They can be a handful, since they are smart enough to know when they are dealing with kind souls who have the potential to say yes to everything. Pisces are diplomats, and they strategically find ways to create peace and harmony. They are also very emotional, and their first response always comes from the gut. Pisces individuals are usually very spiritual. While not basically aggressive, they can hide under a camouflage of bravado. They are really sensitive, but fear showing this side of their personality, as they are easily hurt.

There are two types of Pisces personalities: one is the artist, who almost borders on being a hippie; and the other is the efficient and structured individual who does it all. Leos also have the ability to charm their Pisces parents out of everything they own, and do it with a smile!

Pisces parents may need to develop patience when it comes to their little Leo. And make no mistake about it, this water sign has a lot of love to give. A Pisces parent will read storybooks, play games, and if necessary, put on a show. You think that would be enough for a young Leo, until you hear this little fireball say, "I want more."

Guess what Pisces parents will do? Of course—they will give them more!

The Pisces Mom/The Leo Child

A Pisces mom tends to overcompensate when it comes to taking care of *all* of her child's needs, because she wants to make sure that this little person loves her. Part of this tendency stems from the fact that she is quite sensitive and fears rejection. The challenge for Mom is to learn how to say no to her Leo children, or they may take advantage of her. Leo children don't like the sound of the word *no*. Yet, they really don't respect anyone who lets them have their way all of the time, as this behavior bores them.

Leos have a lot of spunk, and they need a parent who gives them a reason to think. Once a Pisces mother understands that her Leo child needs and wants her discipline, her self-confidence in this area will develop. Pisces Mom must learn to trust her intuition when it comes to deciding whether to discipline her Leo child or whether to back off. A balance between discipline and love is always the most effective way of building and maintaining a solid relationship based on respect. My best advice to my Pisces clients is that they should not fear saying no and adhering to their stance. I can assure Pisces Mom that her Leo children will love her for being the sensitive, giving person that she is, someone who will do just about anything to make her family's life as comfortable as possible.

The Pisces Dad/The Leo Child

Dad is friendly, personable, and sensitive. He can be totally focused on you at one moment, and off in his own world in the next. Dad can sometimes get overwhelmed by his own feelings, so he needs to make time for himself. He can be very charismatic, so the world may not always be aware that he can be something of a loner. Even though he does feel that he needs to be involved in family activities, he still struggles for alone time, and he usually manages to get it.

A Pisces father, like Mom, is good-hearted and wants the best for both his children and himself. Dad enjoys the pleasures of life. He does have a tendency, however, to repress his innermost feelings. On the surface, he may behave as though everything is great, even though on the inside, he's probably worrying about all of life's turmoil. A Pisces man is a dreamer, and if it were up to him, he'd like to get away to some private island on a regular basis. He will always be there to encourage his Leo children to act upon their own dreams and goals, but sometimes, he may be overwhelmed by young Leo's strong leadership skills and personal power. As such, he may subconsciously back off from helping his Leo children make important decisions, assuming that they're already in control of the situation.

The best advice I can give a Pisces dad is to suggest that he try to be involved in and concerned with his Leo children's decisions. These fire kids need the benefit of their father's wisdom. Dad needs to believe in his intuition and convictions instead of relying strictly on his emotions. His Leo children will feel comfortable with Dad's emotional side, as he can be attentive and affectionate, but they will also want to sense his stability. Since we already know that Leo children innately believe they are royalty, they can begin life thinking that a parent is just one of their subjects. Pisces individuals can sometimes have a problem making quick decisions, and if they take too much time struggling, young Leos will probably start to take over at about age two.

Leo children may not always reveal that they need support in their life, but in actuality, they do. Dad has the ability to be an excellent role model, imparting creative input to his Leo children to help them grow stronger and more confident in all aspects of life. Relationships are important to Dad, and if he believes in his own ability to guide his Leo children, he can easily supply both the emotional understanding and the motivation that they need.

SUMMARY

I believe that when parents of Leo children understand that these fire kids are intelligent, assertive, sensitive, serious, and honorable people; and conversely, when these kids respect the character of their parents, there will be a wonderful sense of mutual admiration.

Leo kids can be stubborn and bossy, however, so their parents must show the value of being patient so that they can learn from others. Leos are self-sufficient leaders who need to let people care for them. As long as a parent is honest and trustworthy, he or she shouldn't have much trouble raising these children. Parents, if you encourage your Leo children in all their efforts and support the dreams of these little go-getters, they will grow to love and appreciate themselves!

Chapter Six

♍ VIRGO THE VIRGIN

AUGUST 23–SEPTEMBER 22   ELEMENT: Earth   **KEY PHRASE:** "I analyze"

THE VIRGO PERSONALITY

Virgos are sun signs that are synonymous with the concept of excellence, but they are usually born "possessed by perfection." I truly believe that Virgos are victims of their own need to do everything right. Once they begin to understand the depth of their great expectations and standards of performance, they demand too much of themselves. And these criteria will soon be projected onto other people.

There are two types of Virgo's: I call them "The Perfect Virgos," and "The Messy Virgos." The perfect Virgos are the ones who are the most common to this sign; and they enjoy living a flawless lifestyle in all respects. They have immense powers of concentration and the ability to mentally slot everything in their lives—even people. Everything and everyone has its place. Family and home represent the safety zone, and Virgos find a great deal of pleasure entertaining and working in an environment that has been designed to satisfy their needs. They do have a tendency to dramatize all of the significant or insignificant circumstances in their lives, and can therefore look for trouble when there isn't any. Their nerves are fragile, and as each drama is pursued, a little more damage can be done to their digestive tracts. They can be perfect candidates for ulcers.

153

Can you picture a messy Virgo? The messy Virgos set up a sense of order in their minds, but they do not physically act upon any established sequence or procedure. In fact, they are rather avant garde. The internalized pressure of needing to be perfect seems to overwhelm and scare them. Therefore, they try and maintain a lifestyle that won't inhibit or restrain their freedom. Voilà: unusual clothing, a sloppy home, or a very messy desk at the office or studio. It really doesn't matter if they're messy, though, since they still have the ability to find anything of importance, even if it's hidden under a huge pile of clothes or papers.

Parents would be wise to understand the extreme amount of pressure that their Virgo children can place on themselves. I would never suggest tampering with their high intelligence, or ability to be visionary in nature, but it's important to recognize that their perception of the slightest mistake will be right up there with having a flood in the kitchen. Virgo children are worrywarts, so it's important to use moderation when imposing demands upon them. Virgo children do an excellent job of criticizing their own performance, and it takes them days to forget their real or imagined errors, if they ever do.

A sense of humor is essential when raising a Virgo. I know that most Virgos need to be taken seriously, but Mom and Dad will have to work on "gently poking fun" at the amount of dramas they seem to create for themselves. If humor becomes a part of their growing-up experience, a lot of their personal pain can be alleviated.

Virgos' talents for efficiency, organization, and creativity are remarkable, and they can easily earn the respect of their friends and associates. They have a tremendous capacity for pragmatically and psychologically understanding the big picture, as long as they don't focus their attention on minute details. If they can give themselves permission to eliminate their self-inflicted dramas, they could comfortably achieve great things!

Step by Step

Virgo children need to take one step at a time when working toward their goals. As they begin to understand the puzzle of life, they will instantly look for all of the matching pieces. If one of the pieces doesn't fit into the picture, young Virgo could stay up all night trying to find it. It's important for a Virgo to develop a model worthy of imitation.

No one would believe that Virgos can be vague when instructing others, but they can. In fact, Virgos rarely believe that they can be unclear in any way, since they are not consciously aware of how much significance they place on detail. When details become more important than focusing on the overall project, a Virgo can become nervous, irritable, and impatient with people who want to deal with the big picture. Once Virgos gets frustrated, they can become intimidating, and it's as these times when mistakes are made.

Parents who raise Virgo children would be wise to challenge them with projects that require vision and creativity, instead of giving them menial chores to complete, which will just bore efficient Virgo boys and girls. Exploration and communication are the best ways to enhance their growth. The real test will be to teach them how to focus on letting themselves go at times, while being open to listening to the opinions of others. If Virgos learn to verbally express what they personally need or want, they can free themselves of considerable angst and internal strife. They may even find that sharing their ideas with others can be just as fulfilling as detail, order, and organization. It would be wise for parents to concentrate on introducing creative outlets into the life of their Virgo children, as imagination and artistic development can help to ease their often-rigid tendencies.

It's Time to Let Go

"Learn to let go of the things that are impossible to resolve. Please stop obsessing over the same problems again and again." These words of advice are indelibly planted in my mind, since I continue to repeat them to my Virgo clients. (I must admit that I have been known to sound like a broken record.) Virgos do work on understanding their own motivation, but their need for perfection gets in the way of their need to relax. It's at these times when I recommend a long vacation, which is essential to a Virgo's overall well-being. Getting away forces them to relinquish their hold on their environment and the responsibility they feel to everyone and everything in it.

Virgos can get immersed in an obsessive rut when they feel that someone they care about is making a mistake. In fact, they can exhibit this obsession even when a situation involves someone that they don't know that well or don't care about all that much. This obsessive part of their nature really seems to work against them, though, and they end up being the ones who aren't happy. My broken record still continues with "Let go before it's too late." Most of Virgos' intentions are good, especially when it comes to their family and friends; but they cannot seem to back off from what they believe is right or wrong. Virgos do have the practical ability to resolve any problem, but it all comes down to tempering their need to control.

Debbie had been a client of mine for about a year, and she was working through her feelings of resentment toward her father. During the period of time that she was seeing me, she started dating a young man named Jake. It was our usual Thursday afternoon session when Debbie told me about her problem with him. "Sylvia, I'm beginning to feel intimidated by my boyfriend Jake. He's acting like my father."

I asked, "You mean that Jake is trying to control your behavior?"

"Yes," she answered, "and I'm sick about it."

Debbie, a soft, sweet, good-hearted Pisces, needed to work on facing the realities of life. Her Virgo father's need for perfection and control had diminished her self-esteem. Jake was also a Virgo, and evidently he couldn't control his neuroses in this area, either. I asked Debbie if she might not have subconsciously chosen Jake because he was like her father. "Perhaps you've fallen into a recognizable relationship."

She acknowledged, "Yes, I know, and I think I want to break up with him. Sylvia, it's been a year of hard work. I'm just beginning to stand up to my father, and now I'm having the same problem with Jake."

"Good for you, Debbie!"

She was puzzled. "What do you mean?"

I answered, "You've been working very hard to develop your self-confidence and self-esteem, and now I know that you're making progress. You're rebelling against Jake's need to control you. I think that's progress."

Debbie told me that she was going to confront Jake and see if he would compromise with respect to his need for perfection and domination. I told her that she was taking a huge step forward. Being a Pisces who had a terrible time making personal decisions, she had come a long way. I was very proud of her.

This story is significant because it reveals how two adult Virgos unintentionally hurt their personal relationships by not being able to temper the controlling part of their behavior. Debbie's father wanted a flawless, beautiful child who would do his bidding. Her boyfriend wanted the same type of woman in a mate. Neither of the two men realized how intimidating they could be.

Parents would be wise to help their young Virgos work on letting go of their need to control, which stems from insecurity. Virgos believe that controlling a situation will protect them from having to listen to anyone else's opinions. Virgos' opinions are based on practicality, and they are thorough and steady when they make decisions, but if they can be taught to exchange ideas with others on a give-and-take basis, they would be learning a valuable lesson that they could apply to many areas of their lives.

That's My Family!

Virgos want to be proud of their family members, as they are very important to them. The relationships they form as young children have a strong impact upon their behavior as adults. As such, they live most happily in a stable and peaceful home. For the most part, they enjoy modest, discriminating, and thoughtful parents who respect their privacy. Most people would not consider Virgos people who are easily "damaged" emotionally, but due to their intense self-scrutiny, they may tend to give themselves inferiority complexes. Virgos can be quick to judge or criticize themselves and others, and once they make up their minds, it's very difficult to modify their thinking. The only time they will change their minds will be when they truly honor someone's intelligence and respect what they say.

Parents need to be aware that their Virgo children are subconsciously judging their ability to raise them properly. It's not always easy to understand Virgos, as they can be hard to reach—especially on an intimate level. Virgos' sense of reasoning is based on facts, and their analytical nature can dissect every emotion, which can cause them to destroy their natural spontaneity. If parents can understand that friendship and mental affinity are what really matter to Virgo children, they'll be way ahead of the game. Any extremes in emotion or affection can make them uncomfortable.

It's my suggestion, after years of research, that parents of Virgo children would be wise to work against the basic nature of their kids' distancing personalities, especially when it comes to affection and spontaneity. If Virgo children are raised in an upbeat environment, with happy and positive parents, they will benefit enormously from this lifestyle. Virgos may not overtly respond to affection, but if they are surrounded by this type of behavior, they may end up giving hugs and kisses of their own accord.

The family environment will have a lot to do with Virgos' outlook on life. They may tend to get angry if the family is not living up to their standards, but they are usually quite protective of the other siblings in the household. Virgos can be quite stubborn when it comes to admitting that they're wrong, but respect and honesty provide the best means for getting them to concede.

A Virgo also enjoys being a caretaker. When someone is sick in the household, young Virgo will be sure that he or she gets aspirin, a blanket, or whatever is necessary to make that person feel better. Virgos value family and loved ones more than anything else, although their behavior may belie this fact at times.

They're Both Persuasive and Determined

Virgos are great salespeople, even if sales is not their chosen profession. They are always prepared, as their minds are constantly sorting and indexing ideas in order to have them ready when they need them. They are articulate and convincing speakers who strategically work on developing the art of persuasion.

A story that reminds me of how Virgos will try to persuade others took place at a friend's home at Christmas one year. A group of us were all sitting around singing holiday songs, led by my friend's three-year-old son, Jason. Everyone was singing until…Jason stopped us. He pointed his tiny finger at his Uncle Ken and ordered, "Sing it."

Well, none of the rest of us had observed that Ken wasn't singing, but Jason, the Virgo, didn't miss a trick. Ken wasn't going to let Jason control him, though, so he left the room. I am still of the opinion that Jason won. At the time, everyone thought the scenario was very funny, but as an astrologer, I understood that Jason was already trying to run the show at an early age. It was obvious that he was quite persuasive and determined, and his Uncle Ken didn't want to mess with him.

Parents would never want to stifle their Virgo's determination or persuasive abilities. These are two talents that will be instrumental in their long-term success, but Mom and Dad would be wise to help them understand that they cannot *force anyone* to follow their lead. A Virgo will be a lot happier if parents would try to focus on one of their best traits: the art of patience. Frustration and angst can be eliminated if young Virgo believes that he or she will is able to make things happen without pushing so hard.

☆　☆　☆

PARENT AND CHILD

The Aries Parent/The Virgo Child

Aries and Virgos are not on the same wavelength, but that doesn't necessarily mean that they won't get along; it just means that they're different. An Aries is basically aggressive, while a Virgo is discriminating. The Aries personality has an emotional base, and most of their decisions begin with the heart. Virgos, on the other hand, have a practical base, and most of their decisions stem from facts—cold, hard facts! I believe the difference between them is fairly clear.

An Aries can be impulsive, while the Virgo is generally methodical. Young Virgos may not always be comfortable with the behavior of their Aries parents, as they may move too fast for them. Virgos need to be very careful and accurate, and in their opinion, when someone moves too fast, that person will make a mistake.

Virgo children who live with Aries parents may have a problem understanding Mom and Dad's behavior. Although they won't all react this way, many Aries have a tendency to leap before they look. Virgo children will rarely behave in this manner, but as they grow, they will start to accept the fact that even if their Aries parents *are* impulsive at times, they somehow have an instinct for what's right or wrong. Honesty is important to Virgo children, and they have inherited a parent who speaks the truth. Aries personalities are promoters, and whether they be school teachers or talent agents, they don't like getting involved with minor details. As I've mentioned, a Virgo has a problem overlooking even the slightest detail. Mom and Dad's patience can run out from time to time; but when they have a Virgo in the home, patience will definitely be a virtue!

The Aries Mom/The Virgo Child

An Aries mom can inspire her young Virgo, as she is an independent free spirit. I believe Virgos can learn from a mother such as this one, who is efficient, courageous, and self-contained. She will be an excellent role model. Many Aries mothers are perfectionists, but instead of worrying about the outcome of any situation, they simply handle it. They are action-oriented, and there isn't much grass that grows under their feet. Virgos admire their Aries mother's inner strength and protective nature, and they will have a problem trying to control her. This child will soon learn that Mom is no pushover, and this can be a unique and healthy learning experience: In fact, this child is fortunate to have the opportunity to live with an upbeat, optimistic, take-charge woman. Aries mothers love their children, and they are always there to help. Mom makes quick decisions, so her Virgo children won't have time to dwell on their problems.

The Aries Dad/The Virgo Child

Dad, like Mom, is a quick thinker, and patience is not his virtue. There are those who ponder decisions, and there are those who begin with the bottom line. Guess where Dad fits in?! Dad can help his Virgo children by showing them that there is a lot to be said for making a sound and timely decision without picking every detail of the situation apart. A Virgo is incredibly comfortable with details, but at times, Dad's lack of patience with same can get him into trouble.

Dad is basically a calm man who is capable of dealing with emergencies. If he's nervous, no one will know it. Virgos will appreciate having a father who doesn't get flustered when facing a crisis, as their nerves are often uncontrollable.

An Aries father is usually efficient and orderly, as he values cleanliness and organization. Mom and Dad are both leaders, but at times Dad can appear somewhat militant in his attitude. Rules and regulations are important to him, but he's always fair. Dad's honesty and sense of justice deserve respect, and young Virgo *will* admire him. There are times when Dad can become exasperated and angry, though, and this usually happens when his Virgo child turns into a nitpicker. It's at these times that Dad should try and suppress his impatient nature, so that he can encourage young Virgo to deal with the bottom line when making a decision.

The Taurus Parent/The Virgo Child

Taurus parents and Virgo children are both earthy, and they will share similar values. They both have the need to create a solid foundation in order to build a safe and secure life. This common goal is the basis for their level of intimacy and communication. A Taurus is practical, introspective, and sensitive, while a Virgo is practical and inwardly intense. Virgo children are attracted to the natural vulnerability of their Taurus parents, and tend to protect them in a sense. This leads to the development of a strong bond between parent and child.

Taurus parents provide a safe and secure home for their children, which helps alleviate the daily dramas and traumas of their lives. Taureans and Virgos are quite similar when it comes to inflicting drama and worry upon themselves. So many of my Taurus clients ask me if they'll ever be happy, and my answer is: "If you want to be." They do understand my response, but they cannot seem to eradicate the belief that happiness is ephemeral. They are easily disenchanted, and they tend to own their hurt for a long time. Virgos remember their pain, too, but pain isn't practical. They are great believers in "when something doesn't work, it's time to move on." The differences between a Taurus and a Virgo are simply based on their respective philosophies: a Taurus tends to wear rose-colored glasses, and a Virgo just sees things exactly as they are.

Taureans and Virgos find common ground in their desire to keep the home fires burning. They both maintain high standards for creating a perfect family life. Mom believes that it's important to fulfill her responsibility to raise children; but there will be times when she may quietly withdraw from the pressure of needing to be all things to all people. A Taurus mother would be wise to personally evaluate and develop her emotional maturity when she decides to bear children. Many of my Taurus clients have come to me with the fear of "raising a baby when I'm still a baby."

The Taurus Mom/The Virgo Child

Virgo children need to feel that their mother is stable and loyal, and a Taurus mom certainly fits the bill. We know that Virgo children can be demanding, so it's important for Mom to feel confident about her opinions so she won't give in to all of young Virgo's demands. Virgo children will respect a parent who has the sense to discipline them when they step over the line. A Taurus mom would be wise to develop the courage of her own convictions, as young Virgo may test her to the limit. Mom is patient, but it will be at those times that her child will decide to try that patience to the extreme.

Mom is very dedicated to helping her children achieve their highest potential. She wants their talents to unfold naturally, and she will always try to encourage every bit of personal and professional growth. A Virgo child will appreciate and respect this part of her personality. Although Virgos are very intuitive and may quietly sense that Mom is not always sure of herself; they won't resent her for this quality, but will accept the fact that this aspect of her personality is just one fraction of a substantial person.

The Taurus Dad/The Virgo Child

Dad is far more rebellious than Mom. If life doesn't proceed as he wishes, or if his sense of fairness is challenged, he can be a tough cookie. However, for the most part, he is a low-key person who is friendly and personable. He values family, and will work hard to provide them with the best of everything. There are certain Taurus men who have problems handling anger and anxiety, and these traits manifest themselves in a form of emotional immaturity. Those types of Taurus personalities may not feel good enough to raise a family, and Virgos might have a problem dealing with this type of Taurus father.

Virgo children need a stable dad who believes in tradition, home, and family. They become insecure with anyone who give them an inkling of irresponsibility. In fact they have a tendency to lose respect for someone whose personality reflects a lack of discipline or a sense of unreliability. Virgos may be very independent, but when they get sick or have a problem, they want to be able to rely on a person of strength to guide and protect them.

The stable, sensible, and somewhat rigid Taurus father may lock horns with his Virgo child, as both can be obstinate and narrow-minded from time to time. Dad and his young Virgo have difficulty with personal confrontation, and it will be up to Dad to bring any conflicts out in the open. However, their arguments don't last very long, as their values are essentially the same. For the most part, a Taurus father may have a tendency to limit his personal expression, but so will his Virgo child. Communication takes work, so both Taurus and Virgo will be challenged to air out their problems in an honest and forthright manner.

The Gemini Parent/The Virgo Child

Geminis want to savor all that life has to offer, without restriction. I do believe that raising a family is their ultimate commitment; but even when they commit themselves to this goal, they don't relish the responsibility. They are smart enough to know that parenting is serious and complicated, but they subconsciously resent circumstances that interfere with their freedom.

Geminis are generally excellent parents who will want to do what's right for their children, but...they will instinctively move away from anyone who's too demanding. We've learned that Virgo children can exhibit this trait, and due to their distancing manner, Geminis may simply ignore these demands. They just don't take them too seriously. Gemini parents would be wise to understand that this part of their nature may frustrate their Virgo children, so it would be wise for Mom and Dad to carefully discern what is and what is not important before turning a deaf ear to their little Virgos.

Both Geminis and Virgos can be uncompromising, and this inability to bend can hinder their ability to communicate on a personal level. The main problem that can occur when Geminis raise Virgo children is the way a Gemini relates to a fixed course of action—they *don't!* Young Virgos are not comfortable with a lack of consistency in the home. They need to grow up in a stable and secure atmosphere. I believe that Gemini parents' natural spontaneity is good for their Virgo children. It helps to reduce their natural rigidity.

A Gemini's energy and versatility can also be mentally stimulating for a Virgo child, but a Gemini's changeable or restless behavior may complicate a peaceful lifestyle. I'd like to suggest that Gemini parents try to incorporate a sense of structure and constancy in their rearing techniques, as this mode of behavior will provide little Virgo with a sense of well-being. Interestingly enough, I have found that many Virgos and Geminis are attracted to each other. A Gemini seems to have an affinity for a Virgo's predictability, and a Virgo is attracted to a Gemini's sense of freedom.

The Gemini Mom/The Virgo Child

Mom can be serious, or a lot of fun, depending on which one of the "Twins" raises her Virgo child. I have previously discussed the two sides of the Gemini personality—namely, the serious intellectual, and the fun-loving creative type. The serious mom is outwardly cool, calm, and collected. She has the same energy as her outgoing counterpart, but her self-control is very much in evidence, for all the world to see. The outgoing Gemini's self-control goes incognito; she enjoys dressing in disguise. It doesn't really matter which mom is raising her Virgo child, though, as long as she understands that her child desires roots and reliability in addition to a sense of humor.

Geminis are interested in mental affinity and communication. Virgos are interested in practical possibilities. But even if young Virgo disagrees with the direction that Mom is taking in any particular situation, the Virgo child can rest assured that she will be able to present a plausible and objective explanation for her behavior.

Another aspect of the Gemini mother/Virgo child relationship will be their tendency to be social and to enjoy being with people. This characteristic will contribute much to making them function as friends and not just mother and child.

The Gemini Dad/The Virgo Child

A Gemini dad will usually choose a mate who's both a smart lady and who can also take care of the home and children. He wants the freedom to pursue a variety of interests, with the option of returning to the roost for rest and relaxation.

Gemini men are not comfortable with people who are overly emotional, as they tend to base their relationships on casual friendship, rather than profound feelings. Mental affinity with others is important to a Gemini man, and he is naturally attracted to anyone with intelligence. Dad will be pleased to have a Virgo child, as he or she has the ability to keep up with Dad's energy. They can develop a wonderful friendship, and both will enjoy delving into cultural experiences.

The one difficulty with this Gemini/Virgo relationship can manifest itself in Dad's conflicted "come here, go away" behavior. A Virgo needs a solid, steady parent, and Dad's chosen lifestyle may not always fit that mold. A Gemini man is restless, and boredom can set in every ten minutes when the subject isn't mentally stimulating. This behavior can be his weakness, as he believes that anything less than a challenge is mundane. Geminis are direct, and can quickly reveal irritation with anyone who waltzes around the bottom line. Virgos, however, are very analytical and tend to thoroughly dissect everything. I suggest that Dad try to curb his restless nature and occasionally abrupt way of speaking in order to give young Virgo the option to explain or analyze a problem.

The Cancer Parent/The Virgo Child

Cancers are emotional and tenacious. They hold on to what they love in a firm, stubborn, and persistent manner. They are exceedingly considerate and will extend themselves to the farthest point, without asking for anything in return. They're the ultimate parent figures, and they are very genuine when giving their love. However, their tendency to overcompensate can be attributed to their need for approval.

I advise my Cancer clients to "try and give themselves permission to receive because they may end up feeling that all of their giving was for naught." People shouldn't have to go through life without receiving some appreciation for all they have given. If Cancers decide to be last in the receiving line, they may eventually believe that they're not worth much. My experience in counseling Cancers has revealed that Cancer women, more than men, pay a high price for giving too much.

Virgo children can do any kind of work that requires perseverance and clear thinking. They are intelligent and versatile, and they are experts at research. Most of them are born demanding and critical, and they do not tolerate their own mistakes. Since this behavior is often picked up by those living with them, Cancer Mom and Dad will have to thwart this behavior before it goes too far. They will have to help their Virgo children relax and let up on themselves a little. However, Cancer parents can tend to be perfectionistic as well, so they need to ease up on themselves first.

It's best for Cancer parents to learn how to be flexible in their thinking when they raise these earth kids. Virgo children are skeptical when they perceive a nervous and overly emotional parent. They believe that feelings are not reasonable, and an emotional approach tends to confuse them. They tend to pick on the people they love, and it is usually the closeness that annoys them. The best way for Mom and Dad to approach their Virgo children is to encourage them to work with projects that have a purpose, or which can be useful on their road to success. It doesn't matter how old a Virgo is, he or she needs to live by a definite plan.

A Cancer parent has a lot of love to give, so young Virgos will no doubt receive an abundance of affection, but encouraging their children to be flexible in all areas of their lives will be one of the greatest achievements that Mom and Dad can strive for!

The Cancer Mom/The Virgo Child

Virgo children will benefit from living in a stable environment filled with love and warmth. Cancer Mom is a pleaser who will generally cater to her children, and although young Virgos are independent, they will be easily spoiled. Virgo children seem to enjoy getting a lot of attention when they're very little, but they will begin to claim their independence early in life. They believe that their need for freedom doesn't mesh with affection. Virgos are not naturally demonstrative since their strong practical nature doesn't mix well with emotion. Mom's loving nature can help her Virgo child understand that warmth and intimacy run in the family. If Mom is aware, at the outset, that her Virgo child is a bit cooler than she expects, she won't view it as rejection. Remember, she personalizes everything!

The Cancer Dad /The Virgo Child

A Cancer dad and his Virgo child may have problems deciding who's the boss. Virgos begin to run the show as they sit in their high chairs, and Cancer fathers expect to be the heads of the household. Dad is really a softie, but he has a fear of letting his real feelings come to the surface. He will repress his sensitivity with self-control, and this control is associated with a strong ego. Again, we have a parent who tends to overcompensate.

Dad battles an inner conflict between expressing emotion and repressing it, and this frustrating dichotomy can force him to lash out in an inappropriate manner. If Dad can be direct and honest when he confronts his Virgo children, they will definitely listen to reason. However, if Dad is cagey or inexpressive and doesn't offer reasonable, objective explanations for his behavior in a particular situation, he and his practical Virgo child may co-exist uneasily, both wearing invisible armor.

The Leo Parent/The Virgo Child

Leos' words are etched in stone. They are dependable, reliable, and honestly concerned for the welfare of their families. Their sense of responsibility will easily earn the respect of their children, but it would be wise for them to modify their need to control everyone in their household. Leos believe that if they are in control of family decisions, everyone is properly taken care of. I'd like to suggest that they begin to share their thoughts or ideas (in a tactful, diplomatic way) with their children as soon as possible, as kids begin to fear someone who appears to be so strong and powerful.

There is also another problem. I can just hear the words of Virgo children now: "If Mom and Dad take care of it, then I won't have to." It would be wise for Leo parents to give their children permission to enter into conversations that involve them. Most children, especially Virgos, need to believe that their opinions count. I am the first to acknowledge that Leo parents are bright, and quick to understand the bottom line, but I always offer this suggestion to these parents: let your children know who you really are and where you stand so that they can emulate you.

Virgo children learn to respect their Leo parents at an early age, and do feel that they'll protect them from harm or from proceeding in the wrong direction. Virgos need to achieve, and they avidly seek knowledge, but a Leo parent will have to be careful about his or her high expectations or standards, as Virgos make terrible demands upon themselves. Leo parents would be wise to motivate, but not push, their Virgo children. It is in this way that they will reach their greatest potential.

The Leo Mom/The Virgo Child

A Leo mom will encourage her Virgo children to realize their abilities and talents. She is untiring in her love, and will provide unconditional support to help her kids (and herself) reach their goals. In fact, if something isn't within her reach, she'll stretch as far as she can to make it happen.

A Virgo child feels safe and secure with this powerful parent, but the real difference between them lies in the area of emotions. A Leo mother is quite emotional, while her Virgo child is practical. Mom is attentive and affectionate, though, and young Virgo will be attracted to her demonstrative nature. Even though Leos are very intense, they are basically private people who fear self-expression and personal confrontation. I always lecture my Leo clients on the importance of revealing their personal feelings, and I've had a lot of success (I'm an Aries, and they trust me).

When a Leo mom gives herself and her Virgo child permission to deal openly with conflict and profound emotions, she will be a real asset as a problem solver and as a helpmate. She can also be instrumental in teaching her Virgo child the value of communicating freely and openly.

The Leo Dad/The Virgo Child

Dad is powerful, and he is a very solid, dependable person, but he experiences difficulty when he can't rule the family as all "kings" would. As such, he has to be careful not to place overly high expectations on his Virgo children.

A Leo father believes that his children can do anything as long as he's there to help them, but Virgo children are independent and value their individuality. Since Leo fathers have a tendency to take over, it's important for them to know that they may be stifling their Virgo children's need to analyze and work out a situation on their own when they try to make all of their kids' important decisions for them. Because a Leo father also values freedom and autonomy, though, it should not be too difficult for him to understand that honoring and having faith in his Virgo children's natural abilities will contribute to the formation of a compatible relationship.

Virgo earth children can be skeptical and a bit cynical until they receive reasonable explanations to their questions. They appreciate hearing the truth, and despite their cool outward demeanor, need a lot of attention. Therefore, Dad sets a good example with his protective, honest, and attentive nature. A Leo dad and his Virgo child are both resilient, and they can easily bounce back from defeat. Virgo children are intelligent energetic, and demanding, so Dad must understand that he may have to fight for control in this relationship.

The best thing a Leo father can do for his Virgo earth children is to raise them with a positive attitude, helping them understand that relaxing and having fun will only enhance their lives; it won't prevent them from accomplishing all that they desire!

The Virgo Parent/The Virgo Child

Virgo parents and Virgo children understand each other because they are both practical and their values are the same. These parents provide the stable, secure environment that a young Virgo can thrive on. Both parent and child have the desire to attain what the world has to offer, and neither will get in the other's way. Of course, they all worry, they are all determined, they are all controlled, and they are usually organized.

There is one thing that Virgo parents can do for their Virgo children. They can work on their own resistance to flexibility in the home. Both parents and child have a problem with this issue. They both have definite points of view and do not readily accept people for who they are. If Virgo parents can teach their earth kids to learn how to accept people for their own opinions and decisions, they may not have to change anyone who might not agree with them. If Virgo children learn the importance of tolerance at an early age, Mom and Dad will help them to be easier on themselves and others.

Virgo parents enjoy their independent earth children and want to help them reach their greatest potential. Parent and child are usually carefully and methodical; therefore, they do not make many mistakes. It's important for Mom and Dad to help their Virgos understand that it's okay to make a mistake, though, because "nothing terrible will happen" to them. Virgos are very intelligent and have the power to learn from their mistakes if they do not overwhelm themselves with worry. Their nervous anxiety tends to harm their potential. I always tell my Virgo clients to step back from their anxieties and regroup. If Mom and Dad can try to learn these lessons when they raise these children, they will be the best parents possible!

The Virgo Mom/The Virgo Child

A Virgo mom will insist on good manners so that her Virgo child will act appropriately when in public. Mom will also impart her considerable knowledge on the value of being sensible with money, and how it should be spent in order to improve one's life. In my experience, I have found that a Virgo's advice about money can be contradictory, though. Virgos love beautiful things, and they can spend a lot of money on a gorgeous dress to create the proper image, or on a costly sofa because it would look perfect in the room. Basically, Mom may tend to be penny wise and pound foolish.

There is one suggestion that I'd like to offer to a Virgo mother when she raises her Virgo child: please try to ease your standards regarding your need for perfection, and also try to calm your nerves, as young Virgo will quickly pick up your behavior. Mom can be instrumental in helping her Virgo children suppress their obsessive natures. Virgo children must be assured that it's not always possible to do everything exactly right. I know that when talking about Virgos, this advice presents quite a challenge, but I know that once Mom makes the effort to ease her child's tension, some of her own will diminish. The best gift a Virgo mom can give to her Virgo children is to help them relax when they're feeling overwhelmed.

The Virgo Dad/The Virgo Child

A Virgo father is a determined person. He can be an intense personality who at times may seem intimidating to those outside the family, although his Virgo children will simply view him as a protective parent. Dad will never say no when it comes to helping his children. He may be a bit controlling and practical for some children, such as Aries or Aquarians, but he and his Virgo children have the same dream of living a productive and service-oriented life. Dad can be a strong mentor for a Virgo child, as his knowledge and experience can provide reassurance and encouragement. In addition, he will be there to thwart potential problems, so that young Virgos won't make them over and over again. Virgos really do want to learn their lessons in order to prevent repetition of mistakes!

The Libra Parent/The Virgo Child

Libras have a problem with any condition that inhibits their free spirit. They may be practical, but they always look in the direction of broadening their horizons. They expect peace and harmony to be present in their lives, and they will not comfortably respond to daily drama. They can be hard on themselves, but won't appreciate anyone who tries to add insult to injury. Libras can be unconventional, and I believe that they tend to set up traditional lives for themselves to serve as a comfort zone while they pursue fascinating adventures. Libras are logical and want to believe that their dreams can be realized, but if they ultimately find that they're not, they come home to revitalize themselves and regroup.

Although Libras may choose to live a "safe" life, they would still rather interact with creative people, as they find them far more interesting. Libra parents who raise Virgo children may find their energy to be slightly inhibiting, as the earthy Virgo is quite different in temperament from the spiritual or visionary plane that the Libra is on. It would be wise for Libra parents to try to deal with their Virgo children on a down-to-earth level in order to maintain a healthy mental balance, and to get their children to listen to them.

A Libra's key phrase is "I balance," while the Virgo's key phrase is "I analyze." Libras can assimilate a great deal of information at once, and they have the ability to sort it out and balance it until it all makes sense. Virgos' tendency to analyze isn't all that different, but they don't take the time to sort out or balance. Instead, they have a tendency to focus on what they don't agree with. The subtlety of the compassionate Libra parent's behavior can help a Virgo understand that overreacting can harm rather than heal a situation.

The Libra Mom/The Virgo Child

A Libra mom is a kid at heart, and she enjoys assuming the role of playmate with her children. She identifies with the thoughts and feelings of her kids, and she has the ability to nurture their self-expression. Virgo children are usually self-in-criminating and serious, and Mom may have a difficult time with this part of their personality. She teaches her children to value the pleasure and beauty of life and wants them to believe in themselves. Libras and Virgos are very different in temperament, but Mom can be a positive influence on her Virgo children if she maintains a patient and sensitive demeanor. I'd like to suggest that she stress the importance of playtime, as she's good at reading stories, using her imagination, and preaching tolerance. Virgo children tend to reveal their impatience at an early age, so this type of guidance is particularly helpful. For example, if a friend of a Virgo child should utter an erroneous statement, or use incorrect grammar, young Virgo will be right there to criticize or judge this behavior, and feel that an immediate "punishment" should fit the crime. Libra mothers can do a lot to help quell this somewhat irrational behavior on the part of their Virgo children.

The Libra Dad/The Virgo Child

Dad may often choose an outgoing, talkative woman as a mate so that he won't have to do the talking. When he does decide to speak up, though, he can be charming, poised, and funny. The logical, reasonable, objective Libras are often attracted to the law, as they have a strong sense of justice, and many of them end up in litigation. The artistic Libra man is usually a spiritual and creative person who learns to nurture his free spirit.

Virgo children, on the other hand, have a tendency to personally restrict themselves, although they function freely in groups. It's important for them to fit in, as they need to be socially acceptable. A Libra dad can fit in anywhere if he chooses to place himself in a particular situation, but he can often be a devil's advocate and will not be forced into anything, even if it's to his benefit.

Parent and child are quite different, but Dad has the power to ease the inner tension and nerves of his Virgo child. He won't accept outrageous behavior, and he will be a calming factor when he explains how unwarranted anger can hinder reasonable communication. Dad is outwardly calm and collected, but he's serious about taking care of his family. He'll be there to handle his Virgo children's problems, and he will quietly resolve any dilemmas that crop up. Dad will definitely object to the stirring up of a lot of drama and emotion on a daily basis, but young Virgo will find that he will never just walk away.

The Scorpio Parent/The Virgo Child

Scorpios are perfect examples of individuals with a fixed nature. They are stable, dogmatically hold to their beliefs and values, and don't want their way of life to vary or change. They provide the kind of environment that is just what the Virgo ordered. Scorpios are giving, and will do anything they can for their children, unless their kids invalidate the boundaries or rules of the household. Virgo children will rarely do so, but they are very willful when it comes to their decisions. This is the time when a Virgo and Scorpio may clash.

Scorpio parents and their Virgo children are opinionated and judgmental. They are both problem solvers who are very attentive to detail. When there are decisions to be made that involve young Virgos, Scorpio parents would be wise to offer their earth children the opportunity to choose from a variety of options. And after these kids decide what they want to do, they should be complimented on their efforts.

There are times when Scorpios may be impulsive when making decisions themselves, but they are usually reserved and often secretive about their actions. While Scorpios and Virgos do have a lot in common, Mom and Dad will find that their analytical earth children rarely do anything on impulse, but are methodical and practical. Both parent and child are intelligent, shrewd, proud, and creative, but Virgo earth children rarely take the time to see both sides of a situation. It's best for Mom and Dad to point out that looking at all sides of a situation can prevent a lot of mistakes and can also present a wonderful opportunity for learning valuable lessons.

The Scorpio Mom/The Virgo Child

Mom is very traditional and is attracted to antiques and old-world theories. As a traditionalist, she believes that children should be treated like children until they prove that they can be trusted with mature opinions or decisions. In fact, if a Scorpio mother believes that her child isn't stable or emotionally mature at age 50, she will take care of that kid. Mom abides by a set of customs passed on from one generation to another, and family history will strongly influence the present. Virgo children can easily accept this philosophy, as they will have the same values when it comes to family heritage.

The main problem that I see with a Scorpio mom and a Virgo child can be their tendency to worry and create mountains out of molehills. They both tend to be nervous, so Mom would be wise to calm her apprehensive behavior in order to prevent young Virgo from emulating her.

Mom will help anyone if she feels she is needed, and her humanitarian nature is genuine. She'll have to be careful when trying to impose her will over her Virgo children, though, as they can become dependent or insecure when a parent doesn't validate their thoughts or decisions.

Virgos are young grown-ups, well-behaved and independent. They'll enjoy Mom's rearing techniques as long as she maintains a logical and rational attitude. Mom is usually a perfectionist, but she should try to give her Virgo children permission to be less than perfect. This may be a difficult task to accomplish, as her tendency to be judgmental and critical may stand in her way.

I would like to offer a suggestion to Scorpio mothers: think of the times when nerves have interfered with your need to function normally. Think of how you can overwhelm yourself in order to do the right thing, and think of how it can harm you physically. When you have reflected on the times that these situations have happened to you, you will have less of a tendency to act this way around your Virgo children, and as a result, you can help them relax!

The Scorpio Dad/The Virgo Child

Dad is a true perfectionist who can get very irritable when his children don't learn from their mistakes or work up to their potential. I don't believe he's as intolerant with his family, though, as he is with his co-workers. Dad is a very private man, and his personal feelings are locked inside his heart. He is emotional and deeply intense, but his children may have a problem knowing him on a personal level. A Scorpio man is usually very intelligent and well-versed on any subject. He is an excellent mentor, and his advice and guidance can be of great value to his Virgo child.

We know that Virgos don't like to base their relationships on emotion, so Dad's introspection may not bother them. Virgos are similarly aligned with their Scorpio parent when it comes to repressing their feelings. It would be quite special, though, if Dad could push past his boundaries and open up with his children. Virgo children would benefit greatly from this type of interpersonal communication.

As I have worked with Scorpio men, I have found that self-repression is their biggest problem. In fact, I counsel a number of men who are divorced from their third wives because they couldn't verbalize their feelings. Dad and his Virgo children can build an excellent relationship when they share ideas, values, culture, history, and anything that stimulates their intellectual and artistic tastes.

The Sagittarius Parent/The Virgo Child

Sagittarians can be rigid, but their rigidity is usually connected to their career. When they work, they want structure, organization, and detail; however, freedom to do as they choose is always at the forefront of their minds. This energetic fire sign loves to play and laugh. I've always said, "Keep them on their toes, and keep them laughing." Their behavior and attitude toward their personal life is different from that of their professional life. The creative Sagittarians give themselves the opportunity to acknowledge their free spirit, where the corporate executive types have a tendency to repress this side of their personality. The advice I usually give to my rigid Sagittarian clients is: "Please leave yourself alone, and honor the needs of that special little girl or boy who sits inside, waiting to come out and play."

Virgo children enjoy having an energetic, intelligent parent who loves to learn. Mom and Dad's priority will be to enhance their children's intellect. These earth kids need to be educated well, and they have boundless energy and drive. They thrive on developing a variety of interests—the more things they do, the happier they are.

Sagittarian are capable of doing many things, too. They are impulsive, and there seems to be an irresistible force inside them that provokes immediate action with respect to everything they do. Their earth kids are contemplative and meticulously careful. They do not like to rush! Therefore, Sagittarius parents need to develop patience with their Virgo children's approach to life. It isn't easy, though, because both the fire parent and the earth child have strong opinions and want to do things in their own way. Their wills tend to clash.

One of the nicest things about Sagittarius parents is their jovial dispositions. These individuals are usually funny and can easily make you laugh (especially the men). It's important for these Sagittarius Moms and Dads to teach their young Virgos how to laugh at themselves so they can release their inner tension. Humor is the best way to build a healthy relationship!

It will not always be easy for this parent and child to communicate on a personal level because Mom and Dad tend to be fearful of their feelings, and their child does not relate to emotion, so it's best for these parents to be honest and practical when they want to explain their rationale for making a decision.

The Sagittarius Mom/The Virgo Child

A Sagittarian mom may have a problem dealing with the serious and intense nature of her Virgo child. Her success in raising her children comes through perceiving their assets and liabilities. Once she comprehends the good and the not-so-good, she can be fair in her judgment of their behavior. She's not fixed in her thinking, and her unpredictability can be delightful. A Sagittarius mom and her Virgo children differ in that Mom advocates mental stimulation, but her focus is on abstract, rather than concrete, presentation. Virgos need to connect to specifics, and they can feel confused or unstable when they are faced with any kind of teaching that doesn't seem grounded.

Mom can understand that her Virgo child is not secure without a sense of order, and it is important for her to develop a form of compromise between her free approach to living and a clearly defined lifestyle. Virgos have a habit of remembering the past, and if they aren't raised with a solid foundation, they can inwardly retreat and outwardly rebel.

Mom is fun, and she is also an idealist. Young Virgo needs to be raised by someone like her, who has a sense of humor and believes that dreams can come true. She's a motivator, and may be the one parent who can really help encourage the creative and artistic side of her Virgo child. Make no mistake, though: Mom has a serious side when it comes to wanting the good life for herself and her family. This philosophy will help to secure young Virgo's need for a stable foundation, as this child will have a lot to learn from a mom who's fun to be around, outgoing, and protective.

The Sagittarius Dad/The Virgo Child

Sagittarius Dad is similar to Gemini Dad with respect to needing the freedom to pursue his own interests. He enjoys having a woman in his life who will take care of the essentials of life and the minor problems of the household, yet he will definitely be there in times of crisis. Dad has little patience when it comes to his children, but he will be happy to be there for the social gatherings. He can tell all of his stories and jokes, and he's an excellent host.

The main difference between the Sagittarius father and his Virgo child is their approach to life. A Virgo is outwardly serious, and a Sagittarian is inwardly serious. It's true—Dad is a much more serious person than he presents himself to be on the surface. He, like the Cancer father, fears his sensitivity and feelings. Both use the same type of external protection—they hide behind their humor. When raising Virgo children, Dad will have to work on his patience and make a point of spending time with these kids when they need reassurance and motivation. Virgos are independent and will only expect Dad to be around when they need help with an important decision. They won't have much trouble adjusting to the free-spirited rearing techniques of the Sagittarius dad.

The Capricorn Parent/The Virgo Child

Capricorn parents are usually ambitious and forceful, and they will work very hard to achieve financial security in their lives. Their practical Virgo children have the same desire, and if they could plan their own lives, their methods would be similar to those of their parents. This parent and child have much in common, as their need for perfection is very intense. Their nervous systems tend to be fragile because they are so demanding of themselves and others. Therefore, they both need organization and structure to maintain their sanity. Capricorn parents have the stamina and endurance to fight for what they want, and they have the ability to motivate their earth children to keep going, even when their nervous anxiety overwhelms them.

This parent and child tend to communicate through their ability to analyze and through their sense of reality, which works for them because their practical minds do not get sidetracked by their feelings. It is best for these parents to work on family flexibility, or their young Virgo can turn out to be more intense than they are. Capricorns and Virgos tend to drive themselves, and they need to finish what they start. These parents would be wise to ease up on their own criticism in order to help their earth children. I have found that many of my Virgo and Capricorn clients' critical natures tend to cover up their own insecurities. Parent and child are very competent and intelligent, so they do not need to look for trouble in order to have a productive life!

The Capricorn Mom/The Virgo Child

As far as filling all material needs, a Capricorn mom is at the top of the list. She is interested in anything that can be useful to her children's lives, and her curiosity has made her one of the most informed women in the zodiac. Virgo children won't have to worry about playing with interesting toys, wearing the softest diaper, having the cleanest bedroom, or learning with a purpose in mind. All of the comforts of life will be provided, if at all possible. Mom is the greatest bargain hunter, too. She can find the most outstanding items at the cheapest prices.

It's known that earth signs (Taurus, Capricorn, and Virgo) don't feel comfortable with self-expression or personal confrontation, and this team is no exception. The focus for this parent/child due will be on getting the best education in order to be successful in a chosen career. Both show refinement in intellectual and artistic matters, both are experienced in the ways of the world, and both are concerned with material things. All in all, both Mom and her Virgo child have the ability to present a classy and distinguished image to those around them.

The Capricorn Dad/The Virgo Child

Dad is usually predictable and stable. He works very hard, and he doesn't often sell himself short. He believes in his worth and goes after the highest bidder. He is usually excellent in business and can be quite a showman, as long as he isn't forced to express his feelings. One can't refer to a Capricorn father as emotional, but he could be considered very intense. There are children who may feel that Dad's behavior is cold and undemonstrative, but that isn't really his intention. He just doesn't understand a child's need to emote.

A Virgo child and a Capricorn father should get along very well. Dad is usually a materialist, where the physical world is the only reality. What he can see or utilize makes sense, and what he can't see or utilize he doesn't understand. His Virgo child is also down to earth in this way. The one difficulty that can occur with Dad and his Virgo child revolves around the issue of independence. A Virgo needs the freedom to explore life. Dad, however, can be a strong disciplinarian who may stifle young Virgo, especially if young Virgos pursue things themselves without asking for Dad's approval. Dad would be wise to keep his opinions to himself until he's heard the complete story.

The Aquarius Parent/The Virgo Child

Aquarians, for the most part, are easygoing and enjoy a relaxed life. They are highly intelligent, and as is the case with any air sign, they desire freedom and flexibility. They can be quite successful, or they may be constantly looking for the right job.

Down deep in every Aquarian is a shy person, someone who needs to test the waters before allowing anyone to enter their lives. They place strong emphasis on friendship, yet their own decisions seem to outweigh the opinions of those close to them. They are well liked because their interest involves the masses, and they tend to hold liberal opinions and ideas. They can stand in their own way when they sacrifice their own needs for the sake of others, and tend to procrastinate when it comes to dealing with themselves and circumstances that may enhance their lives. It seems that they put things off because they don't feel safe with the unknown, or with circumstances beyond their control. I believe that new commitments seem to pique their fears. It takes them a long time to make a decision that will ultimately change their lives.

Aquarians are honorable and trustworthy, and they have great admiration for those who seek and tell the truth. They are known to be idealists, rather than materialists, and their reality consists of perceptions and ideas. Their logical minds separate the rational from the irrational, and it is at this time that they can become blindly opinionated. Aquarians will never judge people who can't find their way, as they believe in the betterment of all people, no matter what race, creed or color. One-on-one relationships secretly scare them, as sharing their life with someone may cause them to lose control.

Aquarian parents who have Virgo children would be wise to understand that "going with the flow" won't work for these kids. Mom and Dad need to define their lives through the building of a solid, stable foundation that is consistent and predictable. Mom is a supportive person who has the ability to create an easier life for her children. She's a fine homemaker, great cook, has excellent taste in clothes and furnishings, and also has a tendency to push herself to the wall. At those times, she may retreat, moving into her own private world. When this happens, her Virgo child may run for the hills.

The Aquarius Mom/The Virgo Child

It's known that Virgos are earthy, and they need to keep their feet on the ground, where Aquarians can often be "up in the air." This can be the main problem between parent and child. Mom is an intelligent woman, and it would be wise for her to be aware of her child's need to be grounded and practical. Virgo children need constant reassurance that their world is solid, as it is this type of foundation that allows them to be productive and creative. If their home life is filled with unpredictable behavior, their self-confidence can suffer. Mom is born with a healing quality, which can be a fine asset when raising this child. Her calm demeanor will motivate her Virgo child to understand that extreme tension and self-criticism can work only to his or her detriment.

The Aquarius Dad/The Virgo Child

Dad will promote his child's individuality and personal independence. His mind is his fortune, and he believes in himself totally. He is primarily an idealist, and he will apply that philosophy to his everyday life. He doesn't believe in violent behavior, and he will avoid severely punishing his children—his logic tells him that there has to be a more reasonable way of dealing with right and wrong. He's a teacher, an artist, a philosopher, and a dreamer.

He and his Virgo child live in a different world. Dad believes in reality, but his thinking can be nonspecific, which can be a far cry from his Virgo child's need for concrete behavior. Dad would be wise to understand that he and his Virgo child are not on the same wavelength, so he will have to make a real effort to be there to reassure and enhance young Virgo's sense of stability. This is a perfect way of connecting with this child. Once Dad secures the confidence of his Virgo child, he can easily impart his philosophy, which is that freedom must conquer restriction.

The Pisces Parent/The Virgo Child

Pisces is the culminating sign in the zodiac. Imagine moving through eleven personalities, taking on the aura of each. It seems as though this is the Pisces experience, as these individuals have a habit of psychically absorbing the feelings of those they encounter. The artistic Pisces will usually function through emotion and spirituality, and the perfect Pisces will function through detail and structure. I believe that the perfect Pisces uses these traits to put up a wall to protect their sensitive feelings. Pisces get hurt very easily, and they have a terrible time verbalizing their feelings. They love children and are fascinated by youth and staying young. They are essentially little kids in grown-up bodies.

Pisces are easily intimidated by confrontational personalities, as they are extremely sensitive and dreamy. Since a Virgo child is a direct and practical person, and emotional people confuse them, this parent and child will definitely have some basic problems to overcome.

I always believe that becoming a parent is one of the best steps toward developing emotional maturity, and raising a Virgo will definitely pave the way. I know that a Virgo child's tendency to expect a lot can be wearing on the Pisces parent's ability to maintain composure, and it is at these times when hysteria may set in. However, when Mom and Dad calm down, they do have the ability to deal with the situation. The best way to handle the sometimes off-putting nature of the Virgo is to try and understand the inner fear that has provoked this behavior. When Virgo children feel alone, they can subconsciously demand a parent's attention. Their nerves take over, and they need to feel that their Pisces parents can assuage their anxiety and be there to protect them.

The Pisces Mom/The Virgo Child

Mom is a very good-hearted person, and she will shower her child with love and attention. She is basically emotional, and following the water sign's pattern of behavior, she can fall into the "overcompensating parent" category. She will provide a lovely home environment, which usually reveals her natural creativity. If she falls into the conventional category, her raising technique will be traditional, and her behavior will be socially acceptable. Virgo children won't have a problem with the home life that Mom creates, but they may not react well if she doesn't appear to be solid or predictable. Mom has a problem making important decisions, and this part of her personality can exasperate her Virgo child.

When I counsel Pisces mothers, I suggest that they work on overcoming their fear of making the wrong decision. They are of the opinion that something terrible will happen if they make a mistake. Mom's instincts are excellent, and she can easily come up with the right answer. Virgo children's personal security can be threatened by an indecisive mother, and out of their own frustration, they may try to make all of the decisions. Virgo kids need to be disciplined, so their Pisces mother will really have to follow through on what she says and not back away from her dictates in the face of their rebelliousness.

The Pisces Dad/The Virgo Child

A Pisces dad has a real problem verbalizing his feelings, and he can close them off to the point of self-denial. Inside, Dad is emotional, though, no matter what he says, and his Virgo children are practical. In fact, any display of affection is not easy for them. Therefore, I am saying that the base of each personality is different. Dad tends to spoil his children, as he needs a lot of love and approval to satisfy his personal security. Virgo children can be very demanding, and Dad may create monsters if he isn't careful about giving too much. There is never too much love and attention, but there can be an overabundance of material things.

Virgos are honest, family oriented, and tend to be a bit bossy. Dad can fall prey to their bossiness, as he is very good-hearted. It's important for Dad to learn how to say no to his Virgo children when they are unreasonably demanding. Dad can help by providing a variety of learning projects, as his earth children will always need to be mentally stimulated. Dad is usually creative, and he can encourage young Virgos' ideas, as most of these earth children are born promoters. The best thing that Dad can do for his Virgo children is to teach them to be considerate and understanding—especially when their determination to succeed becomes too intense. Virgos need to learn that flexibility and compromise will help them feel better and develop healthy relationships.

☆ ☆ ☆

SUMMARY

I'm certain that by now you're aware that Virgos are intelligent people who make every effort to get what they need in life. Their success comes through practical direction and fortitude.

They accept psychology as part of their daily life, and will analyze, and at times, overanalyze a set of circumstances that will determine a course of action. Virgos definitely get the job done, but they need to be aware of their tendency to get lost in trivial details. It's really the big picture that counts. If Virgos can learn how to pull back from the demands they make upon themselves, they will be far less likely to criticize or judge.

Self-control and control of others is far too important in the minds of Virgos. They need to realize that the repression of emotion will not yield loving relationships, but will only promote fear and intimidation, which hinders communication. Virgos love family and children, and they have a tendency to impose their strong morals and standards upon them. They are caretakers who will spend hours taking care of people who suffer. I suggest that parents understand how important it is to encourage their Virgo children to follow their need to serve humankind, which will give them a great deal of satisfaction and help them counteract the often-rigid lives they set up for themselves.

"Peace is not a season,
it is a way of life."
— Anonymous

Chapter Seven

....

♎ LIBRA THE SCALES

SEPTEMBER 23–OCTOBER 22   **ELEMENT:** Air   **KEY PHRASE:** "I balance"

....

THE LIBRA PERSONALITY

"I balance" is a Libra's solemn promise or declaration to him- or herself. This key phrase describes how Libras behave with respect to their ethics, principles, and opinions. They're the gentle and caring peacemakers of the zodiac who set out to eradicate violence from the world. In order to do so, it's very important for Libras to learn how to speak up for themselves at an early age, especially when they feel hurt, or when they're sure that they're right. If they learn how to confront others, they'll feel good about themselves, which will give them the self-confidence they need to win the respect of their peers.

Libras have problems making up their minds, and they tend to vacillate when it comes to making important decisions. Therefore, the people who live with them need to understand that these air signs can't be rushed into anything. When it comes to their personal lives, they like to think things through over and over again. They fear making mistakes, and constantly wonder if each one their decisions couldn't be better. If Libras can learn to depend upon their instinctive natures, they won't have to work so hard to make a decision.

☆ ☆ ☆

I was at my girlfriend Jackie's house for her son Johnny's sixth birthday party, and suddenly out of nowhere, Johnny (a Libra) came running into the kitchen and cried out, "Elizabeth pinched me. Elizabeth pinched me on my birthday!"

Jackie looked at him sympathetically and asked, "Did Elizabeth hurt your feelings?"

He nodded. "Yes. It's my birthday. Elizabeth was mean."

Jackie wiped his eyes and said, "Let's go outside and tell Elizabeth that she hurt your feelings and that you never want her to pinch you again."

Johnny looked up with a hint of trepidation in his eyes. Then he said, "You tell her."

"No, Johnny," Jackie told him. "I'll go with you, but you're going to have to tell Elizabeth yourself. If you don't tell Elizabeth that your feelings were hurt, she won't respect you, and that won't make you happy."

Johnny thought about it for a moment and said grudgingly, "Well...if you come with me." So, slowly and hesitantly, he told his little friend how he felt.

Johnny was six years old, so a pinch on his birthday was very painful. His mom had the good sense to help him confront his feelings at the time when he actually felt them, which helped him develop the confidence and strength that he needed to intelligently confront people whenever he was hurt. Johnny's mother recognized the importance of her little Libra learning this lesson at a tender age. I applaud her.

☆ ☆ ☆

The reason why Libras often keep their feelings to themselves is because they think that emotions can't always be trusted. These balance-oriented people don't want to be misled. However, they need to give themselves more credit, because their instincts are excellent. Therefore it's up to the parents of Libras to stress the value of love and honesty within the family. I remember saying to my children when they were very young, "It's so important to love each other. You have to try not to hold a grudge. It's okay to disagree with each other. We are family."

Libras have a tendency to sacrifice their own needs by giving people what they expect, rather than acting on how they really feel. If Libras allow themselves to live this way, they'll start to build up resentment, which will no doubt develop into internalized anger. The severity of this negative emotion is not always clear to them, though, until they lose control. If Libras don't learn to speak their mind at an early age, they can become defensive. Parents must be truthful with these children and offer reasonable explanations for their decisions, as their self-confidence is dependent upon being honest with both themselves and others.

Parents also need to support their Libras' need for private moments. They would be wise to give them permission to sort out their thoughts before they are expected to make a decision. The best way to reach Libra children is to gently lead them into informal discussions about how they feel, and encourage them to talk about their thoughts on any given subject. Libras will genuinely want to please their parents, but harsh, dominant parents can intimidate them. If they should try to impose their ideas on their Libra children without asking them if they have any thoughts of their own, these kids may pleasantly agree to do what is asked of them, but inwardly resent the entire situation. Libra children need parents who are reasonable and logical—those who value their opinions and who give them a series of options, rather than orders.

A Need for Harmony

Libras need to be careful of their need to constantly balance all of the elements in their personal life just to create a harmonious environment. They have a tendency to believe that when something bad happens, it just has to be their fault. Libras need to remember that there are many trying circumstances in life, but these occurrences cannot all be taken personally.

Libras' sense of balance and harmony does, however, give them a natural understanding of what's proper and appropriate. They seem to test themselves by comparing their abilities and talents with the accomplishments of others, such as: "Her dress is prettier than my dress, and his scores were better than mine." This behavior can either challenge them to do their best, or make them insecure. Parents would be wise to honestly compliment their Libra children for the positive things they do in order to build their self-confidence. Parents should never compare them to other children, or make them feel as though they need to compete. If they do something that isn't appropriate, it's best to sit down and rationally discuss the problem. Parents who understand how hard Libras can be on themselves have won the first battle.

Another interesting thing about Libras is that they are outstanding mediators who can easily convince most people to see both sides of an argument. If they accept the fact that their special powers can emotionally heal other people, they will achieve true peace of mind. A Libra's personality never comes off as threatening, as he or she appears to be easygoing, without a worry in the world. However, there's a lot more beneath the surface.

Parents would be wise to encourage their Libra children to make their own reasonable decisions. If these kids believe that they have the ability to make up their own minds, they may not have to go through the unnecessary turmoil of thinking about all of the things they don't want to do before they do achieve this goal. It's best that parents help them balance their intellectual power with logic and sensitivity. It's important for Libras to believe that their own feelings are acceptable, and then perhaps they won't want to deny them. If they are confident in this area, they can fight the intensity of their anger. It's okay to be angry about something that seems unfair and unacceptable, so once a Libra can honestly confront these feelings, their anger can move into a healthy state of mind.

It's important for young Libras to recognize that their need for harmony won't always leave them feeling good about themselves, though. As Libras begin to honestly accept their own natural ability to help others, they can begin to define the power of their calming influence and leadership qualities. Once they do so, they can create a better life for themselves, and for those around them.

Sharing Their Lives with Others

Adult Libras really do prefer to live with others rather than living by themselves, so a harmonious relationship with another person is very important to them. Anyone who lives with these individuals will soon recognize that they need to have the freedom to take their own time and space to resolve their problems. If Libras ever start to become bossy, they are really just trying to claim their independence. Parents would be wise to understand that Libras can become pleasers because of their fear of personal confrontation. So, Mom and Dad must give their Libras permission to talk about their real feelings and assure them that they won't be punished for standing up for themselves.

Libras are mentally alert, self-sufficient, and hard-working. They're adept at socializing in groups, and people tend to enjoy their company, but most of all, they enjoy sharing their lives with their loved ones. In fact, this kind of interdependence between members of a family is mature and healthy. Loving relationships help Libra children fulfill their special need to make the world a better place. These kids constantly worry about balancing everyone's needs (including their own) on a daily basis. Therefore, it's important for parents to clearly explain the "whys or why nots" of any decisions that concern these children.

Many of my Libra clients have suffered as a result of their tendency to try and please everyone. It takes a lot of work, but once Libras accept the fact that this is an impossible task and start thinking of themselves for a change, their lives will improve immensely.

Artistry, Beauty, and Logic

Libras are usually refined, as well as being poised and charming. They have a special understanding of the beauty that life has to offer. Most of them have artistic talent, whether they utilize it or discount it. This talent can manifest itself in the work of a quality craftsman, or in a beautiful pastel painting. Libras can also be fine writers, and their words seem simple, smooth, and effortless. They work hard, but they can often be underrated because they don't brag about their talents or abilities. Many times this behavior can go back to their philosophy of maintaining peace and harmony.

Libras definitely need attention and appreciation, but they have a hard time focusing on their own accomplishments. That behavior just embarrasses them. It's important for parents to teach their Libras that it's okay to gracefully accept the praise that they deserve. Since there are many Libras who may never utilize the creative sides of their personalities, it's up to their parents to recognize their individual talents and to encourage these kids to put them to use. Libras who grow up to be painters, interior decorators, sculptors, or even theologians will begin to reveal their spirituality and artistic ability at an early age. Parents might consider allowing their Libra children to take music, art, or dance classes if their son or daughter shows a predilection for one of these areas.

In opposition to the artistic Libra, the boy or girl who grows up to be the lawyer, the politician, the judge, or even the salesperson is usually concerned with being the voice of justice. The lawyers will probably end up in litigation, since they're very good at defending their fellow men and women; the politicians will be excellent mediators; the judges will make fair decisions; and the salespeople will be able to sell you the shirts off your back. Libras are born to understand balance and harmony, and when they combine this talent with their own excellent human instincts, they are unbeatable. If parents can be open to the individual talents that their Libra children possess, they can be there to help these kids find the road that makes them happy.

Paula, a pretty Libra with long silky blonde hair, is my friend Tom's daughter. She's a loving person, and she'll get up in the middle of the night to help her family, friends, or anyone else who needs her. Paula worries about being overweight, but it has never detracted from her beauty or good nature. However, she did have a difficult childhood, which left her lacking in self-esteem. She wandered aimlessly for a while, and wasn't able to find a job. Basically, this lovely girl felt like a lost soul.

My friend Tom was very worried about his daughter. "I've tried to get Paula a job," he told me. "I tried to take care of her when I got divorced. I've always been there if she needs me. What can I do?"

I knew that he believed that Paula was going to irreparably damage her life, so I told him, "Tom, I think there may be a problem that you've never been aware of."

"What?" he asked, puzzled.

"Perhaps you didn't always give your daughter the impression that you felt she was good at whatever she did."

He looked straight at me in the eye and said, "I always had a fear that she wouldn't be able to get a handle on her life." He looked away and took a long breath. "Do you think she saw that?"

I said quietly, "Usually kids pick up on that stuff." He nodded in resignation.

Several months after that discussion, Paula met a new love interest named Dave, and from the day I met him, I said, "This man is perfect for her." He brought out the best in her because he believed that she was wonderful. He gave her the feeling that he would always be there to protect her from all of life's roadblocks. Paula is now a terrific housewife, who from time to time drives a chauffeured limo and sells peanuts at Cubs Park in Chicago. She's been very happy with Dave, a young man who needed her love and pathos, and who gave her permission to be completely honest about her feelings.

Needless to say, Tom is very pleased that Paula has found someone who understands and appreciates her. Tom had spent a lot of time thinking about his own behavior, and he has initiated many conversations with his daughter that have helped them both understand each other.

PARENT AND CHILD

The Aries Parent/The Libra Child

Aries parents are intelligent, truthful, and loving, but they may have the ability to intimidate their Libra children if they refuse to see the neutral shadings of life. They have a tendency to see life in absolute terms of right or wrong. At first, this part of their personality may tend to rock the boat of this child, whose life is based on balance and harmony. A Libra will want to go towards the center, while an Aries tends to take a position either one way or the other.

Aries parents will encourage their children to reach the highest heights. They are honest and persuasive, and they can be just what the doctor ordered when it comes to raising a Libra. Aries are great motivators, and they want to see everything done RIGHT NOW! An Aries, however, does need to learn patience. We know that most Libras like to think out most of their decisions, so these parents will need to pull back from their own need to take over and make decisions for these kids.

Aries have a habit of trying to take over a situation before they're asked, so Libra children can easily fall into the trap of "Mom (or Dad) will do that for me." But if these children allow their Aries parents to do everything, they won't believe they can do anything for themselves. The key to turning this problem around is knowing when to take over and when to back off. When a quick decision is necessary, a prudent parent may be required to take control of the situation, rather than allowing young Libra to become frustrated. But, when time isn't an issue, it's smart for Aries parents to leave the less significant decisions to their Libra children, such as, "Do you want to wear your green jacket or your tan sweater?" or "Would you like to see a movie or go to the park?"

If Aries parents can give these children the opportunity to make decisions for themselves—even by starting out with very small ones, this will be quite an accomplishment. If these children can learn to form their own opinions, they can feel that they have earned their parents' respect, and this self-confidence will lead them into making bigger and better decisions. It's very important for young Libras to know that their Aries parents aren't always in a rush to get things done. Aries are strong and effective when teaching, as they enjoy imparting their knowledge to their children. An Aries mom or dad has the persuasive skills that can help nurture their Libra child's self-confidence at an early age.

The Aries Mom/The Libra Child

An Aries mother lives a busy life, engaging in a variety of extracurricular activities along the way. Any child that she raises will begin to understand that Mom is independent and listens to the beat of her own drummer. Since she does have a lot to do with a minimum of time to do it, she naturally expects her children to grow up adapting to her schedule.

An Aries mother is usually a late bloomer who can be somewhat naive. While she always acts like a grown-up lady, in many ways she feels like a little girl. She expects her children to be as independent as she is (after all, she gave birth to them), and when they're not, she may try to take care of all of their needs, becoming the perfect caretaker. Mom does everything so well that a more dependent child can begin to believe that he or she is not able to accomplish anything. Even if her children are not as independent as she may like them to be, Aries Mom would be wise to teach them to handle things on their own, gently guiding them along the way.

Libra children appear to be capable of taking care of themselves without much supervision, but they do want to have reliable, dependable parents to come home to. An Aries mother definitely fits that bill. She has no problem providing an environment that's aesthetically pleasant and clean, as she needs a comfortable place to hang her hat. As an Aries, Mom loves intense, deep colors such as red, purple, black, or bronze. Libras also appreciate an atmosphere that is suited to their temperament, and these kids tend to lean more to colors such as pale blue, yellow, soft green, and apricot. Generally, Libras don't enjoy living in a home that's decorated with bold colors, so what is a an Aries mother to do? She can let her little Libras choose the color of their bedrooms, and also allow them to buy clothes in their favorite hues. This type of compromise will promote a wonderful relationship between the two!

The Aries Dad/The Libra Child

Dad believes in raising well-behaved children. His expectations are very high, and at times, he can overwhelm his Libra children, who may end up trying to live up to his standards and dreams, instead of following their own interests. A Libra child usually likes to explore new facets of life, as does his or her Aries father, but this child isn't as much of a risk-taker as Dad is.

Aries Dad should make an effort to take time away from his usual routine whenever his children need him. Dad wants the best for his children, but his rigid demands can make them believe that everything in life is about competition. This can be problematic for Libra children, as they will not enjoy being forced into competing. They want to succeed, but they want to maintain harmony in their relationships at the same time.

Dad can build a good relationship with his Libra children by motivating them to action, and by challenging them on an intellectual basis. Dad has the ability to elicit the adventurous nature of his Libra kids, and together they can share fascinating new experiences. Many Aries fathers become pilots and mountain climbers, which should be exciting enough for young Libras. Dad would be wise to give equal amounts of his dedication to both his children and his career. If he spends too much time at work or devotes himself to his outside interests to the exclusion of his family, his Libra children will feel hurt and neglected.

The Taurus Parent/The Libra Child

Taureans are down to earth, and they need to build a stable foundation. They feel much more comfortable when their home lives and relationships are firmly established. Many Taurus personalities achieve this goal by making family their main priority. Others tend to travel around the world for a while, searching for their real identity—it may take them awhile to settle down. There's really no difference between the Taurus homebody and the adventurous Taurus Bull when it comes to emotional vulnerability, though. A Taurus needs more attention than most sun signs, although most of these feelings stay buried within their psyche. If their parents gave them a lot of love and affection, they can become strong and self-confident adults. If they were born to less demonstrative parents, they can appear to be cool and distant.

When any Taurus decides to settle down, he or she is usually very committed to the idea of home and hearth. Taureans need to work on developing a positive attitude when they raise a family. They tend to worry a lot, and they can be very hard on themselves. When their personal security is threatened, they start believing that nothing can turn out right.

Taurus parents and their Libra children are very compatible, as they are loving, sensitive, and protective. As Libra children grow, they will be very comfortable with, and attached to, their Taurus parents, who are generally very charming, sociable, and reveal a gentle vulnerability that is very appealing to their little Libras.

Libra children are friendly babies who usually smile a lot. They have a mysterious quality of enchantment, which creates an aura of serenity around them. Their peaceful demeanor can easily calm the anxiety of any parent, and Taurus moms and dads are no exception. Libras aren't difficult to raise, as they get along with everyone. When they are little children, they appear to be walking on cloud nine, with their little feet never quite reaching the ground. Taurus parents are very comfortable with their Libra's ethereal quality, as this characteristic contributes to a relationship that is mutually satisfying and tension free. Taurus parents are basically patient and will give their Libra kids the room to reveal their natural personalities. Taurus parents are well aware of what a special joy it is to raise their Libra children, and it is very likely that a feeling of harmony will pervade the home where a Taurus parent and a Libra child co-exist.

The Taurus Mom/The Libra Child

Taureans often feel the need to look just perfect when it comes to their physical appearance, and while Libras are not quite as obsessive in this area, both they and their Taurus parents have similar insecurities when it comes to presenting themselves to others—especially Taurus moms. To overcome this overemphasis on appearance, Taureans and Libras need to work on believing in themselves. Mom can enhance this situation by stressing the importance of developing the beauty within a person, rather than concentrating on the superficial side. It's also up to Mom to try and control her own need to complain about her own appearance. She needs to ease up on herself. If Mom can teach her Libra children how to love themselves from within, she will end up learning from her own lessons.

Libras tend to look at who they're not before they look at who they are. As such, it's important for Mom to dissuade them from comparing themselves to other children. We have learned that because Libras tend to be hard on themselves, they may underrate their abilities. A Taurus mom is usually very intuitive, so she can make a point of noticing the times when her Libra children start to put themselves down. Mom might say to her son, "John, don't be so hard on yourself. That's a beautiful drawing," or, to her daughter, "Come on, Jane, don't be discouraged. I know you're doing the best you can at school." By reacting to her kids in this way, Mom will become even more aware how important it is that she not put *herself* down. The similarities between the Taurus mother and her Libra child can really contribute to an increased level of understanding between them!

The Taurus Dad/The Libra Child

A Taurus dad is charming, poised, and a wonderful host. He usually has a small group of close friends who are very important to him. He and his Libra child have much in common, as they both appear on the outside to be easygoing and fun, but on the inside their approach to life can be much more serious. Dad believes in safety and security in the home, and likes to keep his feet close to the ground. He loves adventure, but will enjoy providing a stable environment for both himself and his children. A Taurus dad also believes in loyalty, and little Libra will welcome this special kind of dedication.

Both Taureans and Libras are idealists, and when their ideals become tarnished, their attitude toward life can become cynical. It's important for both Taureans and Libras to learn to accept the behavior of others without taking it too personally or getting too angry. Dad's spirituality can help him look at the beauty in life, and his Libra child will easily follow his lead. Dad and his Libra are humanitarians who will always fight to promote human welfare. They are visionaries, and their perception that life should be beautiful is a positive and optimistic one.

Dad has strong emotions that he keeps inside a soft shell. These emotions can often be the instrument of his thoughts and actions. When he's upset, the Bull can be stubborn. His Libra children have many of the same tendencies but tend to assume an "I don't care" attitude when they want to cover up their feelings. Of course that's not true, but a Libra will do anything to avoid personal confrontation.

Libras know that Dad is really a softie; and thanks to these kids' sense of diplomacy, tact, and skill, they can wrap him around their fingers. Dad can easily fall under their spell unless he understands that he must try to help them verbalize their real feelings—and not just "act out"—in order to promote healthy communication in the household.

Libras are enthusiastic about starting new projects, but they take their time before pinning themselves down to making a decision. This can be a problem, because they can lose interest in what they're working on, and then they can become bored with the entire project. Dad can help his Libra child in this area, as he has a keen mind and is excellent at deductive reasoning. For example, if he observes that his Libra son is seriously considering doing something but seems to be spending too much time making up his mind, Dad might say, "Jimmy, that shelf in your room looks empty. When do you think you want to build your model boat? I think it would look perfect there." In other words, he can provide his child with logical, sensible reasons for achieving a goal. It's important for Dad to try and motivate his Libra children to complete creative projects for their own good reasons, as anything that smacks of being too structured or that sounds like a command will put them off.

The Gemini Parent/The Libra Child

Gemini parents can easily help develop the mental acuity of their Libra children. Both parent and child are mentally alert, logical, reasonable, sensible, and objective. They see life through the intellect, with both being sometimes reluctant to speak freely when it comes to talking about their feelings. Geminis usually keep their own counsel and enjoy everything that has to do with learning. They need to have a sense of order in their lives, and they have the ability to focus intently on the interests that intrigue and challenge them.

Some Geminis appear reserved, but they're not conservative when it comes to exploring life. They tend to get bored quickly, and so, welcome any diversion that will prove stimulating. Most people find that Geminis are unpredictable people and, unfortunately, a Libra child needs a parent with a stable nature. Gemini parents would be wise to understand that even though their Libra children can adjust to their capricious behavior, this kind of attitude can create self-doubt.

Libras usually have an easygoing, "devil may care" attitude; however, they can be easily hurt, and their Gemini parents need to encourage them to open up and express what they're feeling. A Libra's emotions and thoughts should not be ignored; if they are, these children may grow up and flounder for years, staying in a job that doesn't correspond to their skills, or remaining in an unhappy marriage. Basically, they can end up behaving as other people want them to, instead of being their own individuals. If Gemini parents become too preoccupied with their own needs and interests, their Libra children may feel that Mom and Dad are deserting them. These children need attention and protection; in many ways they are like young grown-ups, and their Gemini parents would be wise to come up with imaginative activities that can stimulate their alert minds.

Gemini parents are wonderful teachers, so they can truly help their Libra children define their goals, which is a crucial starting point in their personal growth and in their quest for a satisfying future.

The Gemini Mom/The Libra Child

Libras look up to their mothers as a source of protection and inner strength. They'd like her to be efficient, caring, attentive, and warm. They won't be disappointed, since Mom *is* energetic and intelligent, and she will help her Libra children set realistic goals for themselves and achieve their dreams.

Mom is an excellent teacher, and both she and her Libra child will seek educational outlets that will enhance their knowledge of the world as a whole. Geminis and Libras have the talent to become very successful in the arts, music, and in the world of communication. They think alike, and Mom's natural talents and abilities will be very compatible with those of her Libra children.

Gemini mothers do not have a strict plan for raising their children; rather, they are quite spontaneous in their behavior. They tend to change their minds quickly, and this lack of inconsistency can sometimes be detrimental to young Libra's need for safety and security. Mom is usually very efficient at maintaining the home environment, though, which is crucial to the Libra child's emotional security. However, she needs to take special care to take her children's feelings into account before making decisions that involve them.

Terry, my friend Judy's son, was a junior in high school, and one day he came home from basketball practice to find that his dog Simon was missing. He had grown up with Simon and, of course, he loved him.

Terry's mother came home from shopping, and he frantically asked her, "Mom, where's Simon? I've looked everywhere for him."

She looked directly into his eyes and calmly said, "Oh, I'm sorry, honey, we had to put him to sleep." Terry (a Libra) stood there, immobilized. "What?" he asked, in shock.

It was at that moment that Judy (a Gemini) realized that she should have prepared her 16-year-old son for his dog's death. She had believed that it was better to be direct, get the task done, and avoid having to endure much pain. Geminis are good parents, but sometimes they have a problem expressing their feelings, so they wind up stating things a little too logically, forgetting that they can hurt the person they're dealing with.

Judy and I talked about what happened, and I told her, "Judy, you are a logical woman, and if you had to put your dog to sleep because he was sick, it is your way to just make the decision and get on with it. But your son is very sensitive, and he adored his dog. This experience is a lesson for you, and it would be wise to consider your child's feelings in the future."

Judy agreed, saying,"I think I'm am going to tell Terry that I'm sorry for what I did, and in the future I will try to discuss any decisions that involve him."

☆   ☆   ☆

The Gemini Dad/The Libra Child

Dad has a tendency to stay out of the everyday humdrum affairs of family life. He's very protective of his family, but his work can demand a lot of his attention. If he's chosen a career that satisfies him, Dad needs to avoid being a workaholic, because Libra children will need their dad around to help nurture and appreciate their accomplishments. Gemini dads tend to be high-strung and nervous. They are restless and easily bored; therefore, they need to pursue a lot of interests. Dad and his Libra child are similar and will enjoy a mental affinity. They are both logical, and *they believe in the facts and nothing but the facts.*

Dad needs to understand that his Libra children thrive on peace and harmony, and they will often say yes, when no should be the answer. They need to please in order to avoid confrontation. A Gemini's base is not emotional, and Dad may also try to avoid anything that appears to be intimate or very personal. It's important for Dad to build a comfortable relationship with his Libra children, as they will look to him for advice. He needs to be truthful with them, as they are very intuitive and can instantly detect deception.

Dad tends to be highly intelligent, and these air children will benefit from all that he knows. My experience has shown me that Libra children tend to be influenced by what their fathers say. Dad can become a mentor, so he needs to be careful about misleading these idealistic children. Libra kids' natural intuition helps them understand what people need, and their first impressions are usually accurate. If they are hurt, they may pretend that nothing bothers them, but that isn't true. Dad can be very instrumental in helping his Libra children stand up for their rights. His own individuality and freedom is very important to him; therefore, he can easily motivate his free-spirited children to confront people that are intimidating or domineering. Dad would be wise to give his air children the opportunity to make their own choices, no matter how long it may take. If Libras believe that someone appreciates their ability to make a decision, they can set a goal and stick to it!

The Cancer Parent/The Libra Child

Cancer parents are loving and affectionate. Since the home is a Cancer's sanctuary, these parents know how to provide their children with a stable and comfortable environment. Most adults think little Libras are precious, because as young tots they look like little angels who run around spreading angel dust. Libras' sweet demeanor is very pleasant to be around, and Cancer parents will feel a strong need to protect them.

Cancers can be possessive, though, and as nice as Libra children can be, they won't want Mom and Dad to invade their privacy. Cancer parents would be wise to understand that it's best to win their Libra children's love by believing in their talents and abilities. Libra kids will always need their parents' support and positive feedback, as they tend to overanalyze and criticize anything they do. It's very difficult for Libras to release negative feelings, especially when they are dissatisfied with themselves, and Cancers have a similar habit. Mom and Dad should encourage these kids to let go of the things they can't do anything about, and help their children understand that obsessing over issues is unproductive and frustrating.

All in all, a solid and healthy relationship can be built through Cancer parents' respect for their Libra children's need for freedom and individuality.

The Cancer Mom/The Libra Child

A Cancer mother is "the parent" of the zodiac, and she can be too protective of her children. If she bases her personal security on how her children treat her, and if she gives them everything they want in order to elicit their approval, she can wind up making them think that she's *always* going to be there to do things for them.

Mom means well, but her possessive nature can be detrimental to her Libra children if she doesn't give them the opportunity to think and do things for themselves. If she doesn't encourage her Libra children to believe in their own opinions and ideas, their self-confidence and ability to make decisions will diminish. Libra children do need to feel protected, and they secretly want someone to take care of their needs, but they want the freedom to make their own decisions and do their own thing. They tend to resent anyone who needs to be involved in every single thing they do.

Libras will value Cancer Mom's ability to serve as caretaker, but these kids can often pay a price as adults if they think that they have to meekly acquiesce to anyone who tries to control their behavior. Mom should try to get a sense of when it's a good time to back off so her Libra children can find their own space to be alone and think. Then, at the right time, and without any pressure, she can help them open up to her about their feelings in order to build mutual trust.

Libra children enjoy affection, so a Cancer mother needs to give herself permission to get in touch with her innermost feelings and to learn how to express them in a demonstrative manner. Once Mom has conquered her fear of revealing her emotions, she can then work on helping her Libra children do the same thing.

Young Libras are like little angels who want to believe in a world of beauty. As they grow older, their idealism can fade when they start to perceive the realities of life, and like their Cancer parents, they tend to take every one of life's disappointments personally. The way for both Cancers and Libras to hang on to their idealism and ultimately achieve their goals is to figure out how to define their own needs.

I would like to suggest that Cancer mothers try and give their Libra children the freedom they need, both to form their own opinions and make their own decisions. Libras need permission to explore life, and with their protective and endearing mother providing them with the shelter and stability they need, they'll be able to accomplish anything they set their sights on!

The Cancer Dad/The Libra Child

Dad is a very sensitive and emotional man who may tend to hide his feelings behind his sense of humor. If he always chooses to see the world as a comical place to live in, though, he may be denying himself the chance to learn from his own sensitivity. Even though he may not always talk about his feelings, he cannot avoid his own emotional intensity.

Cancer Dad is a competitive person who needs to be challenged both personally and professionally. His home is his castle, and he would like his children to always do the right thing. Dad will always be there to help them with any problem, but he can be a little too opinionated about everything. He would be wise to calmly explain his answers to his Libra children's questions, rather than preach. Dad tends to overdo when he tries to get his point across, so he could reach his children a lot better by choosing a reasonable approach to help them understand his feelings. Libra kids want give and take, and they want to feel that their parents are interested in what they have to say. And, as I've mentioned, these children tend to focus on the negative aspects of themselves, before the good. Therefore, when Dad feels that it's necessary to reprimand his Libra children, he should use honesty, logic, and reason; once these children understand that there is a rational basis for his behavior, they will be able to trust him.

Dad is a warm and loving father who loves small children. He, like Mom, will sacrifice a great deal for his family. Dad is a very private man, though, so if he can allow himself to communicate on a personal level, he will achieve a great deal of emotional satisfaction. But, if he continues to deny his own feelings, he will start to lose sight of the emotions of his family or friends. If Cancer Dad can work on allowing his true feelings to come to the surface, he will have fewer problems with nerves. A Cancer father has a tendency to fall into dark moods, which are caused by inner turmoil. However, he can lift himself out of these states by accepting and appreciating his emotional nature. Since Libras also have a tendency to wallow in depression, if Dad can work on talking about his own feelings, he can encourage his Libra kids to do the same, which will enhance their level of communication and trust.

A Cancer man gets along with most people because he's funny, friendly, and loves sports. He'll be happy to discuss a variety of subjects, since he's very curious. If Dad can learn to accept his emotions and balance his feelings with his intellect, he can have a warm and satisfying relationship with his Libra children.

The Leo Parent/The Libra Child

Leos are emotional, self-reliant, and independent. Most of my Leo clients share a common problem that seems to hinder their true happiness: they have trouble asking for emotional support. Most Leos live their entire lives without resolving that one issue. It's not easy to persuade them to give up their need to control everything. They relish the idea of being appreciated for the things they do, but they're so busy doing everything for everyone else that they hardly give anyone a *chance* to acknowledge them.

Leos are the kings and queens of the zodiac; therefore, they like to be in charge. They want to maintain control over both their personal and professional lives, even though they usually end up suffering as a result. Their relationships become a one-way street, because they end up taking care of everything. It all comes back to their need to dominate all situations.

As parents, Leos will give their Libra children all of the necessary love and guidance they need, but they would be wise to pull back on their naturally domineering natures. Libra children resent being controlled by anyone. Leos treat their children as though they're grown-ups, and this is very important for young Libras, as they need the freedom to be their own person. Nevertheless, Leo parents cannot make all of the decisions for these kids, or they will definitely have problems developing self-confidence. Libras have to claim their own individuality, but they can have a problem standing up to dominant personalities such as Leos. Being "royalty," Leos sometimes want to ensure that their "subjects" revere them.

Libra children can easily depend on these strong and protective fire parents, but Leo parents would be wise to permit their Libra children's individuality to blossom, through patient guidance and wisdom. Libras tend to keep to the middle of the road when it comes to making decisions. Since Leos, being fire signs, usually take a firm stand on one side or the other, they will have to be a little patient with their diplomatic Libra children. Libras need a lot of information before they make a final decision and, in addition, it takes them time to carefully consider everything they've learned. Leos quickly do the research on a subject, decide on a direction, and act upon it.

I have always said that Leo parents can learn the value of patience from their Libra children. Libra kids do not want to feel that they're competing with their parents, and decisive parents can be competitive without realizing it. Leo moms and dads should encourage their Libras to make their own decisions, while being there in the background to advise them when their help is requested. Leos have admirable qualities to share with their Libra kids that will strengthen their self-confidence. They are genuinely supportive and creative, and they won't ever hold their children back from achieving their dreams. Leo parents are optimistic, enthusiastic, and affectionate, and will always defend their Libra children's right to stand up for themselves.

The Leo Mom/The Libra Child

A Leo mother can be a wonderful role model for her Libra child. She has spirit and strength, and she loves to be with people. She's proud of her accomplishments, but most of all, she's proud of her children. A Leo mother's house will be alive with friends who share in her activities, and little Libra will be happy being surrounded by energetic adults. Mom is always busy, so life will never be dull. She's wise, understanding, and has a great sense of humor. Her hearty laughter will nourish her Libra children. She has a quality of being "international," which allows her to speak to anyone, no matter what culture they're from.

It's important for Mom to be aware that her Libra children may not be as gregarious as she is. Libras are friendly and fun to be around, but they tend to build their friendships slowly, gradually developing trust as they spend more time with people. Libras will always need their mother's solid guidance, but as these air children grow, Mom will have to be careful about imposing her opinions on them. Libras like explanations as to *why* they should do things, as opposed to simply being *ordered* to do something. Mom needs to encourage the natural development of her kids' personalities without demands or high expectations.

Mom can be an excellent teacher if she can use her natural ability to motivate her Libra child. Libras are creative and love anything that delights the senses and appeals to the mind. So, it's important for parents to make sure that these kids find a particular interest that they really enjoy. Remember: Libras don't enjoy performing for people, unlike some of their theatrical parents. Leo mothers should ask their Libra kids how they feel about any activity they're involved in, to be certain that there is genuine interest on their part. Doing so will ensure that these kids won't feel like they're being *forced* into anything.

The Leo Dad/The Libra Child

Dad is a man to be admired, as he is strong, intelligent, optimistic, and dependable. He's usually a fast thinker and a fast talker. He believes in his family, and he will continually affirm his support for them. No one has to ask him to appreciate his children, because he's always taking care of them. He's emotional, straightforward, doesn't mince words, and gets to the point quickly. Libras are born to believe that there are many gray areas to consider before they speak or act upon anything, so it's up to Leo Dad to understand that these kids will not be coerced into doing anything without thinking through all of the options. A Leo father can help his Libra children progress by quickly getting to the bottom line of any situation, while at the same time being patient with his kids' decision-making processes.

If Dad tries to interfere with his Libra children's need for balance, he can damage the parent/child relationship, which needs to be based on trust. There will be no problem with Dad setting limits and rules for his Libra children to follow, as they need to know that there's a point in time when they need to complete a certain task or come to a decision. If Dad can give his Libra children the opportunity to form their own opinions and ultimately make their own decisions, he will earn their trust and confidence. If he can avoid making these kids feel foolish or unintelligent along the way, his role as a mentor will be respected even more.

Basically, If Dad can accept and nurture his Libra children's need for balance and harmony, he will be their best friend!

The Virgo Parent/The Libra Child

Virgo parents are practical realists, and no one would ever doubt their intention and ability to provide strong roots for their children. They value the concepts and beliefs that work for them, and eliminate the ones that create doubt in their minds. They have wonderful, imaginative ideas, and their taste is impeccable. They make a home for their family that is comfortable and safe.

Libra children appreciate the balanced lifestyle that their Virgo parents provide for them, but they may have a problem dealing with parents who never let up on their need to keep order in the home. Virgos are geniuses at organization, but they may have to accept the fact that their Libra children may not always respond well to the pressure of keeping every facet of their lives organized all of the time. They themselves need a sense of order, but relaxation is also an essential part of life and helps to calm their nerves and preserve their peace of mind. Libras need their Virgo parents to realize that when they do something for the first time, they need the freedom to make mistakes. They definitely want someone who can provide structure and stability, but they don't like to feel as though they are always being watched. Libras enjoy spending time in their own fantasy worlds, so they have to get the sense from their practical, grounded Virgo parents that it's all right for them to do so.

Virgos dislike anyone who's too demanding of them, because they are already so incredibly exacting about themselves. As such, they'll appreciate and even admire their Libras' free spirit and easygoing nature, and they can guide their Libra children by helping them find realistic ways to make their dreams come true.

The Virgo Mom/The Libra Child

Many Virgo mothers can appear to be a little shy, but they actually have a great sense of humor. They are women of the world who are in command of all of the social graces. Their homes are usually places of beauty, where they enjoy entertaining friends on a regular basis.

As children, Virgos are usually very reserved, and other people have to prove themselves before these earth kids trust them. However, as they grow older, they begin to recognize and appreciate their ability to be self-disciplined in order to take control of their lives. Nevertheless, they always doubt that they have enough financial security or personal stability, and they can hurt themselves by scrutinizing everything they do. I would like to suggest that they depend on their natural ability to do the right thing, and not be so hard on themselves. When a Virgo mother raises Libra children, she needs to accept the fact that her sometimes critical and judgmental nature may cause her to look at things a little differently than they do. Libra children are basically calm and easy to raise, and they will feel comfortable and safe with a mother who can be counted on to keep their lives in order. But, they do not respond well to a parent whose expectations and demands are overwhelming, as this tends to makes them nervous. Libra children may want to please Mom and do what she says, but if she isn't careful how she handles them, their nervous anxiety may cancel out any positive lessons that they learn from her.

Virgo mothers would be wise to give their Libra children the freedom to talk about their feelings, or they will withdraw into their own world. Mom must always encourage her Libra children to say what's on their minds, without judging them. Most of all, Libra children need a Virgo mother's appreciation and praise. Mom is a dedicated and concerned parent, so she shouldn't have trouble comprehending that her Libra children need to feel that they can live up to her expectations.

The Virgo Dad/The Libra Child

Dad may be a perfectionist who has strong opinions, but he'll always stand by his children, even if he doesn't agree with their behavior. He's an efficient, detail-oriented person whose decisions are usually based on strategy, fact, and reason. He's hard-working and needs to succeed, but if something in his life doesn't work out, he has both the ability and courage to start all over again. The difference between a Libra child and a Virgo dad is the Libra's need for calm, and a Virgo's propensity for chaos. Dad can have a difficult time learning to relax. With the help of his Libra children, though, he will learn how to stop and smell the roses.

Dad can be helpful in teaching his Libra children how to focus on their goals, and he'll do everything that he can to see that these aims are met. A Virgo dad has strong concentrative powers, and he can be quite a source of strength when he wants to make things happen. Dad would be wise to realize that he may be more emotionally intense than his Libra children, so he needs to approach them in a subtle manner so they won't retreat from him.

Libras tend to intuitively pick up another person's behavior, so Dad should try to calm his own nerves when he is speaking to these kids because they will sense how he really feels. This behavior can also help promote healthy communication and trust between parent and child.

All in all, Dad can be a great help when it comes to teaching his Libra children to stand up for their rights, and it would be a good idea for him to give them permission to pursue all of their loftiest dreams through utilization of their gifts of diplomacy and intuition.

The Libra Parent/The Libra Child

Libra parents and children both start out with similar points of view, believing that the world can be a better place if it is ruled by reasonable, logical people. They have an abundance of tolerance for people who need their help, and are able to view world problems in an objective manner. Ex-President Jimmy Carter is a Libra, and his talent for mediation is beyond reproach. He remains impartial when listening to the viewpoints of others, and he is able to put together proposals that are based on the best interests of all concerned.

Libras function through their intellect. Therefore, they *think* about their feelings, rather than actually feel them. Since Libra parents and their Libra children can both be moody, these moms and dads need to learn how to express their own feelings in order to help their children do the same. Together, this parent/child duo can make an unbeatable team. In other words, they'll feel much better if they communicate with each other. And, as Libra children grow and parents discuss global issues to a greater extent, they will likely concur with the diplomatic, balanced view of the world that their parents maintain.

Libra parents are a great asset to their Libra children because they can relate to the fact that these kids enjoy playing in their private world of imagination. Libra parents will also tend to treat their children as adults, and relate to them on a mature level. These two signs enjoy playing together, and they are always coming up with new activities that are creative and amusing. Overall, this Libra/Libra combination will really enjoy each other's company!

The Libra Mom/The Libra Child

A Libra mother needs to be in charge of her home, and she will tend to be sentimental about the decor—her belongings mean a lot to her, and she won't remove anything from a room that reminds her of a happy memory.

From an emotional standpoint, she's very willing to share both her thoughts and her ideas with her Libra air children in order to give them the respect that they deserve. Mom will love and protect her children, and she will give them the freedom to express themselves; but she has a tendency to judge her own desire for independence as being irresponsible. I suggest that she give herself the permission to balance her need for responsibility with her need to take care of herself. As I've mentioned earlier, there are two types of Libras: one tends to be more "traditional," and the other leans toward being more "artistic." It would be wise for Mom to determine which type of child she is raising. Does her child appear to be a traditional person who is content with the status quo, or is he or she the artistic type who wants to "live out adventures" around the world?

The artistic Libra mother who is raising conservative Libra children can apply her talents to helping them expand their horizons; and the conservative Libra mom who is raising artistic children can help stabilize their dreams. It won't matter which type a Libra mom raises, really, because all of them are logical. Therefore, she can always be reasonable and objective in her efforts to prepare each child to find the road to success. Overall, Libra mothers are sensitive and patient when it comes to handling their children's problems.

The Libra Dad/The Libra Child

Dad is usually a liberal thinker, but there are Libras who can be more conservative in their thinking. Whichever type of Libra he his, he wants to take the logical approach and be absolutely fair with everyone he deals with. He is often a brilliant diplomat who is well informed and stable. However, once Dad makes up his mind, it can take some mighty strong arguments to change it. In fact, some of his opinions can come off as judgmental or overly critical. Some of my male Libra clients have learned to understand that their critical tendencies stem from their inability to resolve their feelings of anger. Once they get in touch with the cause of their anger and learn to forgive those in the past who have hurt them, they tend to stop passing judgment on others.

The first decan (September 23–October 2) Libra dad is usually conservative, while the second decan (October 3–October 12) father tends to be more restless. The third decan (October 13–October 22) dad is the most creative, and he often holds an office or is a public figure. Each one of these personalities will encourage his Libra children to develop in their own way, though, as Dad is basically kind, compassionate, and helpful. He's always trying to make people feel comfortable, and he's usually the one you'll hear asking, "Can I get you some water?" or "Do you want a chair that's better for your back?" People feel good around Dad, as he is an empathetic man who understands how to take care of others' needs.

The Scorpio Parent/The Libra Child

My experience has shown me that Scorpios and Libras like to be in each other's company. Scorpios like Libras because they are well informed, have good taste and manners, and won't talk back to them (even if they want to). Scorpios parent will have a powerful influence on their Libra children. These parents strive to increase their kids' intellectual abilities and help them to develop their social skills. My main concern with this parent/child relationship is that a Scorpio parent often tries to control the Libra child's thinking. This behavior can make a Libra feel very insecure.

Scorpio parents may not always be aware that their behavior may be suppressing their children's individuality. They would be wise to understand that they cannot totally protect their kids from the outside world. Scorpios are very caring parents who will always try and provide the best for their children. However, they do have a tendency to issue commands. They really have to be careful not to make their Libra children feel as though they can't do anything on their own. Libras tend to go off into their own world if they feel that their parents are continually giving them orders.

Scorpios are natural parents who have an unbelievable ability for organization, detail, and structure. They must remember that children need the power to make decisions on their own, based on a series of options. These parents have a tendency to believe that children remain children until they prove otherwise. A Libra child is wise at an early age and likes to be treated as a young adult. These kids may not be grown-up, but they need to know that their feelings have worth. Scorpio parents are inclined to simply assume that they know what their children are thinking, and then they will make decisions for them based upon those assumptions. It's important for Scorpio parents be careful about adopting this way of thinking and acting, though, because they may not always be right. Libras may stop listening to what their parents say to them when their own thoughts are dismissed. It would be a good idea for Scorpio parents to nurture their Libra children's need for personal freedom, while setting certain limits and rules to abide by in order to help them develop their self-discipline.

The Scorpio Mom/The Libra Child

Mom is a genuine, sincere parent. She is emotional, as well as being and intellectually bright, and she can start up a conversation with anyone, eliciting their personal dramas from them. She's very curious about people's lives, but she tends to keep most of her intimate stories to herself, as she is a private lady who makes her own decisions. She is well versed in many subjects and she can speak eloquently on almost any topic. She's also a people watcher who formulates opinions on human behavior by observing those around her closely.

Mom is drawn to her Libra children's soft beauty, and these children will find that they will enjoy Mom's protective nature. Libras do like to have their needs looked after, but only within limits. Mom may do too much for her Libra children, and they may find that behavior intimidating. As these kids grow, a Scorpio mother may have to learn how to let these kids make decisions on their own. The first decan (October 23–November 1) mother is usually the most intense, while the second (November 2–November 11) is the most critical, and the third (November 12–November 21) is the most creative. As a matter of fact, just about every Scorpio mother has creative tendencies if she chooses to recognize them. No matter what decan we're talking about, it's the soft side of a Scorpio mother that is most attractive to her Libra child.

The Scorpio Dad/The Libra Child

Dad is intense, dramatic, and intelligent, and he has a sharp wit. He has the ability to anticipate the needs of others, and he is very willing to help solve their problems. He's also very protective, and he will go out of his way to help his children as long as they do not cross the boundaries that he sets up for them. Scorpio Dad, like Mom, is a private person who will appear to be somewhat of a mystery to his family. I'd like to suggest that a Scorpio father try and verbalize his feelings with his children. He's basically an emotional man, so it isn't wise for him to keep all of this intensity bottled up. If he doesn't release some of the emotional pressure that he places on himself, he can harm himself physically and wind up with quite a bellyache (literally!). Getting his feelings off his chest will allow him to enjoy life to its fullest, because he'll find that he becomes closer to his family.

Dad is a natural scholar who enjoys teaching, and his Libra kids can be excellent students. If Dad will just reveal his loving nature and fully appreciate his Libra children's charm, poise, creativity, and intelligence, he can help enhance every aspect of their lives!

The Sagittarius Parent/The Libra Child

Here we have two free spirits getting together. The motto of both the Sagittarius parent and the Libra child is: "Don't take away my freedom to do what I have to do." Sagittarius parents are explorers who look for adventure. On the other hand, they also need stable roots and a comfortable, secure home.

Sagittarian parents are interested in developing the intellect. In addition, they are stimulated by challenge and competition. Since Libra children crave intellectual stimulation, these parents can easily prod them into action when they become lethargic. Sagittarian parents and Libra children are also good for each other because they find it very easy to communicate. Also, they love to travel and are both fascinated by the study of philosophy and the sciences. Sagittarius parents try to raise their children in a healthy, balanced manner, and a Libra child will be quite content with this lifestyle.

Sagittarians do have a tendency to be blunt, though, especially when their patience runs out. These diplomatic and patient Libra kids can be easily hurt by this behavior, even though they may pretend they don't care. Sagittarius Mom and Dad need to be considerate of young Libra's feelings, as anything that sounds harsh is taken as a personal affront.

Both Sagittarians and Libras have two distinct sides, one that is cheerful and friendly and which is a joy to behold, and the other that is sullen and morose and hard to fathom. These parents can help to assuage such lapses into depression by pushing beyond their own moodiness. When they acknowledge the fact that their own set of emotions can be contagious when it comes to their Libra children, they will no doubt make more of an effort to curb their negative feelings.

Overall, Sagittarian parents and Libra children are intelligent, charming, gracious, and efficient, and they have the gift of making people feel good about themselves. As sincere humanitarians who enjoy helping those who are less fortunate, these fiery parents and peaceful children bring a lot of joy and happiness into the world!

The Sagittarius Mom/The Libra Child

Mom is a strong woman who takes parenting very seriously. She has a great sense of humor, and she likes to do things in her own unique way. Conversations with her are quite interesting, and she'll take great pains to educate her Libra children—she will consider their intellectual pursuits at all times as she parents them. Her concern for advanced education and high levels of achievement will be limitless, and she will always come up with creative ways to increase her children's desire to learn.

Mom is also very friendly, emotional, and sensitive—a woman who will raise her Libra children with the utmost patience and consideration. Her free spirit just seems to naturally encourage her Libra kids. In fact, her creativity, determination, and social graces will all be positive qualities for her children to emulate.

One suggestion that I'd like to make to Sagittarius mothers is to be careful about being too blunt in their criticism of their Libra children, as they are easily hurt and tend to take everything personally. If Mom feels that she may have been inconsiderate, it would be wise for her to open up a discussion with her Libra children. Remember, these air kids needs to be encouraged to openly communicate their feelings, especially if there's a problem afoot that's really bothering them.

The Sagittarius Dad/The Libra Child

Dad usually has an outgoing personality, exhibits good common sense, has an excellent sense of humor, and is extremely intelligent. Sagittarius dads are also very sensitive and emotional, but they tend to cover these feelings by trying to stick to the practical issues at hand. Dad is involved with so many different activities that he may need to remind himself to spend quality time with his kids. If he fails to do so, these Libra children might misunderstand his intentions and think he doesn't love them.

Libra children are friendly and personable. They are lovable little tots, and as they grow, they too reveal good common sense, a sense of humor, and want to learn as much as they can. But Dad should always remember that these air kids are easily hurt, and they have a tendency to exaggerate their angry emotions.

Dad is usually a strong and intuitive man who has the ability to encourage his air children to talk openly. It's best for Libras to talk about their feelings at the time that they are experiencing them. Otherwise, these kids will suppress them and harbor resentment. A Libra's hidden anger supports violence, and can hurt his or her potential. Many of my Libra clients have trouble subduing their violent thoughts and actions. They tend to limit themselves, and their self-confidence and self-esteem can suffer. Libra children need a lot of love and attention even if they appear to be self-sufficient. They need to share their thoughts and ideas with a father who is born with great ideas and a creative mind.

Dad is good with kids, because he's a kid at heart and is always looking for an amusing time. Basically, he likes to work hard and play hard. When it comes to new ideas, Dad is open-minded; he doesn't believe that any principle, belief, or idea is etched in stone. To an explorer like Sagittarius Dad, life is always teaching you something new!

The Capricorn Parent/The Libra Child

Capricorns are solid and stable perfectionists who tend to overwhelm themselves with anxiety every hour on the hour. They do have a great sense of humor, though, which helps them deal with nervous tension. Capricorns clearly have superb taste, as they want to dress beautifully, select the finest in furniture, and always be surrounded by people and material things that are quality oriented. Capricorns have a practical outlook on life, and they put their stock in anything that brings about a desired result.

Capricorn parents can teach their Libra children (who tend to be dreamers) how to apply themselves in their daily lives and how to be more down to earth. They can also encourage them to conceive of ways to make their dreams come true. Once a Capricorn establishes a set of rules to live by, he or she sticks to them. Libras can adjust to regulations, but they may have difficulty adjusting to any rule that stifles their creative approach to life. It's important for Capricorn parents to allow their Libra children to be innovative and spontaneous in the way they think and act. They would be wise to practice flexibility when they raise these children. Capricorn parents don't like to make mistakes, and they may pass this fear onto their kids. Libra children definitely need permission to make mistakes, as they can become insecure when they are told that they must be perfect. Capricorn parents need to avoid being overly critical with these kids, as they function much more happily when they are given clear, logical explanations instead of being handed judgmental dictates.

The Capricorn Mom/The Libra Child

Mom is usually very attached to home and family, since these are the two most important elements in her life. However, there are many highly successful Capricorn women in the business world, as they are very bright and achievement oriented. They have no problem running an organization, and they have excellent interpersonal skills. Still, all in all, most Capricorn women desire a home and children.

Libra children born to a Capricorn mother will soon understand that Mom tends to be a woman of traditional beliefs, a person who staunchly believes in law and order. As such, her children will be well behaved and have perfect manners. They will learn all there is to know about adapting to society at an early age.

A Libra can be a dreamer, but this little air child can become more practical and down to earth with Mom's assistance. She can provide a variety of educational outlets to stimulate her children's intellect, and since Libras can also be quite logical, they will respond well to any reasonable instruction that she gives them. However, these kids are free spirits, so a Capricorn mom really has to make an effort not to be overly protective and authoritative. Once she has assigned a task to her Libra children, she has to let them have the autonomy to complete it on their own. Mom will do anything she can to make her children happy, and the best way she can help her Libra kids come into their own is to recognize their need for freedom.

The Capricorn Dad/The Libra Child

Dad is a serious man who can drive himself to great professional heights. In fact, he may even push himself too far for his own good. Dad is very self-sufficient, but he also depends on a solid home base for both himself and his family. As his Libra children grow up, Dad may have to accept the fact that their opinions may differ from his. And when this Dad makes up his mind, he can be pretty stubborn. Libras need the freedom to make their own decisions so that they can take charge of their lives. If Dad can understand that he must discuss his opinions with his Libra children without imposing his strong will upon them, he will be a parent whom they can truly respect.

A Libra has the heart of an artist and loves beauty. Libras are the inventors and creators who have the ability to visually understand balance, music, color, and design. Think of John Lennon, George Gershwin, T.S. Eliot, and Julie Andrews—all Libras.

Dad needs to be careful not to impose his practical will upon his Libra children; they need to develop their own enthusiasm and spirit. Dad will enjoy his Libra kids' methodical and organized nature, as he thrives on perfection, but he needs to be careful about placing too many expectations upon them. They usually concentrate on one thing at a time, as this behavior seems to temper their nervous anxiety. Dad can motivate his air children, but he cannot dominate the environment. Libras are not always quick when they make a decision, and they often look to their parents to decide for them. If Dad's behavior is too overbearing, his air kids will begin to feel intimidated, and then their insecurities will bloom. If Dad can guide his children into believing in their own talents and abilities, he will definitely win their love.

The Aquarius Parent/The Libra Child

Aquarians have always had to work on their shyness and reserve. As they grow, they seem to sense the pulse of the world, though. They avidly pursue their own interests and tend to listen to the beat of their own drummer. They are highly intelligent and philosophical, and they easily adjust to being alone. Aquarians are very comfortable making their own decisions, and most of their notions stem from logical, deductive reasoning. Once they see the practicality of an idea, they can then apply their outstanding creative ability to it.

Aquarian parents are liberal and will nurture the minds of their children. Therefore, they need to encourage their Libra children to believe in their own decisions without fear of erring. Libras are artists and perfectionists, so making a mistake destroys the beautiful picture they create in their minds. Aquarians are also creative, but once they see the logic of an idea, they apply their outstanding creative ability to it. Aquarians need to help their air children, who are also logical, pull back from unrealistic fears. Once Libras concentrate on reasonable and objective ways of completing a project or making a decision, they will develop considerable self-confidence.

Libra children and Aquarian parents get along just fine. They share the same need for freedom and independence, and they are both humanitarians who need to keep the peace. They are both argumentative and outspoken when it comes to standing up for a favorite cause, but they have a hard time speaking up for themselves when they feel hurt and insecure. Most people enjoy being in the company of Aquarians and Libras, as individuals of both these signs exhibit honesty and amicability. They understand more than they let people know, but when they make up their minds, their opinions are unalterable. Aquarius parents and their Libra children are basically similar in temperament and so, make quite a fine astrological combination!

The Aquarius Mom/The Libra Child

An Aquarian mother is a visionary who will seem to be "ahead of her time." She has a solid understanding of human nature, but she may have trouble verbalizing her emotions. Mom would be wise to develop the ability to communicate her feelings openly, since she is an expert on everyone else's. Generally, she serves as the "family psychologist" whom everyone talks to.

Mom has a liberal way of raising her children, and she will encourage her Libra kids to develop their minds through education. The only problem with an air parent and child living together in the same household is that they may have difficulty communicating on a personal level. This should not be a problem once they see how many traits and interests they have in common, though.

Mom won't have any trouble giving her Libra children permission to explore and play. She will respect their need to be alone, and she will always be there to care for them. Her Libra children will trust her and have faith in her commitment to raise them in an intelligent and objective fashion. Her Libra children will be open to listening to her philosophy of life, which will help them broaden their horizons. Mom will be instrumental in encouraging her Libra children develop their unique talents without making these air kids feel awkward or eccentric.

The Aquarius Dad/The Libra Child

An Aquarius father has great mental acuity. His academic achievements are numerous, as learning has always come easily to him. He feels better when he can deal with people honestly, without any pretense, but his independence can be detrimental to him at times, since he tends to live in his own world. As such, his friends and family may find it hard to help him when he has a problem.

An Aquarian father and Libra child will become fast friends, and Dad will be very protective of his children's need to express their own opinions. After all, he would resent anyone who took his own freedom or expression away from him. Dad and his Libra children will find peace of mind spending time with one another, as they both enjoy doing the same two things: "hanging out" and relaxing. In fact, Dad may have to concentrate on coming up with creative activities that both he and his children can do with one another, because these dreamers enjoy just sitting around doing nothing all day. Dad may have to make a point of setting rules and regulations, as he and his young Libra may tend to be somewhat lazy.

Dad is an idealist who lives by his own rules, which stem from his belief in independence and freedom. He may try to dominate certain situations, since he does get comfortable doing things his way. At those times, he needs to ask the people he's spending time with what *they're* interested in discussing or doing so they feel that they have a say in what's going on.

Like all air signs, Dad enjoys engaging in activities that are mentally stimulating. If Dad is comfortable with his achievements, he will be secure and stable, but if he has never allowed himself the opportunity to focus on his true talents, he can feel empty and alone. It's important for Dad to choose a profession that's suited to his abilities, a place where he has the freedom to work at his own pace (which is usually fast), without anyone standing over his shoulder. His Libra children have many of the same needs, so it's important for Dad to help them focus on their God-given talents at an early age. Aquarian fathers can be instrumental in encouraging their Libra children to believe in themselves and in their ability to make decisions.

The Pisces Parent/The Libra Child

Imagine two dreamers sitting out in a field full of daisies. That's what this parent/child combination looks like.

Pisces parents can encourage the reflective, dreamy side of a Libra child. These signs are both emotional and sensitive, and they can be both creative or administrative, depending upon how they express their feelings. Pisces are loving and attentive and will base their relationship with their children on emotional bonding.

Both Pisces parents and Libra children are idealists and artists. The warm, outgoing Pisces parents give people a feeling of gentility and compassion, and it's easy to recognize why they want to connect with other people and move close to the ones they love. Their Libra children are gentle and sensitive, but they are thinkers.

As they grow, their logical minds can make it difficult for their water parents to get close to them. Overall, these children will be interested in developing their minds, rather than dealing with a lot of affection. Libras need some hugs and kisses, but they want their parents to pay attention to their accomplishments. Pisces parents need to supply intellectual stimulation when they raise these kids, as Libras always seek knowledge feel a great need to be involved in intellectual pursuits.

Both Libras and Pisces tend to be moody, and they can wear their hearts on their sleeves. It's important for Mom and Dad to set an example by not falling into their own trap of feeling sorry for themselves, because these air children are perceptive and will easily pick up on their parents' feelings. These sensitive, caring, water parents need to try and modify their children's moody nature by helping them to talk about what they feel. Mom and Dad can be good listeners, so if their children can release their hurt feelings, they can work through their anger.

Pisces parents and Libra children both like to make people happy, and they tend to be pleasers. Pisces parents who love to dream can help their air children understand that it's important to pursue their own aims without sacrificing them for the sake of others. I know that Mom and Dad tend to have the same problem, but they can learn to advance their own self-confidence by teaching their children to believe that they are good enough to take control of their lives.

The Pisces Mom/The Libra Child

Mom always seems to have a peaceful aura about her, but there is much more to her than meets the eye. She's a worrier, but she tends to keep these anxious feelings to herself. She's a kind, compassionate, and giving woman, but at times she tends to give too much in order to win the love of her children. A Libra will not expect Mom to ever be more than the person she is. Libras like to live in peace, and they will respect anyone who gently nurtures their growth. A Pisces mother has the ability to appeal to her Libra children's soft, sensitive side by raising them to value love and the sharing of emotions with others.

A Pisces mother gets along with almost everyone, as she rarely likes to make waves. However, she will have to create a set of rules for her Libra children to live by, even though they probably won't be stringent ones. Since most Libras view their mothers as the disciplinarians in the family, they may feel uncomfortable if this Mom doesn't try to set some standards for their behavior. Libra children will enjoy the traditional life that Mom can offer them, but if she isn't careful, her mischievous children may take advantage of her good nature. One of the primary tasks that Mom may have to work on is learning to stand up for herself, as her Libra children will look up to her as an example of strength. Overall, Libra children love and appreciate their Pisces mothers because these moms will never laugh at them in an insulting or derisive way, or leave them out of important decisions.

The Pisces Dad/The Libra Child

Dad, like Mom, is supportive and warm. He cares about his children, and he will always be there for them, because he values home and family. Pisces men can be restless and have a problem staying in one place. They crave a variety of interests and are easily bored. It's important for Dad to create adventures to share with his Libra children, as they will welcome these experiences.

Dad and his Libra child both want to make people happy, so they usually choose the path of serving humanity in one way or another. They like to be with people, yet they need their alone time, too. Both Pisces and Libras tend to be moody, so once they begin to overwhelm themselves with too much responsibility, they like to move into their own space and sort things out.

The Pisces dad and his Libra child are alike when it comes to making mountains out of molehills, and they tend to have unrealistic fears. The also tend to be loners when it comes to their personal lives, so they need to talk about what bothers them. Parent and child have two sides: one is friendly and personable, and the other moves them into a feeling of depression.

Libra kids believe in truth, so will always need Dad to be honest with them. They have a sixth sense, and they seem to know when people are lying. If Dad can try to be open and honest with his air children, even when he needs to retreat, he can set an example that will build healthy communication. If Dad distances himself from his Libra children, they will begin to harbor resentment against him, as their anger is easily aroused. Dad is a sensitive man who, like his Libra kids, has the intuitive power to understand how people feel. Dad can be very instrumental in raising these kids if he can motivate them to avoid scattering their energies. Libras are restless and subconsciously fear settling down. They do not like to commit to anything that demands long-term responsibility. Dad will empathize with this behavior, as he tends to feel the same way. If Dad can motivate his children to follow the paths that will enhance their talents and abilities, whether it leads to serving humanity or writing music, he can help these air children choose the road that will ultimately bring them the most satisfaction.

SUMMARY

After reading about the many dimensions of the Libra personality, I'm certain that you've already guessed that they can be far more complex than they appear. Since Libras are symbolized by the scale of justice, it's important for them to judge all sides fairly. It's not easy to balance everything in life, though, as human interaction can be confusing and scary; but if anyone can do it, a Libra can.

People are often attracted to Libras' profound sense of spirituality, and the most significant example is the Hindu leader, Mahatma Gandhi, born on October 2nd, 1869. He was a man of courage who was sentenced to jail terms on a regular basis as a result of his acts of nonviolent rebellion on behalf of his country.

Overall, Libras tend to define themselves through what others think of them, but they function best when they have the freedom to form their own opinions and rely on their special ability to influence others.

Chapter Eight

♏ SCORPIO THE SCORPION

OCTOBER 23–NOVEMBER 21   **ELEMENT:** Water   **KEY PHRASE:** "I desire"

THE SCORPIO PERSONALITY

Scorpios are charming, persuasive, and shrewd. Their smiles can be infectious, but when they frown, look out! A Scorpio's deepest fears have to do with physical suffering and being alone, fears which inspire them to be some of the most powerful caretakers of the zodiac. They are experts at taking care of the needs of others, because they know how *they* would feel if their needs weren't attended to.

On a personal level, these water-sign individuals can seem both mysterious and mystical, and it may not always be easy for outsiders to understand what they're thinking. They invest all of themselves into the problems of others, and yet they can remain very private about their own emotions. In fact, sometimes they only share their innermost feelings with God, since many Scorpios have a spiritual, religious bent.

Scorpios tend to be devil's advocates, and they begin to test their parents at an early age. They may even have trouble acknowledging their parents' opinions or beliefs until Mom and Dad prove themselves. Scorpios continue to challenge themselves with their need for independence and self-reliance. They are intensely opinionated and possess great inner strength; yet beyond all of their know-how, they can feel insecure and frightened if they don't believe that their family is there for them. It's important that all parents who raise water signs understand that these kids need a great deal of love and support, as they are extremely sensitive. In addition, parents can do themselves a favor by securing their trust at an early age.

Scorpios are both emotionally bright and intellectually mature, but they can't help but find ways of testing people because they honestly believe that they're way ahead of everyone else. They already feel that they've come up with the right answers, and they're waiting for others to come up with the wrong ones. I can hear those silent chuckles. They're so serious and confident about their abilities that they wouldn't dare consider the possibility that they might make a mistake. As soon as you pass their tests, though, and they are confident that you're an honest and responsible person, they begin to accept you.

Scorpios are usually dedicated to their family, and they will always put them first on their agenda. They just need a lot of care and attention because they are as hard on themselves as they are on others. What a Scorpio child needs is specific explanations from Mom and Dad as to why a particular view or opinion may not be appropriate or correct. And, in addition to explanations, they may ask their parents to come up with concrete examples to support their positions. These children always like to stay one step ahead of everyone in their lives, but if their parents can catch them at this game, Scorpios will soon realize that they can't always come out ahead.

☆   ☆   ☆

I was invited to a Chicago fundraiser for a well-known politician, and when I arrived, I sat down with a few friends to have a glass of wine. There were some fun people sitting with us, and a fortyish-looking gentleman said to me, "What do you do for a living?"

Since I didn't like the way he phrased the question, I decided to give him this answer: "I enjoy life."

He smiled, knowing that I was playing with him, and said, "No, you know what I mean. What's your profession?"

I told him, "I'm an astrologer and handwriting analyst."

He looked at me in disbelief and asked, "Can you earn a decent wage in that profession?"

"How could you ask me that question?" I asked him incredulously. "I don't even know you!"

He shook his head, and sheepishly replied, "Oh, I'm sorry, I didn't mean to hurt your feelings. I'm just amazed that people make a living doing what you do."

I then asked him, "How can you assume that what I do wouldn't allow me to take care of myself financially?"

Now he was getting very embarrassed, and he said quietly: "I guess I'm out of line."

I nodded and said, "I think so."

He continued, "Can you really understand someone's personality from astrology or from their handwriting?"

I answered, "Definitely."

"Could you tell me about myself if I wrote something down, and then gave you my birthday?"

"Of course I could." So, he took a napkin from the table and wrote down his name, his birthday, and three nondescript sentences, and then I proceeded to tell him about himself. He stared at me in disbelief as I told him things that even his wife didn't know. In fact, she kept shaking her head at me. After I was finished, he looked admiringly at me and stated, "You nailed me."

I laughed and told him, "Be careful when you sit next to a stranger."

This man was a Scorpio who assumed that no one could survive working as an astrologer or handwriting analyst. Before he even knew anything about it, he discounted my profession and thought it was child's play. Just as I was getting up from the table to leave, he said, "Sylvia, you're a very special woman, and I'll never forget you!"

What he said made me feel good, but I was most pleased that a Scorpio who had prejudged me was now acknowledging that this type of behavior was inappropriate. He was contrite, though, and I forgave him immediately!

☆   ☆   ☆

Silent Dignity

Scorpios are poised and can sometimes appear to be reserved in both their appearance and demeanor. This façade can be misleading, though, as they are really quite intense, emotionally.

When Scorpios are children, they are usually well behaved and tend to be reticent when it comes to their feelings. They live by their gut and instincts, so it's important for parents to understand that they may have to penetrate their Scorpio children's silent dignity by helping them talk about what they feel or what they believe in. It can be difficult to fully understand that it sometimes takes so much work to win children's trust. Young Scorpios can be stubborn. Parents cannot force them to listen to their ideas, because it simply won't work. They will just tune out. The best way for parents to reach Scorpio children is by communicating with them honestly and intelligently and by respecting the opinions that they have to offer.

Passion is the hidden force that drives Scorpios, so their silent dignity is really just a cover-up. Their power and strength comes through their intelligence, but inside lurks sensitive little children. Parents must continue to give these emotionally intense children the love, protection, and care that they need, even if their responses remain cool. Parents should be assured that a solid family life gives Scorpios a lot of comfort and security, so even if these kids appear to be living in their own world at times, it just means that they need time to work through their problems on their own.

Parents should try to openly discuss important transitions that are about to take place in the home, as young Scorpio will always want to know what's going on. In fact, it would be wise to ask them to honestly verbalize how they feel about those changes. For example, parents might ask, "What do *you* think of Mom and Dad's idea of painting the house green?" Scorpio children need to be assured that their opinions will be taken into consideration without ridicule and that they can really make a contribution to the decisions that are ultimately made.

Nonverbal Emotional Bonding

Scorpios are very private, and people who are close to them usually understand that they don't like to reveal their emotions. Instead, they demonstrate their feelings through what I call nonverbal emotional bonding. They show love by *doing* things such as giving out presents, rather than expressing their sentiments aloud. However, this type of nonverbal bonding is not really satisfying for everyone, so it's up to Mom and Dad to work on moving beyond their kids' reticence. If Scorpio children can learn to reveal their feelings, their tendency to be secretive will diminish. Also, these children will admire their parents' efforts to draw them out, and this can be the beginning of a healthy relationship.

Scorpios are loyal and devoted friends who will do anything they can for those whom they care about. With a Scorpio, emotional bonding can go on forever, as long as their friend, parent, or partner is intelligent, goodhearted, and loyal. Scorpios choose friends with whom they share similar interests, or from whom they can learn. Scorpios also have great endurance and patience when it comes to their interpersonal relationships. If they wish to avoid personal confrontation, they'll just place the problem on a back burner until it goes away.

Scorpios can have tunnel vision when it comes to their own opinions, and they are quick to tell other people how to run their lives. Parents would be wise to help their Scorpio children understand that there are always two sides to a situation. If they tell them that it's not a good idea to assume anything before they know all of the facts, these kids will conclude that it's only right to examine all of the circumstances before forming an opinion. This lesson may also help them view *all* situations with objectivity.

Scorpios believe in tradition, as well as in values such as truth and fairness, so it's best not to lie to them, as they are quite mature and have the ability to understand if they're not being dealt with honestly. In fact, some of their advice is so wise, that at times they seem as though they could easily switch roles with Mom and Dad!

The Scorpio Sting

What is the Scorpio sting? It is an ability to deeply hurt someone's feelings. Scorpios really do not want to inflict pain on anyone, but they can be the cause of suffering due to their adamant belief in their own opinions, often to the exclusion of anyone else's. If their ideas are challenged, they have a brilliant way of turning things around to favor themselves. In fact, they can even do so with finesse and humor. They're smart, so when they employ diversionary tactics, they know *exactly* what they're doing.

Scorpios know how to get right to the core of any issue, so they tend to believe that those who try to skirt around a problem aren't very intelligent. When they respond in this way, they have a tendency to lessen the importance of another person's feelings. This tactic is part of their sting. It's not easy to oppose Scorpios, because once they've made up their mind to fight the good fight, they do so until they win.

It's important for parents to thoroughly explain how they have arrived at whatever conclusion they have come to that might concern their Scorpio children. If parents try to force them to adhere to their decisions unequivocally, I can assure you that these kids will just turn off; however, if Mom and Dad try to come up with reasonable compromises, parent and child will more amicably co-exist.

It's wise for parents to teach young Scorpio that Mom and Dad may not always make all of the *right* decisions, but they *will* do their best to present them with a fair and balanced understanding of the world around them. It's important for parents to recognize the need for compromise when raising Scorpio children. But even so, parents will find that although their Scorpio children will want to remain attached to their families, as they grow older there will be times when they disagree with Mom and Dad's views on life, and they may have to go off exploring on their own.

A Strong Work Ethic

Scorpios always need to be *doing* something. They view their accomplishments as indicators of their worth in life. They also believe in the work ethic—working hard and tirelessly to achieve their goals. They are very ambitious and have the capability to be quite successful, especially if their parents are behind them, encouraging them to make the most of their true talents and abilities. If they're allowed to scatter their talents and explore too many avenues, they can get caught up in careers that do not suit them, which may cause them great dissatisfaction later in life. When Scorpios really believe that their parents are supporting them fully, they will spur themselves on to do great things!

In addition, Mom and Dad would be wise to let these kids handle chores or projects in their own way. They can be exceptional when it comes to detail and organization. Fulfilling tasks on their own will give these children a feeling of great personal satisfaction. Parents can work on coming up with activities that are intellectually stimulating in order to prepare these kids for life.

☆   ☆   ☆

PARENT AND CHILD

The Aries Parent/The Scorpio Child

Aries parents are self-confident, dramatic free spirits who have a variety of interests. Anything new or exciting fascinates them. These fiery parents are action-oriented, impulsive people who definitely need time to stop and smell the roses. Their Scorpio children are also dramatic personalities, but their organized and strategic natures force them to spend more time dealing with the realities of life. How do emotional parents who want to be close to their children raise reserved and secretive children? It can prove to be a problem if Mom and Dad cannot understand that their water children will always need their privacy. The mysterious Scorpios, more than any other sign in the zodiac, have many secrets that they keep to themselves.

Aries parents are usually strong and protective. As much as Scorpio children want to be independent, though, they rely on the stability of family and strong roots. Basically, parent and child have a different approach to life. Mom and Dad are quick-thinking, honest, impatient, and straightforward personalities. Their water children are careful, patient, and temperamental. The fiery parent makes a decision and acts upon it, while these water children tend to wait in order to get what they want. Aries parents will need to learn how to be patient with their Scorpios' skeptical nature, as they do not trust easily. Scorpio children will admire their fire parents "go get' em" attitude, and they can learn from them as long as Mom and Dad don't force them into doing anything.

Many people will not believe that the Aries view of life is simple; they really do not like to complicate their lives. They want independence, freedom, love, and family. Scorpios tend to muddle up their lives because they are constant worriers. They fret about every dot and dash. An Aries parent's positive attitude toward life can help young Scorpio believe that life does not have to be so difficult. Since Mom and Dad will have a problem catering to their water children's temperamental nature, parent and child may clash when young Scorpio makes mountains out of molehills.

Overall, Scorpios are intelligent, strong, and opinionated, and they like to be in control of their lives. Aries parents tend to believe that taking over and making all of the decisions protects their children. It's important for Aries parents to understand that Scorpio children have their own minds and need the opportunity to make their own decisions.

Aries parents can be quite helpful if they teach these children to forgive at an early age. This water sign tends to hold a grudge and can seek revenge. This lack of forgiveness can hinder this innate caretaker's ability to serve humankind.

The Aries Mom/The Scorpio Child

Scorpio children need to feel that they can really be dependent upon their Aries mothers for safety, stability, and security. Mom may have a problem relating to her children's needs, though, as baby talk and coddling are just not her style. In actuality, she tends to view her kids as miniature adults. Scorpio children can start to resent Mom if they feel a lack of empathy on her part in relation to their own fears, so Mom would be wise to understand that even if she doesn't have anxiety about facing life's challenges, her children very well might! Mom cannot simply expect her Scorpio children to take on her own courageous attitude. These kids need nurturing, and they expect to be limited by household rules, discipline, and order.

If Mom expects her Scorpio children to conform their lives to hers, these water kids may rebel by doing exactly the opposite of whatever she asks. And I assure you (being an Aries mother myself) that this woman will not enjoy being tested in this way. I'd like to suggest that Mom try to compromise with her Scorpio children by balancing their need for continual attention and tender loving care with her own need for freedom and independence.

The Aries Dad/The Scorpio Child

An Aries dad is a good father who works hard and wants to give his children everything that they need. His ability to prove himself in his career may be very important to him, but his true expression of love will be to nurture his Scorpio children's sensitivity. These kids will really appreciate being taken to the playground, having books read to them, and being taken to a movie, and these are simple tasks that Dad will have no problem undertaking in order to build a solid relationship with his Scorpio children.

However, the most important quality that Dad has to offer his Scorpio children is his sense of humor and innate self-confidence, characteristics that they will no doubt emulate. Aries Dad will, though, have to watch his tendency to keep things to himself, as little Scorpio children have a similar predilection for reticence.

Overall, Aries Dad will be an excellent role model for his Scorpio children, especially when it comes to helping them temper their overly competitive natures and their somewhat critical view of those who don't live up to their expectations.

The Taurus Parent/The Scorpio Child

Scorpio children need to raised by parents who are patient. Taurus parents not only possess this quality, but they are steadfast and will continue on despite all obstacles. Scorpio children relate to their Taurus parents because they have a similar approach to life. These water children are fascinated by the charming and poised personality of their earth parents. They feel comfortable in the pleasant environment that Mom and Dad create around them. Taurus parents understand the importance of working toward establishing their own peace of mind, and they can impart this special wisdom to their Scorpio children.

Scorpios, more than their water counterparts, Cancer and Pisces, can be over-whelmed by their need to be perfect in all that they do. This nervous anxiety can make them intense or hyper—unpleasant feelings that Taurus parents can help alleviate. Mom and Dad are usually calm when they handle their children's anxiety. They can be nervous and worrisome at time, but they usually manage to keep these feelings to themselves. Both parent and child are hard on themselves, and they both need to work on tempering the difficult demands they make. If parents can set the example, young Scorpios may follow their lead.

Taurus parents appreciate the beauty of life, and they tend to be friendly and kind. They are good teachers and understand the value of reality. Their intuitive natures help them to understand the intensity of their Scorpio children, and their soft and easy approach to life can be useful when dealing with their children's temper and irritability. If Mom and Dad can try to nurture the creative imagination of their Scorpio children by giving them projects that are both mentally stimulating and artistic, there is nothing they won't be able to accomplish!

The Taurus Mom/The Scorpio Child

A Taurus mother usually isn't the type of person who will add tension to the household, as she allows her children to be who they are, without ever asking too much of them. She would be uncomfortable if anyone forced her into doing what made *her* unhappy, so what is good for her will be good for her children. Both Taurus moms and Scorpio children are very stubborn, but the extreme nervous intensity of these kids can intimidate Mom. Once this happens, she may back off just to create peace in the household, but this is not a good idea; it's important for Mom to be firm with her instructions and discipline. Young Scorpio will respect her for adhering to her beliefs, and she will respect herself for following through, as well.

This mother is sensible, practical, and intuitive. She's usually not a demanding person, but she can be intimidated by people who insist on expecting more from her than she is willing to give. It's very important for Mom to feel self-confident and to feel comfortable saying no when she believes that type of response is called for.

Both Taureans and Scorpios tend to be traditional in their thinking, and they are both fascinated by family history and the past in general. Mom is both moral and fair, and she believes in honesty and the beautiful simplicity of relationships, which include love, friendship, and respect. Mom should be aware that her ability to constantly obsess over all of her choices in life may cause her to feel insecure. She has excellent instincts, and she needs to listen to them. Scorpio children are also naturally intuitive, so Taurus Mom will have to remind her water kids that their opinions are worthy and intelligent just in case they start to wallow in self-doubt.

Both Taureans and Scorpios have a tendency to overwhelm themselves with fear. Both have great imaginations when it comes to a problem, and they know how to create mountains out of molehills. Mom would be wise to control her tendency to get carried away with emotion when she is raising her Scorpio. I would suggest that

Mom try to lessen her need for drama, so that she can teach her Scorpios how to conquer their own irrational, overblown fears.

The Taurus Dad/The Scorpio Child

Taurus fathers come in two varieties: one is the sedate and more traditional father figure, and the other is the free spirit. Either way, young Scorpio will find his dad very appealing. A Taurus man is surrounded by an aura that combines sensitivity and charisma, and through these qualities, he'll definitely capture the devotion and the loyalty of his Scorpio child.

Dad is basically soft-spoken, but if his ire is aroused, he can be a stubborn opponent. Generally speaking, he's not one for personal confrontation, but it would be wise for him to step up and defend his views in a simple, honest manner. Above all, Scorpio children respect honesty. These kids are extremely intelligent, and if you don't let them in on what you're thinking, they'll try to *tell* you what you're thinking. This Dad may need to accept the fact, though, that his Scorpio child cannot always help this behavior. He can just say to his little son or daughter, "Don't assume you know what I'm going to say until I tell you myself!"

A Taurus father can be an excellent role model when it comes to setting practical boundaries and limits for his children. It's important for Dad to weigh the relative importance of a particular problem and decide whether it's something that has to be handled immediately or whether it can wait. It's a good idea for him to set a specific time to discuss the issue with his Scorpio children so that they won't feel that their problem is being dismissed. A Taurus father also has to remember to stand his ground once he comes to a decision, or little Scorpio will seize the opportunity to take advantage of any vacillation on his part. When Scorpio children realize that Dad can't be pushed around, they will not only respect him, but they will be less likely to pull their shenanigans in the future!

The Gemini Parent/The Scorpio Child

Geminis and Scorpios like to be in complete control of their lives. They can both be extremely private personalities, and it can take a while to get to know them. (They will tell you what they want you to know, but beyond that, they will remain a mystery.)

While Geminis tend to function through their intellect, Scorpios depend on their emotional nature. You have to earn Scorpios' trust before they reveal their innermost thoughts and feelings to you. Both Scorpios and Geminis can be excellent strategists, though, with Geminis tending to rely on both logic and reason, while Scorpios tend to rely more on their gut instincts.

Most Geminis are not comfortable dealing with people who are extremely sensitive, so these parents will need to work on understanding that when they raise emotional children, they need to find ways to nurture their feelings. I would like to suggest that Gemini Mom and Dad develop the patience to handle difficult situations when they arise, as Scorpio children need to feel confident that their parents are capable of taking care of crises.

A Gemini's primary focus is on education and related pursuits. Since a Scorpio is continually seeking knowledge, these kids will value the wealth of information that they can elicit from their Gemini parents. Sharing in intellectual pursuits is a wonderful way for this parent and child to communicate. Geminis are particularly adept at developing imaginative activities that they can share with their Scorpio children, and they will buy them as many educational-type toys as they can. These kids will be pleased to have the opportunity to learn as much as possible!

Geminis do not like to stick to a predictable pattern when they raise children, and this behavior may be a bit frustrating for a Scorpio child, who enjoys a more traditional and steady lifestyle. Geminis seek variety in their lives; the status quo bores them. If they need to do the same things over and over on a daily basis, their resultant restlessness can overwhelm them. It's wise for Gemini parents to understand that Scorpio children are uncomfortable with a lot of change, as they like everything to stay the same at home. If Gemini parents can balance their need for spontaneity and change with their Scorpio children's desire for consistency and predictability, they can reach a happy medium.

Geminis have no problem dealing with the practical demands made by their children; however, they also must have their own alone time. Gemini parents should make an effort to make time for themselves without neglecting their kids, because Scorpio children expect their parents to be there for them on a consistent basis. These kids can start to feel abandoned if they feel that they aren't getting enough quality time from Mom or Dad, so these Gemini parents really have to stay aware and alert to the needs of their Scorpio children.

The Gemini Mom/The Scorpio Child

Mom is an interesting, intelligent woman who has strong opinions and usually sticks to her word. She moves pretty fast and always needs to be busy, busy, busy! She's always on the go, and her young children go right with her. Since verbal communication is her forte, she'll concentrate on helping her children develop in this area. Mom can get a little restless when it comes to maintaining regular routines, but once she acknowledges that this trait is just part of her make-up, she will start to relax. She will come to the realization that everything can't be happening all at once, all of the time!

Scorpio children's moods are based on self-judgment and self-pity. For example, if they feel that they did not get the grades that they wanted, they tend to question their intellect, and can fall into a morose mood. If they get hurt or disappointed, they tend to take it personally, and it takes them a while to get over these emotions. This predilection for moodiness can disturb a Gemini mom, as she naturally shies away from excessive emotion. As such, she won't always know how to handle her children when they fall into these depressive states.

My advice for Mom is to give her Scorpio children time to pull out of one of these moods, and then sit down and talk with them to find out what the root cause was. It's crucial for her to make the effort to draw her children out so they know that she empathizes with their problem. Gemini Mom has the ability to use her logical mind to offer her children practical advice, as well as the comfort that they need.

The Gemini Dad/The Scorpio Child

Dad, like Mom, is a mover and a shaker. He has many friends and many interests, and the wheels of his mind never stop turning—he is always looking for his next challenge or adventure. Scorpio children need a lot of attention and they want to think that their dad is a family man. They love their home and relate to the traditional way of life. Geminis look to the future; they may enjoy the familiar, but it's the new and exciting that fascinates them. Dad needs to understand that his water children are rather "old world" in their thinking. This spiritual approach is very different than Dad's.

Scorpio children need their own time and space, and while they will not want Dad to hover over them, they *will* expect to share their ideas and thoughts with him. He needs to be there when they need him, or they will resent his lack of interest in what they're doing. These water children are practical and pretty stable, while Dad tends to be restless. He needs to stay put when young Scorpios ask for his advice. Scorpio children need to be appreciated, although they are very private. Dad can give them the attention they require by sharing his intelligence and providing a variety of projects that can stimulate their minds. Scorpios want to learn, so a Gemini father is the best teacher. When it comes to raising his Scorpio children, he may find it difficult at first to give them the tender, loving care that they need, but once he takes the leap and starts showing his kids affection, he will find it very rewarding.

Dad is basically a thinker, a man of words who will be both a pal and an authoritative figure to his Scorpio kids. He can help his children resolve their problems by using his intelligence and logic, although he may have to make an effort to accept the fact that his little Scorpios come from a much more emotional base than he does.

☆ ☆ ☆

My friend Calvin was reading the newspaper in the den one evening when his 13-year-old daughter Jean walked in. Being a Gemini, his concentrative powers were very strong, so he didn't even look up.

Jean a sensitive and emotional Scorpio, tried to get her father's attention. She was having a problem, and she really needed her father to help her.

"Dad, why is it when you really like someone, they don't like you?"

Her father, who didn't feel very comfortable dealing with a teenager's rampant emotions, just said abruptly, "What are you talking about?"

Jean was starting to get upset because her father wasn't looking at her. "Dad," she persisted, "I'm talking about this boy at school."

This time, her father's eyes peered over the top edge of the paper."What about him?"

She answered, "I like him, and he doesn't like me."

Dad thought for a moment. "Jean, you're only 13, and I bet this young boy doesn't know that you like him."

Jean exclaimed,"Well, you don't expect me to tell him!" Her eyes started to fill up with tears.

Her father noticed her tears and asked, with surprise in his voice, "Why are you crying? He isn't important; he's just a kid."

Jean became very defensive when she realized that her father was just trying to brush off her dilemma. "Oh, Dad, I knew you couldn't help me!"

He finally put aside his paper. "What do you mean? I know you're feeling very bad about this boy, because you don't know if he likes you. But remember, you're a wonderful girl. Believe me, there will be other boys." He returned to his news-paper, and Jean left the room, frustrated and unhappy.

Several days later when Calvin related this story to me, I told him that his Scor-pio daughter was a very private young girl, and it had to have been difficult for her to make the decision to come to him with her problem. Not being comfortable with heavy, emotional issues, Gemini Calvin didn't have a clue that he should have got-ten up from his chair, gone over to her, and given her a big hug. However, he cer-tainly learned a lot from that situation, and in the future, he assured me that he would be more sensitive to the needs of his daughter.

The Cancer Parent/The Scorpio Child

Cancer parents and their Scorpio children have a strong bond between them. Mom and Dad are sensitive, emotional, and caring. In fact, they can tend to over-compensate when it comes to affection because they always want to receive pos-itive attention from their children. Young Scorpios won't mind, as warmth and affection are good for them. Scorpio children may not be as demonstrative when it comes to affection, but they'll definitely enjoy being a recipient. Many Scorpios have difficulty being openly affectionate, so their Cancer parents can give them the emotional security they need. It's natural for these parents to provide the traditional home life that's suited to a Scorpio child. Their home is a haven, and young Scor-pio will always come back to it for support. Cancer parents will know how to nurture their Scorpio children's wounds, but they also need to make sure that these kids talk about how they feel.

When Scorpios want to attain a goal, nothing can stop them. They don't miss very much, and they are very smart investigators. If they like you, there is nothing they won't do for you, but if they don't, they can be dangerous enemies. It's important for these children to understand that they do not have to go to extremes. This kind of intensity is not healthy for them. Mom and Dad need to appeal to their kids' kind hearts and teach them the importance of having compassion for those who make mistakes. It's best to show them that they cannot assume that they know what people are thinking before they hear what is being said.

Scorpios trust their Cancer parents, as these moms and dads will raise them with sensitivity, as well as have a profound interest in their well-being. As children, they instantly feel their support and encouragement. In fact, Cancers always praise their children. This parent and child are on the same wavelength—two sensitive, introspective signs who wish to build a mutually healthy and loving relationship.

The Cancer Mom/The Scorpio Child

A Cancer mother may tend to sacrifice her own needs for the sake of her children, and a smart Scorpio child may try to take advantage of her good nature. Mom would be wise to understand that she can overcompensate when it comes to her children, so she must pull back from giving too much. This may be a Cancer mother's plight. I have had too many Cancer clients who gave too much to their children in order to win their love. When their kids grew up, they looked at themselves and asked, "What about me?"

Cancer mothers would do themselves a favor by allowing themselves to receive the love and attention that they have so often imparted to others. Their self-confidence and esteem would improve, which can only help them become better mothers. Human beings can never understand how special they are if they don't give themselves permission to receive the care they deserve.

Scorpios and Cancers are both inwardly nervous and possessive, but Scorpios need more of their own personal space. They feel stifled by anyone who hovers around them when they need to be alone. Most Cancers and Scorpios tend to be moody, since both of them are very emotional and sensitive. They may be happy in one moment and sad in the next. Many of their moods stem from not being able to express their emotions. If Mom can learn to recognize this kind of sensitivity in herself and work on verbalizing her feelings, she'll be able to help her Scorpio children open up. Both parent and child have to avoid the tendency to repress their emotions, especially when someone they care about has hurt them.

The Cancer Dad/The Scorpio Child

Dad can sometimes wrap himself up in his career. His nervous energy comes from the challenge of trying to make everything perfect. Dad does understand that he's a sensitive and feeling man, but he is afraid to reveal this part of himself, as he regards his emotion to be a flaw in his character. He takes criticism too personally, and he is easily hurt by others. It's important for Dad to understand that his sensitivity is a rare and wonderful quality, and he should be proud that he "feels," instead of masking his emotions with humor. If he begins to deny his own feelings, he can misunderstand those of the people around him.

A Cancer father usually presents himself as a strong personality who knows how to take charge. A Scorpio can sense the emotional vulnerability of this Cancer dad, though. These kids are also intuitive, and they have the ability and inner strength to rebel against anyone who makes their decisions for them. Dad would be wise to explain why he has formed an opinion or made a decision. Scorpio kids will appreciate Dad's consideration of their feelings.

A Cancer father will do everything he can to protect his Scorpio children, as he views himself as a natural caretaker. And because he is a loving father, Scorpio children will feel safe and secure with his love. If a Cancer dad can work on being more open with his Scorpio child, perhaps this son or daughter will also learn the importance of emotional interaction.

The Leo Parent/The Scorpio Child

We know that Leo parents tend to rule their roost. They're interested in everything that happens to the people they care about, and they're right there fixing all of their problems. When I talk about this parent and child combination, I am talking about two emotional people. Leo parents are self-contained personalities who tend to see the world in terms of black or white, while their Scorpio children are introspective individuals who act upon their feelings, impressions, and instincts. When dealing with an issue, Leos tend to go "straight to the point," while Scorpios use a carefully considered course of action.

Leo parents' strong personalities can sometimes overwhelm their Scorpio children. Those kids can become quite rebellious if Mom and Dad try to make all of the decisions for them, as these water children are just as opinionated as their parents are. Leos, however, tend to be risk-takers, while Scorpios are more cautious. Leo parents need to make their Scorpio kids feel as though their own ideas are important by giving these children a set of options to choose from. Then, these kids will feel that they are making their own decisions.

Leos are enthusiastic fireballs who enjoy the limelight, while Scorpios tend to be more quiet and unassuming. There are those who believe that Leos are self-centered because of their assertive behavior. Leos do have the ability to lead, but this kind of self-confidence does not always reveal their inner sensitivity and their lack of personal security. Leos want people to love them, and they take over because they believe that they are making everyone's lives better. I always tell my Leo clients, "You don't have to change your personality, because you are a strong, enthusiastic motivator who helps many people. You just don't have to try so hard!" However,

I would suggest that they understand the understated, introspective children whom they are living with. Scorpios can be dynamic and dramatic, but their need for public attention takes a back seat when compared to that of their Leo parent.

The Leo Mom/The Scorpio Child

Mom takes care of everything, and she likes to do what's right. Scorpio children will enjoy living with this efficient mother, because like their parents, they feel good when they can live an orderly life. Both have strong instincts and place high expectations on themselves. They like to do things their own way, but they can back off from their own opinions if someone presents them with a better idea. As tots, Scorpios will respond to Mom's protective behavior, but as they grow, they may start to rebel if they feel they cannot be in control of their actions—and both parent and child can both be very stubborn! However, a Leo mom does have the wisdom to teach her child the value of compromise. Mom can also be a big-hearted pushover, because she has a problem saying no to her children when it comes to buying them things. She is an energetic, vital free spirit who can often look the other way when it comes to her own need personal needs. She is easily guilt-tripped and must be careful with her Scorpio children, as they are excellent manipulators. If Mom gives her Scorpio children the freedom to develop their own opinions, she will do herself a big favor. She can be there to guide her Scorpio children while they map out their own lives.

The Leo Dad/The Scorpio Child

Dad is a pussycat who growls, a sweetheart who can sometimes be a bit too fiery. The best way to get to Dad is to be affectionate to him and flatter him. Even a subtle, low-key Leo loves kisses, hugs, and compliments. Don't get me wrong: this Dad is no pushover, especially when it comes to making decisions. He's his own person, and he believes in his talent to lead and motivate others.

Scorpio children will admire Dad's natural self-confidence, as he is more than capable of channeling his energy and self-discipline when he sets his mind to accomplishing any project. His Scorpio kids, though, can have a tendency to underachieve because they can question their ability to succeed. Dad can help them believe in their own talents and use his positive attitude to encourage them to move forward. Leos, like their fire counterparts (Aries and Sagittarius) are builders and dreamers. They fantasize about the possibilities in life, and they enthusiastically create exciting, new projects to work on, which need their leadership and constant attention. Their spontaneity, charisma, and glamour can inspire anyone who is hesitant or fearful of getting involved with them. Scorpios have a different approach—they are silent leaders who know how to carefully and systematically build their empires, whether it's their family's foundation, or a conglomerate.

Dad needs to be honest and direct with his Scorpio children. They will not always think alike, and Dad may have to work on understanding that Scorpio children have their own ideas, and they will resent anyone who expects more of them than they want to give. They will respect Dad's intelligence, and if he gently gives them sound advice, they will listen. Scorpios are self-disciplined, and they know how to go after something when they want it. Dad can be an excellent role model if he can gently encourage his Scorpios to believe in themselves whey they're going after what they want in life!

The Virgo Parent/The Scorpio Child

Virgos are usually perfectionists who tend to overwhelm themselves on a daily basis. They need to get everything right. It is also known that they can't help passing on their high expectations and standards to their children. This can prove to be a difficult situation for Scorpio children. It's not the high expectations and standards that concern them, it's just that they feel frustrated when they're pushed into perfection since they are already pushing themselves to the limit. Once they're taught, Scorpios have no problem understanding how to go after a goal, as long as they're dealing with a subject that piques their interest. I work with teenagers, and I have heard many Scorpios say, "I hate my teacher, she's boring," or "What a dumb subject!" I try to tell them that complaining is a way of getting their feelings out, and it's okay to do so, but there are things in life that we need to learn in order to accomplish our real goals in life.

Virgo parents may not always realize that they can sound insensitive when they give instructions; they have to remember that it's not what you say, but how you say it. For example, instead of saying, "Debbie, I can't stand how you look. That blouse is old and ugly," a Virgo parent could say, "I know that you like that blouse, but I bet that pretty red one you have in your closet would look great with your jeans." Virgo parents sincerely care for their Scorpio children's well-being, and they will always want to take care of everything for them, but they have to remember that these kids take everything personally.

Scorpios are comfortable in a structured home environment, as it presents a safe and secure foundation. Like their Virgo parents, these kids appreciate order, detail, and organization. It's really important, though, for Mom and Dad to recognize the level of their kids' sensitivity and to always let them know that they're loved.

Since both Virgos and Scorpios have a tendency to avoid personal confrontation, Virgo parents must try to be open in their conversations with their Scorpio children in order to help them release their feelings. Many Virgos have a deep spiritual nature, which will definitely be a great aid in understanding the needs of these complex Scorpio kids.

The Virgo Mom/The Scorpio Child

Mom is practical, serious, and very efficient. My mother had a favorite comment when she admired her friend Helen's spotless home. She would always say, "Helen, this place is squeaky clean." If I had been into astrology at the time, I would have known that Helen was a Virgo.

A Virgo mom enjoys keeping her house in order, therefore, she expects her children to participate by keeping their rooms clean and by putting things away after they've been used. This mother runs a tight ship—she has wonderful taste, and her children are always neat, clean, and beautifully dressed.

A Virgo mom is moralistic, and she has sound, healthy values. Her ability to teach her children the importance of taking care of both their home and their belongings is important. She's very interested in raising her children to be polite, as this is part of her need to get everything right. Now, Scorpio children will enjoy looking good in the clothes that Mom buys for them, but they really don't worry about being accepted by others. In fact, they can often be rebels who respect individuality and originality. Therefore, Mom would be wise to understand that her Scorpio children may not always follow her lead exactly when it comes to the social graces. They will, however, admire her stability and the way she knows how to get the best value for her money. Like their Virgo parents, Scorpios do not like to waste anything, and they tend to view anyone who does in a negative light.

Overall, the values of the Virgo mom and her Scorpio children will be compatible in many ways, but I'd like to advise Mom to recognize these children's sensitivity. These kids often need a sympathetic ear, and if there is no one around to listen to them, they'll end up repressing their feelings, which will eventually harm the relationship between mother and child.

The Virgo Dad/The Scorpio Child

Dad is impressed with people who are considered authorities in their field. He tends to judge others through their accomplishments, rather than whether or not they can provide him with emotional support. I know that Dad relates to the materialistic side of life, but he would be wise to remember that he is raising a child who is sensitive and philanthropic. Dad himself is well versed in many subjects, and he's always interested in anyone who's both intelligent and self-confident. He's in constant search of information, as he likes to know what is going on in the world.

There are two types of Virgo fathers: one is perfection oriented, and the other is the artist, who could care less about clothes or being accepted by others socially. No matter what type of personality Dad is, he will be very interested in the power of the mind. Dad really enjoys sharing his knowledge, and he is an excellent teacher. Both he and his Scorpio children will enjoy a special mental affinity, as they can be masters of research and detail. They are also both idealistic and fight for what they believe in. In addition, they share a sense of boundless determination and ambition. The only thing that Dad has to watch out for is becoming too critical or too judgmental. Even though he doesn't mean to, he can hurt his sensitive Scorpio children. And even though Scorpios do not always reveal this sensitivity, they will take anything that comes off as too direct as a personal affront, which can lead to resentment.

All in all, a Virgo father is intelligent, strong, and practical. If he can learn to use a gentle approach when he teaches his Scorpio children, he can easily gain the respect he deserves.

The Libra Parent/The Scorpio Child

We all know that Libras need balance and harmony, and they are at their best when they're surrounded by love and beauty. Their wonderful attributes include grace, poise, charm, and good taste, all of which attract many people. They are also socially adept and refined.

Libras are full of all kinds of talents, yet they tend to be very hard on themselves; they can be their own worst enemies. These intelligent, complex personalities aren't as delicate as they appear, as they often have the ability to take care of everyone's problems. One would think that with Libras' sense of justice, they would understand what fine human beings they are and would give themselves a break. But no—they constantly judge their own behavior. I tell my Libra clients to take a compassionate look at themselves before they decide to characterize what they view as "bad" in their personality.

Libras are extremely receptive to those around them and can be very intuitive about how other people feel. In fact, this ability can sometimes make them feel off balance. Their nerves can get a little raw when they encounter anyone who is very angry or upset. I always recommend a "personal service kit" to my Libras. It's very different from their "personal survival kit." They dig into this survival kit at a young age, and its basic motto is "maintain peace at any price." They assume responsibility for the needs of everyone around them. And this pressure can be exhausting. Libras believe that if they can hide their own needs from the people they love, this will lessen the burden on them. It's almost as though they feel that at some point they did something wrong and that they have to find a way to make up for it. It's really an easy way out. Libras can help themselves by giving themselves the chance to stop overcompensating for everyone, and take care of themselves for once. If Libras don't ask for what they need, they might not get it. It's time to discard the survival kit.

A Libra parent's soft and gentle nature will impress his or her Scorpio child. These air parents really enjoy encouraging self-expression, and a Scorpio will love having this freedom. These parents have a strong "mental antenna," and they are adept at calming the nerves of their intense Scorpio children. Libras want to allow their children to grow in their own way, and a Scorpio child can benefit from the freedom that this quality allows them.

Because Libras always like to strike an ideal balance, they can take time before making important decisions. Scorpio children need strong, decisive parents, and if they believe that Mom and Dad are wishy-washy, these kids can start to lose their trust. If Libra parents can try to work on their fear of making a mistake and believe in their ability to make wise decisions for themselves and others, they can easily win the respect of their Scorpio children.

A Scorpio's first reaction to anything tends to be emotional, while Libras tend to react more intellectually to situations, which means that this parent may have to work a little harder to provide the emotional support that these kids need.

The Libra Mom/The Scorpio Child

A Libra mother usually has one of two ways of presenting herself to the world: delicate or feisty. It all depends upon the amount of love she has received in her life. If Mom was raised in a home where she gave and received a lot of affection, she will be more confident about her opinions and decisions and will be less apt to express frustration. However, if she was raised in a home that didn't honor her sensitivity, she will usually have to work through her pent-up inner anger so that she can build her self-esteem and spirituality. The delicate Libra mom may tend to avoid her own feelings and become subservient to the needs of her family without asking for anything in return. The feisty Libra mother is more outgoing and opinionated. She appears to have a stronger demeanor, but on the inside she's just as soft and sensitive as her "delicate" counterpart.

Libra Mom decorates her home in a way that is meaningful to her, and she enjoys anything that involves artistic and creative expression. Her Scorpio children will find this environment relaxing, but if they were to have their way, they would like to have their rooms filled with old-world furnishings.

Mom wants her children to be both independent and self-reliant, so these kids will be given the freedom to make their own decisions. Scorpio children do need independence, but they also want Mom to be there to protect them when they feel frightened or insecure. Scorpios appear to be a lot more together than they actually are, so they need a lot of attention, and they need to be at the center of the family. But if they feel Mom is not focusing on them to the degree they wish, these kids can become very demanding, and at times Mom can feel overwhelmed by her Scorpio children's intensity. However, if these kids grow up in a home that is both warm and nurturing, they won't feel the need to make unreasonable demands.

The Libra Dad/The Scorpio Child

Dad is a family man who enjoys doing his own thing. He enjoys being married to an efficient woman who likes to run the household. A Libra dad can appear to be quiet and reserved when he's around people who talk a lot, but he can be very stubborn at times, and he likes to be in control of his professional life. He can have a problem opening up when it comes to his feelings; in fact, both he and his Scorpio child are usually understated in their behavior. Dad is sweet and kind, but he would be wise to talk about his emotions, rather than letting them build up to the point of an outburst. Libra men are very sensitive and private people, and if they are hurt by someone, they usually keep these feelings to themselves. When a Libra man refuses to make people accountable for their unacceptable actions, his rage will start to build. I have worked with many Libra males, and they usually fear confronting their anger. But once they accept their sensitivity and decide to stand up for themselves, their self-esteem grows.

Dad is very interested in teaching his children about the world and what it has to offer. Scorpio children will share many wonderful experiences with their Libra father, as he is diplomatic and charming, and people really like him. Dad does enjoy his alone time, though, and his Scorpio child may take this tendency personally. Dad likes to makes important decisions by himself because he feels more confident and comfortable solving his problems in this way. Dad might consider sharing some of his problems with his family, though, as they would be glad to help him. In fact, he will make his family a lot happier if they know they have the opportunity to be of assistance. Dad definitely needs companionship, but he doesn't let that desire get in the way of his freedom.

Dad, like Mom, needs to understand that a Scorpio child can often play devil's advocate and can test one's patience to the limit. Since Dad is excellent at making observations, he can utilize this strength by being considerate and attentive when he sees that his Scorpio child needs his love.

The Scorpio Parent/The Scorpio Child

These parents and their Scorpio children will think alike and feel alike. The only problem that can occur between these two fixed personalities is that they each want to do things in their own way. The Scorpio parents will feel their children's deep emotions and intensity. These kids won't have to demand the attention they need—they'll simply get it.

Scorpio parents and their children will all feel very comfortable in their traditional, organized home. Mom and Dad will encourage and help these kids to develop their talents and ability so that they can reach their fullest potential. All of the practical details of their world will be beautifully handled, and these kids will be properly taken care of. A Scorpio understands another Scorpio's feelings, and in fact, both of them may be a little obsessive. It's up to the parents to learn how to let go of the things they cannot resolve and move on to situations that offer solutions. If they can accomplish this difficult task, they will be able to help their children at an early age.

Mom and Dad may feel like they want to take control over their children's activities, so these Scorpio parents will have to be aware that this behavior can turn these kids into nervous wrecks. If Scorpios were raised in a loving family, they may have learned that excessive control isn't necessary. If they lived with parents who didn't understand them, they can overdo when it comes to being protective. Like their parents, these kids take everything that they do seriously and place very high standards on themselves. And like their children, Scorpio parents may have to learn how to ease up on themselves and allow their bright sense of humor to shine through when things seem out of control.

The Scorpio Mom/The Scorpio Child

Scorpios tend to think that even with the best-laid plans, something is bound to go wrong. So, if both sides of this Scorpio duo perceive life in that way, the results could be disastrous. Mom needs to develop a more positive outlook on life so she can be a good role model for her kids. They will often share the same opinions, as long as their stubborn natures don't overwhelm them. Mom has the ability to motivate her Scorpio children to reach their greatest potential, and she will enthusiastically provide them with any information they need.

It's Mom's responsibility to help her young Scorpios move away from their emotional dramas. These children tend to build their disappointments to a high crescendo, so she needs to help them relax, and forgive and forget.

On the one hand, Scorpios need to be very close to their family and friends, and on the other, they fear making strong attachments to anyone. They do not really relish the prospect of being responsible for themselves because they are afraid of having to deal with the world around them. This trait might surprise a lot of people, but it's true. Scorpios might seem bossy at times, but it's actually their method of self-protection. Each time they get hurt, they remember every slight and build up anger and vengeful feelings inside. As such, Mom needs to help soothe her Scorpio children, making them realize that holding on to their pain will only hinder their progress in life.

Overall, Scorpios are very intelligent and efficient individuals who believe in what they are doing and are often unstoppable in their life quests. They are loyal and reliable, but they need to know that a healthy relationship is not built on caretaking, but on being open and intimate with those whom they love. If Mom has overcome her need to keep everything to herself, she can share her knowledge and experiences with her water children and let them know that sensitivity is not a weakness—it's a way to give and receive love freely in order to reap the happiness they all deserve!

The Scorpio Dad/The Scorpio Child

Dad's goal is to provide a stable and secure foundation for his family. He is happy to offer love and support to his children, although at times, he can be too dogmatic in his opinions and try to take control of his kids' lives. Dad needs to accept the fact that his Scorpio children will be as strong-willed as he is. They may seek his counsel, but in the end, they will want to make their own choices. There are times when Dad will need to back off and let his Scorpio children make their own mistakes in order to learn from them. Children cannot grow into self-confident adults if they feel that their parents are always making all their decisions for them.

Scorpio fathers would be wise to remember that they cannot always protect their children from the outside world. Every child has to face a variety of valuable learning experiences when growing up, so Dad just needs to be there to support these water kids as they go through the trials of life. He can certainly give them advice along the way and show them that he is genuinely interested in their welfare, but he should take care not to impose unrealistic expectations on them.

Most Scorpios are very curious individuals who are ripe for yielding to all sorts of temptations. It's at those times that Dad can help his kids control their urges and show that unhealthy desires can destroy their self-respect. Dad, after all, certainly understands how much his own self-esteem means to him!

The Sagittarius Parent/The Scorpio Child

Here is a parent who has an enthusiastic, dynamic, and self-confident personality. Sagittarius parents can be both traditional and unpredictable at the same time, though. Even though they are solidly grounded when it comes to home and family, they will still want the freedom to explore life in ways that can both challenge and mentally stimulate them. Their real goal is to eventually have an easy life, and most Sagittarians are ready to work hard and earn plenty of money to fulfill this dream. If Sagittarians are both positive and determined when it comes to setting goals for themselves, they can accomplish what they set out to do. They seem to have the ability to turn away disappointment, and to drive themselves until they attain their aims. However, if a Sagittarian lacks self-esteem, he or she can easily fall prey to disappointment. These particular fire parents can hold on to their losses for a long time until they begin to understand that their fear must be replaced with a realistic, practical understanding of how they can go about achieving their goals.

When a free-spirited Sagittarian raises Scorpio children who tend to be more cautious about their own behavior, we could be dealing with a parent/child role reversal.

☆   ☆   ☆

My friend Bob, his daughter Angel, and Angel's girlfriend Betty were going shopping for Angel's prom dress. Bob was singing and making jokes while they were driving, when Angel finally said to him, "Dad, your songs and jokes are getting on my nerves."

He looked at her, grinned, and said, "I'm over 21. I'll sing if I want to. Besides, Betty likes my jokes."

Betty laughed and said, "Of course I do, Mr. Martin."

Angel sneered at her friend, and said, "Dad, I don't think you're funny."

Bob was now getting angry. "Angel, I don't appreciate your lack of respect."

She replied, "Dad, I didn't mean to insult you."

He answered, "Well, you did."

Angel muttered, "I just can't understand why you have to be so silly."

"Silly? What's so silly? I was just singing and telling jokes. What's wrong with that?"

"Nothing, I guess," she admitted, "but you're such a baby."

Bob considered this assessment for a moment and then said, "I'd rather be a baby than a young woman who can't talk about her real feelings."

Angel asked indignantly, "What real feelings?"

Bob told her, "The fact that you're worrying about getting the right dress, that any interruption from anywhere seems to bother you." Angel didn't answer.

"I'm your father, Angel, and you can't control me. It just doesn't work." Angel was now very upset, as she didn't yet realize that she had been getting far too serious about getting the right dress.

Finally, after a few minutes, Angel said to her Dad, "I guess I was getting too intense. I'm sorry." They all laughed, and in the end, Angel bought a beautiful dress.

You see, Bob was a flamboyant, free-spirited Sagittarius, while his daughter Angel was a very serious Scorpio. Angel was trying to parent her father; however, she should have known that her dad would never back down, and that as a Sagittarius, he was definitely his own man!

☆ ☆ ☆

The Sagittarius Mom/The Scorpio Child

Mom is more involved with the household than Dad, and taking care of her children is easy for her. She's a free spirit who provides her children with a fine education and a high set of standards to live by in order to sensibly prepare them for the outside world. She's a wise woman who has the patience to understand her children's individuality, and she will recognize the wisdom of giving them freedom to think on their own. She will also encourage them to express their feelings and to be assertive about them, as she herself would never hesitate to give her opinion on any subject. As is the case with all fire signs, Mom can be very direct and frank in her opinions, and her Scorpio child may take what she says as a personal attack without her even knowing it.

Overall, Mom can be a tough act to follow, and I would like to suggest that she try to understand that her commanding presence can sometimes intimidate her Scorpio children. If Mom remembers to ask for her son's or daughter's opinions before making some of the important decisions in the household, everyone concerned will be pleased to find that they can function as friends, as well as parent and child.

The Sagittarius Dad/The Scorpio Child

Dad is a funny guy, and he loves to associate with people who have a sense of humor. But make no mistake about it, he's also very serious about both his family and his professional life. He works very hard, and he has an extremely stringent work ethic. He likes to take the lead, and he won't be happy working in an environment that feels restricting to him. Dad can be quite opinionated, and when he wants to make a point, he can also be intimidating. However, as is the case with other fire signs, Dad really enjoys it when others have the courage to stand up to him. Dad likes to stay on the positive side of life, and he can have a problem with people who are overly negative or gloomy. At times Dad may appear to exaggerate when he tells one of his "larger than life" stories, but after all, he is a showman.

Scorpio children can be dependent on their Sagittarius dad's strength, as they sense how strong and protective he can be. They will also respect his honesty and good nature. Dad needs to remember that his Scorpio children will feel safe in an environment where there are specific rules to live by, so his free-spirited nature may throw them off guard. Dad's sense of humor is good for his Scorpio children, as they tend to take life a bit too seriously, but he would be wise to help these water kids understand that he is a very loving and protective father.

The Capricorn Parent/The Scorpio Child

Capricorn parents believe that their children deserve their utmost attention. Therefore, they work hard to create a comfortable lifestyle that can help them feel safe and happy. Both Scorpios and Capricorns are similar in their need for a stable and predictable environment, as security is important to both of them. Scorpios won't object to living in a structured home as long as they're allowed to maintain their own individuality. However, they do seek their parents' approval when it comes time to make important decisions. It would be wise for Capricorn parents to understand that they cannot force these children to do what they believe is best for them. This is probably the biggest lesson most Capricorns have had to learn. If they can understand and accept their children's personality and help them to grow into empowered, successful people, they can build and sustain a healthy and wonderful relationship.

Scorpio children are very emotional and sensitive, and they take everything personally. Therefore, Capricorn parents should avoid being too critical or judgmental. Capricorns tend to look at life first from a practical sense, while Scorpios tend to look at situations more emotionally. Capricorns are drawn to deep-feeling people, but they can have a difficult time talking about their own emotions. Instead, they tend to demonstrate their love for their family by taking wonderful care of them. Scorpios will enjoy being taken care of, but they do need their parents to display some warmth and affection. Capricorn parents need to make an effort to be more demonstrative so that their Scorpio children will know that they really care. These kids' sensitivity is a great source of strength for them, and their survival instincts are powerful.

Overall, Capricorns and Scorpios get along very well, as both enjoy a stable existence, where organization and concrete plans form the basis for their daily lives.

The Capricorn Mom/The Scorpio Child

Mom can either be domestic, or she can be president of a company—the choice is hers. It really doesn't matter which path Mom decides on, her family will always be first. She'll always want to protect her children from suffering, although she may have to lower her own "emotional defenses" in order to take the best care of her sensitive water kids. Both Capricorns and Scorpios have a great deal in common, as they both became wise at an early age. Their childhoods will always remain deep inside them, and what happens to them as adults will be based on the pictures they mentally paint for themselves as children. Both also tend to keep any sadness to themselves, although this parent/child combo could draw great strength from each other if they talked about their feelings. A few hugs and kisses between them wouldn't hurt either.

Mom will teach her children all of the social graces in life. These kids will be well behaved, well dressed, and sophisticated. Scorpios are not averse to this kind of training, as long as their sense of freedom is never stifled. If Mom becomes too demanding, she may find that her little Scorpios may argue strenuously for their own individuality.

The Capricorn Dad/The Scorpio Child

Dad is a practical and sensible man, but he is not comfortable when he is not in control. It's almost impossible for him to ask anyone for advice, since he has a tendency to distrust anyone but himself. It seems as though Dad was brought into the world older and wiser than most. Therefore, he is surrounded by an aura of sadness, and it doesn't matter whether it was predestined or self-created. His humor is dry, and his appearance is usually somewhat reserved. His devotion to both family and profession demands all of his time.

Dad and his Scorpio children are similar in their approach to life because they both need to live an organized and structured lifestyle. They are both practical, disciplined, efficient, and self-reliant. Details are paramount because they both want to complete their projects and leave everything in perfect order.

Scorpio children are very emotional and sensitive, even if they don't talk about their emotions. They are easily hurt, so they need to be raised in an understanding and reasonable manner. Even though they may appear to be defensive when their feelings are injured, they do require a lot of attention, so they will want Dad to listen to them and help them decide what to do about their issues and problems.

Dad is happy to take care of his children's practical needs, but he has a hard time demonstrating his feelings. My experience has shown me that Capricorns are not particularly affectionate, but when they raise sensitive Scorpios, they have to be attentive to them by appreciating and complimenting their efforts. In addition, Dad needs to offer reasonable explanations when it comes to decisions that concern these kids. Dad is an intuitive man, and his first impressions are usually accurate.

He can truly be an inspiration to his water children, as he can help them set their goals and work hard to make them a reality.

Both Dad and his children are opinionated, and they are not necessarily open-minded. Therefore, it is best for Dad to initiate practical discussions about situations that need to be resolved. He needs to be honest and straightforward in his approach, and this behavior will encourage his Scorpio kids to trust him. Scorpios do not trust people easily, but Dad's ability to make them feel safe and secure provides a solid basis for a mutually satisfying relationship.

The Aquarius Parent/The Scorpio Child

Aquarians are logical and independent free spirits. They base their lives on a desire to find mental affinity with others, as they function through their intellect. Scorpios, on the other hand, usually work through their gut reactions, and their first response to things is usually on a more emotional level. Aquarians are born independent and self-reliant. They tend to flex their intellectual muscles at an early age. Freedom is at the core of their being, and they are usually involved in humanitarian efforts. Aquarians are extraordinarily intelligent, and many become famous. If we think of Abraham Lincoln, Franklin Delano Roosevelt, and Ronald Reagan, we can quickly have an understanding of how complex these air parents can be.

Aquarians must function at their own high rate of speed, and parents need to be careful about trying to place rigid restrictions on them. They will close their minds to anyone who holds them back, and in fact, this situation will only contribute to making them more shy and reserved then they already are. As Aquarians grow, they begin to understand their outstanding capacity to reach people all over the world, since they have a keen sense of human nature. Aquarians and Scorpios can both be devil's advocates, but while an Aquarian tends to be cool and low key, a Scorpio tends to be more emotionally intense.

Aquarians are liberal parents who raise their children with an easygoing approach to life. Aquarian parents will encourage their Scorpio children's individuality, which will allow them to form their own opinions and make their own decisions. Most Aquarians never believe that their children should stick by the book when it comes to following any social trends. The motto is: Be your own person, and enjoy it. They feel they have a social responsibility to all human beings, and that they must be there to ease their pain. In fact, if they tend to concentrate too much on the world outside their family, they can inadvertently neglect the needs of those closest to them. Scorpios also have strong opinions when it comes to human nature. When they decide that they're right, they will fight anyone who cannot see the truth. While Aquarian parents need peace, independence, and harmony, Scorpio children are more like steamrollers who are attracted to adventure and passion.

The Aquarian Mom/The Scorpio Child

Mom is a reliable lady who will do anything for her children. She teaches them the importance of being decent human beings who don't fall prey to hostile behavior. Scorpio children will have very high expectations of themselves and those around them. When they believe someone is unfair, they can be quite nasty. An Aquarian mother may have to teach her Scorpio children that people are vulnerable, and that you sometimes need to give them the benefit of the doubt. She may have a problem getting a positive response from her Scorpio children, though, as they can be very opinionated. However, it's important for her to maintain her stance in this regard in order to teach young Scorpio that people are not always completely right or completely wrong—the truth is usually somewhere in between.

Scorpio children are very bright, and they need a parent who can encourage them to diversify their interests, as they are creative people who can be innovative in their thinking. An Aquarian mother will never discourage creativity or the ability to introduce something new to the world. She is a progressive visionary, and she has the ability to apply a clear and logical perspective to most situations in life, which helps her to objectively make decisions. Young Scorpio can learn a lot from Mom's approach. One area that both parent and child may have to work on, though, is personal communication. This is often the case of a thinker who lives with a feeler.

I would suggest to Mom that she recognize the very serious, sensitive, and emotional nature of her Scorpio child. It would be wise for her to use her diplomatic skills to deal with this child's intense emotional nature. "The mind" is usually an Aquarian mom's concentration when she raises her children, but when a Scorpio lives in her house, it's the heart that counts. An Aquarian mother is more accustomed to processing things in a logical way, but it's up to her to find a balance when raising her little Scorpio. Scorpios do not feel comfortable when their lives are totally surrounded by logic and intellect. They need an parent who will empathize with them as needed. Since Aquarian mothers will do just about anything to make their children happy, they shouldn't have any trouble functioning in this loving and caring manner.

The Aquarius Dad/The Scorpio Child

Dad has strong beliefs when it comes to both his attitudes and values. He won't change his mind unless he believes that someone has intelligently convinced him to modify his views. He likes being a unique individual and tends to resent anyone who tells him he *must* do something. Dad is also a family-oriented guy, but he expects his family to respect his need for privacy. Basically, he's a loner who only comes out of his cocoon when necessary.

Scorpio children need structure and organization to balance their lives. They tend to be very hard on themselves. As such, they need to be loved and appreciated, although they fear making strong attachments to anyone. They do believe in family, like their Aquarius dad, though, and enjoy sharing experiences with him.

Dad is usually very bright, and he will be well versed in many subjects. Therefore, young Scorpio can learn a lot from him. All in all, though, parent and child are different in their approach to life. A Scorpio is emotional and involved, while an Aquarian is logical and distant. Dad's sensible nature can be very helpful in calming his Scorpio child's nervous anxiety, as he has the ability to provide reasonable, objective explanations for his behavior.

Most Scorpio children are full of energy and action. They work very hard to attain their goals, and they have infinite patience. They do like to have things their own way, so they can be difficult when opposed. However, Dad is an independent and self-reliant sort who can easily earn young Scorpio's respect. An Aquarian father is no pushover! His tolerance and penchant for fair play sets a good example for his water child.

The Pisces Parent/The Scorpio Child

Pisces parents can easily bond with their Scorpio children, since the two of them are both sensitive water signs. Pisces parents place high expectations on themselves, and they can be the most critical people they know, especially when it comes to their *own* behavior. This presents a real dichotomy, because these idealistic people tend to dislike criticism of any kind. So why are they are so hard on themselves? I believe the real answer comes from the fact that they want to see the best in everyone, and wonder whether or not they're living up to their own ideals. Pisces parents have excellent intuitive instincts, and they may have to just learn to ease up on themselves. In addition, they also have to remember not to get lost in a world of approval seeking, where they are constantly living up to the expectations of others. Pisces are creative, intuitive, and loving people who have to find realistic ways of making their *own* dreams come true.

Pisces want to be good parents, and they will try to nurture all of their children's needs. They just have to be aware that their Scorpio children may test their patience by compulsively asking them for things. It's at this time that it would be wise for these parents to defend themselves. It's called saying NO. If Pisces parents stand by their decisions, their Scorpio children will listen. Pisces parents can help ease their own anxieties by understanding that their children tend to overwhelm themselves at an early age. In addition, these children will tend to back off from asking for things as soon as they discover that these water parents are sensitive to their feelings. As small children, Scorpios have very little release for their feelings until they can offer support to other people.

The Pisces Mom/The Scorpio Child

Mom is usually a soft, sensitive woman. She loves children because she herself is a child at heart. A Pisces mom wants to be as original as possible when it comes to how she does things; however, a part of her also wants to be traditional because she doesn't want to be isolated from the rest of the world. Therefore, she will enjoy raising her children in a traditional home, and she will teach them to behave properly so they can be accepted by others. Many Pisces are overwhelmed by the realities of life, and they are continually adjusting their dreams to fit the outside world.

Mom may feel the need to take control of her own environment; as such, she will follow a precise course of action so she won't make mistakes. She would be wise to recognize and accept her sensitivity so that she won't have to pay the price of suffering from nervous anxiety. A Scorpio needs a sensitive parent, and a Pisces mom certainly fits the bill. Mom needs to give herself permission to be affectionate and loving, because her Scorpio will relish this behavior. Mom will try not to embarrass her Scorpio children or insult their intelligence. She will be there when her children need her. Young Scorpios will begin to test Mom's intelligence at an early age, as they will want to know if she's both strong and smart. Mom is definitely smart, but she may have to learn that she needs to believe in her own strength.

It's important for these mothers to explain to their Scorpio children their reasons for punishment or discipline, as young Scorpios will feel insecure if they don't understand *why* they've done something wrong. The best way to build a healthy relationship between this parent and child is through Mom's ability to stand behind her decisions, so she will gain the respect that she so desires.

The Pisces Dad/The Scorpio Child

Dad and his Scorpio children take an indirect approach to their personal lives. They work around their feelings because their own emotions make them uneasy and unsure of themselves. Scorpios know how to handle their professional lives; but they do not feel comfortable confronting people in their personal lives in a straightforward manner. They can go through the side door in order to avoid a head-on collision. Pisces fathers also do not enjoy dealing with personal confrontation if they can help it. Since both Scorpios and Pisces are very emotional people, it would be wise for this Pisces father to understand that if he does not try to face up to the important issues that arise between himself and his Scorpio child, the relationship between parent and child may not be an honest one. Scorpio children believe in truth and the importance of family. It won't be very hard for this dad to make the effort to be up front at all times, though, as his natural affinity with this child is very strong.

Dad is a romantic figure, as he's usually very charming, gracious, generous, and loving. His girls adore him because they tend to idealize him. His sons, however, may have a problem with respect, if he is not always honest with them. Dad and his Scorpio child are both very sensitive, and Dad needs to recognize how easily an argument can ensue when a conversation involves two very intense people. We know that Scorpio children can be very stubborn when it comes to their opinions. Therefore, Dad must let his water kids know that there are limits to his endurance. Scorpio children need to be told that there are boundaries, and this is the best way for a parent to earn their respect. Pisces and Scorpios have a great deal of love to give each other, as long as Dad prepares himself to realistically verbalize what he expects from these kids.

☆   ☆   ☆

My friend Derek's son Steve had been an aspiring actor for a long time, and Derek was paying for his rent, his car, and all of the expenses that weren't covered by his infrequent part-time jobs. One evening, Derek and I were sitting in his living room, waiting to go to dinner with Steve, when the phone rang. Derek looked at me and said, "I know it's Steve. Something's come up, and he wants us to wait for him."

Derek picked up the phone and talked to Steve for a few minutes, then he hung up and told me, "Would you believe that he's at his girlfriend's house, and she's doing his laundry?"

I asked, "Is he coming over, or should we leave?"

Derek answered, "Steve said he'd call me back when he's finished."

I then asked, "Do you know his girlfriend's phone number?" He nodded. "Well, don't you think that you should call him back and tell him that we're leaving? I don't know about you, but I'm hungry, and we've been waiting for an hour."

He asked hesitantly, "Do you think that I should?"

"Derek," I said forcefully, "I'm not going to make this decision for you, but your son should know that you have a life, and he can't take advantage of you."

He admitted, "I know. It's my fault. I always wind up waiting until I really get angry, and then we have an argument."

"Then why does he continue to do this?" I asked him.

"Because I let him get away with it."

"Well, Derek, you know it's up to you, but your son will never understand that there are limits to what you will take if you let him take advantage of you."

Derek made up his mind, and said, "I'm going to call him and tell him we're leaving, and after this is over, I am finally going to sit down and have a talk with him."

After a moment, I asked him, "Are you scared?"

He replied, "Of course I am, but I know you're right."

"Derek, it doesn't matter whether I'm right or wrong. Your relationship with your son is good, but he does have a tendency to walk all over you."

He said, "I know. Well, it's about time. I've wanted to talk to him for a while, anyway. I'm not getting any younger."

My friend Derek, who is a Pisces, was around 55 years old at the time, and his son Steve, a Scorpio, had just turned 30. It had taken him all those years to tell his son that his feelings counted, too.

After their talk, Steve learned to have greater respect for his father. Derek learned that it's never too late to communicate honestly with your children. Eventually, Derek gave up acting, became a writer, and dedicated his first book to his father.

SUMMARY

I believe that creativity is a very healthy outlet for a Scorpio's energy. Parents who provide their kids with this opportunity can help ease their inner tension. I have many clients who have told me that painting, sculpture, ceramics, knitting, and music has saved their lives when their nervous anxiety got out of control.

Scorpio children accomplish a great deal in life, as long as they can continue to focus on their intelligence, perseverance, healing abilities, and most important, their truthful nature. Parents need to work on teaching these kids that it's important to see all sides of a situation before making a judgment. They believe they can recognize all problems in an instant and cannot understand why someone else isn't able to handle the situation. Scorpios are very patient when they want to succeed, but they get very irritable when someone makes a mistake. Trust me, they are as hard on themselves as they are on others—anything beyond one mistake deserves a severe reprimand! Parents need to help their little perfectionists learn that people have their own way of doing things. Their patterns may be different, but they can still do an excellent job.

These Scorpio water kids are very sensitive, and they are easily hurt. They may pretend that nothing can faze them, but this is their way of protecting themselves from intimacy and personal confrontation. It may take a while to get Scorpios to talk about their feelings because they do not trust anyone (even Mom and Dad) with their emotions. This task may be the biggest challenge of any parent's life. However, once Scorpio children trust you, their loyalty can be etched in stone!

"I do not feel any age yet.
There is no age to the spirit."
— Anonymous

Chapter Nine

....

✗ SAGITTARIUS THE ARCHER

NOVEMBER 22–DECEMBER 21   **ELEMENT:** Fire   **KEY PHRASE:** "I see"

....

THE SAGITTARIUS PERSONALITY

Most Sagittarians are marked by their spirit. Their soulful eyes reveal a deep sensitivity. There are usually two types of Sagittarians: one is the healer, and the other is the corporate executive. The healers need to nurture the wounds of those who suffer. They can be doctors, nurses, or therapists, all of whom have an instinct for knowing what's wrong. The corporate executives, who can also be spiritual in their own right, welcome challenge and competition, as they strive to bring their idealistic philosophies to the marketplace.

Sagittarians can be devoted workaholics or world travelers. "I see" is their key phrase, and they are visionaries who are always looking for ways to expand their horizons. They need the freedom to investigate and explore, whether it's a different form of civilization or some mysterious castle. Most people like Sagittarians because they are both friendly and very funny. Their positive attitude and sense of humor helps them overcome whatever difficulties they face in life—they always believe that there's a light at the end of the tunnel!

☆ ☆ ☆

It was around eight o'clock in the evening when my friend Lois called me and said, "Sylvia, I'm worried about Alex. He and Stanley left this morning to go see some kind of biological exhibit at the Field Museum, and he isn't home yet." Alex was Lois's seven-year-old son, and Stanley was his little school friend.

I asked her, "Did everyone get on the school bus?"

She replied, "Yes, they left at 8:00 A.M."

I then asked, "What time were they supposed to be home?"

"Well, it's about eight o'clock now, and they were supposed to be home at five."

"Did you call Stanley's mom?"

Lois replied, "Yes, and she hasn't heard from them either."

I then suggested, "Why don't you wait a little longer. Didn't their teacher go with them?"

"Yes, I think so..." Then, all of a sudden I heard Lois shout, "Alex, where have you been?" She got back on the line and said, "I'll call you back."

The phone rang about a half an hour later, and it was little Alex. "Aunt Sylvia," he told me, "I'm okay. Boy, did we have a great day. It was an adventure."

I asked curiously, "What happened?"

"Well," he explained, "the bus broke down, and we had to stay in there until they fixed it. A lot of the other kids were scared, but I thought it was great."

I asked, "Couldn't they get to a telephone?"

He laughed. "I guess not. Don't worry, I was making everyone laugh. I told a lot of jokes, and then I had everyone singing songs. Oh, and then, one of the girls started to complain. And I told her, 'Listen, stop complaining, we'll be home soon.'"

I said, "Well, I'm very glad everything's okay. Let me speak to your mother." Lois got back on the line, and I asked her, "Are you okay?"

She responded with relief, "Yes, another scary situation saved by my very courageous little boy. I think I'm going to take lessons from that kid. He has a great outlook on life."

Alex is a very special Sagittarius, and I have always adored him. His optimism is contagious, and he didn't get scared when the bus broke down because he knew that it would be fixed and that in the end, they'd all be safe and sound!

☆ ☆ ☆

Happy or Sad—There's No In-Between!

Most Sagittarians are outgoing, optimistic go-getters who are determined to get their ideas across, despite any obstacles in their path. They're the ultimate promoters, and they can sell milk to a cow. They win people's attention by presenting themselves as individuals who can improve their lives. They always believe in what they say, so why wouldn't anyone else believe in them, too? I call them the "lovable con artists of the world." They rarely seem embarrassed or awkward, and even when they're trying to do something for the first time, they give you the impression that what they've just done takes very little effort. They also usually appear to be very easygoing, which helps minimize any element of tension or strain from a situation. I guess you could say that they know how to work an audience. Sammy Davis Jr. and Frank Sinatra, two very famous Sagittarians, certainly did!

Sagittarian children create wonderful play worlds for themselves, and as adults, they strive to find a balance between their dreams and cold, hard reality. Since these kids are very intense and nervous on the inside, it's important that they grow up in an environment where they can feel "grounded." They need to live in a stable, happy home where peace and tranquility prevail. This environment will give them a place where they can take the time to relax and ease their anxiety. Even though these kids appear free from worry, it's simply not true. They actually tend to avoid dealing with the more emotional and sensitive sides of their nature, as this proclivity makes it easier for them to take on the harsh realities of life.

Even though many Sagittarians can appear to be "larger than life," it's important to realize that on the inside, many of them feel very shy and suffer great sadness. They have very deep feelings and, as a result, try to avoid intense emotional commitments. The thought of letting real love enter their lives scares them. They also have to avoid becoming obsessed over anything that feels negative because this behavior affects their self-confidence. My advice to parents of these complex Sagittarian kids is to keep them on a positive track. Whenever a negative situation occurs, Mom and Dad should try to come up with positive solutions to solve the problem. It's very important to teach these kids how to transform an unpleasant scenario into a positive one. If they are taught this valuable lesson when they are children, they will carry this philosophy with them throughout their lives!

My friend Joanie's son Jake (a Sagittarian) was a nice young man, and I had known him for a long time. He went to the University of Southern California while my son was attending UCLA, so Joanie and I decided to visit the boys for a week. Joanie told me that Jake's personal life was troubling him because he had just broken up with his last girlfriend. I said to her, "You know, Joanie, Jake is very personable, he's charming and a good-looking young man, but there's always been an inner shyness about him, and something makes me feel like he's a little sad."

She nodded and admitted, "I know." She took a long breath. "Maybe you could talk to him when we see him at school." Joanie and I called Jake, and we met him in his dormitory room. As I walked into his room, I almost collapsed. I looked up to see a noose hanging from the ceiling. I thought Joanie was going to faint.

I exclaimed, "Jake, what in the world is a noose doing hanging from the ceiling?!"

He answered, "I don't know. I've always been fascinated with nooses, so I put it there as part of the decor."

"Jake," I said quietly, "you definitely have a dark side." He laughed, but I didn't think what I'd said was that funny. Both his mother and I had a long talk with him about the ex-girlfriend, and he seemed to feel better. Before we left, he asked if he could call me in case he felt the need to talk to a counselor. I agreed, and for the next few weeks, we talked on the phone many times, and I offered him suggestions on how to stop obsessing over everything in his life. I suggested that he start by trying to recognize his need to create drama in his life, turning even the simplest problems into momentous, operatic tragedies. He had a tendency to obsess over all of the details of a situation until he wore himself out. He used this obsession as a way to punish himself every time he made a wrong decision, and by doing so, he was blocking his natural talents and abilities. Both his grades and general productivity were much lower than his potential.

Jake worked on these problems for a long time, and he has learned to let go of the things he can't solve. And now, he's much happier. I believe his decision to fight his obsessive nature has helped him to come out a winner!

☆ ☆ ☆

"Keep Me on My Toes, and Keep Me Laughing!"

Young Sagittarians have an unrestrained, high level of energy. There's a lot of excitement and enthusiasm when they're around. They can be hunters who are always searching curiously for the next adventure, or explorers, who can ransack the house in 15 minutes. They're quick little devils who enjoy living life to its fullest.

As children, Sagittarians will start by attempting smaller ventures, like emptying all of the cabinets or the closets. But of course, to them, it's really the "big exploration" that counts. Sagittarians look for excitement and challenge at every turn in the road. They're restless travelers who refuse to sit around and be bored.

Parents would be wise to understand that a Sagittarius child's overwhelming energy may not be easy to control. These kids tend to be both mischievous and curious, always looking for a place to apply their energies. As these kids grow up, they need to be taught the concept of limits and boundaries in order to understand that they cannot rummage through everything in life. Parents should be careful not to dampen these children's free spirit and zest for life, though, as these special qualities give them the courage and motivation to accomplish their goals.

Sagittarians search for love and laughter throughout their lives. They tend to pick friends or partners who are both smart and funny. Parents must be aware that raising them in an environment with too many restrictions will stifle their free spirit. They need their independence. And without it, they tend to leave home early, or underachieve in their school work. However, with the freedom to explore, they can enthusiastically seek out wonderful new opportunities, set specific goals, and attain success in school. Of course, they'll need to lighten their load through athletic activities or comedy, though.

It's Their Personal Style!

It's not about the fashionable clothes they wear, and it has nothing to do with the car they drive...so what makes these fire signs so compelling? You guessed it— it's their personal style! Sagittarians' style is reflected in both their charisma and good taste. They love to live the elegant life, and their grace, poise, and creativity give them an effervescent glow that never seems to fade away. Their surroundings are usually neat and clean; in fact, a Sagittarius woman's home is usually filled with beautiful flowers, which reflect her love for nature and beauty.

Sagittarians have an exceptional ability to secure other people's devotion and loyalty. They're usually not intimidating figures, and it's easy to follow their lead. But...beyond a Sagittarian's easygoing personality lurks a very sharp man or woman who definitely knows how to get what he or she wants. There are times when Sagittarians can be driven by ego, and they can get a little overzealous in their determination to succeed, but they are ambitious, intelligent, and sophisticated, and they tend to try to reach beyond their limits in order to find new and exciting challenges. At times, they can appear cool and distant when they're trying to go after an important goal, though, as they may feel that getting emotionally involved will get in their way. Parents would be wise to help their Sagittarian children understand that it's not necessary to overcompensate, because their intelligence, sensitivity, and natural instincts are what will help them achieve their greatest and most difficult accomplishments.

Sagittarians who are in touch with both their spirituality and sensitivity are also hardworking and successful; however, they feel that love is the most important achievement in their lives. They're the ones who have a soft, outer glow that is always evident in their faces. Sagittarians are also known to be able to party with the best of 'em—these fire kids can be likened to a strobe light...staggering the mind and the eyes!

It's My Mind, My Space, and My Body That Count!

"I need to learn, have my own space, and keep fit. After all, it's my mind, my freedom, and my body that count!" When Sagittarians feel confident and free to explore the world, they'd be content to wander until they've seen it all. Parents who raise these children should understand that they have a great need for knowledge, a secure home, and physical activity. Young Sagittarians will also have a natural affinity toward cleanliness and organization. That doesn't mean, however, that they won't need to be motivated to complete household chores or to participate in family projects. It's important that they understand the most basic and necessary lessons in life.

When they first start school, they tend to reject the idea of a formal education. It takes some adjustment for them, as they are usually restless and easily bored. As they grow, parents may have to continually explain to them why it's necessary to attend classes with regularity. These explanations can help them understand that if they can initially try to concentrate on the required subjects and get them out of the way, they will then be able to take the subjects that interest them.

Sagittarians can be vain when it comes to looking good, and these fire kids are also oriented toward physical fitness—they usually *love* sports! In fact, many feel a need to remain physically active all of their lives. Many Sagittarians love to eat, and may become gourmet cooks; however, if they refuse to eliminate the rich food and desserts from their diets, they can tend to be overweight. (If they care more about how they look than about what they eat, though, they'll be sure to stick to the right foods.) It would be wise for parents to introduce these fire kids to a nutritional diet as they grow up, while throwing in some goodies from time to time.

PARENT AND CHILD

The Aries Parent/The Sagittarius Child

Aries parents and their Sagittarius children are an optimistic, self-confident combination. They're emotionally and intellectually compatible. They have an honest and direct approach to life, and in addition, they can be a little self-centered. These signs will enjoy living together as long as Aries parents can control their need to try to dominate their kids' lives. Sagittarians are free spirits with minds of their own. They can also be pretty stubborn, and they won't react well to overly protective parents. Sagittarius children will easily respond to their Aries parents' attentive natures; however, these parents may have to be careful not to compete with their kids.

Sagittarius children are usually positive because no matter what happens, "tomorrow will be a better day"! Aries fire parents agree with this philosophy because without hope, their lives seem meaningless. Aries parents continue to search for things to stimulate their minds. Their fire children will be happy to join in the fun, as they too want to learn everything. Both parents and child are both very spontaneous, therefore, it would be useless for these parents to try and impose their will on these children. This fire combination tends to only deal with what's right and what's wrong, leaving the middle of the road to someone else.

This duo is emotional; they need love in their lives, and they both have a lot to give. It's important for Aries parents to know that their free-spirited children will need more space than they do. They cannot encroach on this space, or these kids will rebel. There is a lot of intellectual compatibility between parent and child, and they will learn from each other, but Aries parents need to help their young Sagittarians overcome their compulsive natures. They tend to scatter their energies. This behavior can hurt their professional lives and lead them into the wrong relationships. These children suffer from pushing themselves to the limit, and this is the time when they can get moody. These parents need to teach them to pull back before they exhaust themselves. They don't have to do everything NOW! Sagittarius children, in particular, are so intense that they definitely need the peace that playtime can offer.

Sagittarius children tend to live in their own world. If they happen to get on the wrong track, they resent anyone who tries to interfere. These kids will respect their fire parents, and they, more than most, have the ability to influence them.

Sagittarius children need an abundance of challenge in their lives. They blindly enter into the wrong situations or relationships because they are difficult to conquer. Many of my clients tell me, "I'm not afraid of anything!"

I tell them, "You may not be afraid of a challenge, but you are afraid of risking your feelings." Sagittarius children cherish their freedom, and their fire parents have no problem letting them go, but they just need to help them focus on building their emotional stability, or they may never grow up!

The Aries Mom/The Sagittarius Child

An Aries mother is a builder who can't be stopped when it comes to going after her dreams. She's an energetic, bright woman who has the ability to live her own life, create her own interests, and raise wonderful children. She's proud of her kids, believing that it's her responsibility to take special care of both their mental and physical needs. Typically, she won't be an advocate of setting down strict rules and regulations for her children to follow. Her Sagittarius children are quite comfortable with this approach, as they need to have as much freedom as Mom does. Also, Sagittarius children will usually trust their Aries mother to stick to her word, and they will appreciate her quick thinking and decision-making abilities.

Mom needs attention and recognition from the public. However, she can be quite direct when she needs to get her point across, and she may find that certain people may take what she says too personally. In fact, she'd rather have someone be truthful with her, as this is the behavior she exhibits with others. Of course, Sagittarius children would never be offended by Mom's demeanor, as they will grow up to be very much like her. It's important, however, for Mom to understand that she can hurt an overly sensitive person if she comes off in too blunt a fashion. She's usually harsh when she loses her patience, but once she tries to rectify this problem, she can help her child understand that being *too* direct with someone can be tactless.

The Aries Dad/The Sagittarius Child

Aries fathers possess a lot of confidence. Dad has an inner strength, and his Sagittarius child will value him as both a leader and confidant. He will have the ability to advise his children as to how to direct and focus their excessive energy into being productive, either academically or athletically or both. These dads have as much energy as their children, and like their fire kids, they will not tolerate any restrictions of their own freedom. This parent/child combo is a solid team because, essentially, they are on the same wavelength. Dad, however, can appear to be somewhat rigid and too concerned with self-discipline. He may also have a difficult time verbalizing the sensitive side of his personality. While it is important to maintain self-discipline when trying to achieve a goal, Dad may have to learn that it is wise to reveal his feelings to his Sagittarius children. This will create an emotional bond that cannot be broken. Honest and open communication will make this relationship unshakable!

The Taurus Parent/The Sagittarius Child

Taurus parents will do *anything* to protect their families. They tend to have very possessive natures. In fact, each important investment they make, whether it be financial or emotional, becomes valuable property. Their key phrase, "I have," is their declaration of a need for both safety and security. Once they love something, they may never give it up, even it means sacrificing their own happiness. They're cautious and prudent people who can find making personal changes very difficult. So how do they handle a free-spirited, spontaneous Sagittarius child who gets bored *without* constant change? Acceptance, limits, and boundaries are the answers, but it won't be easy. If Taurus parents can accept the fact that these kids often ride in on a tidal wave, they'll be prepared for anything. However, they have to realize that the only thing that balances a tidal wave is the earth below it. Earthy Taurus parents will provide the stability that these active Sagittarius children need.

These fire kids are sweet and loving, and they have the ability to charm Taurus parents into doing exactly what they want. Sagittarius children will benefit from their Taurus parents' stable and protective nature, and Mom and Dad will enjoy their kids' positive, good-humored approach to life. These children believe in the goodness of the world, and this upbeat quality can't help but affect those in their world. Taureans, however, can be worldly cynics, and they have to be careful not to inadvertently pass along these beliefs to their Sagittarius children. Dampening a fire child's spirit is the worst thing a parent can do to him or her!

The Taurus Mom/The Sagittarius Child

Mom is ready and willing to provide the kind of security that her young Sagittarius children need. She'll love to carry her fire kids around with her when they are little, and you can be sure that Sagittarius sons and daughters will be right behind Mom as they grow. Mom adores these small bundles of humor and joy, as Sagittarius kids are very easy to love. In fact, most young Sagittarians will have Mom in the palms of their little hands. A stable Taurus mom can easily provide the free-spirited, sensible lifestyle that Sagittarius children enjoy. These fire kids' nerves will be calmed by a stable, pleasant home environment where they are allowed to express their ideas. It's important that Mom allows them to develop their sensitive natures through creative projects.

Mom can be a moralist, concerned with teaching her children good manners. She believes in making sure that her children are accepted by others. Sagittarians don't mind subscribing to rules, but these fire kids have a quality of eccentricity that will always influence their behavior.

Many Taurus women and men have a tendency to dissect everything they do, in both their personal and professional lives. They want to be perfect, and they tend to put themselves down for whatever little things they *don't* do, rather then give themselves credit for the good things that they *do* accomplish. This kind of introspection can unnecessarily thwart Mom's self-confidence and self-esteem. I suggest that Mom believe in herself and her talents. Taurus mothers have a special blend of both the sensible and the creative. It's very important for her to work on having an optimistic viewpoint, as she wouldn't want to do anything to magnify her Sagittarius child's sorrowful side.

The Taurus Dad/The Sagittarius Child

The Taurus dad who allows himself to be both sensitive and creative can be a fine influence on his Sagittarius child. There are Taurus men whose backgrounds have taught them to believe that self-control is what helps them to be successful. These men often lose track of the creative free spirit inside them, which, if applied, could propel them to even greater success. The Taurus dad who does allow his light-hearted inner child to shine, though, can be quite compatible with Sagittarius children. If Dad remains too controlled, he can end up inhibiting these kids, as their creative freedom is essential to their mental and physical health. Taureans and Sagittarians love art, music, and writing—they are inspired by anything creative. Dad and his children can easily bond in these areas if Dad is able to let his spirit soar.

Dad and his Sagittarian children will also love nature and sports. They will enjoy taking long walks in the park together, where they will delight in playing games and creating adventures. In fact, Dad can begin to share his love of sports with his Sagittarius son or daughter at an early age. A Taurus dad has the ability to fulfill most of this child's needs if he just allows himself to be open, sensitive, and practical.

The Gemini Parent/The Sagittarius Child

Geminis are not conventional parents. Like their Sagittarius children, they enjoy change and adventure. Overall, Gemini parents and their Sagittarius children have much in common, including a need for freedom and a desire to develop the intellect. While this parent and child are compatible in many ways, the difference between the two is that a Gemini reacts to the world from a logical point of view, while a Sagittarius tends to react to things more emotionally. It's not easy for Geminis to express their feelings, as their main concentration is usually on how to improve their minds. A Gemini naturally avoids interpersonal communication.

If Sagittarius children feel that their Gemini parents aren't listening to how they feel, they may start to keep their emotions to themselves. Remember, Sagittarians view emotion as the weak link in their personality, and they try to hide their feelings from others. My experience with my Sagittarius clients has shown me that this predilection can hurt their relationships. My advice to Gemini parents is to encourage open lines of communication at all times. Sagittarius children need to trust a parent with their thoughts and feelings. It's important that Gemini parents patiently listen and respond intelligently to what these kids have to say.

When Gemini parents raise Sagittarius children, they always need to provide them with reasonable, honest answers, and allow them to be privy to a wide range of educational outlets. But while these Sagittarius children do love to learn, they also yearn for intimacy in life, and a lack of it can be frustrating for them. I suggest that Mom and Dad make an effort to really work on understanding their children's feelings.

A wonderful way for this parent and child to bond is through any kind of creative expression. I believe that Geminis teach us about emotion through their love of music—think about Cole Porter, Marvin Hamlisch, Barry Manilow, Henry Mancini, and Judy Garland—all Geminis!

The Gemini Mom/The Sagittarius Child

At first, Mom may not define a specific set of household rules for her Sagittarius children, but she will be instrumental in helping them develop and enhance their minds. I'd like to suggest, however, that Mom think about creating some sort of guidelines for these kids. Even though Sagittarius children are free spirits, they still need to understand the importance of responsibility and self-discipline. Without it, they can lose focus and determination, and wind up underachieving.

A Gemini mother will be delighted when her children start to communicate with her. Most Sagittarian children understand what is being said to them—even at an early age. Some of these kids also talk early, but most are involved in physical activity. These kids usually wait until they're three or more to begin clearly articulating what they think and what they feel. At that time, these small children can become both judge and jury with respect to Mom's opinions or decisions. They can defiantly challenge the validity of what she says or does, and they will expect Mom to come up with reasonable explanations for them—especially if they feel that her decision wasn't made entirely on their behalf. These little fire children can really set their parents up by testing their honesty. Sagittarians can be quite authoritative in their own right, and even at a young age, they like to be in control.

Parent and child share a physical vitality, and they both enjoy being active in all phases of life. In fact, they usually wear themselves out in their constant search for ways to relieve boredom. A Gemini mom will never try to stifle her Sagittarians' need to explore, as she relishes this aspect of life as much as they do!

The Gemini Dad/The Sagittarius Child

Both Dad and his Sagittarius children are very independent. Dad doesn't really like to feel he owes anything to anyone. He rarely asks for favors; he likes to hold himself accountable for his own debts, and he makes a point of taking care of them as soon as possible. His Sagittarius children may have a similar problem, but in their case, it's usually because they become caretakers who tend to take on *all* the responsibility for situations themselves. People really touch these fire kids, and they will want to look after everyone.

Both Gemini Dad and his Sagittarius children share a mental affinity. Their competitive natures complement each other well, as they will both find challenges that they can work on together. They enjoy arguing with each other, and they both have their own defiant, dramatic styles. These two will work together as great movers and shakers. They will both search for knowledge, as they are intelligent, quick-thinking, and humorous explorers.

A Sagittarius will appreciate the fact that Dad is intelligent, funny, and organized. Dad can reach his Sagittarius children through kindness and consideration. These kids can be easily hurt, and parents will have to make sure that they aren't trying to pretend that nothing's bothering them. A Gemini father's most difficult task will be to handle both the sensitive and emotional sides of his Sagittarius children. It isn't always easy for a Gemini father to understand his Sagittarian kids' spirituality and emotions, as they themselves feel uncomfortable revealing this part of their personality.

The Cancer Parent/The Sagittarius Child

Both Cancer parents and their Sagittarius children are very emotional. In the beginning, these active little persons may exhaust their Cancer parents; nonetheless, Mom and Dad will become emotionally energized by these unpredictable kids. Cancer parents will fulfill the emotional needs of their fire children, as they easily give love and attention. Close family ties and a stable environment are what a Cancer enjoys in life. A Sagittarius will enjoy this stability, but parents must also remember that these kids are independent free spirits who definitely have their own opinions. When they ask these kids to do something, Mom and Dad will have to avoid making their requests sound like orders, and it's also important to tell them *why* they are supposed to do things. If they feel as if they're being blamed without cause, they will tend to rebel, and repeat the same offense over and over again.

Sagittarians need the support and freedom to express their own opinions. They want a place to come home to, but they don't want too many questions from their parents when they leave. Cancers have a tendency to worry a lot, and they have to be careful not to hover over their children. Sagittarius children will not respond well if they feel that their parents are watching over everything they do. It's perfectly fine for parents to set up guidelines and consistent household rules, as these kids do need to learn self-discipline. However, these children cannot be subdued by Mom and Dad. If this situation occurs, these Sagittarius children will end up saying, "I need my space, lots of space, and if you recognize this fact, I'll adore you."

The Cancer Mom/The Sagittarius Child

A Cancer mom has very strong mothering instincts, and she will do everything in her power to make her children happy. However, Mom has to be careful not to base her self-esteem solely on how happy her children are in life. If this is the case, this parent can lose her own personal security.

Sagittarians are loving and sensitive children. These kids believe that life is beautiful, and their cheerful nature is wonderful to be around. Mom will enjoy her Sagittarius children's idealistic attitudes, as they can help her see the positive side of any situation. There is a fact, however, that a Cancer Mom will have to accept: these children like to do their own thing! If Sagittarian children are made to feel guilty about their need to explore, then as they grow, they will begin to retreat into their own world. And as adults, they may distance themselves emotionally from their parents. It's important for Mom to understand that guilt can damage any relationship.

☆   ☆   ☆

Many years ago, my friend Sarah was having lunch at my house, when she started to complain about her son. She told me, "Joel hardly comes to see me. He lives right in the neighborhood, and he rarely ever stops by."

I asked her, "Why do you think he does that?"

"I don't know. I gave him everything I could, and I can't believe he's treating me this way!"

"Sarah, have you ever told your son how you feel?"

She answered, "What for? He wouldn't understand."

I explained, "Now you're judging him before the verdict is out."

She took a deep breath and said, "When Joel was a little boy, he always did the opposite of what I told him to do. He's always been a rebel."

I responded, "Sarah, maybe it was how you approached him. Perhaps, it was the tone in your voice or the way you asked him to do something."

Sarah said defensively, "Nothing was wrong with the tone of my voice!"

"Don't be angry, Sarah. You know, you can be a little bossy at times. You do like things you're way. It's important to realize that when you tell someone to do something a certain way, you take away their freedom to think for themselves. You know that Joel is someone who likes his freedom, and I'm sure he needed it then, as he does

now. Perhaps you didn't give him enough time alone to figure things out for himself."
Sarah half-nodded, reluctantly acknowledging the truth of what I was saying.

She asked, "What could I do now?"

"Talk to him," I told her.

She thought about this possibility for a moment. "He'll think I'm trying to make him feel guilty. He says I have a tendency to do that."

"Well, do you?"

She admitted, "Maybe."

I then suggested, "Sarah, call your son tonight, and tell him you would like to see him, and then tell him how you really feel."

With worry in her voice, she said, "He'll be angry."

I replied, "I don't think so. He's a very sensitive man."

Sarah, who was a Cancer, did call her son Joel, a Sagittarius, and they discussed how they felt. She tried to tell him how hurt and lonely she was, and he admitted that he did have a bit of a problem relating to her at times. He told her that he feels judged by her, and he doesn't like it when she tells him how to live his life. The conversation turned out to be a real beginning for them, as Sarah told me that Joel started to visit her on a regular basis after that talk!

☆ ☆ ☆

The Cancer Dad/The Sagittarius Child

Cancer dads are sensitive, funny, and have a great love for children. Their natural affinity for fatherhood make them excellent fathers. Even though Dad is regarded as a nice guy, though, he's not a pushover. Overall, he likes to raise well-behaved, disciplined children. Sagittarians are not unruly, but sometimes they need appropriate motivation to stay out of trouble. These little tots have a lot of energy, and their curiosity inspires them to perform devilish acts. Yelling or screaming is never the answer, though, as these kids are very sensitive, and they will wind up doing just the opposite of what Dad tells them to do. These kids want their fathers to be interested in them, so their little "adventures" may sometimes just be ploys to get attention. Overall, Sagittarius children respond well to kindness and humor.

Sagittarians are usually happy, adaptable, and flexible, unless they feel as if their need to express themselves is being restricted. Young Sagittarius will need Dad's approval, appreciation, and honesty. Since Dad is both emotional and a very strong parent figure, he would be wise to try to be open and communicative with these sensitive children, as this will be the way to win their trust. There are times when Dad can seem a little irritable, though, and these optimistic kids may regard his behavior as a personal affront. Sagittarius children are naturally intuitive, and they may think that Dad is upset with them. It's best that Dad explain to these sensitive kids that his behavior has nothing to do with anything they did.

A Cancer father is very loving and affectionate, and he has the ability to give his Sagittarian children the attention that they need. Interpersonal communication can be a very important part of this parent/child relationship. If Dad always ties to make a point of explaining to his little fire children the reasons behind his decisions, and if he openly talks about why he feels the way he does, he will receive everlasting love from these kids. And by sharing his own feelings, he will be encouraging his Sagittarius children to do the same. These kids will always appreciate a sensible approach. A Cancer father who works toward achieving his own emotional balance can effect a wonderful relationship with his fiery Sagittarian kids.

The Leo Parent/The Sagittarius Child

A Leo parent and a Sagittarius child interact in much the same way as an orchestra conductor and his or her devoted crew of musicians would. The parents take the lead, and the children always seem to understand where they're going. Two fire signs burn brightly together! A Leo's self-contained personality is right in tune with his or her Sagittarius child. Most Leos are natural extroverts, whose energy, determination and optimism are responsible for their ability to lead. Sagittarian children also have their own minds and strive toward leadership, but they're not natural extroverts. There's an underlying shyness and reserve until they trust you. These fiery parents can seem a little naive at times, but a Leo mom and dad will be very responsible and serious when it comes to raising their children. They believe that their kids are extensions of themselves, and they will always encourage them to persevere and succeed.

Leo parents have big dreams for their children, but they do have to remember that these kids will need to follow their *own* paths, rather then the ones that their parents set down for them. These fire parents may need to be careful not to lose sight of what their children's own desires might be. Sagittarius children, however, will always appreciate their parents' encouragement, as well as the fact that they will always be able to rely on them. Leo parents can be excellent role models for their Sagittarian children. This parent and child duo enjoy being in each other's company, although it is important for them—especially as they grow older—to communicate their feelings to each other. These fire children must be taught to appreciate and understand their own abilities, as well as their own inner strength. These kids will possess great mental capacity and a lot of physical energy, as well.

Both Leos and Sagittarians tend to see the world in terms of black or white, or right or wrong, and they have little room for "gray" in their personalities. When it comes to expressing an opinion, a fire sign rarely takes the middle of the road. And I can tell you from experience that they wouldn't have it any other way!

The Leo Mom/The Sagittarius Child

A Leo mother will be able to provide a variety of diversions to keep her Sagittarius children happy. She'll read to them, play with them, and make sure that they'll receive a fine education. Most of all, she'll recognize their sensitivity and encourage their creativity. Mom is emotional, intense, dramatic, and a quick thinker.

There are generally two type of Leo women: one tends to be flamboyant, while the other usually tends to be more conservative and understated in nature. Either way, they are both intense on the inside. The flamboyant Leo mom may have to work on being overly dramatic with these kids, as she can overwhelm her reserved sons and daughters. She'd be wise to share the limelight, as her Sagittarius children also like to be center stage. The understated Leo mom can be emotionally supportive, and she will encourage these kids to be self-reliant. This will not be difficult for Mom, as Sagittarian children are innately independent. These fire kids will be comfortable with both her efficiency and her stability. And no matter what type of Leo mother she is, she will always have the tendency to overprotect her children. Mom is kind and caring, but she may have a need to control everything in her home environment, and this can be imposing to Sagittarius children, who need their own space and freedom to grow. Sagittarians want to have the opportunity to experience all of the wonders of life in order to help them fulfill their own aspirations.

Sagittarians can also become defensive and argumentative when they feel that anyone is infringing on their independence. Both Mom and her Sagittarius children can be easily hurt, although these kids may not let Mom know if they're upset about something. Both of these fire signs feel as if they'll lose their control if they admit how they feel. This parent and child combination really need appreciation and approval from each other. They can wind up doing so much for everyone else that they don't take the time to ask for anything for themselves. Mom would be wise to understand that both she and her child need to openly communicate in order to build the most healthy and productive relationship possible.

Overall, this parent and child will instinctively understand each other, as they are alike in many ways—they are both emotional, compassionate, intelligent, honest, and stubborn!

The Leo Dad/The Sagittarius Child

If you think a Leo mother acts like the boss of the family, then you haven't met a Leo dad. Dad, like Mom, can be very aggressive and outgoing, or he can be the strong, silent type. No matter which one he is, he's in charge. He is usually fair and just, and he will have a great sense of humor. These qualities are very endearing to his Sagittarius children, since they, too, are both honest and funny. Dad has one dream: he wants his children turn out to be the most productive, brilliant kids in the world. And he will do anything to help them get there!

Since Sagittarian children are born with many talents and a keen intelligence, Dad will enjoy helping them achieve their dreams. Dad needs to encourage his fire children at an early age, as these Sagittarians need to be inspired by his creative and resourceful mind. But Dad also should keep in mind that these kids need the freedom to live out their own dreams without feeling like they have to live up to someone else's expectations. Dad needs to have confidence in the fact that his young fire children have many unique abilities of their own. As Dad praises his kids for their efforts, their self-esteem will grow.

These fire-sign children will admire Dad for being a man of his word, and they will understand his own need to be appreciated and understood. The one thing that Dad may want to acknowledge is that he cannot control his Sagittarius kids. He can share his knowledge and zest for life, and he can help guide them toward positive and productive goals, but he has to make sure he doesn't stifle their need to express themselves along the way.

The Virgo Parent/The Sagittarius Child

Virgo parents are perfectionists, and they have a resourceful, practical approach to life. They encourage their children to aspire to excellence. They also expect them to be well behaved, disciplined, and socially acceptable to the outside world. These parents believe that they're protecting their kids by teaching them how to get along with others. Sagittarius children do need to be given a sense of discipline and order, but they cannot be overwhelmed. Virgos can get caught up in their own need to try to get everything right, and they may not realize how demanding they can be. They hope that their children follow their practical approach to life, but they may need to realize that these free-spirited Sagittarian kids need the choice to explore life on their own, as they tend to rebel against any kind of restriction.

Both Virgo parents and their Sagittarius children have a need for organization and control. They do, however, tend to respond to situations differently: while a Sagittarian's first instinct is usually emotional, Virgos always lean toward the practical side of any issue. These logical thinkers may need to learn the art of patience when dealing with their emotional kids, as they really need to be assured that their parents are accepting of, and interested in, how they feel!

The Virgo Mom/The Sagittarius Child

Mom can be very patient and methodical when it comes to achieving a goal, and her fire children will learn how to emulate her behavior. A Virgo mother is very consistent when it comes to giving her kids specific instructions.

Mom and her children are both interested in education, so this mother will create ways to help her Sagittarian sons and daughters reach their full potential, as that is her primary goal. Interesting projects will keep these fire kids from getting bored and will also help them learn how to organize their thoughts. A Virgo mom likes to set up rules and standards in her household, and she has high expectations of her children. Virgo mothers tend to be both very caring and overly protective, so if Mom watches over her children too closely, they may then decide to assume a devil-may-care attitude, especially when it comes to taking care of their chores. When these fire kids become upset, they tend to respond to Mom in this somewhat rebellious way, because they may not always be comfortable confronting her about what's really bothering them. Mom's best bet is to explain to these kids the reasons *why* they should or shouldn't be doing something.

Sagittarians respect honesty, and they will listen to the truth. Ask them to help solve a problem, and they'll always be right there for you. Sagittarius children are, first and foremost, free spirits. As such, Mom may need to encourage her Sagittarian kids to stand up for themselves and talk about their feelings.

Both Mom and her Sagittarius children can have a lot of fun together, as they both share a great sense of humor. It's important for a Virgo parent to be extremely positive when raising Sagittarius children, as they tend to view life as joyous and full of possibilities! Children who require a lot of freedom may at first seem like a handful for a Virgo mother, but her intelligent and analytical mind can help these kids find realistic ways of making their dreams come true.

The Virgo Dad/The Sagittarius Child

Dad needs to understand that raising a child who's emotional, sensitive, and idealistic will be quite an exciting challenge. Since Dad needs to depend on his practical intelligence, he may have a problem valuing a Sagittarius child's intuition and idealistic dreams, as his logical mind tends to focus on the facts. This trait provides him with a safety net: if he always has a handle on what's going to happen, there's less of a chance of making a mistake.

Sagittarius children may be free-spirited, but doing the right thing is important to them. The real difference between Dad and his Sagittarius children is their need to feel free. Fire children do not respond to a parent who wants to control their thinking. They need to make their own decisions and act upon them. Dad's practical nature and sound common sense can help these children stabilize their impulsive natures. Sagittarius children will always be spontaneous and impetuous, and they may need to travel the world before settling down. As long as these children know that they have a steady, efficient, reliable father to depend on, they are content. Dad would be wise to work on altering his own need for running his kids' lives, though. Young Sagittarians will rebel, and Dad will be sorry he ever tried to alter their enthusiastic responses to life.

Earth parents usually need to be organized, consistent, and predictable in their behavior, while Sagittarius children do not like anything routine. They may be rigid in the way they like to do things, but they want to choose the time and place. These children will respect Dad as long as he is there to stabilize, not stifle, their emotions and zest for life!

The Libra Parent/The Sagittarius Child

Libra parents and their Sagittarius children both need to maintain their own private place where they can rest and relax. They get so busy that they push themselves too far, and they can become exhausted. Libra parents are creative, so they will decorate their homes to reflect their need for peace and beauty. This environment is a positive one for the Sagittarius child.

Libras have a wonderful gift of diplomacy that wins them great praise from both family and friends. Sagittarius children also believe in what's fair and honest, and Libras enjoy these kids' perspective, as their own inner child is released when they're with them. They play together and have great fun, and then their spirits soar. Sagittarius children will be grateful that they are allowed to play like kids, as they wish to always remain young at heart. In addition, a Libra parent's logical mind can help teach these children how to live productively in the real world. Libras, too, may need to learn these lessons, because like their Sagittarius kids, they are idealists.

What helps these air parents are their logical minds; they always work to find a reasonable, practical approach to things. Libras, however, can view intimate relationships through rose-colored glasses, and they can have a problem telling people whom they care about how they feel. It's important that these parents learn how to defend themselves, because if Sagittarius children begin to pick up on this behavior, they may think it's acceptable, and they will avoid standing up for themselves as well. Sagittarians do not have a problem adhering to their own opinions on most subjects, but like their Libra parents, they have a very difficult time verbalizing their feelings. If Libra parents can learn to discuss the things that really bother them, this kind of open communication can give these sensitive kids permission to talk about their hurt feelings.

Libras like to dominate their environment, and it is in this respect that their Sagittarius children can see the rebellious sides of their nature. They're the bosses when it comes to taking care of the home and family. Now, Sagittarius children are strong and opinionated, too, and they can also be obstinate when they want to get their way. Sagittarians tend to see the world in terms of black and white, while a Libra always works to see shades of gray. Since their approach to life can be different, both parent and child can learn from each other. Sagittarius children can learn that there are times when it's important to see all sides of a situation in order to work through a problem, and their parents can accept the fact that the direct and honest approach to making a decision can be very helpful.

Libra parents and their Sagittarius children can both be rebels in their own right, and each may have a problem discussing how they feel. Libras want peace and quiet, and Sagittarians can be afraid of releasing their deepest emotions. Libras are logical and will have the ability to encourage these children to try to express themselves and make sense out of their feelings. The most important part of this relationship is the Libra's ability to nurture the energetic enthusiasm of his or her fire children.

The Libra Mom/The Sagittarius Child

Mom will enjoy her Sagittarian's natural spontaneity, but at times, this mother can get bored, as her need for safety can override her need for change. Giving up security may mean losing her financial and emotional foundation. I always encourage my Libra clients to try and achieve their dreams and goals by daring to move away from "safe" behavior. Those who have accepted the possibility of risk have often become much happier in their lives.

Mom would be wise to provide a variety of interests for her Sagittarius children, as they too can be restless. She should encourage these kids to learn, explore, and express their opinions. At times, these kids may become arrogant and lose their perspective in a situation. Once they have made a decision, it's difficult for anyone to change their minds, but Mom has the ability to keep them on track.

Some Libra moms are very involved in home and family, while others do their own thing. If a Libra mother is busy with many projects or outside interests, she may expect her children to be as free-spirited as she is. Sagittarius children are independent, but Mom may need to learn that they also need a lot of attention. If she can remember to consider these children's feelings, and be there to listen when they need to talk, these children will gladly do their own thing. Mom tends to be interested in dealing with the intellect, but her Sagittarius children will need her affection. If Mom is the homebody type, she'll be there to take care of all of her kids' needs; however, she will always encourage them to think for themselves and work within their own unique styles. Sagittarius children will thrive as a result of this type of subtle parenting technique. These kids need Mom's permission to be free, but they also need her logic to help clarify their feelings. They need her to provide them with rules, limits, and boundaries within their lives in order to help stabilize their restless behavior.

Mom's need for balance and harmony can mean that it can take her a while to come to a decision. By covering all of her bases, this Mom can avoid dealing with the unknown. She has excellent instincts, and she may need to learn to trust herself. Sagittarians look to the future and will need Mom's support in order to set their own goals. If Mom works on having faith in her own decisions, her Sagittarius children will respect her for the effort. Mom can help with the logical aspects of any decision, and her fire children will appreciate her reasonable judgments. However, once she makes up her mind, Mom may have a tendency to be a little critical about anyone who disagrees with her. She has to remember that her Sagittarius children are independent thinkers who may disagree with even her best thought-out decisions.

Sagittarians can be worrywarts, so they'll need Mom's dry, gentle humor to help cheer them up. She can provide the calm after the storm. These kids are also very restless, so it's important for them to release their inner intensity through physical activity. They tend to fight their emotions and keep their feelings to themselves. A Libra mother is both sensitive *and* logical, but it isn't her emotional side that makes her avoid personal communication. Her self-confidence may not be as strong as it should be, and she fears rejection. Both parent and child don't enjoy stirring the pot, but they may need to learn that telling people how they feel will make them feel better about themselves. It would be a great step forward for Mom to try to help her children bring their emotions out into the open. At first, this may be difficult for both of them to do, but it can be accomplished through Mom's efforts to release her own feelings first, and then help her children do the same.

The Libra Dad/The Sagittarius Child

Dad is a master of reason and good sense. He believes in being able to solve most problems with logic. He is sensitive, and he tends to use his considerable intuition when he raises his Sagittarius children. At their core, these kids are basically emotional and sensitive, and they tend not to let logic stand in the way of their feelings. These kids are both spontaneous and decisive, and they may not always think through all of their actions. Dad has the ability to teach his fire children to look before they leap. He can present a good case for thinking things over carefully before jumping into a situation that may appear to be exciting or challenging on the surface.

Dad can supply both the stability and security that his children need, as he is both intelligent and mentally alert. Libra men can have more of a problem verbalizing their personal feelings than Libra women, though. Many people who've lived with Libra men all of their lives often say they've never heard them express their emotions. If Dad works on communicating with his Sagittarius children, who really need an understanding father, he can also release some of his own inner feelings at the same time. It might be a good way for Dad to start opening up.

All in all, a Libra father is bright, logical, and is a calming force in the family. His Sagittarius children will receive positive feedback from him, and they will reap great rewards from his sage advice.

The Scorpio Parent/The Sagittarius Child

While a Sagittarius child thrives on freedom, a Scorpio parent needs a more organized lifestyle. Scorpios are emotional, but they can get overwhelmed by their own feelings. Sagittarius children do not do well with extreme intensity, so Mom and Dad will need to calm down before they begin to talk to them about anything of importance. Sagittarians feel better when they can discuss anything in a reasonable manner. While Sagittarians understand the need for discipline, it's not best for a parent to make them feel as if every one of their moves is being watched. They'll feel as if they're being treated like babies. These Sagittarius fire kids fear restriction of any kind, so they need to feel like they're are making their own choices in life, even if they're merely options presented to them by their Mom or Dad.

Scorpio men believe that they should be the final authority when it comes to all family decisions, and just like their Scorpio dads, Sagittarius children do need to be focused and centered in their behavior, so Dad can easily set them along a structured course. Scorpio parents want their children to be independent, and they will encourage their growth and maturity. Scorpios, however, can seem a little too judgmental at times, and these Sagittarius children do deal better with explanations then they do with criticism. They have lofty aims, so they can benefit from a Scorpio parent's realistic outlook, which leads them toward concrete ways of making their dreams come true.

Both Scorpios and Sagittarians tend to be spiritual, so this aspect of their personalities will blend well. If Scorpio parents avoid placing unrealistic expectations on these kids, they can build a healthy parent/child relationship. Scorpios have high standards, but they need to sort out what's important and what's not before they make a judgment or criticize. The most important thing for these parents to remember is to try not to stifle their fire children's spirit or thwart their freedom to choose.

☆   ☆   ☆

I was driving one morning with my young friend Andrea when she looked over to me and said, "I don't think my father will ever understand me."

I asked her, "What do you mean?"

Andrea replied, "Dad just doesn't get it. He doesn't understand that I need to make my own career decisions. He thinks he can decide for me because he thinks he knows what my real talents are." She took a long breath, and continued, "I don't want to teach school. Just because I love children doesn't mean I want to be a teacher. I want to be a fashion designer."

I told her, "I can't believe that you think your Dad doesn't understand how creative you are. Just the other day he told me that he thought you would be an excellent fashion designer."

In disbelief, Andrea asked, "He did? He hasn't said anything to me. The only thing he ever says to me is 'Why don't you consider a career in teaching?' "

I suggested, "Andrea, why don't you try and talk to your father? I know that he admires your self-confidence and creative abilities."

Andrea responded, "He's never clear when he speaks to me. I always get a mixed message."

I said, "Andrea, why not just call your father on the car phone and talk to him. I know it's scary to talk to him about this, but I think it will be worth it. You'll be making the first step."

Andrea paused for a moment, picked up the phone, and called her father's office. When she had him on the line, she blurted out, "Dad, I don't want to be a school teacher."

Her father asked with surprise, "What's this all about?"

"Dad, I want to be a fashion designer, and I need your encouragement."

He replied, "You know I believe in you."

Andrea's eyes filled up with tears as she admitted, "Sometimes you intimidate me."

"Andrea, I didn't know you were so definite about what you wanted to do." He paused for a moment. "I respect the fact you're being so honest about it. We'll talk about this later and I'll do my best to help you."

Andrea hung up, and quietly said to me, "That was the hardest thing I've ever done." Being a Sagittarius, what Andrea needed most from her Scorpio dad was his respect. She wanted him to believe in her abilities and allow her the freedom to make her own choices in life. Sometimes all it takes is a little communication!

☆　　☆　　☆

The Scorpio Mom/The Sagittarius Child

A Scorpio mom will do everything in her power to take care of her children's needs. No one will ever question her sincerity when she is raising her kids. Overall, Mom is a bright lady who is well versed in a number of subjects, and she believes that her children should know how to act properly in the outside world. Scorpio moms are artistic, and many can paint or sew.

One thing that Mom needs to be particularly conscious of is her tendency to try to completely take over the household. If necessary, Mom may need to learn how to turn an order into a clear explanation of why she wants something done. I know that Mom's a natural protector, but with Sagittarius children, it's important that she try not to be overly solicitous.

Scorpio moms will give their Sagittarius children the foundation they need to help them turn their dreams into reality. She can offer a solid, stable home in which to grow, and as long as she provides a reasonably free environment, Mom will have happy children on her hands. Scorpio moms may need to understand that when they're raising Sagittarius children, they're bringing up kids who will always look for freedom, challenge, and excitement!

The Scorpio Dad/The Sagittarius Child

Dad can be a serious fellow who is very intense about his accomplishments. He's quite intuitive, and once he makes up his mind about someone, that's it! If he likes you, he'll be a loyal friend, but if he doesn't, he can be a formidable opponent. A Scorpio dad is passionate and magnetic, and he is so determined, that when he sets a goal for himself he won't stop until he has achieved it. When he's off and running, it can be hard for him to see the forest for the trees.

This dad is charming, intelligent, and quite suave. He wants people to listen to his ideas, but if he feels that those whom he's talking to are *not* as intelligent as he is, he won't take them very seriously. Dad loves the enthusiasm, sense of humor, and intelligence of his Sagittarius children. However, on the inside, these kids can also be shy and sensitive. When these children are hurt by someone, they don't share their feelings openly. They want to have Dad's permission to tell him how they honestly feel about things, without fear or judgment.

Dad is both just and fair, and it would be best if he shared his humanitarian and compassionate side with his sensitive children, as both Scorpios and Sagittarians want to be of help to others. This Scorpio dad will pass along to his Sagittarius children his interest in learning about different cultures in the world, and his fire kids will truly value his teachings.

The Sagittarius Parent/The Sagittarius Child

Both Sagittarius parents and their Sagittarius children can build an amicable, warm-hearted friendship. This fiery duo tends to be emotional, straightforward, philosophical, and humorous. Together, they share all of the qualities and traits necessary to live a happy life. These parents will never dream of restricting their children, and these fire kids will have more than enough room to explore. Parent and child both have a tendency to daydream, and they each believe that every wonderful day will bring about another. They love life, and they love each other!

Most Sagittarians understand that they can be compulsive and restless. They search for variety, new adventures, and lots of activity. Sagittarius parents need to help their fire kids learn the importance of focusing on one thing at a time, rather than scattering their energy. When Sagittarians overwhelm themselves, they can become moody, irritable, and difficult to handle. So, Mom and Dad definitely will relate to their kids' tendency to push themselves too much, often reaching a state of collapse before they give up on a task or project. Sagittarius parents need to help calm their kids down by setting up some quiet time that will soothe their restlessness.

Many Sagittarians believe in mythology and heroes. That's one of the reasons they love change, sports, or any kind of competition. They have a tendency to overidealize their heroes, whether it's a brilliant teacher, a football player, or a parent who provides them with everything they need. The Sagittarian idealism and naivete are reasons why they are often misled. It's crucial that parents teach them to view people realistically, rather than through their rose-colored glasses.

Parent and child are basically on the same wavelength, so they have a true instinctual bond. Sagittarius parents will always want to provide materials to stimulate their children's intellect, as they believe that no one can learn enough. In addition, Sagittarians are interested in human diversity, and they find the differences in people and cultures fascinating.

Overall, Mom and Dad should try to help their little fireballs control their impulsive natures and encourage them to scrutinize situations before they take action. These parents will want to provide a solid foundation for their kids, and Sagittarian children will truly appreciate their Mom and Dad for trying to make life more comfortable for them!

The Sagittarius Mom/The Sagittarius Child

Mom and her Sagittarius child have a lot in common, as they are both emotional and free-spirited. It doesn't matter whether we're talking about the serious and administrative variety of Sagittarius or the poet type, they both need complete freedom.

Mom is the best person to inspire her Sagittarius children, as she is honest and diplomatic and can help them reach their greatest potential by encouraging them to develop their intellect and use their imagination. Sagittarians are usually spiritual, and making their dreams come true is very important to them. Mom needs to hold loose reins when she raises these fire children, as she cannot protect them from seeking adventure and exploring new things. If Mom is in touch with her own need for independence and autonomy, she won't try to stifle her children's zest for life.

Mom can work on helping her children calm down when their enthusiasm runs amuck, because scattering their energies will hinder them from attaining their goals. When Sagittarius children push themselves too far, they tend to become moody and irritable. Mom needs to urge them to pull back before they reach their limits.

This fiery mom can be the perfect confidante if she keeps her need to control everything in check. A Sagittarius mother wants to be certain that her family is well taken care of, but there are times when she does too much. She has to accept the fact that her Sagittarius children will need to make their own decisions, but she can be very instrumental in guiding them in the right direction. These kids are lucky to have a mother who empathizes with them and who wants to join in their sense of fun.

The Sagittarius Dad/The Sagittarius Child

There are two Sagittarius personalities: the devilish fireball who looks for trouble and dislikes confining rules, or the honorable and moralistic seeker of justice who fights for his beliefs. If the moralistic father is raising the troublesome fire kid, he may need to develop patience. Fire signs do not possess this quality in abundance, so the best way for Dad to reach his restless child is through experiencing his own free-spirited nature. He would be wise to modify extreme criticism and judgment. Dad is straightforward and persuasive; therefore, if he is sincere and honest with his fire kids, he can inspire them to combine this restless nature with a healthy enthusiasm for helping people. This is one of the best characteristics of a Sagittarius personality. It is also important for Dad to provide a variety of options to learn from, as he certainly understands the value of mental stimulation.

If Dad and his fire child are similar, he can be there to guide and further develop the mental affinity that is natural for both of them. It won't matter which personality Dad is raising—the sense of humor will prevail, and each one's zest for life will help them to build a healthy relationship. Dad is always pursuing a new interest, since variety is very important to his well-being. As his children grow, they will really have the same philosophy of life. Dad and his Sagittarius children are quite intelligent, and they look to the future with optimism. It's vital that Dad maintains his positive attitude when he raises his Sagittarius kids so that these sensitive fire children will follow his lead.

The Capricorn Parent/The Sagittarius Child

Capricorn parents can be proper individuals who aspire to be stable, solid, upstanding citizens. Most of their thoughts and actions are based on a logical, practical approach to life. They try to create as stable a home environment as they can for their Sagittarius child; this is a place that both parent and child can always feel comfortable. However, although Capricorns are very effective in building protective walls around themselves, it doesn't completely negate all the nervous tension that they feel inside.

At first, Capricorn parents may be overwhelmed by their impulsive, spontaneous, and overly energetic Sagittarius children. These kids tend to instinctively "leap before they look," and Capricorn parents may legitimately ask these children if they are actually ready to make that jump. Sagittarius children will always appreciate being given reasonable explanations by their Capricorn parents as to why they have made the decisions they have, as long as Mom and Dad don't sound overly critical. Capricorn parents may hurt these idealistic children's feelings if they give them the impression that individuals who are dreamers are not stable. It's best for parents to refrain from putting out that message, because although these kids may indulge in fantasy at times, they are also independent go-getters who are capable of making their idealistic aims come true.

Sagittarians have great courage and endurance, and once they decide to go for the pot at the end of the rainbow, they will do everything possible to see that they get it! Capricorn parents are exceptional leaders, in that they promote a healthy work ethic, and their Sagittarius children can benefit from their realistic point of view. If Capricorn parents can let their Sagitarius children know that they appreciate their need to explore life, these fire kids will be happy to let these parents help them structure their lives. The philosophy of the Sagittarian child is: "Give me permission to dream, and allow me the freedom to change."

The Capricorn Mom/The Sagittarius Child

A Capricorn mother has the ability to recognize quality in both material goods and people. This special wisdom, combined with her profound level of maturity, can be the keys to accomplishing her goals. This mother can see the big picture, and she has the vision to know what belongs and what doesn't in any given situation. And, once her decision is made, it can be difficult for her to change her mind. Astrologically, Mom is a "fixed" personality who applies self-discipline and hard work to anything she undertakes. Her home and material possessions are extremely important to her life, and she expects anyone who lives in her domicile to respect her values.

Sagittarius children are very comfortable with the solid family life that Mom helps provide, and they will always respect Mom's ability to provide a safe and secure home environment. However, while Mom certainly is very efficient, she can tend to be dogmatic in her vision of what a home and family should be like. Anyone who disagrees with her could find themselves in deep trouble. Sagittarius children like to adhere to their own philosophy, so this attitude won't always coincide with Mom's. Sagittarius kids are idealistic and enjoy change, where Mom tends to be more realistic and likes to maintain her life at a comfortable level. These kids react first from the gut, while Mom tends to first see things more practically. She needs to accept the fact that no matter how practical Sagittarius children can be, they will always need the freedom to follow their dreams.

Overall, Mom is a wonderful guide, and she can give her kids the benefit of her wisdom and clarity when it comes to distinguishing the difference between reality and pipe dreams. She may have a problem releasing the "parental reins" when raising her children, but she'll realize, eventually, that she needs to loosen her grip when her kids start to rebel. Sagittarian children need her protection, but they will not appreciate being hovered over.

Sagittarians are very bright, and although they are serious about their lives, their sense of humor and optimism will always be there to help deal with sadness and pain. Mom can take a lesson from her idealistic child, as she tends to make mountains out of molehills. She tends to see what's wrong in a situation first, in order to set up the perfect picture. Sagittarians need to understand that self-discipline is important, but they will also need to be flattered and receive Mom's approval. A few compliments can go a long way. Capricorn mothers are just trying to make everyone's life as easy as possible, but the pressure that they put on themselves can turn them into nervous wrecks. After all, it isn't necessary to pick up *every* crumb on the floor. All in all, this caring mother has given birth to emotional, sensitive children who will appreciate her understanding and love.

The Capricorn Dad/The Sagittarius Child

Dad is quite adamant when it comes to his beliefs and opinions. He doesn't enjoy deviating from the lifestyle that he's worked so hard to create for himself. Dad wants a simple life, which includes a worthwhile profession, a nice home (and someone to take care of it), well-behaved, bright children, and financial security. Capricorn dads are often tuned into the business world, and their mind power is their greatest strength. Dad's intentions toward his Sagittarius children are always positive, but because he is so ambitious, he can lose sight of what his children really need— that is, his undivided attention. He may express his affection to his little fire children by buying them things, but what these kids need is to feel close to Dad.

This Capricorn dad will understand that his Sagittarius children are bright and emotionally complex, and he will fit into their image of what a strong, responsible father should be. They will admire his efficiency, intelligence, and gift for organization. In fact, many Sagittarians grow up to be a little too rigid in their behavior. These fire kids may need to get more in touch with their free, creative sides. I believe that if parents help nurture this part of their kids' nature, they will help them live more satisfying lives.

Dad can provide the stable family life that Sagittarius children will enjoy, but he would be wise to take the time to communicate with these kids. He needs to learn that these children dislike criticism, even when it seems constructive. Dad can connect with his Sagittarius children by really listening to what they have to say without being judgmental. If Sagittarius children feel that they are not able to speak to their parents openly, they will begin to withdraw into their own little world at an early age. Dad is usually an intuitive man, so he will no doubt pick up on the fact that his Sagittarius children are emotional, creative, and truly crave his attention!

The Aquarius Parent/The Sagittarius Child

If Sagittarius children could offer their parents some words of wisdom before they enter the universe, they would say, "Please fan my flame so I can burn bright." Aquarius parents admire highly spirited, action-oriented children, so they will have no problem living up to their fire kids' earnest plea.

Sagittarius children want their mothers to be romantic and visionary, as well as accepting and understanding. They like their fathers to be strong, honest, stable, and direct. Aquarius parents have many of the qualities and traits that Sagittarian kids look for. First of all, both parent and child need their independence and freedom. If these fire children decide that they need to spend time by themselves, these parents won't place any restrictions on them because they often feel the same way.

Aquarians feel a social responsibility toward others, and they want to raise their children to feel the same way. This won't be a problem, because parent and child are born humanitarians who tend to reach out to those who suffer. Aquarius parents are logical and have a lot of patience. They always try to give others the benefit of the doubt. Their Sagittarius children are emotional and impatient; they can be headstrong and argumentative and do not believe in gray areas. The real difference between these parents and children is that Mom and Dad can wait, but their children leap before they look!

Aquarius parents can help their fire kids by explaining the importance of taking some time to avoid mistakes and by showing them how to be realistic in their life pursuits. These kids need these stable, sensitive parents to help them be persistent and learn to adhere to their decisions.

Overall, parent and child share a special mental affinity, since they both tend to be intelligent and are willing to explore anything that piques their interest. These fire kids are shrewd and move fast, while their parents like to take their time figuring things out. They are a good match for each other, since one thinks, while the other feels.

Aquarius parents would do well to nurture their Sagittarius children's feelings and create a peaceful, harmonious environment in which they can calm their impulsive, restless tendencies!

The Aquarius Mom/The Sagittarius Child

Mom is honest and easy to get along with, but she tends to have an innate shyness that she's always working to overcome. This reserve may keep her at a distance from people, even when she's having a great time at a social function. This Aquarius mother also needs to be mentally stimulated, or she can spend a lot of time in her own thoughts. She does have a great sense of humor, though, and she raises her children to be down-to-earth, easygoing people. Their best interests are always her first consideration. In fact, she often sacrifices her own needs for the sake of her family.

All of the air signs, which include Aquarius, Gemini, and Libra have a strong appreciation for beauty and art. Therefore, an Aquarius mother will provide her Sagittarius children with a home that will both delight the senses and appeal to the mind. These fire kids will be very comfortable in this environment, which will stimulate their creativity.

Mom takes a balanced and realistic approach to life, and she will teach her children to be responsible for their actions. Aquarian moms are usually not tough disciplinarians, though. They are much more interested in encouraging their kids' individuality than punishing them. Sagittarius kids love this part of her personality, but they will still need a structured environment. Mom can gently teach her idealistic Sagittarius children how to make their dreams come true in the real world. Her idealism is always there, and she instinctively understands the need to fulfill one's desires. However, when it comes to making a decision, she can take forever to make up her mind. Mom doesn't ever want to lose what she has and may find it difficult to take personal risks. And, while Sagittarians are very adventurous, they may find it difficult to take chances, as well, especially when it comes to making an emotional commitment. However, if Mom can learn how to be more free and easy with respect to accepting change into her life, she will be able to pass this wisdom along to her child.

The Aquarius Dad/The Sagittarius Child

Dad and his Sagittarius child have a curious thing in common: both can either be lazy or workaholics. The key to determining how they turn out is the degree of challenge in their lives. If they are mentally stimulated by what they're doing, they can become exceptionally productive.

Both parent and child also seem to fear emotional commitment, because to them, that would mean having to give up some of their freedom. Sagittarians have a need to maintain control over their lives, and so do Aquarians. Both Dad and his children need to believe that they are not being forced into anything. If they know that they will have permission to do their own thing, within sensible limits, they can begin to accept a sharing relationship with someone they care about.

An Aquarian father, like Mom, will share a mental affinity with this child. Dad is easily won over by sweet talk and charm, and Sagittarian kids win the prize for being "most lovable." Dad really loves his Sagittarius children, and he always want to be there for them, but he can spend a lot of time in his own thoughts. Sagittarius kids need to know that Dad is emotionally and physically available. They want to be assured that he will be their to listen to them, discuss their problems, or just to share a laugh or two.

On the outside, Dad appears cool and calm, and this is part of his easygoing nature. However, on the inside, Dad is sentimental and sincere. If he can just take the time to relate to his Sagittarius children's feelings, he will be a wonderful asset to their lives!

The Pisces Parent/The Sagittarius Child

Pisces parents are drawn to a Sagittarius child's spirited behavior. However, Pisces are water signs, and they need to remember that water can put out fire. Pisces parents can be overprotective, and they have to be careful not to stifle their optimistic Sagittarius children. Both Pisces parents and their Sagittarius kids are emotional and sensitive, but Sagittarius children's adventurous nature can give them a kind of "blind courage." They're optimistic and believe that each day can be wonderful, while their Pisces parents are worrying about what these kids plan to do next. Mom and Dad would be wise to enjoy the fact that they are raising friendly, fun-loving children. These sons and daughters can exhaust their parents at times, but they're worth it.

Sagittarius children are emotional, but they respond to life with both energy and spontaneity. As small children, they can have a tendency to leap before they look, but as their understanding of right and wrong develops, they will learn where to place their energies. Sagittarius kids need parental guidance when it comes to living in the real world. Pisces, too, can be dreamers, but by using the detailed, organized side of their personalities, they learn to live prudently and practically. When it comes to discipline, Sagittarius children need parents who are calm and sensible, as these kids may try to take advantage of their Pisces parents if Mom and Dad don't adhere to their decisions.

Pisces parents are emotional, and they can view life as a dramatic play that never ends. If there are no problems in their lives, they will create some. Sagittarius children believe that if something goes wrong, tomorrow will be a better day, and their optimism is contagious. These parents could learn a great lesson from their children's wonderful outlook on life!

The Pisces Mom/The Sagittarius Child

While Mom may have a problem letting others know how she feels, those who know her well will understand that she is very emotional. You can see it in the soft, intuitive eyes of this water sign. Pisces mothers are sensitive, loving, kind ladies who can charm anyone. Most people feel good being around them because they are comfortable to be with. Mom loves her children, and she will spend a lot of time playing with them, but her energetic Sagittarius may tire her out. Sagittarius children need a lot of attention, and Mom is capable of giving them the love and affection they need.

On the one hand, both Mom and her Sagittarius child are dreamers who fight reality, and on the other, they tend to be structured, detailed perfectionists who need to control their environment. Mom may be engaged in a continual tug-of-war, though, if she tries to control this child. She will need to apply her whimsical sense to parenting her Sagittarius sons and daughters, and try not to take everything they do so seriously, as humor is one of the best ways to reach Sagittarius kids.

It's important for these children to have rules to live by as they grow, or these fire kids will want to do everything in their own way. Mom needs to explain her decisions in a direct and honest manner. As such, her self-confident behavior will earn these children's respect. There will be times, though, when Mom will have a hard time keeping up with young Sagittarians, as they rarely stop to take a breath. They are active free spirits who are always looking for anything that can stimulate their minds.

There is one issue that Mom needs to work on, which can be beneficial to both parent and child, and that is recognizing the difference between reality and fantasy. This is not always easy for a parent and child who tend to move into their own dream worlds from time to time. But there is one area in which Mom is very comfortable when it comes to raising these children—giving them the freedom to explore life!

The Pisces Dad/The Sagittarius Child

Many Pisces men begin to control their personal feelings at an early age in order to maintain a stable life. They are wise and tend to understand that they are little boys who enjoy living in their fantasies. Most of the Pisces men that I counsel tell me that they fight a constant battle in their efforts to learn to deal with the real world.

A Pisces dad feels a need to be the best father he can be, and he will do everything he can to make his children happy. Both Dad and his Sagittarius children are emotional and sensitive, but their approach to life is different. Dad is a visionary who sees a lot of life's gray areas. This middle-of-the-road philosophy tends to make him indecisive. His fiery kids, on the other hand, see black and white, right or wrong, and very little in between. Therefore, these kids can be impetuous and tend to make quick decisions. Young Sagittarians are restless and do not have a lot of patience. Dad needs to work on being firm and decisive, or these kids will try to make decisions for him—at an early age.

Sagittarius children are usually adorable and fun-loving, so they can easily win Dad's heart. In fact, Dad and his fire children are very compatible when it comes to their charm and sales ability. They are both very intuitive, and their instincts tell them what a person needs to hear most. Most Sagittarius and Pisces individuals tend to have mood swings, though. They both hide from their personal feelings, and their internal frustration makes them irritable and angry. It's up to Dad to recognize that his child's moody nature is similar to his, so he needs to work on being optimistic and playful with his son or daughter. Sagittarians love to laugh, so they will really appreciate Dad's ability to engage in fun, light-hearted activities with them.

Dad tends to have two very different sides when it comes to rearing his Sagittarius kids. One day he's very opinionated and wants to control everything, and the next he's buying up the toy store. Dad needs to be consistent in his actions and reactions, though, in order to win his children's respect.

Dad can be very organized, however, and young Sagittarians will relate to Dad's efficiency because they do need structure in their lives. A Pisces father needs to be honest and straightforward with his fire children, because truth is very important to them. And they, like elephants, never forget a slight! Sagittarius children are very sensitive, and they need to know the reasons why they're being reprimanded. If Dad can learn to express his feelings and talk about the meaningful issues in his life, he will feel a lot better about himself. Parent and child are creative free spirits who can explore the world together, and they are generally kind and compassionate. If Dad can help his fire child understand that the real world is a great place in which to live, they will have many special dreams to share!

SUMMARY

We now know that Sagittarians are optimistic free spirits who have a great zest for life. Put them in a sailboat, and they can roam the world. The best way for parents to build a loving and healthy relationship with their Sagittarian children is to give them freedom of choice and a lot of personal space. I am not suggesting that they do not need guidance to temper their impulsive and overly enthusiastic natures. They want to learn so much that they never can get enough of anything. It's important for parents to understand that these fire kids are so idealistic that this trait can affect their emotional stability. Their parents need to sit down and explain their own decisions and point out the truth in any situation. Sagittarius children believe in honesty, so they will respect and listen to parents who are sincere and forthright in their approach.

I have spoken about the Sagittarians' tendency to fall into mood swings. This generally occurs when they are bored or when they push themselves too far. They tend to be obsessive/compulsive personalities, and this behavior makes them intense and nervous. It's up to parents to say "Time out!" when they see that their Sagittarian kids are being too hard on themselves.

One day I was talking to a Sagittarian associate of mine, and he jokingly asked, "What am I like?"

I replied, "You're a serious free spirit who has a great sense of humor."

He laughed. "Yes, I do need my freedom. I ran away from my parents because they tried to control my entire life!"

"It's too bad they couldn't understand your needs," I told him, "but at that time, many parents raised their children to live up to their own expectations. I'm certain that running away couldn't have helped your relationship with your family."

He admitted, "It took us years to understand and forgive each other."

"I'm glad you were strong enough to put your anger behind you."

"So am I!"

"I have a dream that my four little children will one day live in a nation where they will not be judged by the color of their skin, but by the content of their character."
— Dr. Martin Luther King, Jr.

Chapter Ten

....

♑ CAPRICORN THE GOAT

DECEMBER 22–JANUARY 19   **ELEMENT:** Earth   **KEY PHRASE:** "I use"

....

THE CAPRICORN PERSONALITY

Capricorns understand quality. They know it when they see it in a person or in a piece of artwork. Capricorn kids are also excellent leaders because they know how to combine everyone's ideas and make them all work together. Capricorns are superb at organization, structure, and detail, and they feel like they need to keep their lives in perfect order.

Humor May Help Break the Ice

Capricorns are very serious children, and they tend to see themselves as miniature adults. Most of them are light years ahead of their time and begin to develop their need to take care of others at an early age. They're not very interested in childlike games, and would rather create scenarios where they can play "grown-up." Parents will soon be aware of the exceptional intelligence of their Capricorn children. These kids aren't afraid to own up to responsibility because they like to be in charge of situations. Also, they usually don't require that much discipline because they're always working hard to present their best possible self to the world.

Capricorns don't like making mistakes. They will go to great lengths in terms of both planning and organization to prevent something from going wrong. And even if something incredibly minor does go amiss, these earth kids will tend to be very hard on themselves, running every detail of a given situation over and over in their heads. These kids carry the weight of the world on their shoulders, and it would be wise for parents to try to lighten the load. Mom and Dad should try to create an environment for these children that's both playful and relaxed, and teach their kids that it's okay to make mistakes. After all, it's not possible to fix everything and everyone. If parents can deal with the more serious part of these children's nature with a humorous, light-hearted attitude, these kids may learn to give themselves a break.

They're Strategic Planners

I was at my friend Cynthia's house for dinner, and she related a story about her Capricorn mother.

Cynthia said, "I was telling my mother that each person's astrological sign provides an outline of who they are. So, sounding a little skeptical, my mother said, 'Okay, then, tell me about a Capricorn.' I told her that they're efficient, structured, and that they are the planners of the world. So my Mom tells me, 'I'm not at all like that.' I started laughing and said to her, 'Oh yes you are.' So she sat for a moment, and then said, 'Well, I guess I planned all of my children's birthdays.' So I asked her, 'How did you do that?' Mom said, 'Well, you were first born on August 13th. Your father was born on the third, so I decided I liked the number three. And since you were a C-section baby, I was told that I could schedule each child. So I had your sister Patti on November 3rd, Mary on February 3, and Laura was supposed to be born on the 13th, but the doctor didn't have that day available, so I had her on April 26th. I thought as long as Laura was born on the 26th, I might as well be consistent and schedule Lisa for July 26th.'"

"I looked at my mother at that point and asked, 'Mom, doesn't that story tell you something?' Never much into this sort of thing, she answered, 'I guess I do have some of those Capricorn qualities.'"

Both Cynthia and I laughed and exclaimed simultaneously, "Astrology really works!"

☆ ☆ ☆

Capricorns like to be on top of everything, and even as small children, you'll hear them say, "It's seven o'clock, why isn't the cereal on the table?" or "The bus is two minutes late; where is it?" or "Mom, be sure to pick me up as soon as football practice is over at five." And if Mom is not on time coming to pick up her Capricorn child, he or she will not fail to tell her, "You're seven minutes late!"

Capricorn children are more secure if they can deal with a defined course of action. If these kids have too much to worry about, their nerves take over. They try to be sure that everyone will do the right thing at the right time so they won't have to worry. Even as young children, they begin to envision themselves as perfect. Since they are "young grown-ups," they tend to protect themselves from anxiety by controlling a situation. They do not like to fail, and if they perceive that they have made a mistake, or someone else has erred in some way, they have a problem forgiving themselves, and others as well. It's important for parents to help young Capricorns understand that they can trust Mom and Dad to do the right thing, which includes teaching these kids that if something happens at 3:05, instead of at three o'clock sharp, it won't be the end of the world. If parents can try to nip this type of neurotic behavior in the bud at an early age, their Capricorn children may be able to ease up on themselves.

Capricorn children tend to quietly do their jobs, and since they also usually keep their feelings to themselves, it can be hard for parents to tell when they are in need of attention and affection. We know that Capricorns are usually perfectionists. Therefore, they tend to look at people's foibles, rather than their strong points— no wonder they always want to keep things within their own control! Most Capricorns are results-oriented people who look to strong, intelligent people to provide the assurance and security they need. Capricorns inadvertently test a parent's ability to discipline them, as they're usually clear about what's right or wrong. If parents win this child's respect by revealing strong minds of their own, young Capricorn will adhere to their rules, and be their best friend. No one can condemn Capricorns for their efficient and accurate ways of doing things, but their parents can guide them toward understanding that the world has a lot to offer, and making a mistake will not inhibit their chance to succeed.

Duty, Obligation, and a Need for Perfection

Capricorns feel a great sense of duty and obligation. They definitely feel that it is their moral responsibility to take care of other people's needs—they are wonderful caretakers, so when they watch over other people, they will really do the job right! And when these earth kids are assigned to work with other people on a project, they tend to want to take complete charge. It's hard for them to see the forest for the trees because of their strong determination to get the job done. A Capricorn's ability to put things to use usually forms the basis of their self-confidence. They believe in anything that serves a purpose, and when something doesn't work, it's "outta here"!

Capricorns are leaders whose self-esteem is based on what they achieve. They are self-starters who really do not like to take orders, so they are usually excellent managers who are diligent and meticulous. People have wondered why their Capricorn friends cannot own up to their mistakes, and I have told them that: "If they own up to mistakes, they need to own up to failure. Therefore, it's so important for parents to give them permission to make mistakes at an early age, so they will not be as intimidated by their own real or perceived imperfections."

Capricorns *need* to be perfect, yet they dislike how they feel when they make unrealistic demands upon themselves. A Capricorn appears to be cool on the outside, but tension and turmoil reside within. Individuals such as Capricorns who have problems trusting others wind up doing everything themselves because they are afraid to ask for help. And since they push themselves to the limit, they tend to burn out easily. *Vulnerability* is not a word that exists in Capricorns' vocabulary; they would rather be seen as being stable, responsible, efficient, and self-disciplined. But, although Capricorns' competence is rarely questioned, it's true that their need to be perfect keeps them isolated. This perfectionistic attitude may also tend to intimidate their parents. I have seen this situation occur with quite a few of my clients who have Capricorn children.

PARENT AND CHILD

The Aries Parent/The Capricorn Child

Aries parents are strong, self-motivated personalities who are naturally courageous. Most Aries have great inner strength, and they can easily win their Capricorn children's respect and trust, two qualities that will help these children believe that these parents can take care of their needs. Aries parents are also independent and self-reliant, they have a great zest for life, and they're usually very optimistic. They have a lot in common with their Capricorn children, as they are also perfectionists. While an Aries can also be rigid and disciplined as well, most have an excellent sense of humor and love spontaneity. Even if they appear to be a little stoic at their core, Aries parents are very emotional. They are inwardly intense, even though most of them avoid openly revealing their feelings. Basically, Capricorns tend to view life from a practical and realistic point of view, while their Aries parents are emotional and idealistic.

There are times when both parent and child will want to have things their way. The first thing for a parent to remember is that Capricorn children are methodical thinkers who like to carefully plan out the decisions they make, whereas their Aries parents tend to rely mostly on their instincts. Aries parents and Capricorn children have to learn how to live together, so it's up to Mom and Dad to work on combining their natural instincts with their child's tendency to be conservative and strategic. In this way, parent and child can really learn from each other.

Aries parents will admire their Capricorn's painstaking attention to detail, while they themselves tend to focus on the big picture. These serious children can learn all about optimism and hope from their Aries parents, though, since a parent who is optimistic and spontaneous can help reserved and serious Capricorn children believe that it can really feel good to look on the bright side of life.

My dear friend Roberta had always believed in astrology. While not an avid astrological buff, she definitely believed in the different dynamics of each personality. She called to tell me the following story, which she herself would never have believed unless she'd heard it herself.

Roberta's husband Stan had a cardiovascular problem, and surgery was necessary. At the hospital, Roberta met with the surgeon who was operating on her husband. A gutsy Aries, she naturally wanted to find out all of the technical details about the surgery, and she also wanted to know the doctor's astrological sign.

She asked him, "By the way, when's your birthday?"

Without missing a beat, he asserted, "I'm a second decan Aries." She almost fell over.

When I heard this story, I said, "Thank God, Roberta, here's a man who knows what he's doing!" (I'm also an Aries, if you will recall.) Roberta was amazed that the surgeon even knew what his sign was, but to know what decan he was in was unbelievable.

Since Roberta's husband was a Capricorn who was concerned abut the kind of care that he was going to be receiving. Roberta told him that he didn't have to worry; he had the perfect doctor. "How do you know that?" he asked her.

"He's an Aries!" she replied.

"Ohhh!" Stan said, trying to sound overly impressed. He smiled. "It's a good thing he's got all of the right qualifications!"

In the case of that surgeon, here was a man whose base of knowledge was highly technical, yet he was able to appreciate a completely different dimension in his life. This trait definitely depicts the Aries personality—they are often perfectionists, but that characteristic won't interfere with being open-minded. Aries parents are excellent mentors for Capricorn children for that very reason, as they will encourage their kids to do their best while being open to all the wonderful options that life has to offer.

The Aries Mom/The Capricorn Child

Capricorn children will usually admire their Aries mother because she lives up to their ideal of motherhood. She's honest, strong, outgoing, and intelligent, and she doesn't mince words—once her anger's aroused, it's right out there for all the world to see. Mom is also kind, compassionate, and very caring. She loves her children, and she's very interested in helping them develop their intellect and creativity. Mom tends to move quickly, so she can often be found walking ahead of her Capricorn children, as they tend to move at their own methodical pace. Mom needs to realize that she cannot force her Capricorn children into emulating her behavior, though, as they listen to the beat of a more consistent and predictable drummer. She has to understand that her children need to feel stable and secure with someone who will follow a definite routine within the home.

At times, an Aries mother can almost be too independent and self-reliant. She may give her family the impression that everything she does is easy. One of her reasons for trying to take care of everything is that she has specific ideas on how to run a home, and believes she is more efficient than most people when it comes to getting the job done. It's important for this mother to allow herself to receive recognition for everything she does. An Aries mom's most difficult task is to ask for help. In addition, she needs to give herself permission to share her personal thoughts with those whom she can trust. She should accept the fact that while total control makes her ultimately responsible for things, people, and situations, maintaining this rigid attitude may never give her the understanding, acceptance, and love she truly needs.

Mom always tries to take a positive viewpoint, and her Capricorn will appreciate her outlook on life. Capricorns don't usually trust easily, but they will easily respect and honor their truthful Aries mother. Mom can teach her children the importance of seeing the good in people and how to be objective in terms of their opinions and judgments. Both parent and child can benefit from learning that they are not the only ones in the world who know how to do what's right.

Mom is really a people person, even if she has a practical side. She is an individualist, and remaining that way is important to her. "I am who I am," she might say, and "I can't help it if you don't like the way I am." When Mom raises Capricorn children, she would be wise not to encourage these kids to become independent and self-reliant at too early an age, as they will feel that she has left them too soon. They must develop a feeling of safety and security at home before they're allowed to start exploring life on their own. Capricorns look up to their parents to provide them with a solid foundation.

The Aries Dad/The Capricorn Child

Capricorns need an intelligent and responsible father who has a strong work ethic, as these children believe that striving for success is very important to one's image. Capricorns respect a father who is honest in both business and in his personal life, and who is available to both listen to them and help them with their decisions. They need to depend on someone who's strong and supportive—a father whose first instinct is to motivate, rather than to tell them what they've done wrong.

Any kind of personal confrontation can emotionally upset an Aries dad, as he can't help but take everything personally. Like their Aries parents, Capricorn children can also find personal confrontation difficult, because it can be stressful to express oneself perfectly, and after all, Capricorns are perfectionists. Both parent and child may have to learn that they may find themselves "babbling" when they try to explain how they feel; however, this is perfectly human, and if someone babbles long enough and sincerely enough, they will eventually find their way to the truth.

Many Aries fathers find it difficult to talk about their feelings, and at times they appear to be distant. I have counseled many Aries men, and I often ask them, "Why do you fight your feelings when you can offer so much personal security to your family and your friends?" Many of these Aries have responded that they are very private people who view emotion as a sign of weakness. Also, some have admitted that they have been so busy taking care of others that they haven't paid heed to their own desires. I have often told them that an emotional, sensitive man needs to receive love and attention, and if he doesn't get it, he should ask!

An Aries dad likes to experiment. He takes risks, and he will give himself the opportunity to learn about everything. He often believes that his children can learn in the same manner. In general, Capricorns do not enjoy experimentation, though, as they do not feel comfortable taking risks. They always want to know what's happening, as the unknown holds no fascination for them. This father can be instrumental in helping their Capricorns learn to explore, and he can also show his children how much fun it is to take a few calculated risks. Dad and his Capricorn kids will be friends, as Dad can offer many practical skills that these earth children will enjoy. However, both an Aries dad and his Capricorn children can be a little vain (since they are perfectionists), so Dad would be wise to teach them that their self-esteem has only a small part to do with outer appearances.

The Taurus Parent/The Capricorn Child

Taurus parents will easily fulfill a Capricorn's need for personal security. They can give these kids the solid foundation that they dream about. Taureans would gladly sacrifice their own needs to make sure that these children live in a comfortable home environment where they can grow up with a family that provides an abundance of love and affection. They are stable, sensitive people who will always stand up for their children. However, there are Taureans who are "late bloomers," emotionally immature individuals who fear becoming parents.

Taurus parents are in tune with their Capricorn's organized nature. Mom and Dad will be an asset to these children, as they never try to make them go against their wishes. They will allow these kids the freedom to develop in their own way, since these parents will believe in their earth children's stability. There are times when Taurus parents may feel that their Capricorn children are making too many demands, but by providing these kids with a safe and secure environment, they won't feel like they have to remind their parents that they need to be taken care of.

A Taurean's worst fear is to be abandoned, so Mom and Dad will make sure that their own children know that they will never desert them. Capricorn parents have a tendency to sacrifice their own needs for their children, and so they may expect their Taurus parents to do the same for them. This is the time when a Taurus may have to draw the line. Mom and Dad would be wise to understand that they cannot give up their status as parents—the leaders in the family—and that from time to time they might have to put their young Capricorns in their rightful place.

The Taurus Mom/The Capricorn Child

Mom is an honest and loving lady who raises her children with assurance and grace. In addition, she also has good taste, style, and she really likes people. All of these qualities fit right in with her Capricorn children's way of thinking, as both signs present themselves in an elegant manner.

Both Mom and her children are in tune as far as expecting to live a stable, secure lifestyle, but how they present these needs can be very different. A Taurus mom wants to be taken care of, while her Capricorn child is usually a caretaker. Caretakers are drawn to a Taurus personality, as the latter has a "protectable quality" that can make others want to look after them. Capricorns like to take charge of situations, and these kids may try to boss around their Taurus parents. It's easy for Mom to depend upon her Capricorn children, as they are strong and protective; but she needs to hold her own as a parent, as these children will require her strength in order to give them the emotional security they need.

Taurus mothers can be excellent role models because they have an idealistic and romantic outlook on life. This attitude tends to help soften the Capricorn child's practical view of life. Taureans have a tendency to want to please everyone, so they tend to avoid personal confrontation. It would be wise for Mom to work on her own self-confidence, which will then help her Capricorn children do the same.

Overall, Taurus moms will allow their Capricorn kids to maintain their right to privacy, as well as encouraging their pursuit of excellence!

The Taurus Dad/The Capricorn Child

Dad and his Capricorn child agree on the importance of a solid family life. They both feel secure and stable when living in an environment that provides them with a feeling of mutual support. The traditional, more conservative type of Taurus father wants to maintain a peaceful life, with very little change. Those Taureans who tend to be dreamers, though, sometimes allow themselves to settle down both financially and emotionally before they raise a family.

A Taurus dad can be quite stubborn once he's made up his mind about something, and since his Capricorn child shares this trait, it's up to Dad to work on bending a bit. Capricorn children are usually very serious, and when they are very young, they can isolate themselves from people who might intimidate them. Dad is generally a very intuitive person, so it would be a good idea for him to acknowledge that he can't push his earth children into moving too quickly. Many of these kids are outgoing and friendly, but there are those who tend to be skeptical until they trust someone.

Dad needs to be aware that his Capricorn children may remain silent after an argument and retreat inward. They usually keep their grievances to themselves, and their reticence can be a way of punishing those around them. It's important for Dad to try and break through this silence by opening up discussion in a frank and honest manner. His Capricorns will appreciate the effort!

The Gemini Parent/The Capricorn Child

Gemini parents like to search for new and exciting adventures. And, like their Capricorn children, they have a very realistic approach when it comes to getting things done. Capricorns, however, tend to be planners who always like to know what's going on, while Geminis tend to make things up as they go along and don't usually enjoy being pinned down to a specific time. Gemini parents need to be aware that their Capricorn children tend to fear spontaneity, as it isn't practical. They can feel insecure with an independent parent who may force them to adapt to an environment that does not fit their character. Capricorns may need to know what plans are being made on an hourly basis. Gemini parents cannot totally change their personalities, but they need to try to develop a more consistent pattern, especially when it involves a Capricorn child's needs.

As parents, Geminis will be involved in diverse activities outside the home, but they would be wise to remember that their Capricorn children need their attention at home, too. Geminis don't plan to be restless—they just are by nature; and Capricorns don't plan to be stable homebodies—that's just *their* predilection. So, Gemini parents really need to make an effort to understand how important a Capricorn's home life is to them, as their need for safety is assuaged by growing up in a secure and stable environment. No one would use the word *secure* when describing a Gemini, as their somewhat inconsistent behavior precludes a life filled with a great deal of stability.

The Gemini Mom/The Capricorn Child

Mom's motto could be: "Don't ever stop me from moving!" Gemini mothers may very likely be involved in a number of activities outside the home, including charitable interests. They just have to remember that Capricorn children need to know that their Mom will always be there for them when they need them. It is natural for Mom to distance herself from the everyday humdrum affairs of life, as she is not very interested in domesticity. However, Capricorns *are* very interested in the home and the stability it offers them.

Capricorns are very practical, and Mom will appreciate their intelligence and sense of what's right and wrong. If she can understand that she needs to listen carefully to her Capricorn children's point of view, she will be able to give them the freedom to make their own decisions. Mom's energy and enthusiasm will help her Capricorn kids see that life can be joyous—there's so much to explore and seek out!

Mom will not invade her Capricorn children's privacy; she will gladly give them time to be by themselves. Capricorn children do enjoy their time alone, as long as they feel that Mom is there to listen to them and support them.

Capricorn children are basically serious, and they want to understand how the real world works. They value self-discipline and organization and usually like to live within established household rules. Gemini Mom loves her children, and she will do anything for them, but making time for herself is necessary to calm her restless nature. As long as she explains to her Capricorn children that she's taking time for herself because that is her nature and not because she's ignoring or neglecting them, they won't resent her. In fact, they will respect her honesty, which can only enhance this parent/child relationship.

Capricorns love to learn, and Mom can be very instrumental in helping them enhance their intellectual abilities. Mom is interested in anything that relates to the mind, so practicality, reason, and sensibility are all a part of her personality. She knows how to logically explain her opinions clearly and concisely, and she also has the ability to help her children learn how to be more flexible. This is not an easy task, but if Mom can help her kids understand that it's okay to accept change, her children will see that it can be a valuable learning experience.

The Gemini Dad/The Capricorn Child

Dad is very protective, and he'll do anything for his children, but he may spend a lot of time working. He needs to use his intellect, and staying around the house doesn't always give him the excitement he needs. Dad would be wise to show an interest in everything his Capricorn does, as this child needs his approval. It's okay for him to disagree with his Capricorn kids, as long as he explains his reasons. If he is there to protect his young Capricorns (and he's very good at shielding them from harm), they will feel quite secure. Dad, like Mom, looks at things logically, and most of what he does is based on reason and sensibility.

There are generally two types of Gemini fathers. If Dad is the serious intellectual type, he may take on the role of the authoritarian in the home, as it suits his ability to control most situations. Capricorns accept authority when they learn to respect their parents, so as long as Dad is willing to openly discuss his Capricorn children's opinions with them and give them the options to make their own decisions, he will have no trouble raising these kids. If Dad is the more creative type of Gemini father, he can help his child learn that creativity can be combined with reason in order to give them a broader and more open-minded perspective of the world.

A Gemini father may also enjoy some hobbies that may be thought of as domestic. He enjoys cooking and traveling, which are activities that his Capricorn children will enjoy sharing with him, and he also is interested in collecting valuables from all over the world. All in all, Dad is a well-rounded man who will enrich his children's lives in many ways!

The Cancer Parent/The Capricorn Child

Cancer parents and their Capricorn children share a great affinity for home and family. Cancers are comfortable living in a traditional and stable home environment, and this atmosphere will fulfill Capricorn children's need for safety and security. Cancers feel profound love for their children, and they will give their kids an abundance of love and attention. These sensitive parents do, however, have a tendency to do almost *anything* for their kids simply because they want to receive their approval. Sometimes it's necessary for Cancer parents to remain firm in order to maintain their own self-esteem. Cancers are very emotional people, so it would be wise for them to nurture their own feelings instead of worrying about their children to excess.

The following story illustrates this point.

☆ ☆ ☆

My friend Dina and her son Richard were having dinner at my house to celebrate my son Layne's 29th birthday. After I made a birthday toast, Layne took my hand and said, "I love you, Mom."

Dina smiled. "Layne, that's beautiful."

He responded matter-of-factly, "I always tell my Mom how much I love her." Dina's son Richard glanced quickly over to his mother, and then back down to his salad. I could tell that he wasn't relating to this emotional scene.

Dina then looked at her own son, and said, "I love you, Richard."

He replied uncomfortably, "Thanks, that's great." I could see Dina's eyes filling up with tears. She didn't want to make a scene, so she excused herself and went into the bathroom.

"Richard," I asked him curiously, "is it hard for you to tell your mother you love her?"

He looked down and muttered, "Maybe."

As usual, I needed to get more information. "Richard, your Mom is a very sensitive woman, and she would really love to hear you say those words."

He resisted for a moment, and then said, "I do love my mother."

I pressed him. "Then why can't you say it?"

He was starting to get a little peeved at me. "I have a problem saying it. I show her that I love her by what I do for her." He added, "She hardly ever tells me how she feels!"

I knew that Dina, a Cancer, found it difficult to talk about her personal feelings. Therefore, she never let Richard (a Capricorn) know what she needed—that is, to hear him say "I love you."

When Dina returned, I knew I might be overstepping my bounds, but I said, "Dina, don't you think that you should let Richard know that you need him to pay attention to you?"

She replied, "I guess so."

I thought for a moment, and asked, "Do you believe that you deserve *your son's love?"*

"I suppose I do."

"Well," I continued, "if you constantly give, without asking in return, you'll never recognize your real needs."

Richard was carefully listening to every word. He jumped in with "Mom, Sylvia's right."

Dina replied, "I know she is." She turned toward Richard and gave him a big hug.

As Dina and Richard were leaving, he kissed me goodbye and remarked to my son Layne, "Aren't these ladies wonderful? I love them both!"

Dina really appreciated her son's efforts, and the two started to open up to each other for the first time in years!

☆   ☆   ☆

Most Cancers define their personal worth through their relationships. The more they give, the more worthy they feel. In fact, many of them stay in unhealthy relationships due to their "caretaking" natures. They hang on for years before they're finally forced to let go. Many of my clients are Cancer women, and almost all of them have problems believing that they deserve to be loved. However, many of these same clients have come to understand that their self-worth and self-esteem stem from their capacity to love themselves. Once they see how special they are, they take better care of themselves. People cannot know what they deserve if they constantly give themselves away.

Since Cancers are great advocates of home and family, they naturally remain very strongly connected to their children. These water parents are totally involved in being the best parents that they can be and, as such, they will give their Capricorn children permission to achieve everything that they want in life. They support their kids' special affinity for the practical aspects of life.

The Cancer Mom/The Capricorn Child

Mom's key phrase is "I feel," while her Capricorn children's key phrase is "I use." Capricorns can never resist Mom's attention or affection, but they themselves may not always find it easy to express deep emotions. But if Mom continues to kiss and hug her kids anyway, these kids may follow by example.

Mom's ability to create a stable, secure household will provide a solid foundation for this parent/child relationship. In addition, Cancers parents are excellent at organization and planning, and their Capricorn children will never have to remind them of their responsibility to follow through on a promise. Both Capricorns and Cancers need to be easier on themselves, though. These quick-thinking children place a great deal of responsibility upon themselves. So, it's Mom's job to first try and calm her own nerves if she expects her children to do the same.

What I often advise Cancer moms to do is: "Learn to believe that you're worthy just as you are. You don't need your children's approval. They'll always love you because you truly care about *them*. You don't have to immerse yourself totally into your home just to protect yourself from the outside world. You love your home, but what's more important is to love yourself!" If Mom can realize she's lovable just for being herself, her Capricorn children will be sure to appreciate her. One thing that parent and child have to avoid, though, is guilt. If Mom knows that she's worthy, she won't have to use guilt trips to persuade her children to do something. Her gift to her Capricorn children will be to help them develop their self-esteem.

The Cancer Dad/The Capricorn Child

Dad is usually affectionate and attentive, and his sensitive, protective nature helps him nurture his children when they're troubled. No one would ever question a Cancer father's devotion to his children. Unfortunately, this Cancer father doesn't give himself permission to talk about how he feels. As one of my clients once told me about her Cancer dad, "All my father ever talked about was sports."

Dad assumes the role of "ruler of the house," as this kind of control protects him from personal exposure. If he shows his family how strong he is, he figures that they won't question his actions. Dad tends to inhibit himself by tucking away his real emotions, but a sensitive man cannot deny his feelings without experiencing underlying frustration. This is one of the reasons that Dad tends to fall in and out of moods. Capricorn children can be confused and frightened by this behavior because they will take it personally. If Dad can try to release his anxiety by confronting his own emotional side, his moods won't fluctuate as much, and his Capricorn children will be more content.

All in all, Dad has a lot to offer his Capricorn children, and they will always benefit from his genuine loving care and wisdom.

The Leo Parent/The Capricorn Child

Leos are strong, supportive, emotional parents who take excellent care of their children. These "royal" moms and dads are kind-hearted, energetic, and they always think young. They stand behind their kids, and this tendency will make Capricorn children feel very safe and secure throughout their lives.

Leos and Capricorns are both stubborn and opinionated, and they both have a problem backing away from what they believe. Capricorns will quickly sense a Leo's strong and protective nature, as they admire people whom they can trust. While they enjoy being able to depend on their Leo parents' natural strength and power, though, there are times when they resent the fact that they do just that.

Capricorn children like to do things their way, and if they acknowledge their reliance on their parents, they perceive their own power diminishing. So, it's important for these fire parents to give their Capricorn children the freedom to make their own decisions. Leo parents have a knack for encouraging their earth kids to take advantage of their own potential, and they'll always be there to applaud their successes. Capricorn kids tend to be very hard on themselves, so they need their idealistic Leo parents to help reinforce their personal strength and power.

The Leo Mom/The Capricorn Child

Mom loves to help! She's a good teacher, and her need to take care of people extends beyond her children. When she raises her Capricorn children, she'll easily recognize that these kids mature early. When they grow up, Capricorns become independent, self-reliant adults; but when they're children, they like the idea that they don't have to contend with so much responsibility. And these kids tend to grow up so quickly that it seems as if they hardly spent any time acting like small boys or girls. It would be wise for Leo parents to encourage their Capricorn children to have fun and play so that they can help them to be "little" for a while.

A Leo mother is an emotional person, although she may tend to keep her personal feelings to herself. I have been known to repeat this statement over and over to my Leo clients: "If someone is born an emotional person, then they are doing themselves a disservice by not expressing their true feelings." It's not healthy to inwardly rebel against something that's natural. Leo women tend to hold back their feelings because they think they have to remain strong for those who need them. Many deny their emotions and, instead, focus on being efficient and organized because it's easier to concentrate on the mundane details of life.

A Leo woman's emotions can usually be detected by her playful nature, though. She likes to laugh out loud, and she is a lot of fun to be with. My main concern is her ability to turn her feelings off. I suggest that she get in touch with her real emotions. Nothing terrible will happen as a result—trust me!

Capricorn children enjoy Mom's personality because she takes care of everything and makes life very interesting. However, Mom can be a perfectionist who has trouble trusting others to do things as well as she does. With a Capricorn, she will be raising a child who will probably have a similar problem. Mom may want to roar when someone makes a mistake, and she may need to remind herself that both patience and gentle instruction may be the best ways to get things done right. She doesn't want to hurt the feelings of the people whom she's dealing with. If Mom can learn these lessons, she can then share them with her fellow perfectionist— her Capricorn child.

The best way for Leo mothers to win the hearts of their Capricorn children is to teach them that playing is good for the soul. Mom can have a theatrical side to her personality, which means that she'll be very good at making up games and playing different characters. Both Mom and her Capricorn kids can have a lot of fun together, and this will be instrumental in developing their enthusiasm. These serious, miniature adults will learn that it's important to make time to play, a lesson that they will carry into adulthood.

The Leo Dad/The Capricorn Child

Dad has many qualities that his Capricorn children will admire. He's strong, honest, intelligent, and great at dealing with people. Both Dad and his Capricorn kids are strongly opinionated, and they can all be pretty stubborn when they make up their minds. A Leo dad, more than his female counterpart, believes that he should be the king of his castle. As such, he has to be careful about trying to make all of the important decisions that have to do with his Capricorn children. I know that he believes the entire family is his responsibility, but Capricorns need to be recognized for their ability to make decisions for themselves.

Dad would be wise for to acknowledge that it's important to initiate sensible discussions with his earth kids when it comes to making decisions that can affect them. In addition, Dad can provide his Capricorn children with a series of options to choose from, which will give these kids the opportunity to make their own decisions. A Leo father has great dreams for his children, and he'll do anything he can to help them succeed. As long as he allows these kids to live out their own dreams, he'll be an excellent role model for them. Capricorns are usually ambitious and goal oriented, but they'll need their Leo dad's gentle guidance and support.

Dad is an emotional man, but just like Mom, he tends to keep his feelings to himself. He can be a firm and steady disciplinarian, and his strong presence always makes an impression on those around him. A Capricorn will appreciate this stable, solid father, who will give his children logical, reasonable explanations for his actions and who will defend anyone who has seemingly been unfairly treated. His Capricorn children will witness this type of behavior as they grow up, and they will respect their father for being the courageous and honorable man that he is.

The Virgo Parent/The Capricorn Child

Virgo parents and Capricorn children are very compatible, as they both feel most comfortable in a stable and solid home environment. Young Capricorn will enjoy living in an organized home where household rules are set, and where a series of activities are performed regularly. It's amazing to me, though, that these two methodical, even-keeled personalities can create so much tension and drama in their lives. There are no molehills, only mountains. I keep telling my Virgo and Capricorn clients to work on developing flexibility, as this is a trait that seems to escape them. If both Virgos and Capricorns tried to ease up on themselves, what wonderful lives these brilliant people could have! They could modify their worrisome natures, learn to release those problems they cannot solve, and forgive those individuals who have seemingly hurt them.

Virgo parents and their Capricorn children are fixed personalities, which means that they don't have a problem living a more traditional lifestyle. These Capricorn kids will believe in Mom and Dad's philosophy that self-discipline is crucial if you want to get a job done right.

Capricorn children are very well behaved, and they have proper manners. Both parents and children look at life from a practical point of view, and they're both always trying to figure out the realistic ways of doing things. And like their Virgo parents, Capricorn children put a lot of pressure on themselves because they always want everything to get done perfectly. Virgos do have a great sense of humor, though. So, if Mom and Dad can learn how to laugh at their own mistakes, they can pass this quality on to their Capricorn children. These earth kids need role models who can let up on themselves from time to time, and just enjoy life!

The Virgo Mom/The Capricorn Child

Mom is a planner, and her strategies are usually well thought-out. She wants to know everything about everything in order to make her life perfect, and she detests making a mistake. A Virgo mother can be a harsh taskmaster, but her children have no problem with her attitude, because they are in agreement with her philosophy.

Capricorn children believe in home and family, and they need to live in a stable, organized environment. In fact, all earth signs believe that a healthy foundation is at the core of a satisfying existence. Mom can help her Capricorn kids by inspiring them to go for their goals without ever giving up. She herself never admits defeat; she just persists and persists.

Both Virgos and Capricorns are realists who understand how to use the material things in life wisely, and they are practical when it comes to personal finances. They definitely know how to get the best quality for the least money.

Mom needs to be aware that her strong opinions and critical nature will be easily absorbed by her Capricorn children, so she should make an effort to temper these qualities to the best of her ability. Both Virgos and Capricorns are perfectionists who are much too hard on themselves. Mom should impress upon her Capricorn kids the notion that they needn't make mountains out of molehills, so they don't end up as nervous as she often is.

All in all, though, this parent/child duo will have a fine relationship because these kids will be assured that Mom will always be there for them when needed.

The Virgo Dad/The Capricorn Child

Dad, like Mom, takes a practical approach to life, and he also tends to be a perfectionist. He will enjoy having Capricorn children, as they easily live up to his expectations. He wants intelligent, well-behaved, charming children who look at the world in much the same way he does. He will be always be dreaming about how accomplished and successful his Capricorn children will be. He needs to be careful about placing too many expectations upon his kids, though, as they have a hard enough time handling their own high standards.

When it comes to dealing with emotions, Dad may not always say what he feels. He has to be careful, however, that his silence isn't interpreted by his children to mean that they're not good enough. If Dad lets his Capricorn kids know how he feels, he can help them relax and feel comfortable about what they're doing or thinking.

Dad wants to provide for his family, and he can easily rise to the top of his profession. He has great ideas, and his terrific strategies are excellent for sales careers. He has a lot of inner creativity, and a great deal of curiosity about life. As a matter of fact, Virgos and Capricorns are both excellent in business. They have the ability to understand mathematics and logic, and they make fine managers. Dad can be an inspiration for his Capricorn children as long as he takes his time when confronting them with problems, and if he acknowledges that these children have difficulty dealing with criticism.

The Libra Parent/The Capricorn Child

Libras tend to be more liberal than most parents, but they approach their everyday chores and duties with enthusiasm and intense interest. In fact, they tend to be too hard on themselves. They do have natural social skills, though, and they are in tune with beauty, art, music, and soft colors. They have excellent intuition and can quickly sense whether something is right or wrong.

Capricorn children tend to be serious and conservative. They are comfortable living in an organized and structured environment where everything has its place. They have a tendency to make sure that everything they complete is perfect. Libras can also be very organized, but constant routine stifles their spirit. Overall, their philosophical approach to life is very different from that of their practical earth children. They are visionaries who want to explore all of life, whereas their earth children tend to be conventional and proper. Capricorn children relate to physical objects set before them and quickly understand how to eliminate those items that do not belong, in order to create a perfect picture.

Libra parents may put pressure on themselves, but they have the ability to be a calming influence on their Capricorn children. They are extraordinary diplomats who want to enjoy life. Capricorn kids tend to avoid their seriousness by developing their humorous sides. They need to play and have fun, but all in all, these earth children relate to the world on a practical realistic basis, while their Libra parents tend to look at situations more idealistically. Libras can help their kids recognize the beauty that life has to offer. As negotiators, they will combine both the ideal and the real; their charming natures make both sides feel comfortable, and their way of logically analyzing the facts of a situation—and what's really important to both sides—helps bring about practical solutions to problems. Capricorn children will admire these qualities.

Capricorn kids tend to be strategic and need to live their lives according to plan, while Libras are usually restless individuals who do not like to be tied into set patterns. Mom and Dad will eventually recognize that their practical earth children can become exasperated by this behavior, so it's up to these parents to help their Capricorn kids relax and give themselves some slack. This will be a very difficult task to accomplish, but I know that sensible Libra parents can do it!

Libra parents need peace and harmony, so making important decisions can be troublesome for them. When these parents have difficulty making decisions, their Capricorn sons and daughters will want to take over, as very little stands in their way when they want something. It's important for Libra parents to sit down with their earth kids at an early age in order to give them an opportunity to offer their opinions. Then, parent and child can agree to discuss their issues in a reasonable manner.

Libra parents can bring art and music into the lives of their serious Capricorns in order to help them release their intense feelings and enjoy living in a peaceful, tranquil, and loving environment!

The Libra Mom/The Capricorn Child

A Libra mother is fair, sympathetic, and she believes that anything is possible. Libras do have a tendency, however, to think that everything that happens is somehow their fault, and that it's their responsibility to try and make everyone happy. Libras may have to learn that it's impossible to please everyone. A Libra's self-esteem stems from being able to accomplish what they set out to do. It's important for this Mom to understand that she has to give herself permission to care of her own needs, as well as the needs of her children. Libras are easily guilt-tripped, and they need to learn to move away from these feelings. They have no reason to feel guilty about something they cannot resolve. Mom is a special lady who also needs to realize that nothing terrible will happen to her if she decides to say no. Mom has a powerful sense for what is fair, and she will feel better about the way she runs her life if she makes the decision to stand up for her opinions and beliefs when she feels she is right.

A Libra mother takes great pains to provide a lovely environment for her children, and her innate desire for peace and tranquility can be a wonderful asset to her intense Capricorn kids. Many of Mom's other traits will appeal to them as well, as she is a mother who is intelligent, artistic, and playful, with the ability to help her kids relax.

Many Libras have a lot of anger that they haven't dealt with, however, especially those individuals who are still obsessed with being people-pleasers. So, it would be a good idea for this mom to forgive those in her life whom have seemingly hurt her and to be cognizant of the fact that everyone isn't going to like her. When Libras resolve their inner turmoil in this regard, they will feel much better about themselves.

When Libra mothers raise Capricorn children, they need to learn how to stand up to some of their demands. Capricorn kids can be very opinionated and can try to force their opinions on Mom if she allows it. Capricorns are inspired by a Libra mother's sense of balance and fairness, however, and Mom can be a great help in making her kids realize that their are many ways to deal with a situation. She can teach them to be flexible with respect to their views and decisions, rather than to stubbornly adhere to them, no matter what!

Mom will always be supportive of her Capricorns, and she will give these earth children the reassurance that they need to succeed. She definitely believes in their talents and abilities. Capricorn children are very self-reliant and efficient, and they will want Mom to establish household rules and standards of behavior for them to live by. And if these kids ever become too self-effacing, Mom's combination of patience and wisdom will help them ease up on themselves!

The Libra Dad/The Capricorn Child

Dad is a considerate father and a great friend. He usually appears to be easygoing, but like his Capricorn child, he places very high expectations on himself, and he can drive himself too hard. It's because he is also a perfectionist who can be quite exacting and methodical in his work. Dad may really have to force himself to relax, so one way for Dad to calm his nerves is to take some time away from everyone so he can revitalize his spirit. However, the best way for Dad to calm down is to be open with his emotions.

Dad would be wise to work on his fear of personal confrontation, because he will feel a lot better if he can talk about any hurt feelings he has at the time that they occur. Dad enjoys having his own space, but he needs to accept the fact that his Capricorn children will need him to help them whenever the time comes for making important decisions.

Most people admire Dad because he understands how to get along with everyone on their own level. Dad's tendency to be a loner can lead to problems, though. I've counseled a number of Libra men who have told me, "I didn't know what happened. All of a sudden, my wife was asking me for a divorce." I usually tell them that they can't blame themselves for everything since their wives didn't have the courage to tell *them* how they felt until it was too late. The best advice that I can offer them is that they have to give themselves permission to let people know how they feel, especially those whom they're close to.

Dad is very honest and comforting, and his Capricorn children will seek out his advice and attention. Libras are thinkers, so Dad's logical approach to life will work well with his Capricorn children. A Libra father will always give his children the freedom to learn and explore, and he will show them how to use their practical abilities in order to make their dreams come true.

The Scorpio Parent/The Capricorn Child

Scorpios and Capricorns can live very harmoniously together because they share the same values, which include a sense of order and a need to do everything right. They are both very efficient and organized, and once they set things up, they don't like anything to change. When it comes to emotions, Scorpios feel very deeply, but just like their Capricorn children, they can be very reticent about letting their loved ones know how they feel.

Capricorn children appreciate the kind of structured lifestyle that Scorpio parents can provide, and they will admire Mom and Dad's ability to keep their home environment safe and stable. With respect to how they view their Capricorn kids, Scorpio parents tend to be of the opinion that their children will always be children until they prove otherwise, but Capricorns are usually born old and wise, so Scorpio parents will particularly enjoy their mature little adults.

However, it's important for Mom and Dad to acknowledge that Capricorn children have a tendency to take on too many responsibilities early on in life. As a result, these kids need to learn how to enjoy themselves. Therefore, these Scorpio parents would be wise to encourage playtime for their little Capricorns so they can avoid taking themselves too seriously. Scorpio parents are hardworking perfectionists who give themselves very little time to relax, so if *they* can lighten up at times and take the time to smell the roses, they will set an example for their children that will benefit them throughout their lives.

The Scorpio Mom/The Capricorn Child

Mom likes to take charge of her home environment. Whether she is dealing with decorating, cooking, or the needs of her children, Mom likes to handle *everything!* Her Capricorn children will enjoy helping her, but she cannot overwhelm these kids with too much responsibility. Capricorns seem like they're born with the belief that everything should fall on their shoulders, and Mom has a similar problem. Parent and child need to share their responsibilities in order to lessen their respective burdens. Mom may have to be careful not to try to make all of the decisions that involve her children; when she raises these Capricorn kids, she'd be wise to encourage them to make their own decisions, rather than taking on this task herself. Capricorns need to feel that they can make up their own minds and *then* come to Mom for approval.

Mom will be certain to raise her children with proper nutrition, as well as showing them how to be polite, considerate human beings, and Mom's special degree of intuition helps her understand the underlying needs of her children. Although Mom and her Capricorn children do agree on the need for self-discipline—after all, they are both perfectionists—they might not always agree as to how to get things done. Scorpio mothers may find themselves getting upset when their earth kids start to disagree with them; in fact, these moms may think to themselves, "He's only a kid. What does he know?" Children, however, don't remain children for long, and they develop their opinions at an early age. Mom would be well advised to give her little earth kids reasonable explanations for the actions that she takes, as well as providing them with options to choose from when a decision must be made on some issue. This behavior will give these kids a sense of freedom and autonomy.

A Scorpio mother may believe that her children will suffer in life if they rebel against the norm. She wants her children to live up to their greatest potential, and she feels that if they don't fit in, they won't be able to achieve. Capricorn children, however, also feel this need to conform and will go along with Mom in this regard. If Mom can be careful not to discount her Capricorn children's individuality, she will enhance their self-esteem. Capricorn children get upset when anyone challenges their ability to make decisions and resolve problems. If Mom will take care not to insult her children's intelligence, and allow them to consult on important issues, she can win the greatest battle when raising these kids.

Scorpio mothers have a tendency to make their children feel guilty if they're not living up to their expectations, so it's best that Mom openly discusses these feelings instead of throwing comments at them such as: "I told you that you should have studied more for that test," or "You weren't very organized; you know better than that." Capricorns may avoid personal confrontation, but they would be better off with honest conversation, as they feel guilty when Mom disapproves of their behavior. Remember, like their Scorpio parents, Capricorn children also place very high expectations on themselves, and they don't want to hear that something simply could have been done better. All in all, there is no doubt that Mom will help, protect, and form a loving relationship with her Capricorn children.

The Scorpio Dad/The Capricorn Child

Dad is a powerful man, and like Mom, he likes to run his household in his own way. He's strong and protective, and he can be opinionated, as well. Dad believes that everyone has a right to their own ideas, but when it comes to his own family, he may decide that his ideas are the best. Dad will definitely enjoy his Capricorn children's intelligence and maturity, but he may run into some trouble as they begin to grow because these sharp earth children will be just as opinionated as he is. Dad may need to learn to develop some strategy when it comes to his Capricorn children.

Both Dad and his son or daughter have a high degree of will power, so Dad will need to explain his reasons for ruling against young Capricorn's pronouncements and decisions at an early age.

Parent and child both share the philosophy that a traditional and structured home is a perfect place to live. Dad needs to be independent, and he can be more of a devil's advocate than Mom. He must be careful about trying to test his Capricorn children's intelligence, as they are inwardly shy and insecure. These kids want to feel that Dad believes in their ability to succeed. By intelligently discussing all problems with his children, Dad will pave the way for a healthy relationship.

The Sagittarius Parent/The Capricorn Child

Sagittarius parents can be positive influences on their Capricorn children because they are free-spirited nonconformists. They have the ability to help their serious, rather conventional Capricorns by bringing laughter into their lives. These fiery parents, who have a wonderful sense of humor, are also emotional and imaginative, whereas their kids are practical and realistic. However, as strong and self-reliant as Capricorns tend to be, they are very attached to their family, and they have a powerful need to feel secure.

When Sagittarius parents raise Capricorns, they need to be aware that these kids are usually rigid and self-disciplined and have a real problem with inconsistency when they see this trait in others. Capricorns don't miss a trick, and their parents will not be immune from scrutiny. Sagittarius parents can also be rigid about their lifestyle and hard on themselves, but the main difference between parent and child is that the parents push themselves too far and then find a way to step back and relax, while the child cannot fathom how to relax.

These earth kids are very determined in their pursuits, but one would not characterize them as *enthusiastic.* They plod along and can do anything they set their minds to. Their fire parents, conversely, can be overly zealous about completing a task, and they tend to scatter their energies.

Overall, Capricorn children could do well with a little more verve and spirit, while their Sagittarius parents would benefit by using a little more strategy as they pursue their goals.

The Sagittarius Mom/The Capricorn Child

Mom is very organized and efficient, but she won't allow anyone to stifle her freedom. She'll have an excellent understanding of practical matters, and she can fulfill her Capricorn's desire for a stable home life. This mother loves to travel, and she will gladly share her worldly wisdom with her little earth children. Mom's a restless lady who will never stop learning, and she is also a collector, She enjoys filling her home with many unique items that she has brought back from the various countries that she has visited.

Mom will naturally encourage her Capricorn kids to be playful and self-expressive. Capricorn children can expound on a variety of different topics, and Mom will always be there to listen to what they have to say and to try to answer their questions. Mom has the humor and playfulness that her little Capricorns need, and her innate ability to just have fun will be very comforting to her sons and daughters.

Mom can be very direct when she has something to say, so she'd be wise to use caution with her Capricorn children, as they tend to take everything personally—they're very serious when it comes to their own dignity or pride. Mom may also have a tendency to lightheartedly tease her children, but this behavior just won't work with these kids. Her kind, straightforward approach to life will be much more palatable to these earth children.

Mom is serious about raising her children to be productive human beings, so she tends to worry a lot about their progress in this regard. However, her optimism usually takes precedence over her anxiety. A Sagittarius woman is often a little girl at heart, with a playful sense of humor, which she can use to help ease the serious nature of her Capricorn children. She'll gladly give them permission to stay young as long as they can. If Mom can downplay her Capricorn children's belief that the burdens of the world are on their shoulders, she will have accomplished an amazing feat!

The Sagittarius Dad/The Capricorn Child

Dad can be an "absent-minded professor" type or a corporate executive. Like the easygoing scholar, the corporate executive enjoys spontaneity, but he tends to be more in tune with the practical realities of life, and his Capricorn children can always come to him for sensible, objective advice. This dad is strong and protective, although he tends to keep his emotions to himself. And, since he believes in self-control, he may appear to be more serious than Mom. He tries to influence his children with his common sense and his intelligence, but he tends to avoid confrontation whenever possible. Again, I need to say that emotional people tend to frustrate themselves because they do not verbalize their feelings.

The corporate executive needs to surround himself with order. He can be quite a perfectionist when he works, and as his Capricorn children start to grow, he can help them gain insight into business strategies. A practical Capricorn will welcome this information. Dad is also a lot of fun and has a great sense of humor. When he works, he can spend hours doing his job, and when he plays, he's wonderful to have around.

Unlike the corporate executive, the "professor" type of Sagittarius dad may have a problem with schedules or routine. This father tends to have a dozen ideas at once, and he thrives on inspiration. Dad can be unpredictable, always off on some exciting adventure. However, he needs to make time for his Capricorn child, who thrives on stability. These dads will give their Capricorn children the freedom to make their own choices and provide them with the opportunity to explore life. He may not be viewed as a disciplinarian, but he can win an award for playmate of the year.

Overall, Dad is an emotional man, and I have worked with many Sagittarians who tend to discount their emotions. When a Sagittarius man gives himself permission to share his feelings with someone that he loves, he can progress greatly on the road to personal development.

The Capricorn Parent/The Capricorn Child

This parent/child duo will live in harmony because they both share the same wise common-sense approach to life. Capricorn children flourish in their Capricorn parent's environment, as it offers both safety and security. Capricorn parents will provide these children with the sense of consistency and an understanding of self-discipline that they need.

Capricorns can be solemn children, and their vitality may be stifled by their serious nature. Most of my Capricorn clients recall that their youth seemed very difficult for them. As they grew, they began to feel a tenacious spirit, and this tenacity helped their self-confidence develop. They began to stubbornly cling to their beliefs, and their efficient and self-reliant natures helped them achieve their goals.

It's important for a Capricorn mom and dad to teach their earth children that they cannot be so hard on themselves. I know I have just given them a very tough assignment, but who could accomplish it better than parents who have experienced these feelings themselves?

Capricorns are usually ambitious and want to be successful. They must finish what they start, and then they are ready to go on to something else. These earth people are the most sufficient in the zodiac. They are clever and strategic in their approach, but they need to be considerate of other people's feelings. Parents and children are both practical, determined, and hard-working. It's easy for them to build a healthy and powerful relationship.

☆ ☆ ☆

I was doing astrology readings at a party given by Carol, a client of mine, and I happened to arrive at her home early. I'd known Carol for a long time, so I felt very comfortable talking to her guests until the program began. A young woman came over to me and said, "Are you the astrologer?"

I said, "Yes, I am."

She exclaimed, "I love astrology!" She was holding a small child in her arms, and I remember commenting that this little girl was very well behaved. Her mom remarked, "Thanks, she's a Capricorn." Then she asked curiously, "How does a Capricorn mother get along with a Capricorn child?"

I answered, "You're very compatible."

She smiled, and said, "I've heard that, but I hope she's not as much of a nervous wreck as I am."

I told her, "You can help her by first trying to ease your own tension."
Concerned, she then asked, "Do you think that she'll pick that up from me?"
"I know she will," I answered simply. "If you want to help your little girl, she'll
need a role model—someone who isn't so hard on herself." The woman nodded,
agreeing with me. Capricorns are good at taking constructive criticism, and this
young mother was very appreciative of my comments. I heard from her after the
event, and she informed me that she was trying not to be so self-critical, an effort
that will really help her little earth child in the long run!

☆   ☆   ☆

Capricorn children *do* emulate their parents when it comes to sharing the same kind of intense, perfection-oriented approach to life. A Capricorn mom and dad need to learn how to ease up on themselves, or else their own "personal drama" may eventually be passed down to their children.

The Capricorn Mom/The Capricorn Child

A Capricorn woman feels very responsible to her family. These moms often become businesswomen, or they can turn out to be theatrically creative types. The businesswoman tends to be more structured, while the theatrical type oftentimes is a rebel. No matter which type she is, a Capricorn mother's practical sense is always right on target.

Once a Capricorn woman marries, taking care of the needs of her family is usually her first priority. She will gladly put her own desires aside before she does anything to limit theirs. Mom tends to be very hard on herself, and her personal insecurity may be based on old childhood memories and perceptions. She would be wise to remember and evaluate past lessons in her life in order to avoid acting out dominant behavior. Most of my clients who are Capricorn women tend to remember every bad thing that happened to them in their childhood, and they use these memories as a protective shield when they enter personal relationships. I have suggested that some of the ways they have perceived these crises are blown way out of proportion. Once they realistically look at their background, it's not as bad as it seemed to them. Many of the women who have children have worked through their personal issues, and their self-confidence was strengthened by their discoveries.

Both a Capricorn child's self-confidence and security can grow to powerful dimensions when raised by this earth mom, who is a sensitive listener and confidante. If she utilizes both her wisdom and her intuition, she can encourage these kids to verbalize their feelings whenever they feel hurt. Mom needs to give her Capricorn children a chance to experience what she may have lost in her own childhood.

The Capricorn Dad/The Capricorn Child

Both Dad and his Capricorn children are practical, bright, and serious-minded. Dan can recognize himself in his earth children, as they will usually have strong wills and boundless determination. These kids will need to live in a comfortable home that provides a solid and stable lifestyle. Dad has the same need, so his main focus is on safety and security. Most Capricorn men are hard-working and try to provide the best financial foundation for their families. They are self-reliant, efficient, and constructive. They are often administrators who have an instinct for management and big business.

Capricorn children can easily follow in Dad's footsteps, since they have practical minds and strive for perfection. They will not be impulsive or careless with any project they undertake. Capricorns do not like to make mistakes, so they take their time.

When a Capricorn father raises these kids, he needs to help them learn that it's important to let go of the problems they cannot resolve and move on to the ones that they can take care of. Most Capricorn fathers are persuasive, intense, and hard on themselves. Their powerful determination tends to build up within them and can cause them physical harm if they're not careful. Fifty percent of the Capricorn men and women whom I counsel tend to suffer from ulcers, and a few of them have been stroke victims at an early age. Capricorn men know that they make tremendous demands on themselves and others; therefore, it's very important for them to encourage their earth children to learn how to relax and take it easy at an early age.

Dad is usually a family man and a good father. He will naturally understand his earthy children, since their values and goals are similar. He can guide and inspire his kids to set goals and work to their best potential. He can also relate to the fact that underneath all of their seemingly confident behavior, Capricorns are often insecure. They tend to relate to materialism, and they believe that physical matter is the only reality. Their thoughts, feelings, and beliefs will be explained in terms of matter, as opposed to being abstract or spiritual. This kinds of philosophy can make intimacy difficult to understand. So, it's important for Dad to try and encourage his earth children to talk openly about their feelings. I know this can be a problem for him if he has not dealt with personal communication in the past, but he could do his earth children a great favor by showing them that he is there to help—and a good listener, as well!

The Aquarius Parent/The Capricorn Child

Aquarian parents are charming and likable. They have an easygoing quality that seems to have a calming effect on others. Underneath that calm and collected demeanor, though, lies a person who can be a lot more demanding and opinionated than one might think. Their key phrase is "I know," and anyone who wants to get along with them should be warned not to ever, ever put down their intelligence. When a subject piques an Aquarian's interest, he or she will want to learn as much about it as possible. Aquarians are humanitarians, and they often work to serve the common person. Most Aquarians don't worry about becoming socially acceptable, although they do look for other people's approval when it comes to their opinions and ideas.

Aquarian men, more than women, wear simple and comfortable clothes that very often don't match. However, there are those Aquarians whom I call "perfect peacocks" who are very interested in looking immaculate. They have excellent taste and wear very expensive clothes.

While they do enjoy attending certain social functions, you can't force these air parents to go anywhere. In fact, many of them are homebodies who are perfectly happy to be alone in their own thoughts. I would say that the greatest percentage of Aquarians are independent people who want to do their own thing. Mom and Dad will encourage their Capricorn children to unfold in their own unique and individualistic way. Aquarians are not people who want to condition their children to *be* anything except whatever they're born to be. They won't mind the lighthanded methods of an Aquarian parent, as these kids need to be surrounded by someone whose demands are not severe. However, they definitely need attention, as well as serious consideration of all of their decisions. Mom and Dad may need to remember that it is best to provide a consistent amount of quality time for their Capricorn children, to help point them in the right direction.

The Aquarius Mom/The Capricorn Child

Capricorn children may categorize their mother as too easygoing. At first, these practical earth kids may not know what to do with so much personal freedom and independence. This Aquarian mom may have to learn patience, because although she will encourage these kids to take responsibility for their own projects, her little Capricorns will still like to depend on her to be there whenever they have a question about a problem or decision. However, Mom is very sympathetic to her children's problems, and she will never turn her back on them. If she's wise, she will learn to explain that having freedom isn't scary, as it's supposed to give a person an opportunity to choose from different options in life.

Capricorns want to know that Mom will be there when they need her. With Capricorn children, Aquarian mothers would be wise to determine the importance of their needs, and try to calm them down when they get overwhelmed. In fact, when the task is rather small, it would be a good idea for her to say: "I know you can handle that by yourself. I have seen you do much harder things than that. I'll come back in a little while." When Capricorn children feel challenged, they will want to prove that they can come through in a pinch.

Mom's logical base makes her a thinker and an idealist. She understands the problems of the real world; however, she doesn't set up practical limits for herself. She's always trying to do and learn as much as possible, but she doesn't always put together a time schedule for herself. On the other hand, Capricorns are more practical, and they always like to know what time it is. Mom may need to remember that these children need to be given definite goals and a structured approach that will allow them to attain those aims in a timely and productive fashion.

The Aquarius Dad/The Capricorn Child

Dad can be a hardworking engineer or a creative eccentric, Whichever type of Aquarian he is, Dad is a free spirit who needs to do his own thing! An Aquarius father is not predictable with respect to his behavior. He likes to do a variety of different activities—one moment he might be playing lightheartedly with his kids, and in the next, he could be teaching them how to use a computer.

Dad will not usually take part in everyday family chores, as he is more interested in developing his children's minds. Capricorn kids are usually very intelligent, and they also crave knowledge about all kinds of subjects. They will admire Dad's ability to share his thoughts and ideas with them. Dad and his Capricorn kids do not think alike when it comes to their lifestyle, though. Dad is a much more casual person, whereas I don't think Capricorns know the meaning of the word *casual.* Dad's laid-back persona can inspire his children to take it easier, and let them know that it is not the end of the world when they make a mistake.

Aquarian fathers are usually very individualistic in their manner, while their Capricorn children are conformists who believe that image is everything. If these air parents can encourage their earth children to understand that doing what everyone else does is not as important as maintaining their own individuality, then they may not demand so much of themselves.

Both Aquarians and Capricorns have difficulty revealing their feelings; profound intimacy might be hard to develop, so building a close friendship can be the key to a successful parent/child relationship.

The Pisces Parent/The Capricorn Child

Pisces parents are typically either detailed and structured, or they are creative artists. The more detailed Pisces individual needs to be organized and do things as perfectly as possible. This personality will be a good fit with Capricorn children, as they share the same approach. The Pisces artist fits in with the more rebellious side of the Capricorn personality. There *are* Capricorns, though, who are attracted to the more creative aspects of life such as theater, art, music, and writing. In addition, they are usually more spiritual in nature. These kind of interests, including their affinity for spirituality, blend well with the artistry of the Pisces personality.

When they raise a stability-oriented Capricorn child, Pisces parents need to work on trying to adhere to important decisions once they've made them This child's personal security can be threatened when a parent doesn't appear to be reliable and consistent. Capricorn children need their parents' approval when making their own decisions, so building a trusting parent/child relationship is essential. Pisces parents want to please their children, so they need to be careful not to say yes to everything that their kids want. If Pisces parents give their Capricorn children everything they ask for, they will wrap Mom and Dad around their little fingers. Pisces can enhance their own self-confidence when they can say no to anything that seems unreasonable to them.

Young Capricorns look to their parents for love and support when they're young. As they grow older, though, they recognize their independence and do most things themselves. They have a hard time believing that people can do a better job than they do. Parents would be wise to raise them with the notion that sharing ideas and projects will help them learn things from other people. This attitude can also help minimize some of the pressure they place upon themselves. No matter how independent Capricorn kids may become, they will always return to their roots and family.

The Pisces Mom/The Capricorn Child

Mom is emotional and sympathetic and she will give her Capricorn children a lot of love and attention. A Capricorn enjoys receiving attention from this soft and sensitive mom, as her approach to caring is from the heart and not from a practical point of view. A Pisces mother will first respond with emotion, and then turn to practicality and logic to ensure her stability. Capricorns tend to admire the sensitive nature of a Pisces mom, as this quality brings them a lot of comfort. She can help to temper their intense and serious personalities through her gentle approach to life. She can easily give them the privacy that they need, because she respects the fact that children need their space—a good amount of alone time to go off and think by themselves.

Mom is emotional, so she may have to learn that her Capricorn children's practical minds do not always relate to overt bonding. But if anyone can help these kids respond to sensitivity, it will be their Pisces mother. She really understands children because she is a kid at heart. She will never lose her idealistic and dreamy nature, and she needs to return to her private world from time to time. She is the perfect person to encourage her Capricorn children to let loose, play with abandon, and generally just have a lot of fun.

Like their Capricorn children, Pisces moms can be perfectionists who tend to be hard on themselves when they make a mistake. There are many Pisces mothers who keep their personal feelings to themselves, especially when they're hurt, but this predilection stems from the fact that they always want to appear good-natured and responsible. Mom needs to learn that she is only human and doesn't have to be all things to all people. By balancing her giving nature with her need to display her feelings, Mom will have the perfect formula to raise her Capricorn children.

The Pisces Dad/The Capricorn Child

Dad is idealistic, visionary, and romantic. Most people like him, as he intuitively knows how to get along with them. When people ask me about the Pisces personality, I humorously say, "What you see isn't what you always get." For example,

Dad is usually smiling and friendly on the outside, but he conceals a serious and intense nature within.

Capricorns are private people, but their practical side makes them more predictable. A Pisces father appeals to his Capricorn children because he will be their friend and protector. And, just like them, he has a problem revealing his true feelings. Capricorns appreciate the honest and direct approach to life, but Dad, at times, has a tendency to skirt an issue. If Dad can be straightforward when he doesn't like something that his Capricorn children have done, these kids will listen and try to modify their behavior in the future. But if he doesn't get to the point, these children may silently lose respect for him and end up doing exactly what they please. Dad would be wise to prove himself to be a stable and consistent father so that his children will be comfortable discussing their ideas and problems with him. Capricorns like their parents to listen to them and remember what they say so that they feel that their input has worth.

Overall, Capricorn children love their Pisces dad for his outgoing nature and his ability to interact with all kinds of people. They will gladly emulate those traits in his personality.

SUMMARY

You have learned that Capricorns are perfectionistic individuals who tend to be much too hard on themselves. Therefore, you can understand why they fear making mistakes and why they are often worrywarts. Capricorns do not need a sufficient reason for fretting about anything, so it's important for parents to teach them to forgive themselves and others for real or perceived "wrong" decisions and actions. If they can learn to modify their intense behavior at an early age, they may not make so many demands on themselves as adults. Capricorns have a tendency to try to rationalize their behavior, but there can be no real justification for allowing their nervous tension to overcome their practical natures.

Capricorns have a brilliant sense of humor, and most people find them very engaging and funny, so it's particularly important for parents to allow them to laugh at themselves. Once a Capricorn acknowledges that life doesn't have to be so hard and that their parents are there to protect them, they will more readily ask for support and guidance!

> *"A person's life is dyed the color of his imagination."*
> — MARCUS AURELIUS

Chapter Eleven

....

≈ AQUARIUS THE WATER BEARER

JANUARY 20–FEBRUARY 18 **ELEMENT:** Air **KEY PHRASE:** "I know"

....

THE AQUARIUS PERSONALITY

Aquarians live in the world of ideas. They come in two varieties: one type tends to be more of a focused, conservative perfectionist; while the other tends to be a creative, free-spirited visionary. The perfectionists are also visionaries, but they just like to keep their world more organized, and in their homes, you'll never see a thing out of place. The visionaries also need structure, but not when it comes to their home environment, where you'll typically find stacks of technical journals and overdue laundry scattered about. The perfectionists are intelligent, successful, well dressed, and have a difficult time talking about their personal feelings. The visionaries are explorers who tend to dress for comfort and who spend a lot of time in their own creative worlds. No matter what "type" of Aquarian you're dealing with, though, they are almost all humanitarians who are firm believers in individuality. They understand the suffering of their fellow human beings and, consequently, many Aquarians get involved in politics.

Most Aquarians don't have easy childhoods, as they tend to be introspective and shy. However, they typically seek out people who think the same way they do, and they form close friendships that usually last for life. Parents need to learn that their

Aquarius children won't do anything that they don't wish to do. These free spirits tend to want to explore life in their own way, and they like to figure out their own methods of doing things. Mom and Dad would be wise to teach their little air children that it's important for them to learn from the ideas of others. Aquarians are natural loners who are perfectly comfortable spending time in their own worlds. These air kids, however, will benefit from their parents' encouragement to open up about how they feel.

☆ ☆ ☆

My friend Sheila's son Jack (an Aquarius) was nine years old, and he could spend hours away from his family. Sheila, who was an Aries, encouraged him to do what he liked to do best, which was go off into his room and draw. Sheila gave her child his own time and space, which was very important to him. Jack never gave Sheila a day's worth of trouble, as his lifestyle coincided well with hers. The only problem that she had with Jack was his refusal to talk about his feelings.

It was a Sunday afternoon, and Sheila could see that Jack wasn't very happy. She asked, "What's the matter, honey?"

Jack replied, "Nothing's the matter."

Sheila pressed him. "Jack, if you aren't happy about something, you can share it with me."

He insisted, "I don't want to talk about it!"

Her Aries nature got the best of her, and she said firmly, "Jack, it'll make you feel better if you talk about your feelings."

"How?" he replied curiously.

She pointed to his tummy and asked, "Is there a feeling that you have right here?" He nodded. "Well," she continued, "sometimes, I get nervous there, too. Is that what you feel?" He nodded again. "All I can tell you is that when I talk about what's bothering me, the feeling goes away."

He shook his head and said, "No, it doesn't."

She replied, "Well, only the bravest people try it." Sheila nodded at him reassuringly and left him alone to think about it.

About an hour later, he came up to her in the kitchen and asserted, "I'm brave!" Then he proceeded to tell her a story about an argument he had had with a friend. Afterwards, he admitted, "My stomach does feel better."

Jack hasn't stopped talking to Sheila since! Aquarians tend to be very honest underneath it all, but sometimes all they need is a dose of encouragement.

☆ ☆ ☆

"I Know!"

Aquarians are extremely bright and opinionated, and once they decide that they're right, it could take an army to budge them from their determination. And, if you try to convince them otherwise, these children have the ability to tune you out. They do, however, usually have the wisdom to ultimately accept a sound idea when they've given it some careful rumination.

Aquarians really like to spend time with people who are inventive and honest and whose ideas about life inspire them to think about things differently. Due to their humanitarian natures, they tend to always be there for the people who need them. Parents may have to understand that the best way to deal with these kids is through open and forthright communication. In addition, Mom and Dad would be wise to teach their air kids that sharing their feelings is *not* a sign of a weakness. Aquarians quietly test the love of those around them, but they will always seek out their parents' devotion and approval. If Aquarius children view their parents as both part-time mentors and best friends, they will develop feelings of trust, and they will come to Mom and Dad for advice and succor. If they grow up in an environment that encourages their independence, they will develop into self-sufficient adults. Aquarians tend to want to be of service to others; however, they can wind up giving so much that they don't allow themselves time to receive.

It's up to Mom and Dad to encourage their Aquarian children to enjoy their independent natures, but it's also important for these air children to understand that their parents are there to help them learn as well as to help them solve their problems. Aquarians have an innate sense of morality and good judgment, so it will not really be necessary to place strict rules or restrictions on these kids. They need to be given freedom to make their own choices, and they want their parents to recognize all of their efforts. Once they can understand that their parents will support and guide them without trying to take away their independence, they won't feel like it's up to them to take on every problem alone.

Logic and Emotion

Aquarians are logical thinkers whose quick minds understand how to solve complex problems through reason and objectivity. It's exploration of the intellect that fascinates them. Parents would be wise to stress the value of education to their Aquarius children, while giving them the feeling that they have the right to pursue their own goals. Since Aquarians like to please their parents, they may end up blindly adhering to the future plans that their parents have set down for them, but if they do so, they will never be happy, and as adults, they might tend to move from job to job, and resenting their parents along the way. For this reason, Aquarians will see education as the stepping stone toward expanding their horizons and as the means to achieving the end that *they* aspire to. In school, many Aquarians find that they do not like taking basic courses, as they'd rather just study the subjects that interest them. If they feel that their teachers aren't up to snuff, these air kids won't have respect for them. However, if they can provide a mental challenge, they've won the first battle. Most Aquarians are fast learners, and they can be way ahead of their peer group. Once they feel like they've mastered a subject, they start to become restless or bored. It's very important that Aquarians utilize their special talents and that they feel appreciated for their accomplishments. A parent's support and interest in this child's need to explore is crucial.

Aquarians may sometimes feel that logic and emotion is like oil and water—they just don't mix. These two qualities are, of course, part of the human equation, and parents who raise these children should develop a warm and loving atmosphere in which to bring them up. This kind of environment will teach these air kids the importance of *feeling*. Aquarians need to understand that it's difficult to accomplish anything great in life without acknowledging the need for both logic and emotion. An Aquarian's first priority is mental affinity with others, so it's very important that Mom and Dad discuss their thoughts and feelings with these children. When Aquarians believe that they have permission to voice their own opinions, it appeals to their need for equality.

Parents need to remember that it takes a special effort to win the love of these children, as they can be the ultimate devil's advocates, challenging the opinions of all who cross their paths. What they need most are honest, caring relationships with people who deal with them on equal terms. They often define their own success and failure through the intelligent feedback they receive from both family and friends.

There's a Shy Child Within

Most Aquarians are inwardly shy, even if they appear to be outgoing and personable on the surface. These likable, easygoing air kids can be something of a mystery, as they tend to keep their feelings to themselves. They don't trust others easily and prefer to surround themselves with strong, self-confident people who make them think. Their success lies in their natural ability to solve the problems of the many, rather than the few. Their main challenge is to focus on improving the lives of people in the world.

On the one hand, Aquarians can be very complex, seeing themselves as dynamic orators who want to reach out to the world. On the other hand, they know that they're perfectly happy when they can just be by themselves. In truth, these air kids don't like to feel alone, though; they actually feel more secure when they know that Mom and Dad are around the house somewhere, always ready to listen to their ideas. An Aquarian's real commitment is to help people who can benefit from their sense of justice. Aquarians are best when both their brilliance and their sensitivity can be utilized for the good of all.

A Strong Need for Individuality

Aquarians live in the future. While the here and now always has to be dealt with, what's yet to come always seems more exciting to them. They are the skeptics, always searching for the truth. Their logical minds often move them toward astronomy and astrophysics.

When it comes to interacting with others, they certainly enjoy being social, but they usually wind up doing their own thing. A story about my Aquarian son, Layne, demonstrates this point.

Each year, my entire family would have a reunion where we danced to music, had great food and laughed and generally caught up on where we had left off the previous year. This particular year, we had a dance contest, and all of the children participated. Some of the kids were dressed in costumes, others in bathing suits, but most were wearing jeans and shorts. The music began, and all of the kids began to dance, swaying and shaking their little bodies…and then there was Layne.

I was sitting with my cousin when she asked me, "Why is Layne running around in circles?" I looked over to the children, and saw that Layne was walking around everyone else in a giant circle, seeming to follow his own path. My cousin looked at him curiously. "Whatever is he doing?"

I replied matter-of-factly, "To Layne, that's dancing." It was, in fact, his own unique and unpredictable Aquarian way of expressing himself!

Overall, Aquarians are sentimental. Even though they tend to focus on what's new and progressive, they also have a fondness for what's old and established. Aquarians want to feel that their parents both accept and support their need to make their own choices in life. They can be unpredictable and contradictory. It doesn't matter whether everything around them presents order and stability, their own behavior will be different from the rest. They do, however, always want to feel that they can depend upon Mom and Dad's guidance when they have a question about life. These air kids are both idealistic and futuristic, and while life itself may provide some difficult lessons, none of them will alter these children's optimistic spirit.

They're Independent Thinkers

Most Aquarians want to make all of their own decisions. In the workplace, they tend to want to be their own boss, and many Aquarians eventually start their own companies. Aquarians tend to become independent at an early age. As children, they're often very intelligent, and they can concentrate on their projects for a long time. Aquarians, however, can sometimes take their independence too far for their own good. They may need to learn that it's all right to ask for help. If they take on all of the responsibilities of a project themselves, they can wind up feeling alone, and their self-esteem can suffer. Parents may have to teach these kids that they have to allow themselves to receive, as well as give. Aquarians are so busy thinking up ways to help others, that sometimes they can forget to take care of themselves. Developing intimate relationships is not easy for them, as giving to just one person isn't what they think they were born to do.

If parents are sincere in offering their Aquarian children "honest love," these air kids will come to realize how important it is to share their feelings. And from a child that would prefer keeping his emotions to himself, this is a great accomplishment. A healthy relationship is about sharing, which is built on both giving and receiving, and this may be an Aquarian's most difficult lesson in life!

PARENT AND CHILD

The Aries Parent/The Aquarius Child

Both Aries parents and their Aquarius children believe in their right to be independent and free. Aries parents are go-getters, and they can be involved in many things at once, but this won't be a problem for their Aquarius children as long as they know that Mom and Dad will be there to provide them with both support and guidance whenever they need help with a problem. Aries parents will enjoy raising these independent children, who are typically very mature at an early age. These kids, however, do keep their own timetables.

Aries parents will not repeatedly ask their children to clean their rooms, wash the dishes, or do other household chores because they usually don't have the patience to wait for their kids to finish the jobs. As adults, they know that they can do the job faster; however, they have to be careful not to spoil their little air kids and do everything for them. It would be wise to help these eccentric thinkers learn to understand the importance of discipline by having them follow established household rules.

Another issue that concerns Aquarius children is that of personal appearance. These kids definitely enjoy feeling clean and being neat, but they do not like being told what to wear by Mom and Dad. The following story is a good example of this characteristic.

My girlfriend Helen's son John (an Aquarius) was 25 years old, and he had never owned a suit or a sports jacket in his life. Helen (an Aries) couldn't stand the fact that he didn't care about clothes, and decided he had to buy a sports jacket, even if he had to wear it with jeans. John agreed to go to with his mother to the local department store to shop for a jacket, and when they got there, the two of them immediately started disagreeing with each other.

Helen said, "John, look at this color green. Isn't this gorgeous?"

John responded, "I like blue."

Helen said, "Oh, that jacket is boring."

John insisted, "I like it in blue!"

They finally happened upon a royal blue jacket that appealed to both of them, and Helen said, "That's great. Now, let's look for a pair of slacks."

"I don't need slacks," John said wearily.

"You can't wear jeans to a nice restaurant."

John responded angrily, "Everyone's dressing casual these days, Mom!"

She replied, "Fine. Do what you want."

"Mom, don't get angry."

After a moment, she said simply, "I'm not angry. You should be able to dress the way you want to dress. It's up to you. I have to realize that you're not a little kid anymore."

John responded, "I know that you just want me to look good." He gave her a hug, and told her that the next time he was ready to buy clothes, she'd be the one he'd call. Helen realized that if she became too assertive with John, he tended to argue with her opinion. But, by approaching her Aquarius son logically, the two reached a compromise.

☆ ☆ ☆

The Aries Mom/The Aquarius Child

An Aries mom's heart is with her children, and she can be both loving and affectionate. She's fairminded, and she will always be there to protect and defend her children. Aquarius children will recognize and admire her honesty, strength, and intelligence, as these qualities fit in with their idea of what a mother should be. Aries mothers can be very dramatic and theatrical, and since these kids tend to approach situations logically, Mom may need to remember not to overwhelm them with emotion. Mom, however, can easily make important points through firm, reasonable suggestions. This parent/child relationship works because of Mom's ability to make these children feel confident about their abilities.

Aquarius kids are independent and need to be given their freedom. They do not want a mother who hovers over them. Most Aries mothers are independent and do not possess their children because they themselves are free spirits. I have one strong concern when an Aries mother raises Aquarian children—her need to give orders. Mom is an idealist, and she wants to make everyone and everything look better. She's not a superficial lady, but her image is important to her.

There are some Aquarians who grow up to be as perfect as Mom. They love beautiful clothes, and they care about their overall appearance, but most of them could care less what other people think of them. They are individualists first, last, and always. Aquarius children need to be liked, and they need approval. Even though they may rebel against Mom, they may grow up thinking that she does not approve of them and that they are not good enough. It's important for an Aries mother to be careful about badgering her Aquarian children, as they will never bend to her wishes. If she asks them nicely, though, they may succumb.

Mom is a motivator who needs to move these children along, as they can stay safe and stuck for a long time. Many Aquarians have missed a lot of opportunities because they were afraid of change. The main reason that Mom and her Aquarian children's relationship works is because she has the ability to make these air kids feel confident in their abilities.

The Aries Dad/The Aquarius Child

Dad is quite emotional, but he can have a problem verbalizing his feelings. He has a practical approach when it comes to raising children, since he works long and hard in order to provide for their needs. An Aries dad is strong individual who can be the dominating force in the household. He tends to look at situations in terms of black or white, and that's it! Aquarians tend to study all the gray areas in between, so Dad may have to exercise patience with his little air children, as it may take them longer to make a decision than he would like.

Aquarius children will see Dad as a mentor. He enjoys learning, and then he takes special pleasure in imparting his newfound knowledge to his children. As these kids grow, Aries dads will need to allow them to make their own career choices in life without making them feel like they have to live up to his expectations. Both parent and child are usually very intelligent, and their success as a family unit will stem from their mental affinity, as well as through their understanding of, and compassion for, those in their world.

The Taurus Parent/The Aquarius Child

Taurus parents tend to admire their Aquarian children because they value their natural independence and individuality. These air kids are self-reliant and have no problem taking their own time and space. Earth parents need stability, and once they build a secure foundation that provides a basis for grounding, they do not want anything to change! Aquarius children like to grow up in a safe environment, but these logical thinkers are easily bored and want to explore many interests, near or far from home. Most of these air kids will do all they can to seek knowledge and adventure.

Taurus parents are very protective, but it won't take them long to recognize that their Aquarius children will stubbornly guard their own individuality. These kids will definitely explore life in their own way. When these children are young, some Aquarians can be difficult to handle depending on their level of emotional maturity and their restless natures. Taurus parents are easily unnerved, so they would be wise to set an example early on by letting these air kids know that they are not pushovers! These parents need to stick to their decisions. They have to watch their tendency to be bossy and possessive, though, as this behavior will not work with their free-spirited Aquarians. These kids will rebel and retreat into their own worlds—never to return.

Mom and Dad need to honestly explain their reasons for forming their opinions. Aquarians respect honesty and reason, so they will be accepting of most decisions as long as they can see that they are backed up by substance. In addition, Aquarian children respect parents who believe in themselves and stand up for their rights. There are times when both parent and child may have problems defending themselves, but the Aquarians' logical minds help them move on, while practical Taurus parents can be obsessive and usually have a difficult time letting go of anything they invest in. It's very important for these parents to be flexible when they raise these air kids, since their little thinkers have a problem with flexibility once they make up their minds.

Taurus parents are usually friendly and kind and have great patience and determination when they want to succeed. Both parent and child can be similar, but Aquarius kids can procrastinate over anything that does not mentally stimulate them. It's important for Mom and Dad to set an example, which can motivate their air kids to finish what they start. Both of these signs are rather slow-moving; no one in this family can push each other into anything unless the house is on fire! Overall, though, Taureans and Aquarians have temperaments that complement each other, and they should enjoy a rich and fulfilling relationship.

The Taurus Mom/The Aquarius Child

Taurus Mom is an honest and practical woman who raises her children to be both honorable and moral. She believes in maintaining family traditions, and she upholds the notions that all people should treat each other with decency. Mom won't welcome change, as her personal security is threatened when she faces the unknown.

Aquarians may be comfortable with what is familiar to them, but their need to learn moves them toward new options. Both parent and child need to feel safe at all times, but Aquarians need permission to decide what being safe means to them, and what interesting challenge may constitute their next adventure. As is the case with all earth signs, Mom likes to raise children who are well behaved and mannerly. Aquarians have no problem doing the right thing, though, as long as they do not have to prove themselves to anyone else. Nothing is more important to Aquarian children than having their parents respect their individuality and to acknowledge that they cannot be forced into anything. This mother will definitely encourage her little air kids' individuality. If she ever feels that her children have not done something right, she will explain her reasons in an honest and sensible way. It's important for Mom to encourage honest communication in the home so that there will be an understanding that it's acceptable for anyone in the family to talk about how they feel.

Overall, Mom will benefit from her Aquarian children's fresh and interesting ideas, and she will be invigorated by what she can learn from them. Aquarian kids are wise, mature, and protective, which will help this emotionally intense Mom feel at ease.

The Taurus Dad/The Aquarius Child

A Taurus father is usually realistic and practical, but he can also be spiritual and sensitive. It just depends on how much he wants to be in touch with his real feelings. Dad can also function well as an actor, or he can succeed as a hard-working business mogul. There are two very different fields, but both can be quite challenging. Taurus fathers thrive on competition, and intelligent people fascinate them. Aquarian children are very smart, and they have the ability to learn anything they put their minds to. Dad will admire his air children's intellect and individualistic nature because he will intuitively recognize how inventive and futuristic they can be. However, at times, he tends to question his own talents. Taureans dissect everything they do, and this part of his personality tends to limit their potential. Aquarians, on the other hand, don't waste a lot of time engaged in self-doubt—they just do what makes them feel good!

Dad tends to be earthy, a man who needs a solid home and strong roots. Aquarians crave safety and comfort, too, but their feet never seem to touch the ground. They live in their own space and naturally do their own thing. Aquarians are idealists who are both administrative and creative. I believe they are much happier in a world of artists, rather than fighting the battles in corporate America. Dad is a practical man who must be aware that he cannot set down his own rigid career guidelines for his Aquarian children. He should keep in mind that he's raising independent air kids who want to explore life in their own way.

Overall, Taurus Dad is a wise man with sound common sense who will help his air children realize their goals in a strategic fashion without scattering their thoughts and energies. Aquarian children will be comforted by Dad's ability to ground them, thereby paving the way for a brilliant future!

The Gemini Parent/The Aquarius Child

Gemini parents and Aquarian children have much in common. They are both thinkers who like to have their own space. Gemini parents are free spirits who do not like to follow a clock or calendar unless they have a specific appointment. Parent and child share a similar approach to life, since they both value the intellect, independence, and freedom. These parents can be excellent role models for their

Aquarius kids, as they really like to learn and explore. Both parent and child are always energetically pursuing new interests. As these young Aquarians grow, their primary focus will be on the development of their minds through the application of their natural abilities.

Geminis understand that they cannot be driven into making decisions, and the same goes for their Aquarius kids. Parent and child both have an artistic side, even though their interest in scientific possibilities stimulates them. Therefore, Mom and Dad need to encourage these kids to utilize their creativity. Geminis are personable and communicative and really know a lot about a lot of things. They have the ability to provide the world (and their own children) with fascinating materials, advances, and contributions.

Gemini parents will be pleased to know that their air children have a magnetic ability to attract people, even though they are inwardly shy and reserved. These kids are friendly, but they do not want to be pushed into social situations. They do have the capacity to find the roads that make them comfortable, though. Most people love Aquarians because they are eager and enthusiastic when they believe in something. These parents can inspire their kids to have the courage to develop their intellect and imagination—the best gift they can offer these children!

Personal communication is one area that this parent/child duo may have to work on. Aquarius children can find it difficult to release their emotions, so Gemini parents will have to let these kids know that they have the freedom to open up and discuss their feelings. Mom and Dad must give themselves the same privilege. This is a difficult challenge for parents and children who relate to logic rather than emotion, but with a little work, this duo will be able to succeed!

The Gemini Mom/The Aquarius Child

Mom is a busy bee whose schedule will always be filled with diverse interests and activities. When it comes to decorating her home, a Gemini mother has taste and style, and she enjoys orchestrating parties. Aquarian children will enjoy this free-spirited mom because she will provide these imaginative kids with the opportunity to explore life. Both a Gemini mom and her Aquarius children will live in the realm of ideas, and together they'll come up with new and exciting ways of doing things. Their discoveries will take them on great adventures—from childhood to adulthood.

Aquarian children will relish the fact that Mom will never compare their achievements to others. This is natural for Mom because she values her kids' individuality. These mothers will create a structured home environment for these children, which will provide them with the kind of gentle discipline that they need in order to make their dreams come true.

If Aquarians disagree with you, they won't be afraid to put up an argument. A Gemini mother will need to sensibly explain to her children why she has made the decisions she has. And once a decision has been made, a Gemini parent needs to be sure to stick to their guns in order to maintain their children's respect. The best advice I can offer a Gemini mother is to always be available when her air kids need someone to listen to them. Aquarius children will feel comfortable talking one-on-one with their Gemini parents, and this duo will become fast friends.

The Gemini Dad/The Aquarius Child

A Gemini father can be an important figure in an Aquarius child's life, as he is reasonable, communicative, intellectual, and funloving. As such, they should develop a great friendship if their respective egos don't get in the way. Air signs tend to think they know it all—and most of them do know a lot, but they need to realize that they don't know it all! It's up to Dad to understand that trying to control his Aquarian children is like trying to control his own need for exploration.

Dad and his Aquarian kids will share a natural affinity for one another, as they both believe that developing the intellect is one of the most valuable projects in their lives. Dad, however, is much more amenable to change than his kids; he is always looking for excitement. Aquarians enjoy diversity and new challenges, but first and foremost, they seek educational advancement.

Air signs are not very tolerant, but Aquarians do have much more patience than Geminis. So, these kids can teach Dad a thing or two! He, on the other hand, is a man of action and energy, a person in motion who has the ability to inspire his kids to act, and act now! Since these kids tend to procrastinate when they aren't mentally stimulated, they need to be continually motivated. Aquarian children can get moody when there's nothing new to explore, so Dad needs to be particularly aware that helping these kids release their creative talents will help quell their nervous anxiety. Dad will gladly help his Aquarian children grow in any way he can, and these kids will welcome his efforts throughout their lives!

The Cancer Parent/The Aquarius Child

Cancer parents try to provide a perfect life for their family, as this is what makes them most content. Aquarian children can become attached to the idea of someone taking care of all of their needs, as they have no passion for household chores. Domesticity is more natural for Cancer parents, who generally feel that taking care of their children is what they were born to do. These water parents are emotional, and raising children is the best thing that can happen to them. They will gladly give their kids lots of love and attention, and they will want to be involved with all of their activities.

Cancer parents' personal security comes through raising a family, so it's important for them to realize that their Aquarius children are free spirits who do not want anyone to hover over them. They insist on having their own time and space; and although they are very friendly and sweet, they may not be overly affectionate. Their logical minds do not relate to too much emotion, so it's really the reasonable, sensible, objective person that makes them listen.

Aquarius children usually appear to be cool, calm and collected, even if they are hard on themselves. They tend to distance themselves because they spend a lot of time in their own thoughts. They need their Cancer parents to let them know they believe in and appreciate them, because this type of affirmation helps them develop self-confidence. These kids really do need their parents' approval even though they might not show it. Therefore, too much criticism or bullying tends to push them away.

Cancer parents tend to be quite possessive, but this won't work well with Aquarians. These kids need to be individualistic and free. If Mom and Dad can understand that it's not wise to try to control their Aquarians, they will be way ahead of the game. Aquarians do not like to argue; they love peace and quiet. However, if parents try to force them into anything, they will rebel and get very stubborn. It's best for Mom and Dad to develop patience and flexibility when they raise these intelligent children. These kids are very mature and catch on very quickly. They are usually easygoing and need their parents to let them move slowly and carefully, rather then pushing them to act quickly.

Overall, this parent/child duo will be able to communicate on many levels, with the exception of their personal feelings. But that's okay with Aquarians because emotions are not a priority. Make no mistake about it, though, they love the idea of family and want to live in a home that is filled with love, but their base is logic, and most things are valued through the intellect. Aquarian children are very independent and do not want to be told what to do or how to do it. They just need their parents to sit down and logically explain their reasons for making the decisions that they do. If Cancer parents can give their Aquarius children this type of freedom, these kids will always feel comfortable coming to Mom and Dad for help or advice!

The Cancer Mom/The Aquarius Child

Cancer mothers need to understand that their Aquarian children are very sentimental about both home and family. However, they may find it difficult to allow themselves to become dependent on others. Nevertheless, if a Cancer mom takes care of all of her children's needs, these kids may start to enjoy that personal comfort. In fact, the self-indulgent part of their personalities relish the idea of having parents who do everything for them. All in all, Mom's loving nature is beneficial to her Aquarius children, but she may a have a tendency to spoil them.

Aquarian children appreciate it when they are taught how to do things for themselves, and in return, Mom will receive both their admiration and respect. Mom would be wise to set rules and regulations with respect to household chores; and she will get all the help that she needs if she only *asks!* Cancer mothers need to learn how to receive, as well as give. Mom defines herself through giving to her children, and she needs to remember to tell them that she would like some help at times.

Many of my Cancer clients have been very upset, in retrospect, about their children's lack of consideration as they grew older. As such, Mom needs to realize that her Aquarian children are both logical and reasonable, and when she wants to talk about something important with them, she should always try to present the facts—and all the facts—to them. Also, Mom will have to come to accept the fact that her Aquarian children may not be as affectionate as she is, because the base of their personality is not emotion, but logic. However, in time, her concerned and caring persona will get through to her Aquarian children's hearts, and they will long appreciate the efforts that are made on their behalf.

The Cancer Dad/The Aquarius Child

Dad is a loving man, and his easygoing personality will be very appealing to his Aquarian children. He's very funny and bright, and his terrific sense of humor can ease almost any kind of tension that may arise between him and his kids. A Cancer father will offer his children wonderful advice, and they will gladly appreciate his intuitive wisdom. However, after giving them his "piece of mind," Dad needs to learn to step back, and allow these free-spirited children to figure out how to solve their problems on their own.

Cancer dads can sometimes seem like strict disciplinarians, but they are really softies on the inside. They may have a problem talking about how they feel, and at times, this tendency may make them moody. When they raise Aquarian children, Cancer fathers should acknowledge that these air children are not comfortable with capricious moods.

Overall, Aquarian children are kind and compassionate, so they will take a genuine interest in what Dad has to think or say about any situation. Therefore, he would be wise to try and offer reasonable explanations to assuage his kids' feelings when he has to reprimand them. This dad can really be an excellent teacher who will be a friend and mentor to his children. The best advice I can give a Cancer father is to keep the lines of communication open at all times; this is the best way to build and maintain a healthy relationship with his kids on a long-term basis!

The Leo Parent/The Aquarius Child

Most Aquarian children are inwardly shy and reserved. They may appear to be outgoing and friendly, but they are always watchful in their manner. Even if these Aquarian children tend to be quiet, though, they most assuredly have strong opinions and have a need to express their freedom and individuality.

Leo parents are strong personalities who tend to control their children by making their decisions for them, but this approach would not be a good one to take when it comes to raising Aquarians. These children are very intelligent and have definite likes and dislikes, and they have a need to make up their own minds. As such, it's best that parents offer reasonable explanations and options to choose from before any decisions are made. If Aquarians are forced into anything, they will rebel—they are quite stubborn when it comes to what they believe in. These air kids decide on a course of action, and once they do, it takes a lot of persuasion to change their opinions.

Overall, Leo parents are usually very bright and intuitive—they are action-oriented people who are there for everyone they love, as well as for those they do not. Aquarians are proud and they are easily hurt, so they need approval and appreciation for what they do. Leo parents are born motivators, and the way they can earn these air children's love and respect is to encourage and motivate them into action when they begin to procrastinate.

Leo parents are strong, independent, and very smart, and their Aquarian kids are born with the same traits, so this parent/child duo will have the opportunity to learn from each other. Leos are basically caretakers who want their children to grow up just like they are. While Aquarians admire these fire parents, Mom and Dad must remember that their logical kids are individualists, and they will want to do things in their own unique way. These royal fire parents certainly understand the meaning of individuality, so they will probably not have a problem assuring their Aquarian children that they can make their own choices in life.

The Leo Mom/The Aquarius Child

Mom tends to initially view things from an emotional point of view, while her Aquarian children are more inclined to see things from a logical perspective. Aquarian children will admire Mom's intelligence, honesty, and dependability. Once Mom makes a promise, she follows through on it. Aquarian children will feel secure knowing that if they ever need Mom, she'll always be there for them.

Mom can be a glamorous and dramatic personality, or she can be more on the conservative, responsible intellectual side, but no matter what "type" Mom is, she enjoys being in the limelight. While this energetic mother likes to pursue many interests, she must always make her Aquarian children feel that she'll always be there to listen to their thoughts and ideas. These little air children will gain strength from Mom's wisdom.

These moms will understand their Aquarian children's need to have their own space, and they won't invade on these kids' private time. Aquarian children may be a little overwhelmed by a Leo mother's dramatic approach to life, so it's very important for Mom to understand that she can reach her children by providing intelligent and reasonable explanations for all of her decisions. Her Aquarians will fan her fire, just as long as they are allowed to voice their own opinions.

The Leo Dad/The Aquarius Child

Dad is strong and likes to takes charge of the household. Leo men are the kings of the zodiac, and both he and his Aquarian children will want to help other people. They would both like to take care of those who suffer in the world. Their respective mottos are "I will" (Leo) and "I know" (Aquarius), and together they can make a great team. Dad needs to understand that while his Aquarian children look up to him—even to the point of idolizing him—he will have to ease up on his own expectations when it comes time for these children to decide on their career paths.

If Dad ever tries to insist that his Aquarian children pursue a specific professional goal, these kids will rebel, and they will wind up underachieving.

Aquarians are determined to find their own way in life, and this Dad can help his children by being the role model who can both stimulate and help motivate them toward achieving their goals. Dad has a fair sense of justice, and his Aquarian children will always appreciate his support. Leo fathers and Aquarian children admire each other because they both have a special strength of their own, which helps them to succeed in their own individual ways.

The Virgo Parent/The Aquarius Child

There are many Virgos and Aquarians who are drawn to each other because they tend to be opposites in their approach to life. Virgos are hyper, intense, and structured, and they need to plan everything. These earth people leave little room for personal freedom and flexibility. Aquarian children tend to be passive, and their need for feeling free is as important as their need for food and water. They are liberal thinkers who function in their own time and space, and being placed in a rigid lifestyle stifles their spirit.

It's important for Virgo parents to be careful about giving orders when they raise Aquarians. These air kids do not relate to anything that they feel is unfair and unreasonable—abrupt orders won't work. In fact, they tend to shy away from demanding parents. Both parent and child are independent and self-reliant, but an Aquarius is very uncomfortable when pressured into anything. Aquarians, like Virgo Mom and Dad, can be perfectionists—their image is very important to them.

They are pretty secure in their own decisions, so they may not always depend on their parents for approval and advice, but make no mistake—they do need their guidance and appreciation. Since procrastination is part of the Aquarians' lifestyle, their Virgo parents can help by teaching them to avoid putting things off until tomorrow.

Virgo parents are accurate and precise, and they are hooked into details and perfection. Mom and Dad need to be careful with criticism, though, since their Aquarian children are very sensitive. If Virgo parents want to communicate with their Aquarian children, they need to respect their intelligence and maturity. It's okay to teach them the value of consistency, but they will always need to take care of things in their own way. Virgos and Aquarians can build a relationship based on intellectual understanding. These practical parents will provide their free-spirited children with a comfortable, down-to-earth home environment. Virgo parents are masters of detail, and they will show their imaginative air children practical ways of making their dreams come to fruition.

The Virgo Mom/The Aquarius Child

Mom will be very instrumental in teaching her Aquarius children proper manners, as she believes that her children should treat other people with courtesy. She will expect her Aquarian kids to participate in household chores, and she would be wise to let them choose from a list of things to do. This behavior will appeal to their children's sense of freedom, as well as teach them the meaning of self-discipline. These children are quite mature when it comes to responsibility; however, if Mom and Dad continually ask them whether or not they've finished a task, they may think that their parents don't believe that they can do it.

When Aquarian children are young, they usually do what they're told. They do not want to argue, as it's peace and quiet at any cost with them. Mom needs to sit down and explain her often-compulsive tendencies to her Aquarian children, because both Virgos and Aquarians have trouble expressing their feelings at times. Aquarian children are very bright and eager to please, but they will not appreciate or respect a mother who constantly worries, or who is a nag. Aquarian children are especially intolerant of a mother who keeps repeating herself over and over again. Mom can best reach her Aquarian children through gentle, sensible rules and open, direct conversation. If Mom can learn to step back and give her Aquarian kids the freedom and time to get things done in their own way, these free-spirited children can best live up to their potential.

The Virgo Dad/The Aquarius Child

Dad will do just about anything for his children; his parenting challenge, though, will be to give his kids the freedom to make their own choices. Dad would be wise to affirm and accept his Aquarians' independence at an early age.

Dad is a practical man who will go after anything that serves his purpose in life; his air children are logical, and they will seek out anything that stimulates the mind. Dad is also a perfectionist who is intensely driven. An Aquarian, on the other hand, is quite intense but is not motivated by nervous anxiety. Aquarian children may be hard on themselves, but their practical and objective views on life are quite different from Dad's. Both Dad and his children are patient, for the most part, but Dad has a problem with flexibility, a quality that air children value, because their own actions are often quite unpredictable. Basically, the Aquarians are the idealists who look to the future, and the Virgos are the realists who deal with the here and now.

Dad and his Aquarian children can learn a lot from each other. Dad will admire his bright, sensible kids, and he will be able to teach them that the most successful projects in life have defeats built into them, and that to fulfill a great dream, they need to progress one step at a time.

Both Dad and his Aquarian children may find it difficult to make changes in their lives, but they may have to force themselves to if they feel that they're stuck in the wrong place. As long as Dad understands that he cannot be unjustly critical of his air kids or impose his will upon them, they will be good friends who will always be searching for something new to explore!

☆ ☆ ☆

My friend Hal (a Virgo) was very unhappy that his son Brad continued to change jobs after he graduated from college. For Brad (an Aquarian), it was just one job after the other, because he really wasn't happy being an accountant. He had majored in accounting because his father was a CPA. Hal thought it would be great if his son joined him in that profession so that he could eventually take over the business.

One day, Hal complained to me, "Sylvia, Brad's 25 years old, and he has had three different jobs in three years."

I asked him, "Why does Brad stay in accounting?"

Hal replied, "Because that was his major."

"That was your major, wasn't it?"

He nodded slowly and said, "I wish I could help him."

I remarked, "Well, you've come a long way just saying that. Why don't you encourage Brad to get out from behind a desk, and get into a job where he can communicate with people. He loves to help people, and he could be in sales, community service, or in any position that allows him to interact with people on a daily basis. Right now, he's not utilizing his ability to make people feel better. As for myself, I find him very easy to talk to, and he always makes me feel better."

Hal took a long breath, and then said, "I guess I tried to make his decisions for him."

"Hal," I told him, "the past is gone. It's time to work on the future."

Hal finally spoke to his son and told him that he felt responsible for some of the decisions that Brad had made, and that he would support him if he wanted to move into another field. Virgo Hal learned to pull back and finally give his Aquarian son the freedom to make his own choices in life. Brad is now Executive Director for a child abuse center, and he's helping his fellow men and women on a daily basis. His father is very proud of him!

The Libra Parent/The Aquarius Child

This is a good parent/child team. Libra parents nurture an Aquarian's logical mind and personal maturity. They treat their children as adults, although they have a real talent for understanding their childlike perspectives and fantasies. Libras feed into the abstract thinking of an Aquarian child, and they share great mental affinity.

Libra parents will easily accept their children's individuality, and they will be good influences on them, as they, like their kids, believe in fair treatment and freedom of choice. Also, Libras and Aquarians are both sentimental, and they hold on to the things that are meaningful and reflective of their good taste in life. Aquarians have strong survival instincts, and a Libra parent will respect this strength.

The primary issue that a Libra parent raising Aquarian children has to deal with is helping them to handle their anger. If Libra parents are not encouraged to express their real feelings as they grow, their self-esteem suffers, and they will tend to harbor resentment. Ultimately, these emotions will be detrimental to both themselves and their own children. It's up to Libra parents to learn how to honestly verbalize their sensitive feelings. Their Aquarian children will most likely be very amenable to listening to their concerns and providing any support that they can.

The Libra Mom/The Aquarius Child

Libra Mom will be a great help to her Aquarian children as she encourages them to work at their own pace, never forcing them into hastily making the wrong decisions. If Mom has not dealt with her inner anger and refuses to acknowledge her own desires, though, she can get bossy and negative, which will rub off on her kids. In addition, she has a tendency to compare her lifestyle to what's bigger and better. It's very important for Mom to modify this behavior when she raises her Aquarian children, as they will not respond to demanding people. Any type of negativity disturbs them, and they become especially distressed if a parent compares them to someone else.

Both Mom and her Aquarian children are idealistic and are dedicated to social causes. They both believe in working for the good of all. Mom does have a tendency to look at the negative before the positive, though, which is a predilection she needs to eliminate from her life for the good of both herself *and* her kids. Parent and child function through their logical and factual minds, but under the surface, they both suffer from personal insecurity.

Mom would be wise to offer constructive criticism to her Aquarian children. She must be honest and explain her reasons when she holds them accountable for their actions. Libra parents are very compatible with their Aquarian children—it's mental affinity and exploration of the intellect that counts. When they are at their best, young Aquarians will learn excellent social skills, and Mom will involve them in a variety of social activities. Aquarian children should not have a need to rebel against a Libra mom's lifestyle, because their individuality will always have a way of blossoming.

The Libra Dad/The Aquarius Child

Dad and his Aquarian children will be great friends, as they are bonded through their logic and intellect. Both are free spirits, but Dad has to keep the balance. Many Libra men fight for law and order, as they are natural mediators. They're extremely persuasive when it comes to equal rights, and their charm and poise helps them to peacefully negotiate the problems of the world. Aquarians are also cause-related and will share Dad's sense of justice, but they won't always be as balanced or fair. This parent and child can worry about what others think, especially if they respect those whom they perceive as judging them in some way.

Most people enjoy the company of Libras and Aquarians because they try not to say hurtful things; they like to be as tactful as possible. However, Dad will remember when people hurt him, and he will never trust those people again. Since Aquarians can distance themselves from others, when they get hurt, the pain doesn't make as much of an impression as it does on their Libra parents.

Overall, Dad and his children can build a relationship based on honesty and integrity, and they both could benefit by paying less attention to their own personal interests and more to that of their fellow men and women out in the world.

The Scorpio Parent/The Aquarius Child

Scorpio parents want to live in a traditional and structured environment, and while their Aquarian children won't mind the tradition aspect, they may feel confined in a tightly controlled atmosphere. Scorpio women mainly run the household, and Scorpio men like to be in charge of the entire family. Scorpios believe they have the right to set you straight. Since they assume they know what everybody is thinking before anything is even verbalized, they quickly solve problems without anyone else's input. This tendency could be a problem for Aquarian children, though, because they will always want to make their own decisions. No one can squelch their individuality.

On a more positive side, Scorpio parents want to do the best for their children, and they make every effort to help them live up to their full potential. Aquarians will appreciate the intense interest that their parents show them, but they will not respond to being treated like babies. Scorpio women, more than men, refuse to give up the notion that children are just that until they prove differently. The only problem that may occur is that some of their children stay in the baby stage all of their lives. Scorpio parents say they want their children to be independent and mature, but their own caretaking needs may get in the way.

Aquarians are naturally independent, and they tend to be responsible even when they're very young—maturing early is just part of their basic nature. Overall, if Scorpio parents will just suppress their need to impose their thinking upon these children, they can give them the freedom to develop at their own pace and, as a result, build the self-confidence that is so necessary to a productive and emotionally healthy life.

The Scorpio Mom/The Aquarius Child

Mom is a very bright and competent woman who manages to absorb a lot of knowledge on a diverse array of subjects. As such, she has a lot of information to impart to her Aquarius children.

Many Scorpio women are homemakers, and many are businesswomen, but no matter what path they choose, they almost all want to bear children. Scorpio women who have never had kids seem to suffer that loss on an ongoing basis.

Overall Scorpio mothers tend to be very secretive people who will not verbalize their feelings. They will be very interested in people's problems and want to be aware of every dot and dash, but they will remain a mystery to their family and friends.

Aquarians will not pry into Mom's feelings, as emotions are not easy for them, but they *will* share their intellect with her, which is usually practically and objectively based. Mom will run into a brick wall if she tries to impose her will onto these children. Aquarian kids are logical and realistic, and Mom's protective nature can stifle their need for freedom. Mom really needs her own space, so she can truly appreciate her children's need for alone time.

When discussing issues with her children, Mom would be wise to modify her overly critical behavior. If her Aquarian children cannot speak freely, without judgment, they will stop talking altogether. In fact, they do not offer a lot of information in any case unless they really trust people. Scorpio mothers tend to lecture, and an Aquarian will not tolerate repetitive conversation. Tell them once, or maybe twice, and that's it!

As I have mentioned before, Aquarians do not need to have harsh rules and regulations imposed upon them, as they won't willfully disobey their parents unless they feel forced into a corner.

The Scorpio Dad/The Aquarius Child

Dad is an emotional and intense man who has a great deal of self-control. Once he decides to make something happen, the words *doubt* and *failure* do not enter his mind. He is very emotional, and his opinions are resolute. Dad is also very patient when he sets his mind to a task, and his determination usually propels him to great success.

Aquarian children, on the other hand, are much more subtle in their approach to life. They are very intelligent, and they steadfastly strive to achieve their goals, but they are not emotionally driven. As such, there may be times when Dad will be exasperated by his children's passive behavior, but he might as well just learn to live with it, because his air children won't change. Dad needs to consider both sides of a situation when he raises them, because he won't be able to control his Aquarian sons and daughters. It's best that he try to honestly explain the reasons for his actions so that his kids have the opportunity to question and challenge his decisions. Dad cannot assume that he knows what these children are thinking; if he does, he will encounter a great deal of friction.

Scorpios and Aquarians both love to learn about the world. Aquarians can get a lot of help from a Scorpio father because he absorbs a considerable amount of knowledge, readily offered to his learning-hungry kids. These children will always be open to receiving information, because the development of the intellect is a primary concern to them. If Dad can just develop the patience to deal with a child whose mind is geared to logic instead of emotions, he will be proud to see a son or daughter who grows into a substantial, successful adult!

The Sagittarius Parent/The Aquarius Child

Sagittarian parents' philosophy is to help their children realize all intellectual possibilities, and Aquarians will value the special opportunities presented to expand their mental and physical development. Sagittarius parents give them what they really need—permission to be free, to learn, and to explore.

Sagittarians are energetic, humorous, and intelligent. They, like their Aquarius children, look to the future, wanting to pursue higher levels of education. And since Sagittarius parents and their Aquarian children share a strong mental affinity, they will learn a lot from each other.

Even though Sagittarians are basically emotional, they won't dwell on feelings. They are very sensitive on the inside, but their external demeanor can seem very cool and abrupt. One thing these two signs do have in common is their idealistic and humanitarian nature. They need to live in peace and harmony, without too much personal confrontation, which is something that both of them feel uncomfortable with. Also, both need to acknowledge that they will not be perceived as weak if they ask for help or share their feelings with others.

Recently, I was talking to one of my Sagittarius associates about her fear of confrontation. "Martha, why do you keep everything to yourself?" I asked her.

She answered, "I'm not comfortable talking about myself."

"Well, is it more comfortable to walk around being frustrated all the time?"

"I don't think about it," she replied.

"Well," I told her, "if you don't think about it, you'll never deal with it."

She admitted, "That's right—if I wait long enough, it will just go away!"

It is this type of attitude that needs to be rectified if a Sagittarian parent wants to do right by his or her Aquarian children!

The Sagittarius Mom/The Aquarius Child

My Sagittarius clients can be quite rigid, or they can be loose as a goose! I find that most of them are industrious and efficient, though, and most have a great sense of humor. Sagittarius Mom has a vast storehouse of knowledge. She wants to learn all she can about everything, and she has a definite style of her own. Her taste is usually elegant and subtle, unless she's developed into the eccentric artist type. Mom and her Aquarius children both have a problem with dependency, though. Therefore, each will question their worthiness. Mom would be wise to work on her own need to receive, so she can impart this ability to her children. I find that my Sagittarius clients live with emotional frustration, and my Aquarians live with personal insecurity. Overall, though, Mom's personality coincides with Aquarians' needs. She won't insult their intelligence or discourage their efforts. Instead, she will advocate self-expression. Both Mom and her Aquarian are opinionated, and their wills can clash, but they have the ability to intelligently work out their differences. Mom will always give her children permission to fight for what they believe.

2

Mom tends to be impetuous when she speaks, and so, she may say things that sound a lot more harsh than she intends them to. She is also impulsive in her actions and has a tendency to leap before she looks. Her Aquarius children are very different in their approach to life, though. These kids are prudent and sensible, and they do not like to act on anything without all the facts in hand. These fiery mothers cannot push them to move faster than they wish, though, because they like to take their time.

Mom can help motivate her kids express their feelings and believe in themselves. Aquarians need to be liked; therefore, they want to please. They are rarely troublemakers because they crave peace and harmony in their lives. Most Aquarians, whether they appear to be outgoing or quiet on the outside, do tend to be shy and reserved underneath. However, Mom needs to understand that this shyness doesn't mean they're not opinionated. They will usually do what they want without asking for too much advice.

Aquarian children feel safe and secure when they have a strong mother who is assertive and who believes in the truth, as they do. Even though both of these signs are strong-willed and straightforward, they have no trouble agreeing to disagree.

I find that Sagittarian women tend to live their lives with some degree of frustration, while my Aquarian clients are often withdrawn and personally insecure. No matter how large their egos are, they are both sensitive to the needs of others, and they will serve humanity in one way or another. All in all, it would be wise for Mom to understand that the best way to reach her thoughtful children is through logic and reason.

The Sagittarius Dad/The Aquarius Child

Dad can be the intellectual, or he can be the lovable con man. But it really doesn't matter in which direction he goes—either way he has the gift of persuasion. He's determined, persevering, and intuitive, and he tends to work very hard. So, if Dad does not take the time to relax and play, his inner intensity will translate to irritability. Therefore, it's important for him to have time alone in order to quell his nervous energy.

Aquarian children, on the other hand, can push too hard, but they do know how to relax. As a result, their matter-of-fact attitudes can drive Dad crazy. It's important for Dad to understand that his air children do not think or move as fast as he does, so he shouldn't reveal his impatience with them.

Both parent and child are similar, though, when it comes to their intolerance for mental vacuity. Boredom and depression set in when things stay the same or when they're around people who don't stimulate them. Dad is the kind of man who believes that if you can do it today, why wait until tomorrow? His Aquarian kids, however, definitely believe that tomorrow is a perfectly acceptable day to accomplish things. So, these kids can help Dad try to relax, and he can help them stop procrastinating. They can be good for each other as long as they respect each other's different natures.

Aquarian children, overall, will admire Dad's straightforward demeanor. His sense of humor and protective qualities will be very appealing to them. These air kids are devil's advocates, but their Sagittarius father is one, too. They both have a tendency to doubt anything that may be illogical or which can't be proven beyond a reasonable doubt, so actual experience is their greatest teacher!

The Capricorn Parent/The Aquarius Child

Aquarians are logical, and they are deep thinkers. Capricorns don't have much patience for people who deal in the abstract, as this kind of thinking tends to frustrate these down-to-earth parents. They are materialists who form their decisions in a practical manner and rarely deviate from them. Aquarian children's philosophy is different from their Capricorn parents. They do not function through fixed behavior, and they will not be comfortable living in a rigid and inflexible environment. They have little interest in improving their standards of living, as they base their lives on intellectual pursuits. Aquarians need parents who can be flexible with respect to their views. Capricorns have strong opinions that are not based on concepts or theories. They need to have concrete information!

It's important for Mom and Dad to learn more about their Aquarian kids' abstract, somewhat distant behavior. They need to know that these air children tend to work out their problems in their own heads before asking for advice. Aquarians will appreciate their Capricorn parents' guidance and support, but they need to express themselves freely, without being subjected to unfair criticism. They are protective of their individuality and are easily hurt. Aquarian children will appreciate their earth parents' stability and excellent sense of values. If Capricorn parents respect their kids' desire for freedom and their need to succeed on their own initiative, they can build a healthy relationship. In fact, Capricorns can help their young Aquarians balance their abstract tendencies with practical ideas. Aquarians and Capricorns are born stubborn, so it's up to Mom and Dad to work on developing a good deal of flexibility when raising these kids!

The Capricorn Mom/The Aquarius Child

Mom likes to make the most of her life. She wants to do everything on time, as her calendar tends to be very specific and organized. As is the case with all earth mothers, Capricorns place a tremendous amount of pressure on themselves to get the job done. So, they need to take a step back, and try to formulate a logical approach to any project.

Mom has a tendency to be hyper and dictatorial when it comes to domestic matters. She doesn't mean to be so tough, but she is very focused in her behavior, and is excellent at developing practical ways to utilize everything around her. She is Ms. Fixit, knowing how to get the right products at the right price. It's the material world that fascinates her.

Her Aquarian children, on the other hand, are idealists who exist on another plane. They are fascinated by what is to come, and their imaginations and inventive natures are geared toward building for the future. Their minds are attracted to science, literature, and art; Aquarian children can be artists or travel through space.

Mom lives in reality, while her Aquarian children live somewhere else altogether. She needs to help them understand that the world cannot be seen through rose-colored glasses, however. These air children tend to see the world as they wish it to be, rather than seeing the truth around them. If Mom can help her young Aquarians listen carefully to what is being said to them, rather than moving into their own private worlds, she can save them a lot of disappointment in life.

The Capricorn Dad/The Aquarius Child

Dad is an intelligent man who wants to succeed in the corporate world; however, this Dad can also be involved in the creative arts or in public affairs. No matter what he chooses for a career, though, this father will always project common sense and a practical mind. Dad works hard to create a comfortable home environment, because to him, his home is his castle—he is protective and will take good care of his family. Dad can be opinionated, so he would be wise to understand that his Aquarian children are very bright, and he needs to pay attention to what they have to say. The fact that these two can discuss any issue helps them to build a healthy relationship.

Dad and his Aquarians are responsible individuals who like to take care of other people, but Aquarians tend to see the world in terms of what it could be, while Capricorns usually try to deal with the world as it is. Dad can help his Aquarian children be more in touch with practical values, while his children can teach Dad the importance of looking toward the future. Dad tends to take life a bit too seriously and needs to work very hard to make things happen. His children can help Dad understand that everything is possible when you take things as they come and deal with them in a calm and reasonable fashion.

The Aquarius Parent/The Aquarius Child

Aquarius parents are intelligent, logical, and free-spirited, and Mom or Dad will definitely enjoy the same qualities in their air children. This family of air signs should get along well, since their modes of behavior are the same. They are thinkers who are very patient when pursuing their goals, and they tend to live by an idealistic philosophy. Aquarians may be subtle in their approach to life, but they are not wishy-washy. They have strong likes and dislikes, and they can be very stubborn when they feel that they're being forced into something against their will. Air signs are logical, for the most part, and feelings don't always make sense to them. Therefore, this parent and child will never relate to attacks of hysteria.

Aquarians are not usually aggressive. Most of them have a casual or relaxed persona, so they crave peace of mind. Air signs are also service oriented and enjoy helping other people. They will sacrifice their own needs for the sake of others because, to them, it's the masses that count. I have found that many of my clients who raise or who are married to Aquarians are frustrated by their lack of intimacy. They are usually cool and distant in their behavior. It's important for Aquarians to understand their boundaries and their priorities; they need to acknowledge that the people closest to them require their attention as much as those in the rest of the world. Unfortunately, Aquarians tend to shy away from talking about their feelings and, as such, they do themselves a disservice. It's important that Aquarian parents communicate with their Aquarian children openly, or there will be a lot of repressed emotions and frustration in the household.

Air signs desire safety and security, but they are keenly interested in the future. Aquarians are intelligent individuals who cannot seem to turn their minds off. One thought builds a bridge to the next and the next, and so on. Aquarian parents will appreciate their kids' efforts in many areas and will encourage them to pursue their dreams, but the most important thing these parents can do for their kids is to be their friends—good listeners who will always be there for them when they have problems!

The Aquarius Mom/The Aquarius Child

Mother and child should have no problem communicating, because they think alike. They are both logical and look at life in an objective, reasonable, and sensible way. Mom will teach her Aquarius children that it's important to be tolerant of others, and she will help them learn how to develop relationships that allow them to live in harmony with the world. An Aquarian's freedom is a given when he or she is raised by this Mom, as she doesn't value restrictions or rigid rules. It is important, however, for Mom to set some household rules and give these children a series of choices to select from. Otherwise, these young freedom seekers may have a tendency to think they can do whatever they want.

Both Mom and her Aquarius children are very strong-willed and easily hurt. If she can ask her air kids to share in the decisions that concern them, they will be very pleased. When Aquarians begin to worry, they may not always explore their ideas in a clear manner. Both parent and child are worriers. Therefore, it's up to Mom to encourage these children to worry less and take action when they believe they're right.

Mom and her Aquarian kids are independent and self-reliant. It feels good for Aquarian children to be raised by a calm and intelligent parent who will not pressure them. If Mom is there to support their decisions and ideas and motivate them into action, this is all they really need. This is a family of free spirits who do their own thing, in their own time. They have their own opinions and dislike obligation. They want to give freely without being forced into anything, and they can speak to anyone without given up their individuality. Mom and her Aquarian children also possess a shy quality—no matter how friendly they are, they have a tendency to distance themselves from intimacy. Mom and her Aquarians peacefully love each other, and they intelligently share their thoughts and ideas in a gentle and sensible manner.

The Aquarius Dad/The Aquarius Child

Dad will always encourage his Aquarian children to develop their intellects and fight for their beliefs. His motto is: "Take charge of your own life, and go after your dreams." Now, claiming to love your fellow human beings (which this Aquarian dad does) is one thing, but he may also have to give himself permission to express his feelings to his children. Aquarians tend to feel more comfortable dealing with the masses instead of developing intimacy with one person. Intimacy relates to emotion, and Aquarians would rather figure out their feelings in a logical manner.

Overall, Aquarians worry too much, and they are extremely concerned with financial security. This attitude often prevents them from taking the risks that can help them to accomplish the things they really want to do. Many of my male Aquarian clients regret that they have not utilized their innate talents and abilities. Many tried to live up to their parents' expectations, rather than go for what *they* really wanted. It's important for Dad, as the father figure, to encourage his air kids to take chances in life—this tactic may be risky at times, but it will ultimately yield a great deal of satisfaction!

If Dad has not worked through his own fear of the new and challenging, though, he may pass this trait on to his children. Many Aquarians tend to overlook the wonderful possibilities in life that can be actualized. Dad needs to encourage and motivate his children to move toward their goals in a proactive manner and not sacrifice them for the sake of others.

The Pisces Parent/The Aquarius Child

Pisces and Aquarians are both intuitive and imaginative. Therefore, this parent and child can share many special experiences through their rich imaginations and artistic abilities. The main difference between Pisces and Aquarians is their response to life. Pisces are emotional, and Aquarians are logical. (The parents feel, and the children think!) Aquarius children are geared toward the future, where they can pursue new and innovative ideas that can improve the world. Pisces love new ideas, but everything in the past tends to affect them. Aquarius children will love the safety and security connected to what's familiar, but what's new is far more exciting.

There can be times when this parent and child may have difficulty understanding each other because one is emotional and the other is logical. The best way for Mom and Dad to reach their air children is to try and develop a relationship that relates to them through objectivity, reason, and sensibility. I know that most Pisces parents want to feel an emotional bond when they raise their children, and a young Aquarius can be sweet and affectionate, but it will take some work to reach a happy medium. It's best for Pisces parents to be honest and direct when they raise their children, as they will not relate to wishy-washy explanations and decisions. Aquarians believe in the truth, and they tend to doubt people who do not clearly express themselves.

If Pisces parents can honor their own feelings, they can build the kind of self-confidence that's necessary to enhance their personal strength. These strong feelings can help them open up to others. Pisces parents can be very wise, and Aquarian children can listen to them for hours at an end as they talk about their experiences in the world. Aquarians like to learn, and Pisces like to teach. A sense of freedom and individuality is very important to Aquarian children, and these air kids will appreciate parents who encourage them to work on developing themselves through their own talents and abilities!

The Pisces Mom/The Aquarius Child

When a Pisces mother raises Aquarius children, she would be wise to work on developing intellectual compatibility, as these kids need to share both their thoughts and their ideas with their parents. Most Pisces mothers like to create an emotional bond with their children. They are affectionate and caring and respond with their hearts, rather than with their heads. They are feelers, and the logic and practicalities of life tend to envelop their emotional nature. Their Aquarius children are logical thinkers who are usually objective and reasonable. Emotional reactions tend to confuse them because they do not view them as stable or sensible. A Pisces mother can be a good role model for her Aquarius children, as they need to understand the value of warmth and giving. They really need to receive affection at an early age. These logical air kids may not show it, but they really enjoy being hugged and kissed.

Aquarius children tend to be wise before their time, and this sense of maturity will enhance their independence and their ability to take care of themselves. However, they need to please and will want Mom's approval. At first, it may be difficult for Mom to accept the fact that her Aquarians are so independent, as she likes her children to need her, but in time she will learn to admire their original points of view.

As these children grow, they will reveal a very strong-willed nature. They want to do things their own way, and it can be difficult for Mom to handle these little ones, as they are restless and may continually change their minds. Aquarian children need to develop respect for their parents. Therefore, Mom needs to be decisive, or they may walk all over her. It's important for Pisces mothers to work on their fear of making the wrong decision. they need to be straightforward and honest when they reprimand their Aquarian kids. In addition, when Mom makes a decision, she needs to stick to it. Once Aquarian children discover that they can control their mother, these clever kids will take advantage of this facility as much as possible.

Aquarians are usually very bright, sweet, and shy when they are young, and they need to know that Mom can provide safety and security when they need it. If Mom can keep these restless children busy and mentally stimulated, they will rarely bother her. Mom will admire her children's ability to be self-sufficient and responsible. Aquarians are honest and straightforward, and there may be times when Mom's indecisive nature can exasperate them. Mom and her Aquarius children are creative visionaries, so it's important for parent and child to share playful and creative projects, which will be wonderful for helping open up lines of communication on a personal level.

The Pisces Dad/The Aquarius Child

Dad truly loves his children, so he's usually attentive and demonstrative. He admires his Aquarian children's intelligence; therefore, he will gladly seize on every opportunity he can to help them learn. Aquarian children tend to idolize their father, and they want him there to share thoughts and ideas with them.

Overall, a Pisces father tends to be permissive with his children. He buys them a lot of material goods, and he caters to their whims. Many Pisces fathers are efficient and organized, but they make time to play. Therefore, Dad is a lot of fun, and he and his Aquarian children will enjoy engaging in a variety of activities together. Dad's moods can be changeable, though, and he isn't always comfortable making important decisions. Aquarians need to have a stable father, so it would be wise for Dad to stick to his guns once he decides on a course of action.

Pisces men are usually very kind, and they will do anything for those they love, but they seem to doubt their ability to make an impression on others—especially those whom they regard as strong people. They are very intuitive and their instincts are excellent, however, so there is no real reason for them to doubt themselves or their opinions. Aquarian children like to turn to their fathers when they need help, and a Pisces dad really does have the ability to comfort them if he will just believe in his ability to do so!

SUMMARY

You have learned that Aquarians enjoy serving the masses, and that's true...but it's a good idea for them to acknowledge that committing themselves on a personal level doesn't have to take away from their need for freedom. It's a difficult lesson to learn, as Aquarians guard their individuality, but if they can make the decision to share love with one special person, they'll understand that it feels good to be in a one-on-one relationship.

When I ask my Aquarians clients why they have a problem receiving, I always seem to get the same answer. They say, "I want to serve others, and I'm happy that way."

I ask them, "Don't you ever feel that you want something in return for all you've given?"

Most of them respond, "I don't think about it."

I skeptically retort, "I can't believe that comment. Is it because you fear commitment?"

Many of them tell me, "You're probably right."

Then I ask, "Don't you get lonely?"

They respond, "Not too often."

I try not to laugh when I hear their logical, short, right-to-the-point answers. Many Aquarians truly enjoy their own company, and they have the ability to develop many resources, but I have found that as they grow older, they seem to regret that living in this way didn't give them the opportunity to share their lives with someone special who wants to give them the love and affection they deserve.

Chapter Twelve

....

♓ PISCES THE FISH

FEBRUARY 19–MARCH 20   **ELEMENT:** Water   **KEY PHRASE:** "I believe"

....

THE PISCES PERSONALITY

Pisces are both spiritual and intuitive. The symbol of Pisces showing two fish swimming in opposite directions represents the difference between the spiritual and the more realistic sides of their nature. On the one hand, Pisces are sensitive dreamers who can create fantastic imaginary worlds; on the other hand, they know that there's a need to deal with reality. If it were up to them, they'd stay in their own world, since reality can be harsh and frightening. Typically, these creative individuals like to be around strong, self-confident people whom they can rely on whenever they feel insecure or uncertain. They need a lot of love and attention, and the tiniest slight threatens their safety.

Pisces tend to understand other people's needs at an early age. They have a powerful intuition that seems to be influenced by a strong psychic ability. They tend to come into the world wearing rose-colored glasses, which helps them to see people as they want them to be, rather than as they really are. They want to see the good in people, and each time they get hurt, they move further into a protective cocoon that helps shield them from the real world. Parents need to help their sensitive water children understand that their protective walls can prevent them from using their powerful talents and abilities. Pisces children can appear to be listening to what their parents are saying to them, when they may actually be far off in their own private world of make-believe. That's one of the reasons why they only tend to remember those things that are either convenient or comfortable to them. All in all, it would be wise for parents to use a gentle approach when disciplining these ultrasensitive water children.

Pisces can be idealists who want to make everything perfect in their lives, and they can create a very high set of standards for themselves to live up to. However, these water kids may have a tendency to want to behave perfectly for everyone; Pisces will tell you what you'd like to hear, rather than face rejection after telling you something that you might disagree with. They can be actors who tend to camouflage their lives by acting out different roles, instead of just being themselves. It's important for parents to stress honesty in the home and always encourage these children to express their emotions openly, without fear of judgment or punishment. If Pisces children do not learn to talk about their disappointments, they tend to take a negative approach to life. It's very important for parents to help these children recognize their special attributes so that they can feel worthy and deserving of a good life. If Pisces children are not taught to be honest about their feelings, as well as being accountable for their actions at a early age, they may subconsciously attract personal and professional experiences that will diminish their self-esteem.

They're Very Emotional Underneath it All

Pisces' ability to control their feelings has nothing to do with a lack of emotion. There's not a Pisces in the universe who isn't emotional at heart. Depending on how they were brought up, these perceptive kids usually deal with their sensitivity in a couple of different ways—one way is to maintain a very organized approach to life, and the other is to be artistic and free-spirited. The more organized Pisces children tend to want to keep everything in their lives in perfect order. Since they know that they can't always accurately detect how other people feel, they know that by keeping everything neat and orderly, they can at least maintain control over their own environment. The sensitive artist type is usually a free spirit, so it's important that parents who have water children who fit this description allow them to explore projects that interest them.

When Pisces children repress their feelings, a combination of anger and frustration builds within them. These layers of inner intensity can cause them to lash out inappropriately, which tends to make them misunderstood by others. So, it's crucial that parents encourage their young Pisces children to express their feelings at the time they are hurt. This guidance can help these children say what they mean at the time they feel it.

When Pisces children need to figure out a problem, they may move off into their own private world in order to think things out, so parents would be wise to give these kids the freedom to do so without interference. If parents try to make all of the decisions for their Pisces children, these kids may expect Mom and Dad to assume this responsibility forever. Since Pisces kids can have a problem making up their minds, they may subconsciously take advantage of their parents' protective nature. And while parents will always want to protect these sensitive children, it would be a good idea if they allow their kids to make as many of their own choices as possible. This behavior will not only help build their self-confidence and self-esteem, but when they're older, they will look back and appreciate the autonomy that their parents allowed them to have.

☆   ☆   ☆

My friend Beth's son Mark (a Pisces) rarely wore a happy face, and most of the time he seemed to look at life in a negative way. Beth was a very strong Aries mother who never realized how her own behavior helped to diminish her son's self-confidence.

It was a week before Mark's wedding, and I came over to Beth's house to visit her. Mark was sitting on the couch, looking exhausted and miserable. I asked him, "What's the matter with you? You're getting married next week."

He replied unhappily, "I wish the wedding was over."

I was shocked. "How can you say that? It's going to be one of the best days of your life."

He sat back in his chair and yawned. "I guess so," he replied, "but all of the arrangements have just worn me out."

I almost laughed. "It's been a lot of work?"

He admitted, "Well, Mom has done most of it, but Sylvia, I don't care about fancy weddings. I would have been happy to elope."

I asked him, "Then why didn't you?"

He replied, "Mom would have been disappointed."

"Your Mom may have been disappointed," I told him, "but she would have understood." He slowly shook his head. I continued, "Mark I've known you for many years, and I think it would be healthy for you to start to look at the bright side of things, especially since you're about to enter a new and exciting part of your life. I believe that the reason you get depressed is because you've resigned yourself to allow your mother to take care of everything for you, because that's what she loves to do. But I want to tell you something—you've got a lot of things going for you. You're intelligent and you're sensitive, and I think it's time for you to begin making your own decisions as to how you deal with your life."

"You know Sylvia," he responded, "I guess it is time to start doing more for myself." He gave me a hug. "Thanks, Sylvia, you've given me a lot of food for thought."

I do care about Mark, and since he was starting a new phase of his life, I thought it was important for him to understand his own need for personal expression and self-motivation.

☆   ☆   ☆

Adaptable and Charming

Pisces are charming, socially adept, and they are natural caretakers. They have an innate ability to sense how other people feel, and they can intuitively pick up on others' behavior patterns. Therefore, they know how to adapt themselves to a variety of situations, and their popularity and success in the professional world can stem from this special ability. They want people to like them; however, these water kids may have to learn not to try so hard to get along with everyone because they can wind up sacrificing their own self-esteem. They must remember that their opinions and feelings count, too. Self-esteem only comes from believing in yourself.

Pisces can release their true feelings through development of their creative talents, which can include art, music, or writing. By encouraging these water children's creativity at an early age, parents will give their spiritual selves a chance to grow. In addition, when Pisces children are given the opportunity to develop their own special talents, their self-confidence will increase considerably.

These water kids tend to live in a private world of their own, and they may have a tendency to dwell on the more negative experiences in their lives, so their parents may need to teach them to focus on what's positive in their lives, and never to take anything for granted. These children always want to be involved in decisions that are important for them, and parents must always remember to ask them for their opinions. Pisces children need to feel that their parents believe in them.

Pisces children are very sensitive, and they may find it difficult to admit when they've done something wrong because they don't want Mom and Dad to be mad at them. If parents can teach these water kids that's it's okay for them to make mistakes and that they should always be proud of themselves when they tell their parents the truth, they won't try to avoid confrontation as they grow into adults. Many of my Pisces clients tell me that they hate to argue; however, if parents don't teach these kids to let other people know when they're hurt by them, they can continue to dwell on these unresolved feelings for a long time to come. By learning to tell the truth, these kids will learn to accept responsibility for their actions.

Creative Souls

Most Pisces have the ability to be creative, as many of them are both visionaries with a strong spiritual core. They tend to relate to the old world, old masters, or to long-gone eras, and they definitely have a feeling of nostalgia for their own pasts. As such, many Pisces are musicians, artists, and writers. Their ability to intuitively understand quality allows them to incorporate both the old and the new into their work. If Pisces children are raised in a very structured and rigid environment, they may wind up spending more time being detail oriented rather than using their artistic abilities, though. These detailed Pisces usually grow up to have neat homes and offices. It's important for parents of Pisces children to be aware that these kids can release their feelings by developing their creative talents. Parents would be wise to help these water kids by encouraging them to draw, paint, or listen to music. It doesn't matter whether they draw a stick figure, paint the moon and stars, or bang out notes on a keyboard—each of these skills can help them develop their need for self-expression. If Pisces children can learn to express their artistic abilities when they're young, they will start to understand that creativity can be a wonderful way to define themselves as an adult. Whether Pisces children grow up to be business managers or accountants, they'll always need to work on the part of their being that's special—their creativity.

Building Protective Walls

Pisces personalities may not always let people know how sensitive they are. If they are not encouraged to talk about their feelings as children, they may take on a manner that seems distancing as they become adults.

☆ ☆ ☆

I once had a Pisces client who used to keep her feelings to herself whenever she was afraid of getting hurt. "I'd rather deal with my emotions by myself," she told me.

"But you won't feel as good about yourself if you keep this 'protective barrier' around you," I responded.

She replied, "I like to think of it as my own white picket fence."

"Why a white picket fence?"

She answered, "It's pure, and it seems strong."

"A picket fence sounds kind of romantic."

She laughed and said, "Well, I'd hate to think of it as a stone wall."

I asked her, "But don't you think that a white picket fence is less protective than a stone wall?"

She paused for a moment and told me, "Maybe someday my family can tear that fence down."

"Well, you've got to let them."

She explained, "I really don't like having to protect myself, but I'm afraid of getting hurt."

"Were you ever allowed to talk about your feelings when you grew up?" I asked.

She shook her head and said, "As soon as I got started, I'd get cut off. They didn't have the patience. So, every time I felt pain, I ran behind my white picket fence."

Most Pisces have a problem summoning up the courage to talk about their feelings. Wise parents who raise these water kids need to work on helping them get rid of their protective picket fences. Too much time behind that fence and these kids will wind up building even greater walls, which they will use to protect themselves from dealing with confrontation. In order for these children to reach their full potential, parents must first give them permission to believe in and accept themselves for the sensitive individuals they are. Parents who are both kind and loving can help these children face the realities of life, while at the same time gently supporting the sensitive and artistic sides of their natures. Mom and Dad may need to help these children understand that the real world isn't perfect, but it does offer them the opportunities to develop their own talents and abilities, which will help them fulfill their dreams!

PARENT AND CHILD

The Aries Parent/The Pisces Child

Aries parents and their Pisces children are sensitive, emotional people. These parents are strong, dynamic personalities who respond to the most challenging tasks, and their natural self-confidence can make them a tough act to follow. Pisces are charming, introspective personalities who are very intuitive when it comes to people and who often need to express themselves creatively.

Aries parents can do a lot to motivate these little dreamers and inspire them to turn their ideas into reality. Aries parents may have a tendency to dominate their environment, and at first, Pisces children can be a little intimidated by this kind of behavior, but Aries parents can help these kids if they can back off a bit and teach them that it's okay for them to do things in their own way. If Aries parents try to take charge of every situation, these children may depend on them for the rest of their lives. As they grow, Pisces children do not really enjoy being dependent on their parents; they want to feel that they can make decisions without always needing their parents' approval. If these self-confident parents can teach these children that their opinions count, too, and if they can encourage them to make their own decisions and stick by them, they can help these water kids develop a great deal of self-esteem. Helping children take responsibility for their own actions is an excellent way of preparing them for entering the real world later on in life.

The Aries Mom/The Pisces Child

The most outstanding quality that an Aries mother brings to her Pisces children is optimism. Aries concentrate on the good things that life has to offer, rather than the sorrows of the world. Most Pisces tend to overwhelm themselves with emotion, and this lack of clarity can cause them to believe that life is difficult. Mom can help to correct this kind of thinking, because of her natural ability to motivate her water children. She idealistically believes that "life can be beautiful," and she definitely imparts this feeling to her kids.

Mom is loving, independent, and a pioneer, and she would like to see her children grow up to be as independent and self-reliant as she is. These kids can intuitively sense that Mom is a go-getter who can accomplish practically anything. Many Pisces children tend to be dependent on strong parents, so Mom needs to help her youngsters believe in their own talents and abilities so that they can succeed on their own later in life. However, if these moms begin to take charge of all of their Pisces children's needs without giving them the opportunity to make their own decisions, they can cause these water kids to doubt their own ability to accomplish anything. On the other hand, if these motivated moms encourage these children to recognize their own skills, they will begin to feel self-confident and responsible.

An Aries mother believes in truth most of all, so she will raise children with a strong sense of conscience. It's up to Mom to win her little Pisces' trust by creating an atmosphere that encourages these children to talk about their feelings. She needs to use a gentle approach, as this is not usually her way of communicating. Mom is direct and straightforward, and young Pisces may view her manner as intimidating.

It's important for Mom to gently and fairly set up rules and boundaries for her Pisces kids to live by in order to help stabilize these little dreamers. They need to be encouraged to finish projects that they have started. If Pisces children grow up with a lack of responsibility, they may move toward wishful thinking, instead of facing the realities of life.

The Aries Dad/The Pisces Child

An Aries father is strong, and very much like his fire counterparts Leo and Sagittarius, he likes to be the king of his household. He never means to boss his children around, but he may need to work on giving them permission to make their own decisions. He has to remind himself that these kids may need time to "feel their way" when it comes to figuring out any new problem or experience, and he should make a point to be there to listen to them when they have questions.

In my experience, I have found that many Aries men feel that as their children grow older, they don't take enough time to help and support them. I explain to them that when children learn to be very dependent on a strong parent, they don't ever take into consideration that their father does have his own needs, too. So, it's up to Dad to reveal his expectations and desires and to ask for what he wants. Most Aries fathers do not like to feel vulnerable, though, as feeling needy can be foreign to them. They believe that vulnerability makes them weak. I believe that if an Aries man can learn to accept and share his emotional nature with his family, he would be much more satisfied with his life.

An Aries father can be an excellent role model for his Pisces children, as he has a knack for getting along with people, and he will be able to encourage his kids to believe in their own abilities. As these Pisces children utilize their talents to a greater and greater extent, their self-confidence and self-esteem will build to new levels!

The Taurus Parent/The Pisces Child

Taurus parents are practical, sensitive, and truthful. They believe in building a traditional lifestyle, as they're influenced by past cultures and customs—in fact, the foundation of their lifestyle is based on time-honored practices. They want to create a safe and secure environment for their family, so these earth parents work on building strong, healthy relationships with their family members.

Taureans, like their Pisces children, are natural skeptics. They tend to see the negative in something before they see the positive; therefore, it's important for Mom and Dad to teach these children that it's possible to believe in people, and that they shouldn't assume the worst before they actually know the outcome of any situation. If these children are striving to attain a goal, and they've given it their best effort, they need to congratulate themselves for the work they have put into their efforts. And, if these kids are praised by their Taurus parents, they will be even more motivated to continue in a positive direction.

Taurus parents will willingly and joyfully give their children love and attention, as they enjoy this kind of interaction themselves. In addition, these earth parents will stress good manners, as well as honesty and integrity, in order to teach their children that they must treat others with respect and dignity.

Taurus parents understand the practicalities of life, and their values are stable and consistent. And like their Pisces children, they can also be both spiritual and sensitive. When it comes to solving a problem, these water kids tend to rely on their instincts. Taurus parents have the ability to offer them a sense of emotional understanding, as well as the freedom that they need to pursue their dreams in their own way. Young Pisces will appreciate these efforts, and their strong compatibility will be based on mutual trust and understanding. In addition, these earth parents will provide these children with a safe and comfortable environment to live in, which will allow them to develop their own talents and abilities naturally.

It's important for Taurus parents to develop their own ability to talk about their personal feelings in order to set an example for these children, or else these kids may wind up repressing their emotions. If these parents can win the trust of their sons and daughters and make them feel comfortable with their own feelings, parent and child can build a mutually satisfying relationship.

The Taurus Mom/The Pisces Child

A Taurus mom and her Pisces children are very sensitive and get hurt very easily. Both of them need peace and harmony in their lives, and they have a difficult time standing up for themselves. Mom and her water kids both tend to have hidden sorrows and a weak sense of self-preservation. It's very important that Mom understand that she needs to work on being optimistic, positive, and decisive when she raises these kids; otherwise, they can both be competing for "who creates the biggest drama."

Most people like Mom because she is charming and patient. Her main interest is home and family. She loves beauty, and she will create a very comfortable environment for her Pisces children, who will never have to worry about feeling safe and secure when they live with this earth mother. She will nurture their sensitivity, and she will be there to listen to their problems. Mom is very practical and she can help stabilize her idealistic kids. Pisces children tend to live in their own dream world of fantasy, yet their intellects need mental stimulation. So, it's important for Mom to keep them busy without pressuring them. Mom is a practical woman who is positive and determined; she will succeed in teaching her water children that it can feel good to live in the real world.

Both Mom and her water children fear the unknown, and they do not like to take risks on a personal level. Mom appreciates people who are go-getters and who act upon what they say. Therefore, she needs to encourage her Pisces children to set goals and finish what they start, or they may lapse into unproductive habits. Both Mom and her child are creative and love music, so if she sees that her young Pisces children are overwhelmed by nervous anxiety, music is an excellent remedy.

Mom and her Pisces are very compatible because they are both sensitive and kind. They want to serve humanity, and both can be very giving. However, I have found that both my Taurus and Pisces clients seem to expect the worst before it happens. So, it's important for Taurus mothers to point out the positive aspects in most situations so that her Pisces children will always expect the good to win out over the not-so-good!

The Taurus Dad/The Pisces Child

Taurus fathers are sensitive men, and they can be loyal friends to their Pisces children. Both parent and child appear to be easygoing and a lot of fun, but they are also introspective and hard on themselves. Like Mom, Dad is practical, and his family is very important to him. He's a wise man and a good listener. He can easily win his Pisces children's trust, and they will feel comfortable with him.

Dad and his Pisces children usually share an artistic side; they love music, art, and theater. These interests give them an outlet for releasing the intense emotions that reside within them. Another trait common to both signs is their ability to sell and promote their ideas. As his Pisces kids grow up, Dad can share his special talents with them and function as their mentor in many areas.

Parent and child will have a lot of fun together, as they are both kids at heart, and one of Dad's favorite pastimes is to play with abandon. In addition, Dad's ability to see things in a practical light can help him teach these children how to live with consistent rules and patterns that will help them maintain a sense of balance in their lives.

The Gemini Parent/The Pisces Child

Gemini parents are excellent teachers, and they can easily offer the kind of intellectual support that will encourage their Pisces children to pursue their goals. They can provide these water kids with the balance and objectivity that will help them clarify their thinking. However, it's very important for Mom and Dad to understand their Pisces children's strong emotional needs. The only way these kids believe that their parents care about them is through an abundance of love and affection. If their needs are ignored, their personal security will suffer.

When it comes to reacting to any given situation, Pisces feel first and think second. Geminis, on the other hand, tend to analyze first, as it can take a bit longer for their feelings to settle in. So, a Gemini parent can learn from a Pisces child's sense of intuition, and a Pisces child can develop a wonderfully sensible approach to life.

Geminis are very comfortable spending time by themselves, just thinking about things. This behavior can frustrate Pisces children, because even though these water kids are also dreamers, they can still begin to feel that their parents aren't paying attention to them during these moments. Geminis can work on developing a healthy relationship with their Pisces children by making consistent time to be with them, and by always offering honest and logical explanations as to why they've made their decisions. Gemini parents are reasonable and sensible; therefore, they can clearly and gently explain their intentions to their children. In addition, Mom and Dad should try to provide these kids with a safe and secure environment where consistent household rules are followed on a daily basis. This behavior will provide these free-spirited water kids with the sense of stability they need.

A Pisces child can be a creative spirit, and many Geminis are musically and theatrically talented. Think of Marvin Hamlisch, Sir Lawrence Olivier, and Barry Manilow. Since Geminis are not naturally born with emotion, and it's the intellect that really matters to them, they may need to work a little harder when raising emotional children, who are sentimental and tend to hold on to familiar experiences.

Gemini parents would do anything to make their children comfortable, but their logic and somewhat distant manner can prevent them from becoming too intimate. Pisces children thrive on intimacy; therefore, Mom and Dad will need to try and balance their thinking in order to give these water kids the attention they crave.

Gemini parents have the ability to help these kids logically defend their own decisions. Many lawyers and judges are Geminis, and of course, they have strong opinions. The most forceful part of the Gemini personality comes from the ability to persuade anyone to believe in an idea through the use of their wisdom and logic. This intelligent approach can help young Pisces learn how to express themselves, as reason allows them a way to determine the value of their ideas and feelings.

The Gemini Mom/The Pisces Child

No matter how old her children are, Gemini Mom will feel a need to protect her sweet and vulnerable Pisces children. But remember, Mom: Pisces are very vulnerable, but they aren't as fragile as they seem. Even though Pisces children may have done every conceivable thing in the world to make something happen, and that includes not overlooking a single detail, they still worry whether or not that situation will work out for them. There will be times when Mom will have little appreciation or patience for indirect behavior, especially when this behavior stems from emotion. Her Pisces children will soon learn that they cannot make mountains out of molehills. Mom needs to learn how to temper her frustration and guide young Pisces into making wise and solid decisions. Most of the time, Pisces children grow into efficient, well-organized adults, but Mom needs to remember that they will always have to contend with their feelings.

☆ ☆ ☆

My friend Liz and I were sitting in her living room when her three-year-old Pisces daughter Analisa suddenly burst into the room, sobbing uncontrollably.

"What happened?" Liz asked. "What happened?" Analisa just kept crying. Liz tried to ask again, but Analisa just kept crying.

By this time, Liz began to lose her patience, and her voice went up an octave, "If you don't tell me what happened, I can't help you!"

Liz is a Gemini, and I'm an Aries, so my emotional nature hooked right into that of this little girl. I asked her, "Do you want Mommy to hug you?" Still crying, she nodded and put her head on her mother's lap and kept crying. "Analisa, tell Mommy what happened to you."

She calmed down and said, "I hit my head on the table, and it hurts."

Liz said, "Let's see if you have a bump on your head." Liz looked her over and saw that the damage was minimal. She put Analisa down and said, "You're just fine. Don't worry about it."

Analisa just looked at her mother uncomprehendingly and insisted, "It hurts!"

Liz responded, "I know it hurts, but you didn't break anything. It's just a scratch." Liz then assured me, "She's okay."

Analisa understood that her mother was finished with the ordeal, so she went downstairs to play, wearing a dejected look on her face. Liz was trying to teach Analisa how to temper her feelings and let her know that there was no need to get highly emotional over everything.

As the years wore on, although Liz and I often talked about Analisa's need for affection, her answer was always, "If the problem's small, there's no need for hysteria." While I generally agreed with this assessment, I usually told Liz that perhaps she should try to nurture her daughter's emotions for a few moments longer, rather than dismiss her when she was still frightened and tearful.

"Well, she can't cry about everything." Liz would reply.

As a result of her mother's behavior at times like this, as Analisa grew up, she had a tendency to control her emotions in most situations, almost believing that it wasn't right to have them.

Liz is a wonderful woman and very bright, but she should have been more patient and tolerant with her daughter. In this way, she could have balanced her own logical reaction with her child's need for attention. A few long hugs, along with some calm and reasonable explanations, could have shown Analisa that her mother accepted her hurt feelings, and that it was okay to cry.

☆ ☆ ☆

The Gemini Dad/The Pisces Child

Dad has a very protective nature; he's perfectly willing to help resolve problems in his family, and both he and his Pisces children can build a fine relationship by openly discussing their concerns. Young Pisces can learn a lot from Dad, as he is able to converse intelligently on a variety of subjects. He is usually wonderful with words, and he will always participate in a variety of interests with his water kids, showing them interesting and amusing ways to stimulate their minds.

If Dad is the very serious intellectual type, he may initially not understand how to handle small children because he doesn't relate well to childish behavior. When his little water kids get too silly or too emotional, Dad might try to distance himself from the situation. So, it's very important for Gemini dads to understand that their Pisces children are very intuitive, and they can always sense whether or not their fathers are interested in them. If these water kids find it difficult to get Dad's attention, they may retreat into their own world, believing that what they're doing simply isn't good enough to impress him. Then, they may tend to start working overtime just to try to get Dad's approval. Dad needs to empathize with his children whenever they need him and let these kids know how much he appreciates what they're doing or saying. When these Pisces children are assured that Dad is there to listen to them, their self-esteem will grow, and Dad will receive a special reward: his kids' love and affection!

The Cancer Parent/The Pisces Child

The Cancer parent is lucky to have Pisces children, as these sensitive and emotional water signs belong together. Pisces children tend to be extremely vulnerable and easily hurt. Therefore, they will enthusiastically respond to an affectionate and loving parent. Cancer are very devoted parents, and most of their personal satisfaction comes from sharing their lives with children. A comfortable home means safety and security to these water parents, and it usually turns out to be their sanctuary. They believe that if they can create a solid foundation, this base can protect them from the outside world.

Parent and child have similar traits and values. Most of their reactions come through their feelings, and they usually bond on an emotional level. No one can fault Cancer parents for being protective caretakers, but there are times when their unrealistic fears can overwhelm an already fearful child. Pisces children need to feel that the real world offers many wonderful possibilities. They need to learn that it's okay to form their own opinions and fight for them. I know how much Cancer parents want to do for their children, but they need to explain their reasons for making a decision and offer these water kids a series of options to choose from. Pisces children's self-esteem is built on having the ability to make up their own minds and being responsible for their actions without Mom and Dad taking over. I know that Cancer parents mean well, but doing too much for these water kids keeps them indecisive and dependent. Love will never hurt Pisces children, but parents who shelter them from the outside world do them a disservice.

Both parent and child are givers who are very goodhearted and sympathetic to those who suffer, but both tend to have a problem taking care of their own personal needs. Through years of counseling, I have found that both Cancers and Pisces do not really know how to accept compliments and attention, as they cannot understand how to celebrate their efforts and accomplishments. They do love affection and consideration, but my research has shown me that they tend to lack self-confidence and have unrealistic fears about relationships. They are the creators of the phrase "making a mountain out of a molehill." Cancer parents have to set an example for their water children. They need to develop the courage of their own personal convictions and act upon them. Pisces children need parents who can affirm their worth and help them believe in themselves.

A Cancer parent's protective nature is very comforting to his or her Pisces children. Parent and child are an emotional team. In fact, they both have a problem letting go of anything they invest in. These water kids will be happy to live with strong parents who will never let anything happen to them. However, as Pisces kids grow up, they start to recognize their emotionally dependent natures, and they tend to resent their parents for doing too much for them. If they can be responsible for their actions and make their own decisions at an early age, they may understand the value of feeling independent and self-reliant.

Cancer parents understand how sensitive they are, but most of them are very private people. They are easily hurt and cannot openly discuss their feelings of sadness when someone hurts them. Cancers and Pisces both tend to build up personal resentment, and they often hide their real emotions. Cancer parents need to try and discuss their feelings with their Pisces children in order to build healthy communication. They must be careful about worrying so much and expecting the worst to happen. Their water children can also be negative and worrisome and will pick up on their behavior. It's important for Cancer parents to help their water children understand that there is so much good in the world and that they deserve to take advantage of the wonderful opportunities that are waiting for them. Once this compatible team can appreciate the value in asking for what they need, they will develop an enviable relationship.

The Cancer Mom/The Pisces Child

Mom is usually pretty, charming, and gracious. She enjoys teaching her children the appropriate social skills because she believes they should be well-behaved and have good manners. Mom, more than Dad, has a tendency to equate her identity and personal security with motherhood. As her children grow and start to learn how to take care of themselves, it's important for this self-sacrificing Mom to understand that she needs to make time in her life for herself. She must learn to create goals for herself and then make time to achieve them. Otherwise, she may wind up basing her happiness entirely upon her children's accomplishments.

Mom is very sensitive, and as with all water signs, she tends to keep her feelings to herself. Unfortunately, when an emotional woman works against her real nature, she begins to build internal resentment. A Cancer mother's anxiety can often create nervous conditions, even though she may reveal a "devil-may-care" attitude to the outside world. Mom needs to learn how to ask others for what she needs in terms of love and attention. She has to give others permission to do as much for her as she has for them.

Cancer women are very intelligent and know how to get things done, and Pisces children will always appreciate her efforts. Mom can be very helpful to these kids, as she appreciates their deep-seated sensitivity. She will gladly accept this trait as an inherent part of their personality, so Mom and her Pisces children will very likely have a close relationship. A Cancer mother is usually kind and compassionate to her children, so they will trust her to take care of their needs as long as she refrains from making *all* of their decisions for them.

The Cancer Dad/The Pisces Child

Dad and his Pisces child are water signs who usually share the same values and have no trouble connecting on an emotional level. A Cancer father can easily relate to his responsibility as a parent, since he rates himself at the top of the list of caring dads. He is there to protect his kids from all things that can harm them. On the other hand, Cancer fathers can be moody because they tend to keep their feelings to themselves. Dad may need to learn that it's important to let people know when he's been hurt. This behavior will serve as an excellent example to his Pisces children, who will better learn to openly express their own feelings. If Dad tries to develop some objectivity when raising his sensitive young Pisces kids, an honest and communicative relationship will be sure to grow.

Dad has a tendency to tease, and Pisces children do not like anyone to make fun of them since they take everything personally. Dad should know better, though, because he also tends to personalize anything that suggests criticism. Pisces children have a good sense of humor, but they can overreact to anything that feels like an insult.

Overall, though, Dad is usually personable and lovable. He has a big heart, and he would literally give his children the shirt off his back!

The Leo Parent/The Pisces Child

Pisces children will benefit from the love and inspiration that they receive from a fiery Leo parent. Mom and Dad are usually caring and affectionate and will intensely protect these children. Leos are proud parents who will gladly support their children's talents and potential. Their expectations and standards are high, and they always try to help their children work up to their potential. Leo parents are quick-thinking movers and shakers, and they can inspire their intuitive, imaginative Pisces children to put their ideas into action. Mom and Dad can encourage these talented kids to be confident in their own abilities and pursue their own creative vision.

Leos, the kings and queens of the zodiac, are pretty opinionated, and it's been said that they usually end up getting what they want. They are kind and compassionate people who genuinely want to help people, but their unshakable determination can be threatening to anyone who doesn't recognize the soft side of their personality. Leos are independent and hardworking, ready to do anything to accomplish their goals. They would be wise to understand the difference between their own personalities and those of their Pisces children. A Leo parent's assertive behavior may unintentionally minimize a Pisces' self-confidence. Their priority, of course, should be to help their children enhance their self-confidence and self-esteem.

These fire parents may appear to be more intense than their easygoing water kids, so Mom and Dad may have to remember that Pisces children have a tendency to retreat from anyone who expects them to live up to their expectations. Leo parents may need to be careful not to ask these water kids to justify themselves every time they make a mistake. It's important to ask them to be accountable for their actions and learn to be responsible for their behavior, but too much criticism makes them very insecure. Leo parents will lead their Pisces children into making the right decisions as long as they allow themselves to sit in the wings while their water kids are on stage.

The Leo Mom/The Pisces Child

The best way to describe a Leo mother is to say that she's intelligent, independent, efficient, and strong. She's a "take charge" lady who has little use for being placed in secondary positions. She has a lot of love to give, and her children are very important to her. Leo moms empathize with their Pisces children's sensitivity, and they will always be protective of them. She will always be an attentive, loving mother; however, once she begins to sense that her Pisces children are having problems making decisions, she may have a tendency to take over and make up their minds for them. At these times, Leo mothers may need to develop patience and understand that in order to improve their self-confidence, it's important for these children to learn how to do things on their own. Otherwise, these Pisces children may start to feel that their own choices aren't good enough, and they may tend to depend on Mom's ability to take care of everything for them. Leos are symbols of independence, and they have the ability to encourage the same strength in their Pisces children. Since Mom's approach with her children will be straightforward, her Pisces children will always know where she stands.

Mom has fine taste, and she understands how to take care of her home. In addition, her charismatic behavior makes her welcome anywhere. She is usually a sophisticated woman, and her Pisces children will easily pick up on her style and sophistication without too much training. Her innate strength can be used in a positive manner. Mom tends to compliment her children, and she is happy when they live up to their potential. She has the ability to teach her Pisces children how to appreciate their own abilities. And with Mom's help, these children will understand that they are special so they won't need to seek approval from others as much. Pisces children are very sensitive to other people's needs, and they may have a tendency to want to try to please everyone else. In her straightforward, gentle manner, a Leo mom can teach her Pisces children that while it's beneficial to have others like you, you don't have to do things that make you dislike yourself in order to attain that goal. Leos are excellent teachers, and they can be the perfect role models. Therefore, Mom can encourage these children to believe that they can take charge of their own lives.

Mom is the best person to nurture the Pisces' artistic nature, and she can supply the emotional support and leadership that can motivate these water kids to finish what they start. A Leo mother will never shirk her responsibility to help her Pisces children choose the best paths leading to success!

The Leo Dad/The Pisces Child

Pisces children will idolize a Leo father figure. In their eyes, Dad is to be admired. He is strong and believes that it is his responsibility to take care of his family and make many of the decisions. However, in this relationship, Dad needs to understand that as Pisces children grow up, it's very important for them to learn how to take care of their own lives. If Dad tries to make all of his water children's decisions, they can vacillate between adoration and resentment. Pisces kids tend to be emotionally dependent personalities who look up to strong parents for protection. Leo Dad will gladly take charge if he believes his vulnerable sons and daughters need him, but his sometimes overwhelming strength may diminish his children's independence and self-confidence.

Pisces children are often indecisive, and they have a difficult time making up their minds about things that are important to them. They are very hard on themselves, and they believe that making a mistake may ruin their lives. Of course this is foolish, but water signs have a tendency to be negative and make mountains out of molehills. Pisces children will admire Dad's natural strength and self-confidence, though. They will want to emulate him, but may also view him as a tough act to follow. Leo fathers need to affirm their Pisces children's special talents and abilities by giving them permission to offer their opinions and make their own choices before he makes any decision for them. In addition, he needs to explain the rationale behind his actions.

Dad may not realize that his strong and commanding nature can diminish his children's ability to make up their minds or be responsible for their own actions. Dad's self-assured nature can be the cause of his children's dependency and jealousy. He would be wise to concentrate on helping young Pisces kids learn to retain information through their own experiences. Dad's always learning, and he need to share his knowledge with his little dreamers.

All in all, his action-oriented, optimistic nature and sincere zest for life can set a find example for his water children. When Pisces children are raised by a Leo father, they will have the opportunity to look at the bright side of life!

The Virgo Parent/The Pisces Child

Virgo parents are perfectionists, and no matter what they're working on, they want to take the time to get everything exactly right. These parents are also logical and practical, so they will provide a solid foundation for their spiritual Pisces children. These earthy parents have a common-sense "can do" approach to life. You give Virgos a problem, and they will figure out how to solve it. These perfectionists are expert at analyzing just how to get a job done, and this trait will benefit Pisces children, who want to figure out how to turn their ideas into concrete reality.

It's important for Pisces children to live in an organized household, which Virgo parents will gladly provide. While a Pisces will enjoy these parents' practical approach to life, Mom and Dad must never forget that these water kids are emotional free spirits who need to be given permission to pursue their own creative abilities. By providing a stable home where these children can be allowed to express themselves, Mom and Dad will be helping them enhance their self-esteem.

In a Virgo parent's home, Pisces children will learn everything they need to know about manners and good behavior. These kids can benefit from living in a traditional, clean, safe home environment, but the more conservative Virgo parents may need to learn to allow their Pisces children to figure out things in their own way. Even though Mom and Dad will understand ahead of time what their Pisces sons and daughters need to do in order to get a job done, these parents may need to exercise patience so these kids can learn from their own mistakes. Pisces children often like to be given time alone to think about things, and parents would be wise to let them have their own space for as long as it takes. Since Pisces children often have problems adjusting to reality, Mom and Dad need to give them permission to fantasize from time to time.

Being practical individuals, Virgos tend to show their children how much they love them by how much they *do* for them. Therefore, they may need to learn how to verbalize their love for their kids and give them as much affection as possible!

The Virgo Mom/The Pisces Child

Mom is very smart, and she can accomplish anything that she puts her mind to. She is a woman of quality, and she has excellent taste. She tends to set up very high expectations for herself, which can be projected onto her children. She needs to be careful about being so hard on herself, as this lovely lady can turn herself into a nervous wreck. A Virgo mom also worries about how well her children will do, and she has to be careful not to pass this sense of anxiety down to her Pisces children, since these little water kids are already dealing with their own high standards. Mom needs to realize that most people cannot do everything right, and it's important for her to develop some flexibility when she raises these sensitive free spirits. Pisces children will appreciate a Virgo mom's understanding that they cannot be forced into anything. Once a parent continually stifles their freedom, young Pisces will drift into a private world, never to return. Young Pisces needs a firm, yet gentle, approach to facing the world. Anything harsh or severe tends to frighten these kids.

Pisces children can benefit from Mom's outstanding ability to give them a sense of security, and Mom can build an excellent relationship with her Pisces children if she allows them to evolve through their wonderful imagination and insight.

The Virgo Dad/The Pisces Child

Dad is a strong humanitarian, and he will always be there to make his children's lives better. He's often misunderstood because of his need to get everything in his life to work perfectly. As such, there may be times when Dad may lose patience with his Pisces children's ability to express their ideas or feelings. Pisces children are sensitive and easily intimidated, and they tend to live in their own dream world. Dad is curious and mentally alert; in fact, most of my male Virgo clients see themselves as amateur psychologists who need to analyze everything. Strangely enough, these earth dads aren't very good at guessing what their children are thinking about. Pisces children are somewhat of a mystery, and they tend to hide their true feelings.

Pisces children, on the whole, can present themselves in two different ways. There is the Pisces who is tied into details and organization, and there is the one who is very creative and loves music, art, and theater. Dad can be an outgoing idealist who loves to sell and promote his ideas, or he can be the serious corporate businessman, who works by hard set rules. Whoever Dad is, he has the ability to improve any situation he is involved with, and his strong determination usually gets the job done. A Virgo father can be very instrumental in helping his water children learn how to be accountable for their actions. In addition, Dad has a positive attitude, and he can be a good role model when it comes to looking on the bright side of life.

I have encountered one recurring problem that seems to occur between Virgos and Pisces, though, whether they are parents and children, mates, or business associates. Virgos tend to intimidate the indecisive Pisces because of their powerful need to control everything. Virgo parents need to know that Pisces children's self-confidence and self-esteem need to be nurtured from an early age because they are so hard on themselves. Dad will feel very protective of his Pisces children, as they usually appear to be vulnerable and sensitive. These kids can be quite dependent on a strong parent, so Dad would wise to help them take control of their lives by taking on responsibility at an early age.

The Libra Parent/The Pisces Child

Libra parents are usually intelligent, responsible, amiable, and kind. Since balance and harmony are essential to their lifestyles, they tend to fear and reject anything that's harsh, severe, or violent. Therefore, their personal comfort lies with people whose personalities reflect reason and sensibility. Libras who were raised in a dysfunctional home, where the beauty of life was supplanted by abuse, overbearing control, or neglect, tend to repress what they really feel and pretend that nothing affects them. Their moods are unpredictable, and it may take them years to find themselves. When Libras learn to stand up for what they feel, they develop spiritual power and inner strength.

Libras and Pisces have a lot in common, as they both tend to idealize life. They are both easily hurt and tend to find confrontation difficult. Libras are born diplomats, and they do not want to make a situation worse than it already is. However, they need to take their own feelings into account and recognize that they'll ultimately feel better about themselves if they both honestly and simply let other people know when they've been hurt. If these air parents spend too much time taking responsibility for everyone else's feelings, they'll begin to build up inner resentment and anger, because no one will ever seem to be worrying about them. These calm peacemakers may need to remind themselves that when there are two people in a relationship, both of them need to look out for one another. Only in these situations can Libras find contentment and discover their true ability to teach through love, peace, and harmony. These visionaries are kids at heart who can understand a child's perspective. And these creative kids will appreciate Libra Mom and Dad's gentle nature, as well as their strong sense of balance.

The Libra Mom/The Pisces Child

Mom enjoys her children, and she's a lot of fun to be with. She will provide a beautiful environment for her water kids and will do everything possible to help them work toward their best potential. As with all air signs, Mom believes in the ideals of personal freedom and individuality, and she will never try to stifle her children's ideas. These kids will be encouraged to pursue their own goals. Pisces children need their freedom, but they fear being given too much independence when they're young. Even though Mom is a logical woman, she needs to understand how important it is to nurture her water child's emotional dependency. Pisces children will need a lot of affection and attention because they are very sensitive.

Mom usually likes to live her life in an organized manner; therefore, she tends to be a disciplinarian. It's very important for Pisces children to understand their responsibilities, but Mom needs to be careful with her criticism of young Pisces. Pisces children do not understand how to depersonalize what people say to them. Since Mom is a reasonable lady, she has the ability to reach her water children by offering sensible explanations for her actions.

It's known that Pisces children can live in their own imaginative play worlds, as they have very strong creative abilities. Being creative herself, Mom can be instrumental in helping her Pisces children develop their own ideas.

The Libra Dad/The Pisces Child

My experience has shown me that my Pisces and Libra clients are both very attached to the father figure and seem to see Mom as the disciplinarian. Pisces children need parents who are both honest and gentle in their approach to discipline. These idealistic kids enjoy being raised by parents who act like protective playmates, rather than those who give them a lot of orders. "Tough Love" is not the answer for a Pisces child.

Libra fathers are interested in the intellect. A Libra dad can choose to be either unconventional and creative, or traditional and stable, depending upon which road he travels. If he's a spiritual man, he can be of great assistance to his Pisces children as they seek to grow, in addition to helping them stimulate their minds. Most Libra fathers are usually easygoing, attentive, and funny, but they are very serious about the way they handle their lives. Dad's first reaction to most situations is usually logical, while his Pisces children's reactions are usually based on their feelings. Dad may need to learn to put his logic aside when it comes to his children's deep-seated sensitivity.

These air Dads are great friends, and they often treat their young children as though they are already grown up. However, Dad would be wise to understand that these little water kids will still have a need to be treated like children, as they will look to Dad for both attention and affection. Dad is usually both objective and reasonable because he likes to look at things fairly. Libra dads tend to avoid personal confrontation and many choose to keep their feelings to themselves. It would be a good idea for Dad to encourage his young Pisces kids to talk about how they feel in order to help these impressionable water children express their genuine emotions. Dad needs to give his Pisces children unconditional support, and through his sense of balance and wisdom, he will be able to help these kids deal with the outside world.

The Scorpio Parent/The Pisces Child

A Scorpio parent and a Pisces child are both sensitive and sympathetic human beings. They both like to help people, and tend to be natural caretakers. Mom and Dad will have an emotional affinity with these children, and this special connection will help these water parents to both nurture and understand their kids' feelings. Most water signs tend to fear revealing their emotions and usually keep them to themselves. Mom and Dad would be wise to communicate with young Pisces on a personal level and calmly listen to what they have to say. It's best to guide these kids without being overly critical or judgmental. These children tend to hide from their real thoughts, and they need to have an opportunity to release their honest feelings.

Scorpios deeply love their children, and they could spend all of their lives taking care of their needs; however, when they raise Pisces children, they need to be careful not to make all of these kids' decisions for them. If these water children are not given permission to make up their own minds about things, or form their own opinions, they may start to retreat into their own private worlds. Once this happens, the special emotional connection between parent and child can suffer. Scorpio parents should include these children in any discussions regarding issues pertinent to them, giving them permission for feedback and honest response. And when Mom and Dad make these kids feel like their opinions are important, they won't feel left out. By letting these children be who they are, Scorpio parents can build an excellent relationship with their kids that will get better with each passing year.

Scorpios enjoy living in an organized, structured home. They will provide a safe, stable environment for their Pisces children, and this will provide these water kids with a sense of personal security. Pisces children like to take time by themselves to think about things, or just to keep up with their fantasies. Mom and Dad need to give these water kids the freedom to help them develop both their talents and abilities. Scorpio parents may have a problem believing that their Pisces children can take care of themselves. It's important for these kids to believe in themselves without having to depend on their parents for everything. If Scorpio parents can encourage their young Pisces to make their own decisions (with gentle guidance, of course), these water kids can build the self-esteem they need to become productive and self-confident adults.

The Scorpio Mom/The Pisces Child

Mom is efficient, self-reliant, and artistic. She will take excellent care of her Pisces children, making sure that these kids receive the best education possible. She will also make every effort to help them accomplish their short- and long-term goals so that they can succeed both personally and professionally. Pisces children have the ability to intuitively understand people, and they usually don't have any problems getting along with others. Mom needs to remember that these water kids are very hard on themselves, and they will always look to her for both approval and recognition of their own talents and abilities.

It's important for Mom to teach these children to learn to look at the positive aspects of a situation, since these kids have a tendency to see what's wrong with something before they see what's right. And by pointing out how well they are doing, Mom will help these children develop self-confidence.

Both Mom and her Pisces child are cause-related humanitarians; they have a deep compassion for those who suffer. This same quality will allow a Scorpio mom to sense her Pisces's children's vulnerability, and she will be there to support their emotional needs. Both Mom and her Pisces child are usually very creative; and when they share artistic talents, the time that they spend together will most likely be emotionally and intellectually fulfilling.

The Scorpio Dad/The Pisces Child

Scorpio fathers work very hard to build a strong foundation for their family. Dad is usually an honorable man, and his ethics are typically beyond approach. His Pisces children can learn a lot about truth and honor from him. When it comes to raising his Pisces kids, it would be a good idea for Dad to reveal his soft side when he does so, as they will crave his personal attention. Dad is a very private man, and he can have a difficult time talking about his emotions. In fact, many Scorpio men live their entire lives without sharing their real feelings with anyone. If Dad doesn't learn to open up, young Scorpio will emulate his behavior. Water signs are very sensitive, and it's much easier for them to keep their feelings to themselves than it is to reveal them. If Dad can really make an effort to open up the lines of communication with his Pisces children, he will find that this special effort can be very rewarding.

It's important for Pisces children to recognize their own unique abilities and to maintain their own individuality. It would be wise for Dad to recognize this need. He can be a wonderful teacher and help these kids understand the value of responsibility, as well as teach them how to be accountable for their actions. Dad should be careful not to make too many of his Pisces children's decisions for them, as their self-confidence will begin to diminish. At times, Dad may tend to play devil's advocate, and he may have a tendency to tease his children. At first, Pisces children may not react in any way, but simply remain silent; however, they will not enjoy the fact that Dad is making fun of them. A Pisces child can begin to personalize everything Dad says if he continues to poke fun at them, and this behavior can intimidate these sensitive water children. Instead, Dad might concentrate on nurturing his child's emotional nature and try to modify his need to control his son's or daughter's thinking.

Scorpios are usually spiritual, and they are attuned to other people's feelings. Dad will always be there to listen to his children's thoughts and ideas, and together, they will build a warm and comfortable relationship.

The Sagittarius Parent/The Pisces Child

Sagittarius parents and their Pisces children are both visionaries, so their dreams are very important to them. They both have the ability to come up with great ideas, and they also have the talent to execute them. Sagittarius parents usually focus on developing their children's intellect, but these caretakers can also help nurture these kids' emotions. Even though Sagittarius Mom and Dad tend to concentrate on developing the mind, they are also sensitive to feelings. Sagittarians are optimists, and even if they get hurt, they tend to move on, thinking to themselves, that "tomorrow will be better." This attitude is beneficial for Pisces children, as they enjoy living with bright and sunny parents. Sagittarius parents and their Pisces children are both emotional, so these fire parents will be sensitive to their children's problems, and they will always be ready to help them.

Pisces children will need to depend on their parents' strong emotional support, so Mom and Dad would be wise to allow these water kids to share their own opinions when it comes time to make important decisions in the family unit. Many Sagittarians fear opening up about their personal feelings, even though they are emotional at heart. It's important for Mom and Dad to set an example for young Pisces by trying to develop the personal side of their personality. This effort can lead to a very trusting relationship between parent and child.

Sagittarians have an excellent sense of humor, but they have a tendency to make light of certain situations when they get overwhelmed by their own sensitivity. They have to be careful not to use sarcasm as an emotional cover, as they can accidentally hurt someone else's feelings.

☆　☆　☆

My friend Laura's son Ken was about to turn 21, and she thought it would be a great idea to have a dinner party for him. Laura, a Sagittarius, is a fabulous hostess, and her son Ken, a Pisces, is a charming, articulate young man who decided to offer us a special toast before dinner.

He rose to his feet and said, "I want to thank all of you for sharing this special night with me, and I hope that we'll all be together for years to come. My parents are lucky to have such wonderful friends, and I have grown to love you all." We applauded, as we all were very touched.

Later that evening, Ken, Laura, and I were in the kitchen cleaning up, when I said, "Ken, that was a wonderful speech. Your mom is lucky to have you." I guess the emotion of that moment was too heavy for Laura, so she thought that she would break things up by saying something funny.

"I am lucky, all right," she said flippantly. "I'm lucky that he's leaving home." Laura quickly realized that she had said the wrong thing, and she added, "I'm sorry, Ken, I was just kidding." But Ken didn't say anything; he just left the room.

Both Laura and I knew that he was very hurt, and she looked at me and winced. "I don't know why I say those things!"

I took a long breath, and said, "Laura, you have to realize that you can be a little too sarcastic for your own good."

She nodded. "I'm always doing that instead of just appreciating a serious moment. I've got to work on changing that part of my personality."

"Laura," I told her, "you're a wonderful woman, but you just need to learn how to catch yourself when you feel like being funny. Sometimes a situation really calls for you to show people how much you care for them."

I think that Ken's 21st birthday party made a real impact on Laura, as I have personally witnessed a change in her demeanor. She seems to be more considerate of other people's feelings and no longer feels that she has to use her sense of humor as a cover.

☆ ☆ ☆

The Sagittarius Mom/The Pisces Child

Mom is a wise lady and a good mother. Her kids are very important to her, and she has the ability to create a better life for everyone in her family. Mom sometimes seems to be working "overtime," doing ten things at once, and she may need to be careful that the family motto doesn't become: "Ask Mom, she'll take care of it for you." A Sagittarius mother can sacrifice her own needs for the sake of her children, but this "one-woman show" needs to give herself permission to make time for her own interests. It's important for Mom to let her family know that she has her own needs and that she would like them to be considerate of her feelings. A Sagittarius mother has difficulty releasing her need to control, and many times the price she may pay isn't worth the frustration she might suffer in the future.

Since Mom's a free spirit, her real desire is to learn as much as she can, and to travel all over the world. This need for freedom and exploration will be passed on to her children so that they can seek out new horizons.

Mom has the ability to create a practical and creative home environment. She's ambitious, and she always looks toward the future. This fire mother will encourage her Pisces children to go after and achieve all of their goals. Mom is a motivator, and her children believe in her ability to provide a good life. Some Sagittarius moms are perfectionists and the expectations they place upon themselves are very high. It's important for these mothers to remember that their Pisces children also place very high standards on themselves, and that they need to be allowed to do things in their own way and in their own time. When Pisces children feel as if they can't live up to their parents' wishes, they tend to justify their behavior by making a lot of excuses. Sagittarius moms would be wise to give their children permission to simply do the best job that they can. With their fire mom's love and support, these water kids will be able to fulfill any dreams they can visualize for themselves.

Mom and her child are creatively compatible, as they both believe that life can be magical. Even though Mom tends to be a little more realistic in her approach, she still believes that anything is possible in life! Mom is a caretaker, and these sensitive, vulnerable children will win her heart. It's always important for Mom to reveal her soft and sensitive side to her Pisces children, though, as they will relate to this aspect of her personality and reward her with attention and affection.

The Sagittarius Dad/The Pisces Child

Dad is energetic, optimistic, and unpredictable. Both friendly and outgoing, this fire dad is a pleasure to be around. However, like his Pisces children, Dad sometimes needs to have his own space, where he can think about things by himself. Pisces children need a lot of attention, and if Dad appears to be neglecting them, they start to feel insecure. Dad has the right to take his own private time, but he would be wise to make his water children feel that he will always be there when they need him to help solve a problem.

Dad can be a bit of a chauvinist, so he may let Mom take care of the household while he works hard to provide a comfortable life for his family. This attitude may be a bit old-fashioned in this day and age, but I have found that most fire signs share this philosophy.

Dad can be the perfect playmate for his Pisces kids, as he loves to have fun, and he will give his sons and daughters permission to explore life. This father is usually a calm, rational, self-assured person, and his water kids will depend on him for advice. Dad is wise, and by always listening to what's on his Pisces children's minds, he can be a valuable asset in helping them make the right decisions. Most of my male Sagittarius clients tend to keep their feelings to themselves; they don't not want to bring anyone down by being too serious. Dad is an emotional man, and he needs to understand that it's okay to feel. He should be able to share his thoughts with his family without experiencing discomfort. I always remember the quote: "The unknown is frightening until experienced, then it becomes familiar, and holds no terror."

Dad can be an inspiration to his Pisces children, as he is a man of action. He is a decision maker, and will quickly act upon his findings. Pisces children need help in this direction, and Dad has the ability to encourage his water kids to research a problem, make a decision, and then stick to it.

The Capricorn Parent/The Pisces Child

Capricorn parents can provide all of the safety and security that these kids will ever need. They're excellent role models when it comes to responsibility and efficiency, and these perceptive earth parents know quality when they see it. They have the ability to finish any project that they start, and adversity never scares or stops them. They just move along, never missing a trick. These grounded parents set a good example for children whose feet barely touch the ground. They are self-reliant, determined people who can easily teach these water children the value of responsibility and resiliency, even when things go wrong.

Capricorn parents can help their Pisces children learn how to take their ideas and apply them to their lives from a practical point of view. Mom and Dad are fixed personalities who expect their children to conform to living in an organized and structured household, and this sense of order and stability is beneficial to a Pisces child. After counseling many Pisces clients who were born to Capricorn parents, I have found that lack of self-confidence comes from Mom and Dad's extremely high standards. Capricorn parents can be demanding, and they need to understand that they are raising highly sensitive and emotional children who feel more comfortable with gentle rules and reasonable expectations. Pisces children are very hard on themselves. They tend to concentrate on their imperfections, and they rarely celebrate their talent and intelligence.

Capricorn are usually authoritative parents who can be too critical. They may be harsh when they need to be kind. They don't always think about the way they say things, because their first concern is *perfection.* This behavior can enhance their sensitive children's need to be raised with freedom and objectivity, as they dislike feeling compelled to do anything. If parents try to overwhelm them, they can rebel by looking for negative attention. In addition, they will retreat into their own world, distancing themselves from reality. It's not easy for practical earth parents to relate to emotion. The best way for Mom and Dad to reach Pisces children on an emotional level is to help them develop their creative talents. Pisces usually have a natural ability for music, art, literature, and theater, even if they just engage in these pursuits as a hobby.

Pisces children's approach to life is different from their Capricorn parents. They are feelers who look for affection and attention. They fear intimidation, so they need their parents to be calm and gentle. Their personal security contributes to their self-confidence and self-esteem.

The Capricorn Mom/The Pisces Child

Mom is an intelligent and caring person who always wants the best for her children and who has the ability to solve any problem. When determined Capricorn mothers put their mind to something, they are unstoppable. Their homes are impeccable, their children are well taken care of, they volunteer for school activities, and they always look unruffled and unperturbed. Mom needs to learn to slow down a little, though, so her Pisces kids can keep up with her. Pisces children do not approach life with Mom's kind of intensity. They are moving in slow motion in comparison to this earth woman.

Pisces children appear to be easygoing, but they are actually very hard on themselves. In fact, both parent and child tend to be inwardly nervous, so they both need to relax their rigid expectations of themselves.

A Pisces child is emotional, but it's not natural for this earth mother to concentrate on feelings. She tends to deal with the practical realities of life. Therefore, it's important for Mom to work on understanding her kids' extreme sensitivity, or she will tend to judge her children's emotional nature as a weakness in their characters. Pisces children may want to do everything right, and push themselves to the limit, but they are almost always soft and gentle inside. If Mom can try to use a firm, yet sensitive, approach when raising these children, she will be instrumental in helping them bridge the gap between reality and creativity.

The Capricorn Dad/The Pisces Child

Capricorn men are practical and intelligent, and many of them base their self-esteem on how well they do in their careers. They are very hard workers who act effectively with a minimum of waste or effort. Their personal goal is to build a secure foundation for their families. However, they have to be careful about spending most of their lives at work. Many of my Capricorn male clients come to me saying: "I guess I never realized that my career became a priority. I just wanted to take care of my family." So, it's important for Dad to understand that his Pisces children will need his undivided attention at times, and they will want to just sit around and have fun and play with him.

Dad's temperament is generally serious, but he can reveal a dry wit that stems from his intuitive understanding of people. He has a tendency to mock human behavior, and he can be very funny. Dad, more than Mom, may be unwilling to change his mind once he makes up his mind about something. He must, however, always make sure that his Pisces children are part of any important decisions that involve them, as it's very crucial for the sake of these children's self-esteem to know that Dad will be there to listen to their opinions. Pisces children need to believe in themselves, and Dad would be wise to gently impress upon these kids the fact that they have the ability to succeed. Dad can teach these kids the kind of self-discipline that they need to make their own dreams become a reality. With his support and encouragement, these children will grow into efficient and organized adults.

The Aquarius Parent/The Pisces Child

Aquarian parents are gifted with patience and flexibility. These air signs are stable and tend to approach situations logically. They are blessed with tolerance, and they can handle life's highs and lows even when things seem like they're getting out of control. They seldom lose their cool, calm, and collected manners, so they can be wonderful during a crisis. Since Pisces children tend to worry a lot, they will enjoy the protective nature of their Aquarius parents.

Both parent and child tend to be imaginative dreamers who like to go off by themselves and think about things. (Interestingly enough, Aquarians tend to spend most of their private time engaged in creative problem solving, while Pisces tend to use their time to create wonderful stories.) Aquarius and Pisces individuals are both idealists, but Aquarian parents will help these kids take their ideas and move them into reality.

Parent and child have a lot in common, as both need the freedom to be accepted for who they are. Both need to please, and they do seek others' approval, but Mom and Dad's independence and logical minds help them reason things out and move forward. Aquarian parents have the ability to influence their Pisces children by offering sensible reasons as to why they should not agonize over mistakes, or bemoan the fact that some people might not like them. These parents need to understand that their water children tend to obsess about these things because of their insecurity over not being "good enough."

Aquarius parents can be a bit too casual in their rearing techniques, as they themselves have little need for rules and discipline. However, a Pisces child does need a home environment with a sense of structure, and Aquarian parents should create a series of tasks that these water kids should complete so that they can understand the idea of responsibility. Aquarians have the highest respect for someone else's individuality, and they want their children to develop through their own unique abilities and talents. Pisces children can have a problem with parents who don't seem to place specific expectations on them, because that means they have to make their own decisions for themselves.

Aquarian parents can help their Pisces sons and daughters by always being there to listen to them whenever they're trying to figure out what to do. By encouraging their kids to develop their natural talents, these air parents will increase their self-esteem. Aquarians tend to see life through both the mind and the intellect, and they are comfortable when they can communicate with their children. However, Aquarian parents need to remember that it's important to make time for these kids when they want to talk about how they feel. These air parents are excellent listeners who have the wisdom to help their Pisces children understand what's bothering them. I'd like to suggest that Mom and Dad try to understand and nurture their Pisces children's emotional nature. Remember: Pisces children feel, while Aquarius parents think!

The Aquarius Mom/The Pisces Child

Mom is a devoted parent who wants her children to live in peace and harmony, and she will do her best to provide a safe and secure home for them. Her own humanitarian concepts fit in with her Pisces children's kind and compassionate nature. Mom will teach her Pisces kids that other people should be treated with fairness and respect, so that they will learn to live harmoniously with all human beings. Mom believes in honesty and she will expect her children to tell her the truth. And when Mom senses that her kids are lying, she can be very direct in her approach to them. Her straightforward behavior can be perceived as cold by Pisces children, though, and it may tend to frighten them. Mom would be wise to use a firm, but gentle, approach with these children in order to get them to be forthright. Mom's genuine respect for honesty will inspire her Pisces children, who will learn that it simply feels good to be truthful. As I have said before, it is very important for Mom to share her sensitive human nature with her Pisces children, as emotion is at the foundation of their mutual existence.

The Aquarius Dad/The Pisces Child

Dad is an idealist, and he enjoys being unconventional. His personal philosophy does not have anything to do with materialism, however. He may enjoy a nice home and comfortable surroundings, but when it comes to human suffering, he has an altruistic regard for people who need help. Dad does not always thrive in one-on-one relationships, though, especially when it comes to intimacy. He is much better at keeping his distance and working with groups of people. Dad feels that a good education is of the utmost importance, and he will strive to help his children develop their minds.

Pisces children are bright and since they value intelligence, they will have a special affinity with Dad. They will look to him for advice, as they will want to share their feelings and ideas with him. Dad will need to learn how to nurture young Pisces' emotional nature in order to help them feel secure. If his water children can feel his love and support, they will have the ability to succeed in all aspects of their lives.

The Pisces Parent/The Pisces Child

It's easy for a Pisces parent to raise a Pisces child, since both share a strong emotional affinity. They will be good friends who motivate each other. Young Pisces kids will never be alone, as these parents will always want to be there for them. They also have the same need to create a family love nest. Most Pisces hold on to their dreams, because dealing with reality is an ongoing struggle. Many of them work at creating perfection in the real world so they can survive the emotional burdens of life. This is one of the reasons why they are so hard on themselves and tend to concentrate on every detail.

Pisces parents understand that it's very important to believe in what they are doing and stand up for themselves. Therefore, they need to teach the philosophy of Abraham Lincoln to their children: "If we never try, we shall never succeed."

If Pisces parents have not learned that their negative tendencies can be detrimental to their well-being, now is the time! These loving parents need to be careful when raising their Pisces children because they easily attach themselves to expecting the worst out of life, rather than believing in a positive future. It's up to

Mom and Dad to raise them in a positive and stable environment. Parent and child are sensitive and supportive personalities. They are both gifted with intuition, and they seem to sense the feelings of those around them. They instinctively know how to treat people, and this behavior is the key to their popularity, but they can lose their own identity and character by obsessing about what other people think. These parents need to help their Pisces kids believe in and value their own opinions and decisions. It's up to Mom and Dad to give these water kids the opportunity to choose from a variety of options and help them make their own decisions. Most Pisces tend to live with unrealistic fears; therefore, they may alter the truth and avoid personal confrontation. Pisces parents need to set an example by being as honest as they can be, and teach their kids to follow their lead. This lesson will do wonders for their children's self-esteem!

Pisces parents must be cautious about being too critical, as young Pisces will take everything personally. Most water children lack objectivity and can be influenced by others. Therefore, the best teachers will be their parents. It's important that Mom and Dad do not project a lack of self-expression when they raise their water children. They need to encourage their kids to talk about their feelings. And, those Pisces parents who have not developed their creative abilities need to observe their children's special talents and help them develop them. Pisces parents need to help their children explore life in their own way, even though they should always be there to listen when their kids ask for help. These sensitive water parents need to provide their children with opportunities they may not have received in their own upbringing.

The Pisces Mom/The Pisces Child

It doesn't matter how precise, efficient, and organized Mom is, she will always be a sensitive little girl who doesn't want to give up her dreams. Most Pisces are good mothers because they genuinely love children. Mom will give her Pisces children a lot of attention and affection because it's natural for her to believe in love. She is wonderful at playtime, and she will enjoy coming up with different games for her children. Her spiritual nature makes these kids feel that it's always safe to tell her how they feel. It's important for Mom to be truthful with her Pisces children, and she always need to follow through when they require discipline. If she believes in herself, so will her water children.

A Pisces mother needs to take some time to sort out her feelings when she becomes overwhelmed by her emotional nature. She understands how mixed signals make her feel when she needs to depend on someone for strength and comfort. Pisces children must have structure and ethical standards with which to shape their lives. Mom ought to concentrate on building her children's self-confidence at an early age so that young Pisces can develop the ability to decide between right and wrong. A Pisces mom can inspire her Pisces children to recognize how important it is to make their own decisions and believe in themselves!

The Pisces Dad/The Pisces Child

Dad can be a mentor to his young Pisces, as he is very knowledgeable and has a great sense of humor. A Pisces father will want to give his family everything they need. After counseling many Pisces clients, I have learned that they need to be close to their fathers because they tend to view them as strong men who will protect them from all evil. Most Pisces men tend to be emotional and dependent, and they often choose strong women to take care of their everyday needs. They leave the rearing to Mom so that they can just be involved in the family's more pleasurable moments. This won't work with their Pisces children, though. It's very important for Dad to present the image of a loving, stable, and strong father who can be called on at any time to help with decisions and solve problems.

It's important for Dad to think about the things that made him feel insecure as he grew up. If he lacked the attention he craved or if he felt alone in his own world, he can relate to the right ways to nurture his water children's sensitivity. When Pisces children feel sad or insecure, they will be comforted by Dad's positive support.

Dad can help his young Pisces kids act upon their decisions by believing in their own ability to make them. Dad needs to maintain an optimistic attitude, so he can inspire his children to confidently go after their goals. Most Pisces are intuitive and respond with their feelings. Parent and child can share deep love and a beautiful friendship if Dad will believe in his ability to know what's right. With his guidance, his children will live up to their greatest potential!

SUMMARY

Pisces children are sensitive dreamers. They have excellent imaginations and are often involved in creative fields such as art, music, or writing. In fact, they can be very articulate and may provide very interesting insights and commentaries on other people. Pisces children need stability, safety, and security, and they will always want to depend upon their parents for this support. I feel that parents who raise Pisces children need to work on helping them accept responsibility for their actions by teaching them that it's all right to make mistakes. When parents encourage these children to believe in themselves, they can teach them to face the world with self-confidence, and maintain their own individuality. Since most Pisces personalities tend to see what's wrong with a situation, rather than what's right with it, it's important for parents to stress the positive aspects of their kids' personalities. Once these water kids believe that they can be successful, they won't be afraid to apply their special talents and abilities to their own lives, which will give them the self-esteem that they deserve.

It's important for parents to guide these water kids toward making their own decisions and to help them stand up for themselves when they have something important to say. And most of all, Pisces children need to believe that they are loved!

Appendix

Afterword

The one consistent message that flows through this book is the importance of nurturing and preserving a child's individuality. No one can say that it's easy to live in a complicated world, where struggle always seems to be around the corner. The only deliverance we can count on is our ability to maintain our courage and believe in ourselves.

When children are born, they are innocent and free of sin. As they begin to grow, the crossroads of life tend to lead them in different directions. As parents, we are given the responsibility of understanding both our children's personality and behavior, as well as our own. Only through this knowledge can we help guide our kids in a positive direction—where their natural talents and abilities can flourish. Kids need their parents' permission to be themselves in order to feel secure and self-confident. All human beings have to deal with their feelings of insecurity, and as we know, these emotions usually come about when people are overly critical of us. Therefore, we, as parents, must apply the same standards to our children, and realize that too much criticism can only intensify a child's insecurities. Parents need to help their children understand how to depersonalize constructive criticism. If children learn that they can intellectually grow through parental guidance, they will respond. Kids will never learn to understand who they are if they have to live up to their parents' vision of what they should be. Families cannot isolate themselves from personal communication simply because they choose to follow the paths set by their parents and grandparents. We must remember that intimacy does not have to be scary. In fact, it can bring about a special bond that most people will welcome.

Parents must learn how to come to terms with their children's need for acceptance. The definition of *acceptance* is so simple ("to receive willingly") that it's difficult to fully understand why some parents need to try to totally change their children's basic nature, and try to make all of their choices for them. Astrology provides a special wisdom that can help parents understand their children and gently guide them through their lives.

The issue of control is an ongoing battle between parents and children. The freedom to choose and make decisions on their own is very important to our kids. They need to grow up believing that they can be selective and decisive. When families learn to communicate on a personal level, emotional control may become a thing of the past. We all have to exercise self-discipline in order to make intelligent decisions and work toward healthier relationships. If parents can try to develop a positive out-look on life, and then pass this attitude on to their children, the latter may not fall prey to mood swings and self-pity. In addition, patience is truly a virtue, and par-ents need to serve as role models in order to help their kids avoid making mistakes through impulsive decisions.

The fire signs—Aries, Leo, and Sagittarius—are not very patient, but they are optimistic. The earth signs—Taurus, Capricorn, and Virgo—are gifted with both patience and strategy, but they are worrywarts. The air signs—Aquarius, Gemini, and Libra—are patient and highly intelligent, but they think too much. The water signs—Cancer, Pisces, and Scorpio— are very patient, but they do make mountains out of molehills. Each child is unique to his or her own sign, and astrology points the way toward understanding each child's wonderful differences.

I hope *The Stars in Your Family* has helped you, the reader, to understand your children, your parents, and finally, yourselves. I am grateful to astrology, as it has been my special angel in helping me feel that I did a good job in raising my own children. Astrology offers parents and children a unique opportunity to understand each other better, and especially gives parents the assurance that they are guiding their children in the right direction!

—Sylvia Friedman

*"You can't change
the color of your child's eyes.
But you can make them glow
with the light of true love."*
— ANONYMOUS

About the Author

SYLVIA FRIEDMAN has been an astrologer, handwriting analyst, and consultant on human behavior for over 20 years, and she also facilitates seminars on family dynamics. Currently a resident of Chicago, Illinois, Sylvia has appeared on numerous television programs as a guest expert, including *Oprah* and *AM Chicago*.

Sylvia is available for:

☆ Personalized astrological readings—she will provide you with a full-length cassette (specifically geared to your birth chart) that delves extensively into the nature of your personality, and which also gives you a month-by-month overview of the upcoming year;

☆ Private consultations on family matters, parent/child issues, and any subject related to an individual's emotional and psychological well-being; and

☆ Lectures and workshops for groups and corporations.

You may contact Sylvia in Chicago (during business hours) by calling: **(312) 472-7688.**

☆ ☆ ☆

☆ ☆ ☆